MATHEMATICS FOR PROFIT

a business mathematics text

JAMES HEALEY
MARK JONES
Chabot College

Prentice-Hall Inc., Englewood Cliffs, New Jersey

ISBN : 0-13-562595-5

Library of Congress
Catalog Card Number: 74-37391

10 9 8 7 6 5 4 3 2 1

Prentice-Hall International, Inc., *London*
Prentice-Hall of Australia, Pty. Ltd., *Sydney*
Prentice-Hall of Canada, Ltd., *Toronto*
Prentice-Hall of India Private Limited, *New Delhi*
Prentice-Hall of Japan, Inc., *Tokyo*

Printed in the United States of America

contents

preface

This textbook is specifically designed for the growing number of college students enrolled in lower division business mathematics courses. It is directed to them not in the role of youthful consumers, but as undergraduates ready to identify themselves with the business community. Consequently, the book is written from the point of view of the business firm, not the individual consumer. Particular care has been taken to make this text compatible with the textbooks the college student encounters in his other business courses. Every effort has been taken to make it precise in its terms, accurate in their usage, and reflective of current business practice.

Because business mathematics is one of the first college courses in any business sequence, it is imperative that the elements of profit be fully explained. No student can be expected to appreciate the point of view of the business firm until he has an understanding of profit. The text teaches the student the elements of profit, their calculation and their presentation in a manner consistent with the format of financial statements. The all important income statement and balance sheet serve as the basic structure for the presentation of material. Every business transaction considered is viewed in terms of its effect upon these statements.

Many students lack competency in basic arithmetic which would hamper their progress if proceeding through the text from chapter 1. Therefore, appendix I includes a complete review of the fundamental arithmetic processes involving whole numbers and fractions. Every problem in the text can be solved by using one or more of the arithmetic processes explained in this appendix.

Appendix II presents certain statistical methods such as statistical averages, tables, and graphs. This material has particular pertinence since all business transactions are summarized in figures and the best possible methods must be employed to present data in a meaningful manner.

Appendix III presents number systems, other than the decimal system, which are in common use today. This material has particular application to computer mathematics.

Appendix IV is comprised of *Financial Compound Interest and Annuity Tables* which are essential in many business calculations. We are indebted to Kenneth R. Scott, President of the Financial Publishing Company, for granting us permission to use these tables.

We must also credit John Pritchard and Dean Olsen of Prentice-Hall for launching us on this project and Edward Francis of Prentice-Hall for seeing us through it. The material used in the insurance sections and tailored to our needs was provided by Jack Healey of the Jack Healey Insurance Company. We were also blessed with most capable reviewers who made a great contribution to the finished product. Our thanks to: Mrs. Lillian Haverland; Robert Landry, Massoit Community College; Martin K. May, Bronx Community College; Robert W. Rolfe, Modesto Junior College; and Robert S. Russell, Bryant & Stratton.

We particularly want to express our thanks to our wives. Colleen Healey, the mathematician, contributed Appendix III on number systems and Patricia Jones, the executive secretary, typed and proofread the entire manuscript. In addition, they gave us the assistance and encouragement required to complete the project.

James Healey
Mark Jones

1

introduction
to profit

Profit is an incentive and a reward. In the anticipation of profits, a businessman engages in activities to provide goods or services which he feels people need and consequently will buy. No amount of compassion and empathy for others can enable him to attempt to satisfy these wants for any length of time without receiving an income to sustain himself and to buy the materials necessary for him to remain in business. It is the hope for profits which stirs him to forego the security of a fixed income and accept the risks of owning and operating a business.

Many make grievous mistakes in their estimate of what society wants or in what manner or form a product or service is wanted. Many risk their time, talent, and money only to find that what they have produced is not wanted—or at least is not wanted so much as what is produced by someone else. Regardless of how sincere and diligent they may have been, such persons are not rewarded, they realize no profit—they did not provide people with what they wanted, or did not provide it as efficiently as someone else. However, the economy continues to operate, which means that others were better attuned to the wants of society and that their efforts were being rewarded with profits. In essence, when society profits (gains or benefits in goods or services), a great many individual businesses have profited.

Society, then, actually administers profits by accepting or rejecting goods and services. It channels the efforts of businessmen in the allocation of the

BUFFINGTON'S DEPARTMENT STORE INC.
INCOME STATEMENT
FOR THE YEAR ENDED JANUARY 31, 19XX

SALES			
Gross Sales		$2,120,000	
Less Sales Returns and Allowances		120,000	5.7%
Net Sales		$2,000,000	100.0%
COST OF SALES			
Beginning Inventory at Cost, February 1.....		$ 350,000	
Gross Purchases at Cost.................	$1,395,000		
Less Purchase Returns and Allowances	50,000		
Net Purchases		$1,345,000	
Transportation Charges on Purchases		25,000	
Total Merchandise Available for Sale		$1,720,000	
Less Ending Inventory at Cost, January 31...		400,000	
Gross Cost of Goods Sold.............		$1,320,000	66.0%
Less Cash Discounts Earned		50,000	2.5%
Net Cost of Goods Sold		$1,270,000	63.5%
Net Alteration and Workroom Costs		10,000	.5%
Total Cost of Goods Sold		$1,280,000	64.0%
GROSS MARGIN OF PROFIT		$ 720,000	36.0%
OPERATING EXPENSES			
Payroll.............................		$ 380,000	19.0%
Advertising		60,000	3.0%
Delivery		16,000	.8%
Supplies		24,000	1.2%
Depreciation		22,000	1.1%
Mortgage Expense		60,000	3.0%
Insurance		14,000	.7%
* Interest		20,000	1.0%
Taxes and Licenses		26,000	1.3%
Utilities.............................		20,000	1.0%
Miscellaneous		28,000	1.4%
Total Operating Expenses		$ 670,000	33.5%
OPERATING PROFIT....................		$ 50,000	2.5%
OTHER INCOME		20,000	1.0%
NET PROFIT—BEFORE FEDERAL INCOME TAXES......................		$ 70,000	3.5%

*The concept of "imputed interest", found on actual store statements, is omitted for purposes of simplification.

THE FINANCIAL STATEMENTS

BUFFINGTON'S DEPARTMENT STORE INC.
BALANCE SHEET
AS OF JANUARY 31, 19XX

ASSETS

CURRENT ASSETS:			
Cash on Hand and in Bank		$180,000	15.0%
Notes Receivable		5,000	.4%
Accounts Receivable	$310,000		
Less: Estimated Bad Debts	10,000	·00	25.0%
Merchandise Inventory (at cost)		ʾ0	33.3%
Supplies		ʾ	.9%
Prepaid Expenses			.4%
Total Current Assets		$ 900,000	75.0%
FIXED ASSETS:			
Furniture, Fixtures and Equipment	$125,000		
Less: Accumulated Depreciation	45,000	$ 8	6.7%
Delivery Equipment	$ 50,000		
Less: Accumulated Depreciation	30,000	20,000	1.7%
Building	$250,000		
Less: Accumulated Depreciation	50,000	200,000	16.6%
Total Fixed Assets		300,000	25.0%
TOTAL ASSETS		$1,200,000	100.0%

- -

LIABILITIES AND PROPRIETORSHIP

CURRENT LIABILITIES:			
Notes Payable		$ 50,000	4.2%
Accounts Payable		220,000	18.3%
Expenses Payable		5,000	.4%
Total Current Liabilities		$ 5,000	22.9%
LONG-TERM LIABILITIES:			
Mortgage Payable		125,000	10.4%
Total Liabilities		$ 400,000	33.3%
PROPRIETORSHIP:			
Preferred Stock		$100,000	
Common Stock		500,000	
Retained Earnings		200,000	
Total Proprietorship (net worth)		800,000	66.7%
TOTAL LIABILITIES AND PROPRIETORSHIP		$1,200,000	100.0%

country's resources of land, labor, and capital to the production of goods and services that people want. It may not be a perfect system—as evidenced by the continuing numbers of business failures and the many unfulfilled needs of society—but it has provided, in the United States, the greatest output of goods and services and the highest standard of living that the world has known.

Profit is measured in money, and thus serves as a yardstick for business efficiency. We shall be concerned with the *mathematics of profit*—the calculations necessary to arrive at a figure which realistically reflects how efficiently a business has served society over a period of time.

In our society, probably no other concept is misunderstood and criticized so much as the concept of *profits*. Not only is there a basic lack of understanding of the capitalistic system, but also a misconception of what constitutes profit, how it is calculated, and how it is reported by the business community. An interesting experiment in any introductory course in business is to have the students estimate the net profit of the better-known corporations in the community. In nearly every case the estimates will range from 1 to 50% of sales and, in a few instances, some may even suggest 100% or 200%. In contrast to these estimates, the 1969 median profit after taxes for the five hundred largest industrial corporations in the United States, according to an article in *Fortune* magazine, was 4.6% of sales ("The 500 Largest Industrial Corporations," May 1970). For food and beverage manufacturers in this group, *Fortune* listed profits of 2.7%, for motor vehicles 3.9%, and for pharmaceuticals 9.2%. The retailing company reporting the largest sales and profit in 1969 was Sears, Roebuck & Co., whose profits were 5.0% of sales. The next three retailers ranked by sales showed net profits as follows: Great Atlantic & Pacific Tea Co., 0.9%; Safeway Stores, 1.3%; J. C. Penney, 1.1%.

Every commitment a business makes to a supplier of goods or services, to employees, or to customers has some eventual monetary value attached to it and subsequently will affect profits. Money or promises to pay are received every day by a business as a result of its sales. Likewise, every day a business makes payments or promises to pay for goods, supplies, and services which are required to continue its operations. A record must be made of all these transactions and commitments to pay. This accumulation of such information about all of the company's operation is called the *books of the company*; the method and manner of recording the information is called the *accounting system*; the act of recording the information is called *bookkeeping*.

At least once a year a summary of all the records must be made. The main purpose of this is to determine by how much the income from sales exceeds the total of the cost of those sales and the expenses incurred in operating the business. If there is an excess, it is termed *profit*, but if the income is less than the costs and expenses, a *loss* has been incurred. This summary, called the *income statement*, is the most important financial statement which a business prepares. The profit or loss determined on this statement is used in the preparation of another essential financial statement, the *balance sheet*—so called because, when properly made up, it shows the value of everything the business possesses to equal the total of what the business owes to others for these items of value plus the investment of the business owners.

In this chapter we shall discuss both these statements in detail and carefully examine the elements of profit. The example of an income statement and balance sheet at the beginning of this chapter is that of a fictitious—but realistic—firm, Buffington's Department Store, Inc. This text will explain all calculations necessary for the preparation and analysis of financial statements using Buffington's as an example from chapter to chapter.

EXERCISE 1-1 INDUSTRIAL PROFITS

Calculate the net income of each company as a percent of sales and as a percent of invested capital. Rank the companies on each of these factors from 1 for the highest percent to 10 for the lowest percent. The percents are to be rounded to tenths of a percent.

The 10 Largest Industrial Corporations
(Ranked According to 1968 Sales, 000)

| | | | | Net Income | | | |
| | | | | As Percent of Sales | | As Percent of Inv. Capital | |
	Sales	Net Income*	Invested Capital†	%	Rank	%	Rank
1. General Motors	$22,755,403	$1,731,915	$9,756,810	7.6‡	____	17.8§	____
2. Standard Oil (N.J.)	14,091,337	1,276,681	9,855,796	____	____	____	____
3. Ford Motor	14,075,100	626,600	4,946,600	____	____	____	____
4. General Electric	8,381,633	357,107	2,493,448	____	____	____	____
5. Chrysler	7,445,251	290,729	2,066,324	____	____	____	____
6. IBM	6,888,549	871,498	4,569,140	____	____	____	____
7. Mobil Oil	6,220,996	428,239	4,071,780	____	____	____	____
8. Texaco	5,459,771	835,530	5,418,029	____	____	____	____
9. Gulf Oil	4,558,548	626,319	4,750,791	____	____	____	____
10. U.S. Steel	4,536,703	253,676	3,344,482	____	____	____	____

Source: "The 500 Largest Corporations," Fortune, May 1970.

* After taxes.
† Capital stock, surplus, and retained earnings (i.e., net worth) at year's end.
‡ $1,731,915 ÷ 22,755,403 = .0761 X 100 = 7.6%.
§ $1,731,915 ÷ 9,756,810 = .1775 X 100 = 17.8%.

EXERCISE 1-2 RETAILING PROFITS

Calculate the net income of each company as a percent of sales and as a percent of invested capital. Rank the companies on each of these factors from 1 for the highest percent to 10 for the lowest percent. Round off answers to nearest tenth of a percent.

The 10 Largest Retailing Companies
(Ranked According to 1968 Sales 000)

	Sales	Net Income*	Invested Capital†	Net Income As Percent of Sales %	Rank	As Percent of Inv. Capital %	Rank
1. Sears, Roebuck	$8,197,992	$418,030	$3,173,453	___	___	___	___
2. Great A & P Tea	5,425,000	45,250	640,000	___	___	___	___
3. Safeway	3,685,690	55,061	430,586	___	___	___	___
4. J.C. Penney	3,322,622	109,252	595,271	___	___	___	___
5. Kroger	3,160,838	34,003	281,733	___	___	___	___
6. Marcor (Montgomery Wards)	2,500,705	53,810	817,615	___	___	___	___
7. F.W. Woolworth	1,907,284	65,739	726,147	___	___	___	___
8. Federated Dept. Stores	1,818,765	80,270	612,026	___	___	___	___
9. S.S. Kresge	1,757,750	47,611	319,450	___	___	___	___
10. Food Fair Stores	1,371,781	10,797	117,155	___	___	___	___

*After taxes.
†Capital stock, surplus, and retained earnings (i.e., net worth) at year's end.

EXERCISE 1-3 INDUSTRIAL PROFITS

Calculate the net income of each company as a percent of sales and as a percent of invested capital. Rank the companies on each of these factors from 1 for the highest percent to 10 for the lowest percent. Round off answers to nearest tenth of a percent.

The 10 Largest Industrial Corporations
(Ranked According to 1968 Sales, 000)

	Sales	Net Income*	Invested Capital†	Net Income As Percent of Sales %	Rank	As Percent of Inv. Capital %	Rank
1. General Motors	$24,295,141	$1,710,695	$10,227,904	___	___	___	___
2. Standard Oil (N.J.)	14,929,849	1,047,639	10,092,612	___	___	___	___
3. Ford Motor	14,755,600	546,500	5,222,000	___	___	___	___
4. General Electric	8,447,965	278,015	2,539,977	___	___	___	___
5. IBM	7,197,295	933,873	5,276,991	___	___	___	___
6. Chrysler	7,052,185	88,771	2,100,896	___	___	___	___
7. Mobil Oil	6,121,393	434,515	4,309,070	___	___	___	___
8. Texaco	5,867,860	769,804	5,896,811	___	___	___	___
9. International Tel & Tel	5,474,743	234,034	2,081,309	___	___	___	___
10. Gulf Oil	4,953,281	610,558	5,039,891	___	___	___	___

*After Taxes.
†Capital Stock, surplus, and retained earnings (i.e., net worth) at years end.

EXERCISE 1-4 RETAILING PROFITS

Calculate the net income of each company as a percent of sales and as a percent of invested capital. Rank the companies on each of these factors from 1 for the highest percent to 10 for the lowest percent.   Round off answers to nearest tenth of a percent.

The 10 Largest Retailing Companies
(Ranked According to 1968 Sales, 000)

	Sales	Net Income*	Invested Capital†	Net Income As Percent of Sales %	Rank	As Percent of Inv. Capital %	Rank
1. Sears, Roebuck	$8,862,971	$440,954	$3,439,802				
2. Great A & P Tea	5,700,000	52,000	640,492				
3. Safeway Stores	4,099,647	54,593	457,192				
4. J.C. Penney	3,756,092	110,927	656,423				
5. Kroger	3,477,164	38,730	309,299				
6. Marcor (Montgomery Wards)	2,715,150	66,950	859,347				
7. F.W. Woolworth	2,272,570	70,658	795,327				
8. S.S. Kresge	2,185,298	54,089	367,519				
9. Federated Dept. Stores	1,998,863	85,942	653,319				
10. Food Fair Stores	1,555,431	12,062	123,998				

*After Taxes.
†Capital stock, surplus, and retained earnings (i.e., net worth) at year's end.

SECTION 2—THE INCOME STATEMENT

The *income statement*, being a summary of a company's operation for a period of time, is like a motion picture of the company's transactions. It is sometimes called the *profit-and-loss statement*, emphasizing that its main purpose is to determine the amount of profit or the amount of loss the company has incurred during a certain period of time. It may also be called the *operating statement*, a term which stresses the statement's role as a summary of all operations and its importance in planning operations for the subsequent period.

The income statement may summarize operations for any period of time. However, it must be made at least once a year because it is the basis for the payment of income taxes. Most large companies prepare the statement each month. The precise period is included in the heading. Since it reflects transactions from the first day through the last day, the heading is specified "for the year ended" (or "... month ended," or "... three months ended," etc.), plus the date of the last day for which transactions are included in the statement. Thus, Buffington's income statement is "For the Year Ended January 31, 19XX."

Any period for which an income statement is prepared is referred to as a *fiscal period*. A twelve-month accounting period is known as a *fiscal year*, which may or may not coincide with the calendar year. In Buffington's case (which is typical of most merchandising businesses), the natural break in the year's activities comes at the end of January. After the peak Christmas buying period, clearance sales are necessary to eliminate the odds and ends and broken size ranges. Then, in January, comes a *physical inventory* or count of merchandise on hand when it is at its lowest level for the year. With the information from this inventory an income statement can be prepared. Also, at this time the merchandising emphasis is shifting from winter to spring goods.

Many industrial companies and government organizations have fiscal years ending June 30, when lower production or workload may make it more convenient to summarize a year's operation.

Referring to Buffington's income statement, we note that the word *profit* is used at three different points. Upon subtracting cost of sales from sales, the result is a *gross margin of profit* of $720,000. By no means is this the amount of money which may be distributed to the owners. Following this subtraction of *costs* of the goods which were sold must come a subtraction of the *expenses* of operation. The result is an *operating profit* of $50,000. This is the reward the company has earned for its merchandising activities, the main purpose of its operation. The final or *net profit* may be more or less than this because of income and expenses from nonmerchandising activities. Examples are financial operations—for instance, the investment of company funds, or landlord operations such as the rental of excess storage space. When the $20,000 of net "other income" is added to "operating profit," the final result is a net profit of $70,000. This is the amount on which income taxes must be paid.

EXERCISE 1-5 THE INCOME STATEMENT

Arrange the following items into an appropriate trading section of an income statement. The income statement for Buffington's Department Store at the beginning of this chapter may be used as a guide.

Cash discounts earned
Sales returns and allowances
Total cost of goods sold
Ending inventory
Net alteration and workroom costs
Net sales
Gross margin
Transportation charges on purchases
Net cost of goods sold
Gross sales
Gross cost of goods sold
Gross purchases
Total cost of goods sold
Beginning inventory
Purchase returns and allowances
Total merchandise available for sale
Net purchases

EXERCISE 1-6 THE INCOME STATEMENT

Arrange the following items into an appropriate income statement. The income statement for Buffington's Department Store at the beginning of this chapter may be used as a guide.

Depreciation
Other income
Gross margin
Insurance
Total merchandise available for sale
Net sales
Supplies
Net purchases
Gross cost of goods sold
Net profit
Beginning inventory
Payroll
Net cost of goods sold
Advertising
Total cost of goods sold
Operating profit
Cash discounts earned
Ending inventory
Net alterations and workroom costs

EXERCISE 1-7 THE INCOME STATEMENT

At the beginning of the year a store's merchandise inventory was $50,000; at the end of the year it was $45,000. When it closed its books at the end of the year, the following information was revealed. Prepare an income statement for the year's operations.

Net purchases	$150,000
Net sales	300,000
Rent income	1,200
Cash discounts earned	3,000
Payroll	40,000
Advertising	6,000
Supplies	5,000
Alteration costs	2,000
Depreciation	1,800
Insurance	1,000

SECTION 3—THE BALANCE SHEET

Just as the income statement is like a motion picture of a company's operation, a *balance sheet* is like a photograph. As of a specific date (i.e., at one instance), it gives a picture of the items of value possessed by the company, how much is owed to others for the acquisition of these items, and how much is owned by the company. Thus, Buffington's balance sheet is "As of January 31, 19XX." The balance sheet may also be called a *statement of financial position.* Just as a photograph of a child is often compared with that taken a year earlier, so is a balance sheet at the end of a period often compared with that at the end of a previous period to determine the amount of change.

The balance sheet has three principal groupings: *assets, liabilities,* and *proprietorship* or *net worth.* An asset is anything tangible or intangible which has a monetary value. Every asset must be owned by someone, and ownership rights are called *equities.* The balance sheet sets forth two kinds of equities, those of creditors of the business and those of the owners of the business. Creditor equities or ownership rights in the company's assets constitute liabilities. They are listed first because in the event the business discontinues operations, its creditors must be paid before the owners can exercise their rights to the assets. The business owner's equities or ownership rights constitute proprietorship. Thus, we arrive at the *accounting equation:*

$$\text{Assets} = \text{Liabilities} + \text{Proprietorship}$$

On Buffington's balance sheet, the total assets of $1,200,000 equal the total liabilities of $400,000 plus the proprietorship of $800,000.

Assets

In the balance sheet, assets are subdivided into current assets and fixed assets.

current assets

Current assets include cash and those items which are intended to be converted into cash or used up in the near future (approximately one year). *Notes receivable* are promises of payment from customers. A promissory note is a written unconditional promise to pay a certain sum of money on a definite date to a specified person or to the note's bearer (the person in possession of the note). Consequently, it may be readily converted into cash at a bank or transferred to others in payment of obligations. *Accounts receivable* are claims against others for the sale of goods or invoices. In Buffington's case, this is $310,000 less $10,000; the latter sum is their estimate of the amount which they will not be able to collect due to a lack of character, capacity, or capital on the part of their customers. In some cases this estimate may be referred to as "bad debt allowance" or "reserve for bad debts."

Merchandise inventory is the goods which are purchased or produced for resale. Another commonly used term for these goods is *merchandise stock*—or just *stock*, although such a term is seldom found on balance sheets. Merchandise inventory must not be confused with *supplies*. Supplies are not resold, but are consumed in the operation of the business; they are, in essence, an expense paid in advance—or more accurately, a *prepaid expense*. However, because they are tangible and important, they are listed separately under the term "supplies." Other expenses paid in advance are of an intangible nature—such as insurance premiums—and these intangibles constitute *prepaid expenses* on the balance sheet. The total of Buffington's current assets is $900,000.

fixed assets

Tangible assets of a more or less permanent nature, which are used in carrying on the normal functions of the business and which are not for sale, are called *fixed assets*. However, as they are used they will gradually lose their usefulness or value. A measure of this loss of value is called *depreciation*. Each year a certain amount is charged as an expense against the year's operations for the estimated loss of value of the fixed assets. This depreciation expense is listed on the income statement along with all other expenses. Each fixed asset is, then, shown on the balance sheet at its original cost less the *accumulated depreciation* or *reserve for depreciation*, which is the total depreciation expense for this asset since the time of purchase.

When Buffington's $300,000 of fixed assets is added to the $900,000 of current assets, the total assets are shown to have a value of $1,200,000. This total asset value makes up the left side of the accounting equation (p. 10). Now we must look at the right side, the liabilities and proprietorship, which detail the equities or ownership rights to the assets.

Liabilities

Liabilities are the amounts owed to "others" (the creditors of the business). These amounts represent the creditors' equities or ownership rights in the assets. In terms of the accounting equation,

$$\text{Liabilities} = \text{Assets} - \text{Proprietorship}$$

Liabilities are divided into two groups in a manner similar to the asset grouping—current liabilities and long-term liabilities.

current liabilities

Those debts which must be paid in the near future, usually within one year, are classified as *current liabilities*. Just as Buffington's accepted the promissory notes of others, so have they borrowed money or received credit by giving promissory notes to others. These obligations to pay are *notes payable*. Rarely does a business pay cash on delivery for all of its needs. At any time it will owe others for goods or services received. These obligations which have not been acknowledged by promissory notes are termed *accounts payable.* There are certain other debts which are already owed but for which payment is not yet due. These are listed on Buffington's statement as *expenses payable*, but are often referred to as *accrued expenses payable.* Among these owed but unpaid expenses are interest expense on notes payable, wages, and taxes. Buffington's total current liabilities are $275,000.

long-term liabilities

Those obligations which are not payable within one year are called *long-term liabilities* or fixed liabilities. These would include long-term notes, mortgages, and different types of bonds which a corporation may issue as a means of financing the business. If these long-term commitments are being paid in installments, those installments due within one year would be classified as current liabilities and the remainder as a long-term liability.

In Buffington's case, a mortgage payable of $125,000 is its only long-term liability. This amount added to current liabilities of $275,000 results in total liabilities of $400,000.

Proprietorship

Proprietorship represents the equities or rights of the business owner or owners in the assets of the business. As previously stated, if the business fails these rights are secondary to the rights of the creditors. By transposition of the accounting equation we find:

$$\text{Proprietorship} = \text{Assets} - \text{Liabilities}$$

Other terms often used for proprietorship are *net worth*, *capital*, or—in the case of a corporation—*stockholders' equity.*

There are three types of business ownership: *single proprietorship*, *partnership*, and *corporation.* Assuming each of these ownership possibilities in the case of Buffington's, the proprietorship section would vary as follows:

Single proprietorship		
James P. Buffington, capital		$800,000
Partnership		
James P. Buffington, capital	$500,000	
Ralph R. Meyer, capital	300,000	
Total proprietorship		$800,000
Corporation		
Preferred stock	$100,000	
Common stock	500,000	
Retained earnings	200,000	
Total proprietorship		$800,000

The balance sheet of the corporation differs from the others in that it shows the source of the capital but not the names of the owners. The preferred and common stock constitute the *paid-in capital* of the corporation. The accumulated earnings which have not been distributed to the stockholders as *dividends* are shown as a separate part of the proprietorship section and entitled *retained earnings.*

Preferred stock is so named because its owners are given certain preferential rights over the owners of common stock. Primarily, these rights include being first to participate in dividends or in claims to assets in case the business should be liquidated.

SECTION 4—ANALYZING FINANCIAL STATEMENTS

To analyze something is to study the nature and relationship of its parts. Any figure on a financial statement lacks significance until it is related to other figures on the statement; it becomes even more meaningful when it is then compared with corresponding figures from previous company statements or from the statements of other companies in the industry.

Intrastatement analysis

The first step in financial statement analysis is determining relationships within a given statement. This may be termed *intrastatement* or *vertical analysis*. Thus, in Buffington's income statement, the net sales figure is used as a base and all of the subsequent figures are related to it on the basis of 100 or as percents. Thus, the $70,000 net profit figure becomes meaningful when it is recognized that it is only 3.5% of sales. Similarly, on the balance sheet, each asset figure is shown as a percent of total assets. Likewise, each liability and proprietorship item is percented to the total liabilities and proprietorship figure. Thus, each part is proportionately related to the whole.

In addition to relationships expressed on a percent basis, they are also expressed as ratios. For example, the $900,000 of Buffington's current assets may be related to its $300,000 of fixed assets as being three times as large, or as a ratio 3.0:1 (or simply 3). Likewise, the relationship between the $900,000 of current assets and the $275,000 of current liabilities may be expressed as a ratio of 3.3:1. This is computed by dividing current assets by the current liabilities and rounding to the first place.

Interstatement analysis

After intrastatement analysis, the next step in financial statement analysis is to compare the dollar figures and the intrastatement percents and ratios with those of previous periods or with those of other companies. This may be termed *interstatement* or *horizontal analysis*. Buffington's net profit of $70,000 or 3.5% of sales becomes even more meaningful if it is related to last year's profit of $76,000 which was 4% of sales. A further insight is gained if it is compared with a national average of 4.3% of sales for similar stores for the same year.

Intrastatement and interstatement analyses may be illustrated using the condensed comparative income statement for Buffington's in table 1-1.

TABLE 1-1   comparative income statement, Buffington's Department Store, Inc.

	1970	1969	Increase (or Decrease) ($)	Increase (or Decrease) (%)	Percent of Net Sales 1970	Percent of Net Sales 1969
Net sales	$2,000,000	$1,900,000	100,000	5.2	100.0	100.0
Cost of goods sold	1,280,000	1,196,000	84,000	7.1	64.0	62.9
Gross margin	720,000	704,000	16,000	2.3	36.0	37.0
Operating expenses	670,000	650,000	20,000	3.1	33.5	34.2
Operating profit	50,000	54,000	(4,000)	(7.4)	2.5	2.8
Other income	20,000	22,000	(2,000)	(9.1)	1.0	1.2
Net profit	70,000	76,000	(6,000)	(7.9)	3.5	4.0

Looking at the 1970 figures alone, Buffington's has few guidelines for improving operations. Much more meaningful information for management planning, however, will be gained by comparing the 1970 data with that of the previous year. This will highlight areas where improvement is needed. The analysis shows that the increase in sales was accompanied by a greater percent increase in cost of goods sold. Consequently, even though there were more dollars of gross margin, the rate of margin was lower. Fortunately, a better job was done in controlling operating expenses, which decreased from 34.2 to 33.5% of sales. Nevertheless, there was a decrease in operating profit, which was compounded by a drop in other income. The result was a net profit of 3.5%, contrasted with 4.0% for the previous year. The absolute dollar amount of profit decreased 7.9%.

Management will now make every effort to increase gross margin while maintaining a tight control over expenses. They will also seek means of increasing other income. They will be spurred to even greater effort if comparison with industry averages shows that profit margins for similar stores increased during the past year.

Common analytical meas

The financial condition and operating efficiency of a business is of interest not only to the owners but to others such as creditors, employees, investors, and government agencies. Just as there are common tests to determine the health of an individual, so are there common tests or measures of business health. Some of those most often used are explained below and applied to Buffington's operation.

current ratio

Current assets must be used to pay those debts which fall due within a year. Consequently, the best known test of financial statements is the *current ratio*. This is calculated by dividing current assets by current liabilities:

	Current Year	Previous Year
Current assets	$900,000	$940,000
Current liabilities	275,000	245,000
Net working capital	$625,000	$695,000

Current ratio:

$$\frac{\$900,000}{\$275,000} = \quad 3.27:1$$

$$\frac{\$940,000}{\$245,000} = \qquad\qquad 3.67:1$$

The amount of current assets in excess of current liabilities is termed *working capital*. It is recognized that certain current assets may decline in value and that a business must have funds for opportunity purchases, for peak seasonal periods of business activities, and for contingencies. Consequently, a 2:1 current ratio has been the traditional rule-of-thumb standard. However, no one test can be a complete measure of financial condition. Although Buffington's ratio has declined, it would appear to be more than adequate.

acid-test ratio

Certain current assets such as inventories and prepaid expenses may require considerable time for conversion into cash. Upon conversion, the amount realized may be less, due to a decline in market price or a reduction in demand. Thus, a second measure of solving, called the *acid-test ratio*, is often used. This is calculated by dividing the sum of cash and receivables (called *quick assets*) by the current liabilities:

	Current Year	Previous Year
Quick assets		
Cash	$180,000	$275,000
Accounts receivable	300,000	290,000
Notes receivable	5,000	5,000
Total	$485,000	$570,000
Current liabilities	$275,000	$245,000

Acid-test ratio:

$$\frac{\$485,000}{\$275,000} = \quad 1.76:1$$

$$\frac{\$570,000}{\$245,000} = \qquad\qquad 2.33:1$$

An acid-test ratio of 1:1 is considered desirable. Buffington's decline from 2.33:1 to 1.76:1 confirms the decrease in liquidity indicated by the drop in the current ratio. Further steps may be taken to measure this.

inventory-to-net-working-capital

A closer look at the elements of current assets and their liquidity is obtained by relating inventory to the net working capital. Although inventory constitutes the largest investment of a merchant, too much inventory in relation to cash and receivables may pose problems in meeting current obligations. The relationship is usually expressed as a percent, and is calculated by dividing the merchandise inventory by the net working capital:

	Current Year	Previous Year
Merchandise inventory	$400,000	$355,000
Net working capital	625,000	695,000
Inventory-to-Net-Working-Capital ratio:		
$\dfrac{\$400,000}{\$625,000} =$	.64 or 64%	
$\dfrac{\$355,000}{\$695,000} =$		.5108 or 51.1%

There may be cause for concern if this relationship exceeds 80%. Although Buffington's percent has increased from 51.1% to 64%, this does not mean impending insolvency. However, it does indicate that perhaps they are not utilizing inventory as effectively as in the previous year. This can be more adequately measured by calculating the turnover of average inventory, which is discussed in detail in chapter 3.

accounts receivable turnover and age

The extension of some type of credit is almost essential today for most businesses (with the exception of food stores), and is a major item in current assets. The amount of credit sales is a matter of business policy, which involves appraisal of the amount of increase in total sales due to the extension of credit, the revenue in the form of service charges on long-term accounts, the cost of financing the business, the potential losses due to bad debts, and the resultant effect on profits.

If goods are sold on credit, the store will not receive payment for its credit sales until the end of the *credit period*. The credit period is the length of time granted the customers before full payment is required. Consequently, the firm requires additional capital proportional to the length of the credit period. The relationship between sales volume and accounts receivable is termed *accounts receivable turnover* and is an aid in determining the amount of capital necessary to finance the credit business.

It is calculated by dividing net sales by the average accounts receivable. To get a representative yearly average, the accounts receivable balance at the end of each month should be used. If this is not available, the amounts at the beginning and end of the year may be averaged.

	Current Year	Previous Year
Net sales	$2,000,000	$1,900,000
Accounts receivable (net but including notes receivable)		
Beginning of year	295,000	230,000
End of year	305,000	290,000
Total	$600,000	$520,000
Average	$300,000	$260,000
Accounts receivable turnover:		
$\dfrac{\$2,000,000}{\$300,000} =$	6.7 times	
$\dfrac{\$1,900,000}{\$260,000} =$		7.3 times

It can be seen that there is a greater dependence on credit sales in the current year than in the previous year. The next steps are to determine the effectiveness of the collection policy and to test the stated value of the receivables. The longer an account is past due, the more difficult it is to collect. Accounts on which there have been no payments for six months usually lose about 50% of their value. *Aging* the accounts—comparing their age with the company's normal credit period—is standard practice in any financial audit of a company. This can only be accomplished by listing all account balances, separating the past-due portions, and determining the number of months' delinquency for each account. The allowance for bad debts can then be developed to cover perhaps 50% of portions three to six months past due and 75% of those over six months.

Efforts are sometimes made to determine average age of accounts receivable—the effective collection period—by relating receivables, sales, number of days in the year, and the company's credit period. The results are of dubious value due to the variety of credit terms offered, the seasonal variance in credit sales, and the wide divergence in size of accounts. In Buffington's case, dividing 365 days by the 6.7 turnover figure would give an average age of accounts receivable of 54 days, a figure which would be of doubtful significance without a detailed aging. Aging is discussed in detail in chapter 5.

fixed-assets-to-net-worth

Proceeding to other than current assets, a relationship is often determined between fixed assets and net worth. The total depreciated book values of tangible fixed assets is divided by the net worth. This measurement is related to the current ratio in measuring the adequacy of operating funds to cover obligations which must be met in the near future. The usual practice is to express this relationship as a percent.

	Current Year	Previous Year
Fixed assets	$300,000	$210,000
Net worth	800,000	780,000
Fixed-Assets-to-Net-Worth		
$\dfrac{\$300,000}{\$800,000} =$	37.5%	
$\dfrac{\$210,000}{\$780,000} =$		26.9%

In the current year, a larger amount and percent of Buffington's capital is being devoted to building and equipment than in the previous years. The relationship of fixed assets to net worth probably wouldn't be considered excessive until it reached 60 or 70%. In Buffington's case, this year's higher percent could reflect management's foresight in maintaining facilities which will enhance sales and increase efficiency.

capital turnover

The effective use of total assets is measured by dividing sales by average total assets, yielding a figure termed *capital turnover*. If turnover is too rapid, it indicates too much dependence on borrowed funds. If turnover is too slow, it means that the return on investment is not what it could be and that perhaps too much is tied up in fixed assets.

	Current Year	Previous Year
Net sales	$2,000,000	$1,900,000
Total assets		
Beginning of year	1,210,000	1,220,000
End of year	1,200,000	1,210,000
Total	$2,410,000	$2,430,000
Average	$1,205,000	$1,215,000
Capital turnover:		
$\dfrac{\$2,000,000}{\$1,205,000} =$	1.7:1	
$\dfrac{\$1,900,000}{\$1,215,000} =$		1.6:1

With very little change from last year to this year, greater attention would probably be given to measuring how effective specific groups of assets are being used.

return on average total assets

The productivity of all assets and the competency of management is indicated by dividing net income (after income taxes) by total assets. The equities of creditors or owners are disregarded and consequently businesses with different types of financing may be compared.

	Current Year	Previous Year
Net profit after taxes	$ 42,900	$ 46,020
Total assets		
Beginnihg of year	1,210,000	1,220,000
End of year	1,200,000	1,210,000
Total	$2,410,000	$2,430,000
Average	$1,205,000	$1,215,000
Rate of return:		

$$\frac{\$42,900}{\$1,205,000} = \qquad 3.6\%$$

$$\frac{\$46,020}{\$1,215,000} = \qquad\qquad 3.8\%$$

The drop of .2% indicates that assets have not been so productive. The significance of this can only be determined by looking at industry averages and at possible trends over several years.

net-profit-to-average-net-worth

This relationship is sometimes termed *net profit on tangible net worth* or *rate earned on stockholder's equity*. This is a narrower measure than that relating profit to assets, since it eliminates the equity of creditors. It reflects the productiveness of the owner's investment. It could be used in comparison with alternative ways of investing capital.

	Current Year	Previous Year
Net profit after taxes	$ 42,900	$ 46,020
Proprietorship		
Beginning of year	780,000	700,000
End of year	800,000	780,000
Total	$1,580,000	$1,480,000
Average	$790,000	$740,000
Rate of return:		

$$\frac{\$42,900}{\$790,000} = \qquad 5.4\%$$

$$\frac{\$46,020}{\$740,000} = \qquad\qquad 6.2\%$$

The decrease of 1.2% not only reflects the decrease in actual dollars of profit, but also the greater reliance on ownership equity than on creditor equity. The traditional goal has been a 10% return to provide for growth as well as an annual distribution of profits to the owners.

In the case of public corporations, the rate of return to stockholders is particularly important because of the detachment of the majority of stockholders from management of the business. The attraction of additional equity financing is difficult if the rate of return to potential investors does not give promise of being equivalent to that being achieved by other companies. Consequently, the rate earned on common stockholders' equity and earnings per share on common stock are quite often highlighted to attract investors to the company.

total-liabilities-to-proprietorship

The financing of a business with borrowed funds is termed *trading on the equity*. The extent to which borrowed funds are used is found by dividing total liabilities by the proprietorship. If the return on the borrowed money is greater than current interest rates, then the owners benefit. However, creditors must be paid, and if these fixed charges are too high, it may put too great a strain on the business during slack periods and the creditors may gain control of the business.

	Current Year	Previous Year
Total liabilities	$ 400,000	$ 430,000
Total proprietorship	800,000	700,000
Liabilities as a percent of proprietorship:		
$\frac{\$400,000}{\$800,000} =$	50%	
$\frac{\$430,000}{\$700,000} =$		61.4%

Most bankers will look at this relationship before approving a business loan. The customary standard is 50%, which provides an adequate margin of safety for the creditors. If the relationship were to exceed 100%, then the creditors would have a greater interest in the business than the owners. It would be extremely difficult for a business to operate under such a situation, even if the creditors did not gain outright control.

EXERCISE 1-8 INCOME STATEMENT ANALYSIS

Complete the following income statement. Calculate percents to two decimal places.

THE REGAL SUPPLY COMPANY
Income Statement
For the Year Ended December 31, 1971

			Percent of Net Sales
Sales			
Gross sales	$150,840		
Sales returns & allowances	4,840		
Net sales		$ _ _ _ _ _ _ _	100%
Cost of Sales			
Beginning inventory	$ 16,000		_____
Net purchases	96,000		_____
Total merchandise available	$ _ _ _ _ _ _ _		_____
Ending inventory	17,000		_____
Gross cost of goods sold	$ _ _ _ _ _ _ _		_____
Cash discounts earned	1,800		_____
Net cost of goods sold	$ _ _ _ _ _ _ _		_____
Alteration & workroom costs	550		_____
Total cost of goods sold		_ _ _ _ _ _ _ _	_____
Gross Margin		$ _ _ _ _ _ _ _	_____
Operating Expenses			
Selling expenses	$ 27,000		_____
General & administrative expenses	9,250		_____
Total operating expenses		$ _ _ _ _ _ _	_____
Operating profit		$ _ _ _ _ _ _ _	_____
Other income		500	_____
Net profit		$ _ _ _ _ _ _	_____

EXERCISE 1-9 INCOME STATEMENT ANALYSIS

Complete the following income statement analysis. Calculate percents and ratios to two decimal places. (The calculation of ratios may be reviewed in appendix I, pp. 265)

A & B HARDWARE COMPANY
Comparative Income Statement
For Year Ended January 31, 1970 and 1971

	1971	1970	Increase (or Decrease) ($)	Increase (or Decrease) (%)	Ratio: 1971 to 1970
Sales					
Gross sales	$92,750	$84,500	_____	_____	_____
Sales returns & allowances	3,950	3,500	_____	_____	_____
Net sales	$88,800	$81,000	_____	_____	_____

	1971	1970	Increase (or Decrease) ($)	(%)	Ratio: 1971 to 1970
Cost of Sales					
Beginning inventory	$22,500	$29,700			
Net purchases	66,500	46,375			
Total merchandise available	$89,000	$76,075			
Ending inventory	27,000	22,500			
Gross cost of goods sold	$62,000	$53,575			
Cash discounts earned	950	775			
Net cost of goods sold	$61,050	$52,800			
Alteration & workroom costs	450	400			
Total cost of goods sold	$60,600	$53,200			
Gross Margin	28,200	27,800			
Operating Expenses					
Selling expenses	21,500	19,400			
General & administrative expenses	7,900	7,200			
Total operating expenses	29,400	26,600			
Operating profit	(1,200)	1,200			
Other income	(400)	400			
Net profit	($1,600)	$1,600			

EXERCISE 1-10 INCOME STATEMENT ANALYSIS

Complete the following income statement analysis. Calculate percents to two decimal places.

DAWSON MANUFACTURING CO.
Income Statement
For Year Ended December 31, 1970 and 1971

	1971	1970	Increase (or Decrease) ($)	(%)	Percent of Sales 1971	1970
Sales	$260,000	$210,000				
Cost of Sales						
Beginning inventory of fixed goods	25,000	19,000				
Goods manufactured	193,000	151,000				
Total finished goods available	$218,000	$170,000				
Less: ending inventory of finished goods	30,000	25,000				
Cost of goods sold	$188,000	$145,000				
Gross Profit	$ 72,000	$ 65,000				
Operating Expenses						
Selling expense						
Salesmen's salaries	$ 21,000	$ 16,000				
Advertising	8,500	7,500				
Sales promotion	1,750	1,500				
Total selling	$ 31,250	$ 25,000				
General expense						
Administrative salaries	20,000	18,000				
Depreciation	750	800				
Bad debts	850	700				
Miscellaneous	2,150	1,500				
Total general expense	$ 23,750	$ 21,000				

	Increase (or Decrease)		Percent of Sales	
	($)	(%)	1971	1970
Operating profit	17,000	19,000	____ ____	____ ____
Other income and expense				
Rent of warehouse	3,200	2,400	____ ____	____ ____
Interest expense	2,800	2,600	____ ____	____ ____
Net other income	$ 400	$ (200)	____ ____	____ ____
Net profit	$ 17,400	$ 18,800	____ ____	____ ____

EXERCISE 1-11 THE BALANCE SHEET

Complete the following balance sheet, calculating percents to two decimal places.

THE JONATHON COMPANY
Balance Sheet
as of December 31, 1971

		Percent of Total
Assets		
Current assets		
Cash	$ 8,400	_____
Accounts receivable	12,600	_____
Merchandise inventory	22,800	_____
Supplies	1,200	_____
Prepaid expenses	400	_____
Total current assets	$_____	_____
Fixed assets		
Furniture and fixtures (book value)	$ 9,200	_____
Delivery equipment (book value)	3,400	_____
Buildings (book value)	32,600	_____
Total fixed assets	$_____	_____
Total assets	$_____	100%
Liabilities		
Current liabilities		
Notes payable	$ 1,200	_____
Accounts payable	11,800	_____
Expenses payable	2,200	_____
Total current liabilities	$_____	_____
Long-term liabilities		
Mortgage payable	$14,400	_____
Total liabilities	$_____	_____

		Percent of Total

Proprietorship

Ezra Jonathon, Capital	$ _ _ _ _ _ _	_____
Total Liabilities and Proprietorship	$ _ _ _ _ _ _	100%

EXERCISE 1-12 BALANCE SHEET ANALYSIS

Complete the following balance sheet analysis. Calculate percents and ratios to two decimal places.

A & B HARDWARE COMPANY
Balance Sheet
For Year Ended January 31, 1970 and 1971

	1971	1970	Increase (or Decrease) ($)	(%)	Ratio 1971	1970
Assets						
Current assets						
Cash	$ 2,200	$ 4,800	___	___	___	___
Accounts receivable	7,800	2,200	___	___	___	___
Merchandise inventory	27,000	22,500	___	___	___	___
Supplies	800	600	___	___	___	
Prepaid expenses	500	400	___	___	___	
Total current assets	$38,300	$30,500	___	___	___	___
Fixed assets						
Store equipment (book value)	10,400	8,200	___	___	___	
Office equipment (book value)	2,200	2,400	___	___	___	
Building (book value)	17,800	18,600	___	___	___	
Total fixed assets	$30,400	$29,200	___	___	___	___
Total assets	$68,700	$59,700	___	___	___	___
Liabilities						
Current liabilities						
Accounts payable	$ 9,600	$ 4,400	___	___	___	___
Expenses payable	7,600	6,800	___	___	___	
Total current liabilities	$17,200	$11,200	___	___	___	___
Long-term liabilities						
Mortgage payable	12,000	12,800	___	___	___	
Total liabilities	$29,200	$24,000	___	___	___	___
Proprietorship						
George Abbot, Capital	$19,750	$17,850	___	___	___	___
Robert Burrows, Capital	$19,750	$17,850	___	___	___	___

EXERCISE 1-13 BALANCE SHEET ANALYSIS

Complete the following balance sheet analysis. Calculate percent to two decimal places.

DAWSON MANUFACTURING CO.
Balance Sheet
as of December 31, 1970 and 1971

	1971	1970	Percent of Total 1971	1970	Increase (or Decrease) $	%
Assets						
Current assets						
Cash	$ 12,200	$ 16,400	____	____	____	____
Accounts receivable	25,400	18,600	____	____	____	____
Inventories						
Finished goods	30,000	25,000	____	____	____	____
Work-in-process	14,600	9,200	____	____	____	____
Raw materials	15,800	14,600	____	____	____	____
Total inventories	$ 60,400	$ 48,800	____	____	____	____
Supplies	2,500	1,400	____	____	____	____
Prepaid expenses	1,500	1,200	____	____	____	____
Total current assets	$102,000	$ 86,400	____	____	____	____
Fixed assets						
Office equipment (book value)	6,600	6,800	____	____	____	____
Factory equipment (book value)	72,000	72,600	____	____	____	____
Buildings	58,000	59,000	____	____	____	____
Total fixed assets	$136,600	$138,400	____	____	____	____
Total assets	$238,600	$224,800	100%	100%	____	____
Liabilities						
Current liabilities						
Accounts payable	$ 19,400	$ 14,200	____	____	____	____
Expenses payable	8,200	6,200	____	____	____	____
Total current liabilities	$ 27,600	$ 20,400	____	____	____	____
Long-term liabilities						
Mortgage payable	46,800	48,800	____	____	____	____
Total liabilities	$ 74,400	$ 69,200	____	____	____	____
Proprietorship						
Common stock	$ 80,000	$ 80,000	____	____	____	____
Retained earnings	84,200	75,600	____	____	____	____
Total Proprietorship	$164,200	$155,600	____	____	____	____
Total Liabilities and Proprietorship	$238,600	$224,800	100%	100%	____	____

EXERCISE 1-14 ANALYSIS OF FINANCIAL STATEMENTS

Compute the following ratios for the A & B Hardware Company, using the income statements and balance sheets shown in exercises 1-9 and 1-12.

	1971	1970
1. Current ratio	_____	_____
2. Acid-test ratio	_____	_____
3. Inventory-to-net-working-capital ratio	_____	_____
4. Accounts receivable turnover	_____	_____
5. Fixed-assets-to-net-worth ratio	_____	_____
6. Capital turnover	_____	_____

	1971	1970
7. Return on average total assets	_____	_____
8. Net-profit-to-average-net-worth ratio	_____	_____
9. Total-liabilities-to-proprietorship ratio	_____	_____

EXERCISE 1-15   ANALYSIS OF FINANCIAL STATEMENTS

Compute the following ratios for the Dawson Manufacturing Company using the income statements and balance sheets shown in exercises 1-10 and 1-13.

	1971	1970
1. Current ratio	_____	_____
2. Acid-test ratio	_____	_____
3. Accounts receivable turnover	_____	_____
4. Fixed-assets-to-net-worth ratio	_____	_____
5. Capital turnover	_____	_____
6. Return on average total assets	_____	_____
7. Net-profit-to-average net worth ratio	_____	_____
8. Total-liabilities-to-proprietorship ratio	_____	_____

ANNUAL REPORTS

The size of a company is usually measured by sales, net income, or invested capital. As this chapter has pointed out, the health of the company or efficiency of its operation can only be determined by analysis of its financial statements. Accordingly, every public corporation makes an annual report to its stockholders on its yearly operation. These reports vary as to form and manner of presentation, but their main purpose is to disclose to the stockholders all factors which would affect the return on their investment. Consequently, an income statement and a balance sheet are always incorporated in this report. These also vary considerably in form. Examples from the reports of some of the largest corporations are presented on the following pages. They illustrate the variation in data, terminology, and manner of presentation.

Sears, Roebuck and Co. and Consolidated Subsidiaries

Statement of Income

	Year Ended January 31	
	1970	1969
Net Sales	$8,862,970,649	$8,197,992,298
Equity in Income of Unconsolidated Subsidiaries	109,436,654	110,769,126
Dividends	3,733,991	2,982,046
Total	8,976,141,294	8,311,743,470
Costs and Expenses (note 10)		
Cost of sales, advertising, selling, administrative and general expense	7,482,063,515	6,958,680,626
Rents (properties and equipment)	91,868,388	84,538,912
Repairs and maintenance	51,413,650	49,949,289
Depreciation (note 3)	106,752,712	104,519,371
Interest expense	154,520,371	112,849,520
Contribution to Employes Profit Sharing Fund (note 4)	88,174,784	77,203,484
Taxes (other than income taxes)	162,993,391	144,944,886
Federal and state income taxes (note 9)	397,400,000	361,027,000
Total Costs and Expenses	8,535,186,811	7,893,713,088
Net Income	$ 440,954,483	$ 418,030,382
Per Share		
Average shares outstanding	153,821,000	153,233,000
Net income	$2.87	$2.73

Statement of Retained Income

	Year Ended January 31	
	1970	1969
Balance Beginning of Year	$2,804,998,546	$2,586,192,850
Net Income	440,954,483	418,030,382
Deduct Dividends to Shareholders		
($1.35 and $1.30 per share respectively)	207,647,749	199,224,686
Retained Income for the Year	233,306,734	218,805,696
Balance End of Year	$3,038,305,280	$2,804,998,546

Sears, Roebuck and Co. and Consolidated Subsidiaries

Statement of Source and Use of Funds and Changes in Working Capital

	Year ended January 31,	
SOURCE OF FUNDS	1970	1969
Net income	$ 440,954,483	$ 418,030,382
Depreciation	106,752,712	104,519,371
Changes in deferred charges (future tax benefits)	10,130,252	1,272,351
Undistributed net income of unconsolidated subsidiaries	(101,128,560)	(103,169,619)
Funds provided from operations	456,708,887	420,652,485
Cash for stock issued under options	33,042,365	15,528,119
Proceeds from long-term debt issue	—	100,000,000
Total Source of Funds	489,751,252	536,180,604

USE OF FUNDS		
Cash dividends to shareholders	207,647,749	199,224,686
Property additions, less dispositions	211,043,228	130,797,997
Reduction of long-term debt	28,000,000	20,000,000
Changes in investments and other assets	9,132,785	(8,000,213)
Total Use of Funds	455,823,762	342,022,470
INCREASE IN WORKING CAPITAL	$ 33,927,490	$ 194,158,134

CHANGES IN WORKING CAPITAL	Increase		
Cash and marketable securities	$ 30,115,351	$ 225,827,311	$ 195,711,960
Receivables	253,889,846	3,552,887,620	3,298,997,774
Inventories	80,582,721	1,215,028,627	1,134,445,906
Prepaid advertising and other charges	2,708,993	53,587,194	50,878,201
Total Current Assets	367,296,911	5,047,330,752	4,680,033,841
Notes payable	166,646,395	1,770,696,993	1,604,050,598
Accounts payable and accrued expenses	42,988,549	544,936,455	501,947,906
Income and other taxes—currently payable	63,778,001	211,027,205	147,249,204
deferred	59,956,476	657,840,232	597,883,756
Total Current Liabilities	333,369,421	3,184,500,885	2,851,131,464
WORKING CAPITAL	$ 33,927,490	$1,862,829,867	$1,828,902,377

Sears, Roebuck and Co. and Consolidated Subsidiaries

Statement of Financial Position

	January 31	
	1970	1969
ASSETS		
Current Assets		
Cash	$ 223,276,902	$ 194,361,551
Marketable securities (market value $28,315,817)	2,550,409	1,350,409
Receivables	3,552,887,620	3,298,997,774
Inventories (note 2)	1,215,028,627	1,134,445,906
Prepaid advertising and other charges	53,587,194	50,878,201
Total Current Assets	5,047,330,752	4,680,033,841
Investments (note 1)	923,326,437	812,553,293
Property, Plant and Equipment	1,088,736,634	984,446,118
Deferred Charges (future tax benefits)	17,384,656	27,514,908
Unamortized Debenture Discount and Expense	2,524,223	3,036,022
Total Assets	$7,079,302,702	$6,507,584,182
LIABILITIES		
Current Liabilities		
Notes payable	$1,770,696,993	$1,604,050,598
Accounts payable	330,245,365	293,796,257
Accrued expenses	214,691,090	208,151,649
Federal income taxes accrued	78,568,419	34,201,594
Deferred income tax credits—net	657,840,232	597,883,756
Other accrued taxes	132,458,786	113,047,610
Total Current Liabilities	3,184,500,885	2,851,131,464
Long-Term Debt (note 5)	455,000,000	483,000,000
Total Liabilities	$3,639,500,885	$3,334,131,464
SHAREHOLDERS' EQUITY		
Common Stock (including capital in excess of par value)		
$1.50 par value—authorized 200,000,000 shares, outstanding shares 154,187,115 (notes 6 and 8)	$ 401,496,537	$ 368,454,172
Retained Income	3,038,305,280	2,804,998,546
Total Shareholders' Equity	$3,439,801,817	$3,173,452,718

Financial Position Detail

	January 31	
	1970	1969
RECEIVABLES		
Customer installment accounts receivable		
Easy payment accounts...	$2,221,017,167	$2,126,265,545
Revolving charge accounts...	1,372,874,725	1,220,638,565
	3,593,891,892	3,346,904,110
Other customer accounts...	101,904,882	98,805,738
Miscellaneous accounts and notes receivable..............................	96,446,334	80,752,252
	3,792,243,108	3,526,462,100
Less allowance for collection expense and losses on customer accounts........	236,826,866	225,387,123
	3,555,416,242	3,301,074,977
Deduct installment accounts sold—less portion of proceeds withheld		
pending collection..	2,528,622	2,077,203
	$3,552,887,620	$3,298,997,774
INVESTMENTS		
Unconsolidated subsidiaries and Simpsons-Sears (note 1)		
Allstate Insurance Company..	$ 580,720,285	$ 492,198,451
Allstate Enterprises, Inc...	58,845,798	57,714,517
Foreign Subsidiaries..	74,034,216	66,776,111
Simpsons-Sears Limited (50% of voting stock).........................	60,863,583	56,845,066
Other Subsidiaries..	83,661,952	93,974,831
	858,125,834	767,508,976
Other investments and advances (principally at cost).....................	65,200,603	45,044,317
	$ 923,326,437	$ 812,553,293
PROPERTY, PLANT AND EQUIPMENT (at cost)		
Land..	$ 213,537,550	$ 167,179,534
Buildings and improvements...	1,053,480,607	971,065,783
Less accumulated depreciation..	390,670,536	348,025,770
	662,810,071	623,040,013
Furniture, fixtures and equipment...	597,541,645	540,917,348
Less accumulated depreciation..	385,152,632	346,690,777
	212,389,013	194,226,571
Total property, plant and equipment..	1,864,559,802	1,679,162,665
Less total accumulated depreciation......................................	775,823,168	694,716,547
	$1,088,736,634	$ 984,446,118
LONG-TERM DEBT		
Sears, Roebuck and Co. (note 5)		
4¾% Sinking Fund Debentures, due 1983..............................	$ 230,000,000	$ 258,000,000
6⅝% Sinking Fund Debentures, due 1993..............................	100,000,000	100,000,000
Sears Roebuck Acceptance Corp.		
4⅝% Debentures, due 1972...	50,000,000	50,000,000
5% Debentures, due 1982..	50,000,000	50,000,000
4⅜% Subordinated Debentures, due 1977	25,000,000	25,000,000
	$ 455,000,000	$ 483,000,000

Statement of Income
Statement of Reinvested Earnings

J. C. Penney Company, Inc.
and Consolidated Subsidiaries

Statement of Income	53 weeks ended January 31, 1970	52 weeks ended January 25, 1969
Sales	$3,756,091,636	$3,322,621,612
Costs and expenses		
Cost of goods sold, occupancy, buying and warehousing costs	2,675,191,295	2,357,372,360
Selling, general and administrative expenses	809,442,134	707,489,380
Interest	50,406,233	30,563,031
Total costs and expenses	3,535,039,662	3,095,424,771
Income before Federal income taxes	221,051,974	227,196,841
Federal income taxes	110,125,000	117,945,000
Net income	$ 110,926,974	$ 109,251,841
Per share of common stock		
Primary	$2.15	$2.12
Fully diluted	2.08	2.08

Statement of Reinvested Earnings

Reinvested earnings—beginning of year	$ 548,298,205	$ 485,019,818
Net income for the year	110,926,974	109,251,841
Dividends	(52,012,328)	(45,973,454)
Reinvested earnings—end of year	$ 607,212,851	$ 548,298,205

31

Balance Sheet

Assets	January 31, 1970	January 25, 1969
Current assets		
Cash	$ 62,446,854	$ 59,329,260
Receivables, net	65,135,904	86,100,257
Merchandise inventories	696,646,510	613,246,304
Properties to be sold under sale and leaseback agreements	—	18,637,151
Prepaid expenses	26,817,198	15,082,740
Total current assets	851,046,466	792,395,712
Investment in subsidiary companies	139,586,749	95,240,887
Properties, net	368,950,131	289,698,786
Other assets	1,449,047	10,223,215
	$1,361,032,393	$1,187,558,600

Liabilities		
Current liabilities		
Accounts payable and accrued liabilities	$ 332,715,780	$ 334,356,567
Due to J. C. Penney Financial Corporation	107,197,222	—
Dividend payable	12,921,100	12,496,900
Federal income taxes	11,175,643	29,634,203
Deferred credits, principally tax effects applicable to installment sales	100,400,000	78,400,000
Total current liabilities	564,409,745	454,887,670
Long term debt	125,000,000	125,000,000
Deferred credits, principally tax effects applicable to depreciation	15,200,000	12,400,000
Stockholders' equity		
Preferred stock without par value: Authorized, 5,000,000 shares—issued, none		
Common stock, par value 50¢: Authorized, 75,000,000 shares—		
issued, 51,684,213 shares	49,209,797	46,972,725
Reinvested earnings	607,212,851	548,298,205
Total stockholders' equity	656,422,648	595,270,930
	$1,361,032,393	$1,187,558,600

STATEMENT OF CONSOLIDATED INCOME AND RETAINED EARNINGS

For the 52 Weeks Ended December 27, 1969 (With Comparative Figures for the 52 Weeks Ended December 28, 1968)

	1969	1968
Sales	$4,099,646,656	$3,685,690,368
Cost of Sales	3,249,166,866	2,894,774,935
Gross profit	850,479,790	790,915,433
Operating and Administrative Expenses	737,583,565	672,375,975
Operating profit	112,896,225	118,539,458
Other Deductions		
Interest on debentures and long-term notes	1,518,246	1,602,924
Earnings of unconsolidated foreign subsidiary	(15,263)	(56,945)
Minority interests in earnings of overseas subsidiaries	101,814	64,280
Dividends on preferred stock of Canadian subsidiary	228,357	242,123
Other charges—net	2,453,278	1,160,815
	4,286,432	3,013,197
Income before provision for income taxes	108,609,793	115,526,261
Provision for Federal, Canadian and other Income Taxes	57,304,534	60,465,309
Income before extraordinary item (per share: 1969, $2.01; 1968, $2.16)	51,305,259	55,060,952
Gain on Sale of Securities — net of applicable income taxes (per share: 1969, $0.13)	3,287,707	—
Net Income (per share: 1969, $2.14; 1968, $2.16)	54,592,966	55,060,952
Retained Earnings at Beginning of Period	341,928,965	314,884,206
	396,521,931	369,945,158
Deduct:		
Cash dividends on common stock (per share: 1969, $1.10; 1968, $1.10)	28,036,356	28,036,067
Additions resulting from stock acquisitions	(26,309)	(19,874)
	28,010,047	28,016,193
Retained Earnings at End of Period	$ 368,511,884	$ 341,928,965

Safeway Stores, Incorporated and Subsidiaries

ASSETS	December 27, 1969	December 28, 1968
Current Assets		
Cash	$ 38,840,224	$ 43,908,844
Receivables	23,322,268	13,377,549
Merchandise inventories—at lower of cost or market (first in, first out or retail method)	337,153,455	288,370,538
Prepaid expenses	12,623,051	12,011,039
Properties for development and sale within one year	6,757,539	9,955,964
Total Current Assets	418,696,537	367,623,934
Other Assets		
Notes receivable, licenses, and miscellaneous investments	8,641,273	8,229,073
Excess of cost of investment in subsidiaries over net assets at date of acquisition	4,356,215	4,054,488
	12,997,488	12,283,561
Property, at Cost		
Buildings	38,752,532	27,075,961
Leasehold improvements	78,717,332	68,652,358
Fixtures and equipment	483,687,340	453,663,541
	601,157,204	549,391,860
Less accumulated depreciation	288,786,348	264,626,847
	312,370,856	284,765,013
Land	44,649,090	33,815,366
	357,019,946	318,580,379
TOTAL	$788,713,971	$698,487,874

See accompanying notes to financial statements.

CONSOLIDATED BALANCE SHEET

As of December 27, 1969 (With Comparative Figures as of December 28, 1968)

LIABILITIES AND STOCKHOLDERS' EQUITY	December 27, 1969	December 28, 1968
Current Liabilities		
Notes payable to banks, short-term	$ 8,785,360	$ 676,062
Long-term notes and debentures, current maturities	3,360,000	3,290,000
Payables and accruals	246,267,575	192,628,221
Federal, Canadian and other income taxes	19,527,862	16,470,375
Total Current Liabilities	277,940,797	213,064,658
Long-Term Liabilities and Reserves		
Notes and debentures	27,179,785	30,735,789
Deferred income taxes	17,593,605	14,689,922
Minority interest in capital stock and retained earnings of subsidiaries:		
Preferred stock of Canadian subsidiary	5,592,600	5,918,900
Overseas subsidiaries	43,850	635,610
Reserve for self-insurance	3,171,296	2,856,976
	53,581,136	54,837,197
Stockholders' Equity		
Common stock	42,480,640	42,478,890
Additional paid-in capital	46,199,514	46,178,164
Retained earnings	368,511,884	341,928,965
	457,192,038	430,586,019
TOTAL	$788,713,971	$698,487,874

ASSETS

	Dec. 31, 1969	Dec. 31, 1968
CURRENT ASSETS		
Cash	$ 339,693,352	$ 368,650,131
United States and other government securities and time deposits—at cost, which approximates market:		
Held for payment of United States and foreign income taxes	464,831,576	445,526,091
Other	1,019,885,620	1,084,061,964
Accounts and notes receivable (less allowances)	2,112,672,324	2,013,856,620
Inventories—at the lower of cost (substantially first-in, first-out or average) or market	3,760,525,690	3,423,340,337
TOTAL CURRENT ASSETS................................	7,697,608,562	7,335,435,143
INVESTMENTS AND MISCELLANEOUS ASSETS		
Investments in subsidiary companies not consolidated—at equity in net assets	932,251,336	754,967,715
United States Government securities maturing 1972—at cost	39,880,108	39,469,496
Other investments and miscellaneous assets—at cost (less allowances)...	68,790,009	65,917,325
TOTAL INVESTMENTS AND MISCELLANEOUS ASSETS	1,040,921,453	860,354,536
COMMON STOCK IN TREASURY — Available for Bonus Plan and Stock Option Plan (1969—1,810,724 shares; 1968—1,765,421 shares)	144,358,725	145,692,193
REAL ESTATE, PLANTS, AND EQUIPMENT		
Gross real estate, plants, and equipment—at cost	12,700,178,000	11,882,241,727
Less accumulated depreciation and obsolescence	7,566,487,195	6,983,939,787
Balance	5,133,690,805	4,898,301,940
Special tools—at cost less amortization	511,086,248	539,754,024
NET REAL ESTATE, PLANTS, AND EQUIPMENT...............	5,644,777,053	5,438,055,964
PREPAID EXPENSES AND DEFERRED CHARGES......................	228,986,270	167,194,840
GOODWILL, PATENTS, ETC........................................	63,442,466	63,442,466
TOTAL ASSETS..	$14,820,094,529	$14,010,175,142

and Consolidated Subsidiaries

BALANCE SHEET

1969 and 1968

LIABILITIES, RESERVES, AND STOCKHOLDERS' EQUITY

	Dec. 31, 1969	Dec. 31, 1968
CURRENT LIABILITIES		
Accounts payable	$ 1,504,429,830	$ 1,343,980,914
United States and foreign income taxes	571,240,168	589,238,158
Other taxes, payrolls, and sundry accrued items	1,266,661,995	1,168,710,145
Dividends payable on preferred stocks	3,232,068	3,232,068
TOTAL CURRENT LIABILITIES	3,345,564,061	3,105,161,285
3¼% DEBENTURES DUE 1979 (less reacquired debentures in treasury: 1969—$132,109,000; 1968—$139,635,000)	36,522,000	39,556,000
FOREIGN DEBT OF SUBSIDIARIES DUE 1971-1992	280,463,800	244,724,000
OTHER LIABILITIES	514,262,007	467,974,904
RESERVES		
Deferred investment tax credit	162,876,000	155,264,000
Contingent credits under Stock Option Plan	39,800,000	41,500,000
General reserve applicable to foreign operations	141,667,396	141,667,396
Other (principally unrealized intercompany profits)	71,035,625	57,517,794
TOTAL RESERVES	415,379,021	395,949,190
STOCKHOLDERS' EQUITY		
Capital stock:		
Preferred, without par value (authorized, 6,000,000 shares):		
$5.00 series, stated value $100 per share, redeemable at $120 per share (issued, 1,875,366 shares; in treasury, 39,722 shares; outstanding, 1,835,644 shares)	183,564,400	183,564,400
$3.75 series, stated value $100 per share, redeemable at $101 per share (issued and outstanding, 1,000,000 shares)	100,000,000	100,000,000
Common, $1⅔ par value (authorized, 500,000,000 shares; issued, 287,573,265 shares at December 31, 1969 and 287,560,358 shares at December 31, 1968)	479,288,775	479,267,263
Total capital stock	762,853,175	762,831,663
Capital surplus (principally additional paid-in capital)	764,323,456	763,588,810
Net income retained for use in the business (earned surplus)	8,700,727,009	8,230,389,290
TOTAL STOCKHOLDERS' EQUITY	10,227,903,640	9,756,809,763
TOTAL LIABILITIES, RESERVES, AND STOCKHOLDERS' EQUITY ..	$14,820,094,529	$14,010,175,142

GENERAL MOTORS CORPORATION and Consolidated Subsidiaries
STATEMENT OF CONSOLIDATED INCOME
for the years ended December 31, 1969 and 1968

	Year 1969	Year 1968
NET SALES..	$24,295,141,357	$22,755,402,947
Equity in earnings of subsidiary companies not consolidated (dividends and interest received amounted to $26,565,128 in 1969 and $26,189,441 in 1968)	50,590,859	51,940,123
Other income (principally interest earned) less sundry income deductions.	102,401,880	78,285,857
TOTAL...	24,448,134,096	22,885,628,927
LESS		
Cost of sales and other operating charges, exclusive of items listed below	18,106,500,181	16,639,105,990
Selling, general, and administrative expenses	1,120,094,647	1,028,499,009
Depreciation and obsolescence of real estate, plants, and equipment	765,776,522	729,142,369
Amortization of special tools	891,767,582	853,066,782
Provision for Bonus Plan and Stock Option Plan	110,000,000	111,000,000
Provision for United States and foreign income taxes.................	1,743,300,000	1,792,900,000
TOTAL...	22,737,438,932	21,153,714,150
NET INCOME for the year......................................	1,710,695,164	1,731,914,777
Dividends on preferred stocks.....................................	12,928,272	12,928,273
AMOUNT EARNED ON COMMON STOCK........................	$ 1,697,766,892	$ 1,718,986,504
Average number of shares of common stock outstanding during the year	285,414,606	285,441,990
AMOUNT EARNED PER SHARE OF COMMON STOCK..............	$5.95	$6.02

Standard Oil Company (New Jersey)

Consolidated statement of income for the years 1969 and 1968

Revenue	1969	1968
Sales and other operating revenue	$16,433,143,000	$15,473,909,000
Dividends, interest, and other revenue	467,217,000	399,397,000
	16,900,360,000	15,873,306,000
Costs and other deductions		
Crude oil, products, materials, and services	7,357,416,000	6,668,899,000
Taxes and other payments to governments	5,897,267,000	5,607,094,000
Wages, salaries, and employee benefits	1,275,558,000	1,246,387,000
Depreciation and depletion	856,840,000	849,163,000
Interest and other financial charges	213,919,000	177,961,000
Income applicable to minority interests	56,721,000	47,121,000
	15,657,721,000	14,596,625,000
Income before extraordinary charges	1,242,639,000	1,276,681,000
Per share	*$5.78*	*$5.94*
Extraordinary charges *(see page 28)*	195,000,000	
Per share	*$ .91*	
Net income	$ 1,047,639,000	$ 1,276,681,000
Per share	*$4.87*	*$5.94*

Consolidated statement of changes in working capital for the years 1969 and 1968

Sources	1969	1968
Income before extraordinary charges:		
Accruing to Jersey shareholders	$ 1,242,639,000	$ 1,276,681,000
Accruing to minority interests	56,721,000	47,121,000
Depreciation and depletion	856,840,000	849,163,000
Sales of property, plant, and equipment	115,732,000	71,870,000
Net increase in long-term debt	91,079,000	582,306,000
Other—net	28,626,000	51,500,000
	2,391,637,000	2,878,641,000
Uses		
Additions to property, plant, and equipment	1,690,716,000	1,944,067,000
Additions to investments and advances	52,165,000	32,535,000
Cash dividends to Jersey shareholders	806,450,000	785,139,000
Cash dividends to minority interests	37,257,000	39,430,000
Cost of shares reacquired, less proceeds from shares sold	4,373,000	11,095,000
Net changes in deferred charges and credits	47,327,000	(15,676,000)
	2,638,288,000	2,796,590,000
Net (decrease)/increase in working capital	$ (246,651,000)	$ 82,051,000

Standard Oil Company (New Jersey)

Consolidated statement of financial position, December 31, 1969–1968

Assets	Current assets	1969	1968
	Cash	$ 408,123,000	$ 462,673,000
	Marketable securities, at cost, which approximates market	868,107,000	904,189,000
	Notes and accounts receivable, less estimated doubtful amounts of $77,679,000 and $71,032,000	2,764,997,000	2,545,995,000
	Inventories		
	Crude oil, products, and merchandise	1,154,785,000	1,193,282,000
	Materials and supplies	168,695,000	174,159,000
	Prepaid taxes and other expenses	269,321,000	243,849,000
	Total current assets	5,634,028,000	5,524,147,000
	Investments and advances	988,874,000	936,709,000
	Property, plant, and equipment, at cost, less depreciation and depletion	10,563,375,000	10,077,164,000
	Deferred charges and other assets	351,674,000	248,343,000
	Total assets	17,537,951,000	16,786,363,000
Liabilities	Current liabilities		
	Notes and loans payable	1,093,702,000	975,571,000
	Accounts payable and accrued liabilities	2,041,686,000	1,804,668,000
	Income taxes payable	653,885,000	652,502,000
	Total current liabilities	3,789,273,000	3,432,741,000
	Long-term debt	2,173,800,000	2,082,721,000
	Annuity, insurance, and other reserves	453,796,000	465,021,000
	Deferred income tax credits	485,429,000	431,755,000
	Other deferred credits	88,107,000	85,777,000
	Equity of minority shareholders in affiliated companies	454,934,000	432,552,000
	Total liabilities	7,445,339,000	6,930,567,000
Shareholders' equity	Capital	2,228,773,000	2,233,146,000
	Earnings reinvested	7,863,839,000	7,622,650,000
	Total shareholders' equity	$10,092,612,000	$ 9,855,796,000

40

Consolidated Statement of Financial Position

General Electric Company and consolidated affiliates

December 31	1969	1968
Assets		
Cash on hand and in banks	$ 201,570,000	$ 285,580,000
Marketable securities	127,705,000	87,745,000
Current receivables	1,367,862,000	1,455,685,000
Inventories	1,590,657,000	1,482,108,000
Current assets	3,287,794,000	3,311,118,000
Investments and advances	417,893,000	353,589,000
Plant and equipment—less accumulated depreciation .	1,814,961,000	1,677,651,000
Other assets	486,842,000	401,416,000
Total assets	$6,007,490,000	$5,743,774,000
Liabilities and equity		
Short-term borrowings	$ 340,720,000	$ 280,600,000
Accounts payable	386,868,000	418,805,000
Progress collections and price adjustments accrued . .	709,041,000	528,181,000
Dividends payable	58,756,000	58,718,000
Taxes accrued	213,521,000	216,542,000
Other costs and expenses accrued	657,748,000	601,435,000
Current liabilities	2,366,654,000	2,104,281,000
Long-term borrowings	673,310,000	749,075,000
Other liabilities	240,178,000	227,155,000
Miscellaneous reserves	145,098,000	129,675,000
Total liabilities	3,425,240,000	3,210,186,000
Interest of other share owners in equity of affiliates .	42,273,000	40,140,000
Preferred stock (2,000,000 shares authorized; none issued)	—	—
Common stock (issued shares, $5 par value per share) .	458,657,000	458,324,000
Amounts received for stock in excess of par value . . .	300,287,000	296,880,000
Retained earnings	1,781,033,000	1,738,244,000
Share owners' equity	2,539,977,000	2,493,448,000
Total liabilities and equity	$6,007,490,000	$5,743,774,000

Consolidated Statement of Current and Retained Earnings

General Electric Company and consolidated affiliates

For the year	1969	1968
Sales of products and services to customers	$8,447,965,000	$8,381,633,000
Other income	98,727,000	86,299,000
	8,546,692,000	8,467,932,000
Costs		
Employee compensation, including benefits	3,510,787,000	3,324,526,000
Materials, supplies, services and other costs	4,126,105,000	4,062,360,000
Depreciation	351,282,000	300,141,000
Taxes, except those on income	81,714,000	78,245,000
Interest and other financial charges	78,113,000	70,461,000
Provision for income taxes	231,504,000	312,271,000
Less increase in inventories during the year	− 108,549,000	− 31,453,000
	8,270,956,000	8,116,551,000
Earnings before interest of other share owners . . .	275,736,000	351,381,000
Interest of other share owners in net results of affiliates .	2,279,000	5,726,000
Net earnings applicable to common stock	278,015,000	357,107,000
Dividends declared	− 235,226,000	− 234,783,000
Amount added to retained earnings	42,789,000	122,324,000
Retained earnings at January 1	1,738,244,000	1,615,920,000
Retained earnings at December 31	$1,781,033,000	$1,738,244,000
Net earnings per share	$3.07	$3.95
Dividends declared and paid per share	$2.60	$2.60

42

EXERCISE 1-16 CALCULATION OF RATIOS FROM ANNUAL REPORT EXHIBITS

1. Calculate the current ratio for Sears, Roebuck and Company for 1969 and 1970.
2. Calculate the acid-test ratio for J. C. Penney Company for 1969 and 1970.
3. Calculate the inventory-to-net-working-capital ratio for Safeway Stores for 1968 and 1970.
4. Calculate the accounts receivable turnover for General Electric Company for 1969.
5. Calculate the fixed-assets-to-net-worth ratio for Standard Oil Company (New Jersey) for 1968 and 1969.
6. Calculate the capital turnover for General Motors Corporation for 1969.
7. Calculate the return on average total assets for General Motors Corporation for 1969.
8. Calculate the net-profit-to-average-net-worth ratio for Safeway Stores for 1969.
9. Calculate the total-liabilities-to-proprietorship ratio for J. C. Penney Company for 1969 and 1970.
10. Calculate the percent of net income distributed to shareholders as dividends in 1969 and 1970 by Sears, Roebuck and Company.

BUFFINGTON'S DEPARTMENT STORE INC.
INCOME STATEMENT
FOR THE YEAR ENDED JANUARY 31, 19XX

SALES			
Gross Sales		$2,120,000	
Less Sales Returns and Allowances		120,000	5.7%
Net Sales		$2,000,000	100.0%
COST OF SALES			
Beginning Inventory at Cost, February 1		$ 350,000	
Gross Purchases at Cost	$1,395,000		
Less Purchase Returns and Allowances	50,000		
Net Purchases		$1,345,000	
Transportation Charges on Purchases		25,000	
Total Merchandise Available for Sale		$1,720,000	
Less Ending Inventory at Cost, January 31		400,000	
Gross Cost of Goods Sold		$1,320,000	66.0%
Less Cash Discounts Earned		50,000	2.5%
Net Cost of Goods Sold		$1,270,000	63.5%
Net Alteration and Workroom Costs		10,000	.5%
Total Cost of Goods Sold		$1,280,000	64.0%
GROSS MARGIN OF PROFIT		$ 720,000	36.0%
OPERATING EXPENSES			
Payroll		$ 380,000	19.0%
Advertising		60,000	3.0%
Delivery		16,000	.8%
Supplies		24,000	1.2%
Depreciation		22,000	1.1%
Mortgage Expense		60,000	3.0%
Insurance		14,000	.7%
* Interest		20,000	1.0%
Taxes and Licenses		26,000	1.3%
Utilities		20,000	1.0%
Miscellaneous		28,000	1.4%
Total Operating Expenses		$ 670,000	33.5%
OPERATING PROFIT		$ 50,000	2.5%
OTHER INCOME		20,000	1.0%
NET PROFIT—BEFORE FEDERAL INCOME TAXES		$ 70,000	3.5%

*The concept of "imputed interest", found on actual store statements, is omitted for purposes of simplification.

THE INCOME STATEMENT

2

mathematics of sales

In this chapter we shall focus on those calculations which are involved in arriving at the income statement figures shown above—namely, gross sales, sales returns and allowances, and net sales. Although the examples used will be taken from a retail business, the pricing principles are basically the same for all firms having goods to sell.

In pricing its goods, Buffington's Department Store must consider a number of important factors. Among these are:

1. the price it pays for the merchandise to be sold
2. its cost of doing business
3. the prices charged on the same or similar goods by its competitors
4. the existing demand or sales record for the goods it sells
5. special sales or promotions, which may call for special pricing strategy

Some of the pricing terminology that will be discussed in this chapter is as follows:

Original price. The initial or first price tagged on an item of merchandise. This is the price the store initially asks its customers to pay.

Merchandise cost or *Gross delivered cost.* The amount paid to purchase and receive an item of merchandise. For example, Buffington's might pay $220 each for refrigerators and an additional $18 in freight charges for shipment from the vendor to the store. The merchandise cost per refrigerator received is $238.

Markon. The dollar amount added to the merchandise cost of an item to arrive at the original price. Buffington's might add $112 to each $238 refrigerator to make the original price $350.

Markup. Any addition to the original price.

F.O.B. factory. Transportation term, meaning freight is "free on board" to the vendor's delivery platform; buyer pays transportation charges from there to the store.

F.O.B. store. Transportation term, meaning freight is "free on board" to the store; buyer pays no transportation charges.

Markdown. A reduction in the original price; the difference between the original price and the new, lower retail price, at which the merchandise is sold.

Markdown percent. The amount of the markdown compared to (divided by) the new, lower retail price.

Markdown off percent. The amount of the markdown compared to (divided by) the original price.

Maintained markon. The difference between the gross cost of merchandise (cost plus freight) and net sales.

When reading the definitions above, it will help to refer back to the income statement at the beginning of chapter 1.

SECTION 2–CALCULATING MARKON

When Buffington's receives a refrigerator for which they pay $238, they do not instinctively know that they need a markon of $112. Instead, they think in terms of a certain percent of markon. Most large retailers calculate markon as a percent of the retail or original price. This is logical for at least three good reasons: (1) most goods do sell at their original price (original price and actual selling price are the same); (2) it is easier to keep track of the value of inventory according to retail prices, then later to convert the retail value to a cost value for income statement purposes; (3) as we have seen in the Buffington income statement in chapter 1, all items except for sales returns and allowances in the income statement are measured against net sales.

The basic equation for calculating the markon percent is:

$238	$112	$350
Cost	Markon	Retail

$$C \quad + \quad M \quad = \quad R$$

Calculating markon percent based on the retail price

Referring to the basic equation above, finding the markon percent is a simple problem in percentage. The dollar markon is compared to the retail price and this relationship is expressed as a percent value.

$$M = R - C$$
$$M = \$350 - \$238$$
$$M = \$112$$

Markon % = $\dfrac{\text{(Percentage)}\ \$112}{\$350\ \text{(Base)}}$ = .32 or 32% (Rate)

Calculating markon percent based on the cost of merchandise

If markon were to be calculated as a percent of the cost of merchandise, the cost would become the base.

Markon % = $\dfrac{\text{(Percentage)}\ \$112}{\$238\ \text{(Base)}}$ = .4705 or 47% (Rate)

The key to solving problems in markon percent is to let the base (whether it is cost or retail) be equal to 100%.

Returning to the refrigerator example, Buffington's would calculate the markon as follows:

$$(\$238)$$
$$C + M = R$$
$$68\% \quad 32\% \quad 100\%$$

Explanation: A markon of 32% of the retail price is desired. Since the markon is based on the retail price, retail is equal to 100%. The cost portion of the retail price must account for 68% of the retail price in order to allow 32% for the markon. When we know one dollar amount ($238) and its relationship to the base (68%) we can divide and find the retail price:

Retail price = $\dfrac{\text{(Percentage)}\ \$238}{.68\ \text{(Rate)}}$ = $350 (Base)

and then,

$$\text{Markon} = \$350 - \$238 = \$112$$

If the markon percent had been based on the cost of the merchandise, the solution would have been as follows:

(Base)   (Percentage)

$238

$$C \ + \ M \ = \ R$$
$$100\% \quad 47\% \quad\quad 147\%$$

Retail price = 147% of the cost

So,

$$\$238 \ \times \ 1.47 \ = \ \$349.86 \quad \text{or} \quad \$350 \text{ (rounded off)}$$

Markon = $350 - $238 = $112

If in this example, only the original price and the markon percent based on cost were known, the cost itself could have been found using the same basic markon equation:

(Base)   (Percentage)

$350

$$C \ + \ M \ = \ R$$
$$100\% \quad 47\% \quad\quad 147\%$$

$$C \ + \ M \ = \ 147\%$$

Thus,

$$\$350 \ = \ 147\% \text{ of the cost}$$

$$\text{Cost} = \frac{\$350}{1.47} = \$238$$

Calculating the cost of merchandise

Although Buffington's as well as every other merchant will know the cost of goods at the time they are received, these cost figures can still be calculated without benefit of purchase records. Since Buffington's knows that its $350 refrigerator carries a markon of 32% based on the retail price, they can find the cost quickly by using the basic markon equation:

$350

$$C \ + \ M \ = \ R$$
$$68\% \quad 32\% \quad\quad 100\%$$

$$\text{Cost} = .68 \ \times \ \$350 \ = \ \$238$$
$$\text{(Base)} \quad\quad \text{(Percentage)}$$

Converting markon based on retail to markon based on cost

When the markon percent based on the retail price is known, it can be converted to an equivalent markon percent based on cost:

$$\text{Markon \% based on cost} = \frac{\text{Markon \% based on retail}}{100\% - \text{Markon \% based on retail}}$$

$$= \frac{32\%}{100\% - 32\%} = \frac{.32}{.68} = .47 = 47\%$$

Converting markon based on cost to markon based on retail

If the markon based on cost is 47%, the retail price must be 100% + 47%, or 147% $(C + M = R)$ of the cost. Therefore,

$$\text{Markon \% Based on Retail} = \frac{\text{Markon \% based on cost}}{100\% + \text{Markon \% based on cost}}$$

$$= \frac{47\%}{100\% + 47\%} = \frac{.47}{1.47} = .32 = 32\%$$

EXERCISE 2-1 MARKON BASED ON RETAIL

A. Calculate the markon and markon percent based on the retail price.

	Cost	Original Price	Markon	Markon %
1.	$ 3.00	$ 5.00	_____	_____
2.	500.00	360.00	_____	_____
3.	7.20	9.00	_____	_____
4.	6.50	10.00	_____	_____
5.	1.90	3.60	_____	_____
6.	.65	1.25	_____	_____
7.	9.85	12.00	_____	_____
8.	.12	.25	_____	_____
9.	34.20	58.00	_____	_____
10.	3.50	5.22	_____	_____

B. Calculate the cost of merchandise.

	Original Price	Markon % Based on Retail	Cost
1.	$ 2.00	40%	_____
2.	220.00	20	_____
3.	32.00	28	_____

Original Price	Markon % Based on Retail	Cost
4. $ 7.50	30	_____
5. .25	24	_____
6. 9.95	35	_____
7. 16.75	27.5	_____
8. 1,050.00	37.5	_____
9. 59.50	$22\frac{5}{8}$	_____
10. 300.00	$16\frac{2}{3}$	_____

C. Calculate the original price.

Cost	Markon % Based on Retail	Original Price
1. $ 3.00	40%	_____
2. 12.00	28	_____
3. .15	50	_____
4. 1.25	43	_____
5. 22.50	25	_____
6. 6.88	18.5	_____
7. 100.00	30	_____
8. 4.20	$33\frac{1}{3}$	_____
9. 75.00	$20\frac{3}{4}$	_____
10. 270.00	$16\frac{2}{3}$	_____

EXERCISE 2-2 MARKON BASED ON COST

A. Calculate the markon and markon percent based on the cost of merchandise.

Cost	Original Price	Markon	Markon % Based on Cost
1. $ 3.00	$ 5.00	_____	_____
2. 10.00	15.00	_____	_____
3. 22.50	40.00	_____	_____
4. .08	.15	_____	_____
5. 120.00	240.00	_____	_____

B. Calculate the markon and the original price.

Cost	Markon % Based on Cost	Markon	Original Price
1. $ 1.80	60%	_____	_____
2. 4.00	50	_____	_____
3. .18	68	_____	_____
4. 56.50	46	_____	_____
5. 325.00	$72\frac{1}{2}$	_____	_____

C. Calculate the cost of merchandise.

Original Price	Markon % Based on Cost	Cost
1. $ 16.00	40%	_____
2. 5.00	60	_____
3. 84.50	54	_____
4. 350.00	75	_____
5. 110.00	$62\frac{1}{2}$	_____

EXERCISE 2-3 MARKON BASED ON COST AND RETAIL

A. Calculate the equivalent markon percents.

	Markon % Based on Retail	Markon % Based on Cost
1.	22%	_____
2.	30	_____
3.	35	_____
4.	40	_____
5.	$26\frac{1}{2}$	_____
6.	_____	54%
7.	_____	$66\frac{2}{3}$
8.	_____	75
9.	_____	44.4
10.	_____	38

B. Fill in the blanks.

	Cost	Markon	Markon % Based on Retail	Markon % Based on Cost	Retail Price
1.	$ 7.20	_____	_____	_____	$ 16.00
2.	_____	_____	35%	_____	65.00
3.	85.00	$40.00	_____	_____	_____
4.	26.50	_____	_____	50%	_____
5.	_____	2.75	22.5	_____	_____
6.	_____	18.00	_____	$66\frac{2}{3}$	_____
7.	_____	_____	20	_____	12.98
8.	58.00	33.00	_____	_____	_____
9.	_____	_____	_____	48	88.00
10.	_____	64.00	_____	_____	260.00

EXERCISE 2-4 MARKON PROBLEMS

1. A stereo set sells for $1,200, which represents a 60% markon based on the retailer's cost. What is his cost?

2. A & R Tire Center buys one grade of tires at a cost of $7.45 apiece and sells them for $10.95. What is the markon percent based on retail?

3. Buffington's Department Store is currently selling a certain brand of hair dryers for $11.88. This price represents a 32% markon on retail. What is the store's cost on these hair dryers?

4. In problem C, above, what would be the markon percent based on cost?

5. A merchant buys wallets at $3.51 each to be sold at a markon of 35% based on the retail price. What will be the original price on these wallets?

6. Corley's Variety Store put a markon of $2.40 on a new heavy-duty shovel. If the cost per shovel is 70% of the retail price, what is the retail price?

7. Don's Donuts sells glazed donuts for 90¢ a dozen or 8¢ each for quantities under a dozen. At a markon of 25% of retail, what is Don's total markon on the sale of a half-dozen donuts?

8. The Modern Furniture Mart purchased two dozen dining room sets at a cost of $3,960.00 plus transportation charges amounting to $177.60. The retail price on each dining room set should represent a $66\frac{2}{3}$% markon based on cost. What retail price will each set carry?

9. The Pharmico Wholesale Drug Co. buys and sells one brand of aspirin tablets realizing a markon of 15% of the selling price. What is the equivalent markon percent based on cost?

10. A markon based on cost of 60% is equivalent to what percent based on the selling price?

11. To beat the price of competitors, Music Unlimited is selling a popular record album for 20% less than anyone else in town. If this album is being sold by competitors at $4.98, what must the purchase cost be in order for Music Unlimited to make a 20% markon based on their selling price?

12. Sir Knight, a men's wear shop, purchases handkerchiefs direct from one manufacturer at a cost of $72.00 per gross plus a shipping charge of $3.00. What is the markon percent based on a selling price of 3 for $2.50?

13. For part of the year, Kline's Sporting Goods sold a certain golf ball at $1.00 apiece. Later in the year these golf balls were sold in packages of 3 for $2.88. Assuming a constant year-round cost of 60¢ per ball, what was the difference in markon per ball based on retail for packaged sales versus single sales?

14. The Popcorn Palace pays $16\frac{1}{2}$¢ each for its large-size box of candy-coated popcorn. If the store seeks a 34% markon based on retail, what price should they ask for each box of popcorn?

15. Two vendors are competing to sell their line of spray paint to the Towne Hardware Co. One line costs $4.68 per case of 12 cans; the other carries a 25% markon based on a suggested retail price of 79¢ per can. If Towne Hardware were to sell spray paint at 79¢ per can, which line would offer the bigger markon?

16. The Three Bells, a cash-and-carry grocery store, calculates markon as a percent of cost. What percent of markon based on retail is equivalent to the 62% markon on brooms in this store?

17. In one store, lightbulbs carry a 27% markon. What is the equivalent markon as a percent of cost?

18. What is the dollar difference between markons for goods costing $6 carrying a 37% retail markon and the same goods with a markon of 68% based on cost?

19. In terms of base, rate, and percentage, why is the markon percent based on cost always higher than the markon percent based on retail when the same dollar figures are involved?

20. Why cannot a markon percent based on the retail price ever be as high as 100%? Use an example to prove your answer.

SECTION 3—ADJUSTING THE ORIGINAL PRICE

There are times when a business firm must adjust the original price of goods up or down. Prices may be adjusted upward when the cost of goods or raw materials increases or when business expenses—such as wages, rent, or insurance—increase. Prices may be reset at lower figures when increased sales result in a lower unit cost per item sold or when it is believed that lower prices will result in increased demand and a larger quantity of goods sold. In essence, the original price represents an estimate of what the customer will pay. Many times this estimate is too high or too low.

Markup

If Buffington's Department Store learns that the cost of refrigerators is about to rise and that their price for refrigerators is below the prices of competitive stores, they may raise their price on refrigerators. This upward adjustment in the original price is called a *markup*. The total of the original markon plus any additional markups is called the *marking*. For example, Buffington's might decide to raise prices on refrigerators by raising the markon percent from 32% to 33%. This would mean a new price of $355.22 ($238 ÷ 67%), or a markup of $5.22. The store would probably drop the 22 cents, leaving a price of $355 ($350 original price + $5 markup). The complete calculation is as follows:

$$\begin{array}{ccccc} \$238 & & & & \\ C & + & M & = & R \\ 67\% & & 33\% & & 100\% \\ & & \text{(Originally)} & & \\ & & 32\% & & \end{array}$$

Since the new price must now reflect a total markon of 33%, the cost portion is now 67% of the new, higher retail price. So,

$$\$238 \ = \ 67\% \text{ of retail}$$

$$\text{New retail} \ = \ \frac{\overset{\text{(Percentage)}}{\$238}}{\underset{\text{(Base)}}{.67}} \ = \ \$355.22 \qquad (\$355)$$

$$\text{Markup} = \$355.22 - \$350 = \$5.22 \qquad (\$5.00)$$

Technically, retailers restrict the term *markon* to mean only the *first* amount added to merchandise cost to arrive at the original price. The $5.22 increase in the original price in this example is called *markup*, meaning the original price was *marked up* to a higher price. The difference between the cost ($238) and the new, higher retail price ($355.22) is really composed of a markon of $112 and a subsequent markup of $5.22. Together, these amount to a marking of $117.22.

Markdown

Should Buffington's find that its refrigerators are not selling fast enough at the original price of $350, they might decide to feature them in a special promotion in hopes that a lower price will bring out more buyers. Let us assume that the price is reduced to $300. (NOTE: in practice, this reduction would probably be from $349 to $299.) The *markdown* taken on these refrigerators remaining in stock at the time of the sale is $50 ($350 − $300).

markdown percent

The *markdown percent* in the above refrigerator example is the result of comparing the $50 markdown to the new $300 selling price:

$$\text{Markdown \%} = \frac{\text{(Percentage)}\ \$50}{\$300\ \text{(Base)}} = \frac{1}{6} = 16\frac{2}{3}\%$$

It should be emphasized that if the refrigerator sells at the price of $300, this is the net sales figure in this transaction.

markdown off percent

From Buffington's point of view, the markdown percent is the amount of the markdown divided by the new, lower retail price. In the preceding example, a $50 markdown divided by the reduced price of $300 represented a markdown percent of $16\frac{2}{3}\%$.

However, people who bought these refrigerators on sale would not look at it this way. From the consumer's point of view, the reduction is $50 based on a regular price of $350. These refrigerator buyers would think of their markdown or discount as about 14% of the selling price:

$$\text{Markdown off percent} = \frac{\$50}{\$350} = \frac{1}{7} = .1428 \quad \text{or} \quad 14\%$$

For this reason, Buffington's would not advertise these refrigerators at $16\frac{2}{3}\%$ off. They would have to advertise from the prospective customer's point of view at 14% off. Once again, the difference is that the store views the markdown as a percent of the selling price ($300), while the customer sees it as a percent of the original price ($350).

Maintained markon

Now that Buffington's has sold all of its remaining refrigerators at a price of $300 each, the maintained markon can be calculated. The *maintained markon* is the difference between the gross merchandise cost and the actual selling price. The merchandise cost on refrigerators was $238, and the actual selling price after the markdown was $300. It can, therefore, be seen that the markon which was maintained on this sale was $62 ($300 - $238). Despite the fact that Buffington's tried for a markon of $112 ($350 - $238), they maintained only $62 of that original markon. The maintained markon percent can be calculated this way:

$$\text{Maintained markon } \% = \frac{\$62 \text{ Markon}}{\$300 \text{ Actual selling price}} = .2067 \quad \text{or} \quad 20.67\%$$

The maintained markon percent on all merchandise for the whole year for Buffington's Department Store can be found on the income statement heading chapter 1 by subtracting the gross cost of goods sold percent (66%) from net sales (100%). The maintained markon for the year is 34%. In dollar figures, Buffington's maintained markon is calculated this way:

Merchandise cost		Transportation		Gross cost of goods sold
$1,295,000	+	$25,000	=	$1,320,000

Then,

Net sales		Gross cost of goods sold		Maintained markon
$2,000,000	-	$1,320,000	=	$680,000

And

$$\text{Maintained markon } \% = \frac{\$680,000}{\$2,000,000} = 34\%$$

Notice that the maintained markon is calculated *before* earned cash discounts are deducted from, and net alteration and workroom costs are added to, the cost of goods sold. These two factors will be discussed fully in chapter 3 in connection with calculating the gross margin.

SECTION 4—RECORDING SALES

Sales taxes

Most states levy a tax on goods sold at the consumer level. These state tax rates vary from less than 1% to 5% or more. In some states, cities may likewise have the authority to levy a sales tax on consumer purchases, although these local taxes are not charged on goods delivered outside the municipality.

Retailers are responsible for collecting sales taxes, and must remit them periodically to the appropriate government agency. When Buffington's Department Store sells a refrigerator at $350 and the sales tax rate is 4% of the selling price, the tax on this sale is $14 ($350 $\times$ .04). For the sake of convenience, retail sales personnel will often use a sales tax chart like the one shown in table 2-1. This chart helps to minimize mathematical errors, and solves the problem of what to do about the fractional parts of the tax dollar.

For example, the sales tax on a purchase of $114.35 would be calculated as follows using the percent method:

$$\$114.35 \times .04 = \$4.5740 = \$4.57$$

Calculating tax from tax chart is as follows:

$$
\begin{array}{ll}
\text{4\% of \$114.00} & = \$4.56 \\
\text{Tax on \$.35} & = \underline{.02} \\
\text{Total tax} & = \$4.58
\end{array}
$$

At Buffington's, each sales slip will show the total amount collected or charged to the customer's account. The sales tax will of course be shown separately. We can calculate the amount of sales tax collected by Buffington's from the net sales figure shown on the income statement:

$$
\begin{array}{cccc}
& \text{(Rate)} & \text{(Base)} & \text{(Percentage)} \\
\text{Sales taxes} = & 4\% & \times \ \$2,000,000 = & \$80,000
\end{array}
$$

If we started with a revenue figure of $2,080,000, which includes sales taxes, we could have found sales taxes just as easily:

$$\text{Net sales (100\%)} + \text{Sales Taxes (4\%)} = 104\%$$

TABLE 2-1

STATE OF CALIFORNIA 4% SALES TAX REIMBURSEMENT SCHEDULE   Revenue and Taxation Code, Section 6052.5

Transaction	Tax	Transaction	Tax	Transaction	Tax	Transaction	Tax	Transaction	Tax	Transaction	Tax
.01– .12	.00										
.13– .34	.01	16.88–17.12	.68	33.63–33.87	1.35	50.13–50.37	2.01	66.88–67.12	2.68	83.63–83.87	3.35
.35– .59	.02	17.13–17.37	.69	33.88–34.12	1.36	50.38–50.62	2.02	67.13–67.37	2.69	83.88–84.12	3.36
.60– .87	.03	17.38–17.62	.70	34.13–34.37	1.37	50.63–50.87	2.03	67.38–67.62	2.70	84.13–84.37	3.37
.88– 1.12	.04	17.63–17.87	.71	34.38–34.62	1.38	50.88–51.12	2.04	67.63–67.87	2.71	84.38–84.62	3.38
1.13– 1.37	.05	17.88–18.12	.72	34.63–34.87	1.39	51.13–51.37	2.05	67.88–68.12	2.72	84.63–84.87	3.39
1.38– 1.62	.06	18.13–18.37	.73	34.88–35.12	1.40	51.38–51.62	2.06	68.13–68.37	2.73	84.88–85.12	3.40
1.63– 1.87	.07	18.38–18.62	.74	35.13–35.37	1.41	51.63–51.87	2.07	68.38–68.62	2.74	85.13–85.37	3.41
1.88– 2.12	.08	18.63–18.87	.75	35.38–35.62	1.42	51.88–52.12	2.08	68.63–68.87	2.75	85.38–85.62	3.42
2.13– 2.37	.09	18.88–19.12	.76	35.63–35.87	1.43	52.13–52.37	2.09	68.88–69.12	2.76	85.63–85.87	3.43
2.38– 2.62	.10	19.13–19.37	.77	35.88–36.12	1.44	52.38–52.62	2.10	69.13–69.37	2.77	85.88–86.12	3.44
2.63– 2.87	.11	19.38–19.62	.78	36.13–36.37	1.45	52.63–52.87	2.11	69.38–69.62	2.78	86.13–86.37	3.45
2.88– 3.12	.12	19.63–19.87	.79	36.38–36.62	1.46	52.88–53.12	2.12	69.63–69.87	2.79	86.38–86.62	3.46
3.13– 3.37	.13	19.88–20.12	.80	36.63–36.87	1.47	53.13–53.37	2.13	69.88–70.12	2.80	86.63–86.87	3.47
3.38– 3.62	.14	20.13–20.37	.81	36.88–37.12	1.48	53.38–53.62	2.14	70.13–70.37	2.81	86.88–87.12	3.48
3.63– 3.87	.15	20.38–20.62	.82	37.13–37.37	1.49	53.63–53.87	2.15	70.38–70.62	2.82	87.13–87.37	3.49
3.88– 4.12	.16	20.63–20.87	.83	37.38–37.62	1.50	53.88–54.12	2.16	70.63–70.87	2.83	87.38–87.62	3.50
4.13– 4.37	.17	20.88–21.12	.84	37.63–37.87	1.51	54.13–54.37	2.17	70.88–71.12	2.84	87.63–87.87	3.51
4.38– 4.62	.18	21.13–21.37	.85	37.88–38.12	1.52	54.38–54.62	2.18	71.13–71.37	2.85	87.88–88.12	3.52
4.63– 4.87	.19	21.38–21.62	.86	38.13–38.37	1.53	54.63–54.87	2.19	71.38–71.62	2.86	88.13–88.37	3.53
4.88– 5.12	.20	21.63–21.87	.87	38.38–38.62	1.54	54.88–55.12	2.20	71.63–71.87	2.87	88.38–88.62	3.54
5.13– 5.37	.21	21.88–22.12	.88	38.63–38.87	1.55	55.13–55.37	2.21	71.88–72.12	2.88	88.63–88.87	3.55
5.38– 5.62	.22	22.13–22.37	.89	38.88–39.12	1.56	55.38–55.62	2.22	72.13–72.37	2.89	88.88–89.12	3.56
5.63– 5.87	.23	22.38–22.62	.90	39.13–39.37	1.57	55.63–55.87	2.23	72.38–72.62	2.90	89.13–89.37	3.57
5.88– 6.12	.24	22.63–22.87	.91	39.38–39.62	1.58	55.88–56.12	2.24	72.63–72.87	2.91	89.38–89.62	3.58
6.13– 6.37	.25	22.88–23.12	.92	39.63–39.87	1.59	56.13–56.37	2.25	72.88–73.12	2.92	89.63–89.87	3.59
6.38– 6.62	.26	23.13–23.37	.93	39.88–40.12	1.60	56.38–56.62	2.26	73.13–73.37	2.93	89.88–90.12	3.60
6.63– 6.87	.27	23.38–23.62	.94	40.13–40.37	1.61	56.63–56.87	2.27	73.38–73.62	2.94	90.13–90.37	3.61
6.88– 7.12	.28	23.63–23.87	.95	40.38–40.62	1.62	56.88–57.12	2.28	73.63–73.87	2.95	90.38–90.62	3.62
7.13– 7.37	.29	23.88–24.12	.96	40.63–40.87	1.63	57.13–57.37	2.29	73.88–74.12	2.96	90.63–90.87	3.63
7.38– 7.62	.30	24.13–24.37	.97	40.88–41.12	1.64	57.38–57.62	2.30	74.13–74.37	2.97	90.88–91.12	3.64
7.63– 7.87	.31	24.38–24.62	.98	41.13–41.37	1.65	57.63–57.87	2.31	74.38–74.62	2.98	91.13–91.37	3.65
7.88– 8.12	.32	24.63–24.87	.99	41.38–41.62	1.66	57.88–58.12	2.32	74.63–74.87	2.99	91.38–91.62	3.66
8.13– 8.37	.33	24.88–25.12	1.00	41.63–41.87	1.67	58.13–58.37	2.33	74.88–75.12	3.00	91.63–91.87	3.67
8.38– 8.62	.34	25.13–25.37	1.01	41.88–42.12	1.68	58.38–58.62	2.34	75.13–75.37	3.01	91.88–92.12	3.68
8.63– 8.87	.35	25.38–25.62	1.02	42.13–42.37	1.69	58.63–58.87	2.35	75.38–75.62	3.02	92.13–92.37	3.69
8.88– 9.12	.36	25.63–25.87	1.03	42.38–42.62	1.70	58.88–59.12	2.36	75.63–75.87	3.03	92.38–92.62	3.70
9.13– 9.37	.37	25.88–26.12	1.04	42.63–42.87	1.71	59.13–59.37	2.37	75.88–76.12	3.04	92.63–92.87	3.71
9.38– 9.62	.38	26.13–26.37	1.05	42.88–43.12	1.72	59.38–59.62	2.38	76.13–76.37	3.05	92.88–93.12	3.72
9.63– 9.87	.39	26.38–26.62	1.06	43.13–43.37	1.73	59.63–59.87	2.39	76.38–76.62	3.06	93.13–93.37	3.73
9.88–10.12	.40	26.63–26.87	1.07	43.38–43.62	1.74	59.88–60.12	2.40	76.63–76.87	3.07	93.38–93.62	3.74
10.13–10.37	.41	26.88–27.12	1.08	43.63–43.87	1.75	60.13–60.37	2.41	76.88–77.12	3.08	93.63–93.87	3.75
10.38–10.62	.42	27.13–27.37	1.09	43.88–44.12	1.76	60.38–60.62	2.42	77.13–77.37	3.09	93.88–94.12	3.76
10.63–10.87	.43	27.38–27.62	1.10	44.13–44.37	1.77	60.63–60.87	2.43	77.38–77.62	3.10	94.13–94.37	3.77
10.88–11.12	.44	27.63–27.87	1.11	44.38–44.62	1.78	60.88–61.12	2.44	77.63–77.87	3.11	94.38–94.62	3.78
11.13–11.37	.45	27.88–28.12	1.12	44.63–44.87	1.79	61.13–61.37	2.45	77.88–78.12	3.12	94.63–94.87	3.79
11.38–11.62	.46	28.13–28.37	1.13	44.88–45.12	1.80	61.38–61.62	2.46	78.13–78.37	3.13	94.88–95.12	3.80
11.63–11.87	.47	28.38–28.62	1.14	45.13–45.37	1.81	61.63–61.87	2.47	78.38–78.62	3.14	95.13–95.37	3.81
11.88–12.12	.48	28.63–28.87	1.15	45.38–45.62	1.82	61.88–62.12	2.48	78.63–78.87	3.15	95.38–95.62	3.82
12.13–12.37	.49	28.88–29.12	1.16	45.63–45.87	1.83	62.13–62.37	2.49	78.88–79.12	3.16	95.63–95.87	3.83
12.38–12.62	.50	29.13–29.37	1.17	45.88–46.12	1.84	62.38–62.62	2.50	79.13–79.37	3.17	95.88–96.12	3.84
12.63–12.87	.51	29.38–29.62	1.18	46.13–46.37	1.85	62.63–62.87	2.51	79.38–79.62	3.18	96.13–96.37	3.85
12.88–13.12	.52	29.63–29.87	1.19	46.38–46.62	1.86	62.88–63.12	2.52	79.63–79.87	3.19	96.38–96.62	3.86
13.13–13.37	.53	29.88–30.12	1.20	46.63–46.87	1.87	63.13–63.37	2.53	79.88–80.12	3.20	96.63–96.87	3.87
13.38–13.62	.54	30.13–30.37	1.21	46.88–47.12	1.88	63.38–63.62	2.54	80.13–80.37	3.21	96.88–97.12	3.88
13.63–13.87	.55	30.38–30.62	1.22	47.13–47.37	1.89	63.63–63.87	2.55	80.38–80.62	3.22	97.13–97.37	3.89
13.88–14.12	.56	30.63–30.87	1.23	47.38–47.62	1.90	63.88–64.12	2.56	80.63–80.87	3.23	97.38–97.62	3.90
14.13–14.37	.57	30.88–31.12	1.24	47.63–47.87	1.91	64.13–64.37	2.57	80.88–81.12	3.24	97.63–97.87	3.91
14.38–14.62	.58	31.13–31.37	1.25	47.88–48.12	1.92	64.38–64.62	2.58	81.13–81.37	3.25	97.88–98.12	3.92
14.63–14.87	.59	31.38–31.62	1.26	48.13–48.37	1.93	64.63–64.87	2.59	81.38–81.62	3.26	98.13–98.37	3.93
14.88–15.12	.60	31.63–31.87	1.27	48.38–48.62	1.94	64.88–65.12	2.60	81.63–81.87	3.27	98.38–98.62	3.94
15.13–15.37	.61	31.88–32.12	1.28	48.63–48.87	1.95	65.13–65.37	2.61	81.88–82.12	3.28	98.63–98.87	3.95
15.38–15.62	.62	32.13–32.37	1.29	48.88–49.12	1.96	65.38–65.62	2.62	82.13–82.37	3.29	98.88–99.12	3.96
15.63–15.87	.63	32.38–32.62	1.30	49.13–49.37	1.97	65.63–65.87	2.63	82.38–82.62	3.30	99.13–99.37	3.97
15.88–16.12	.64	32.63–32.87	1.31	49.38–49.62	1.98	65.88–66.12	2.64	82.63–82.87	3.31	99.38–99.62	3.98
16.13–16.37	.65	32.88–33.12	1.32	49.63–49.87	1.99	66.13–66.37	2.65	82.88–83.12	3.32	99.63–99.87	3.99
16.38–16.62	.66	33.13–33.37	1.33	49.88–50.12	2.00	66.38–66.62	2.66	83.13–83.37	3.33	99.88–100.12	4.00
16.63–16.87	.67	33.38–33.62	1.34			66.63–66.87	2.67	83.38–83.62	3.34		

Thus,

$$\$2,080,000 \ = \ 104\% \text{ of net sales}$$

Then,

$$
\begin{array}{llll}
& \text{(Percentage)} & \text{(Rate)} & \text{(Base)} \\
\text{Sales taxes} = & \$2,080,000 \ \div & 104\% & = \$2,000,000 \\
\text{Sales taxes} = & \$2,080,000 \ - & \$2,000,000 & = \quad \$80,000
\end{array}
$$

Applying this same calculation to the sale of one $350 refrigerator, we have:

$$
\begin{array}{lllll}
& \text{(Percentage)} & \text{(Rate)} & \text{(Base)} \\
\text{Sales tax} = & \$364 & \div \ 104\% & = \$350 & \text{(Net sales)}
\end{array}
$$

$$= \$364 - \$350 = \$14$$

$$
\begin{array}{l}
\text{(Base)} \\
\text{Net sales} = \dfrac{\$364}{1.04} = \$350
\end{array}
$$

$$\text{Sales tax} = \$364 - \$350 = \$14$$

Sales returns and allowances

When merchandise is returned to the store after it has been sold, one of two things will usually happen. Either (1) the customer will return the merchandise and be given a full cash or credit refund, or (2) he will keep the merchandise and be given a partial cash or credit refund. The first transaction is called a *return*, the second an *allowance*. Both of these cause a reduction in the gross sales figure on the income statement.

Sales returns and allowances are distinguished from markdowns in one important way: they occur *after* goods are sold. As an example, if after taking delivery of a refrigerator from Buffington's the purchaser should discover that it has a sizeable dent on one side, he and the store may agree on an allowance of $5. On this transaction, gross sales is reduced by $5. A reference to the income statement beginning chapter 1 will reveal that sales returns and allowances are calculated as a percent of gross sales as follows:

$$\text{Percent of sales returns and allowances} = \frac{\$120,000}{\$2,120,000} = 5.7\%$$

In retailing, a high degree of professional salesmanship can go a long way toward keeping returns to a minimum. Goods tend to stay sold when salespeople take care to match their merchandise to the particular needs of each customer.

EXERCISE 2-5 MARKDOWNS

A. Calculate the markdown, markdown percent, and markdown off percent.

	Original Price	Selling Price	Markdown	Markdown %	Markdown Off %
1.	$210.00	$200.00	_____	_____	_____
2.	$32.50	$28.50	_____	_____	_____
3.	$10.00	$6.00	_____	_____	_____
4.	$99.00	$79.00	_____	_____	_____
5.	$1.00	$.88	_____	_____	_____
6.	$8.00	$6.80	_____	_____	_____
7.	$540.00	$395.00	_____	_____	_____
8.	2 for $9	2 for $7.50	_____	_____	_____
9.	$31.35	$29.95	_____	_____	_____
10.	$.40	2 for $.41	_____	_____	_____

B. Calculate the maintained markon and maintained markon percent given the monthly data below.

	Original Price	Markdown	Merchandise Cost	Transportation	Maintained Markon	Maintained Markon %
1.	$60,000	$4,000	$30,000	$2,000	_____	_____
2.	$145,000	$8,350	$87,400	$9,175	_____	_____
3.	$44,000	$2,360	$22,100	$1,540	_____	_____
4.	$234,000	$14,000	$152,000	$8,000	_____	_____
5.	$86,200	$5,100	$49,175	$4,080	_____	_____
6.	$76,200	$6,200	$38,000	$2,000	_____	_____
7.	$15,700	$1,265	$7,500	$680	_____	_____
8.	$184,000	$12,800	$129,400	$4,700	_____	_____
9.	$36,750	$2,882	$21,600	$1,260	_____	_____
10.	$8,420	$602	$6,400	$336	_____	_____

EXERCISE 2-6 PROBLEMS IN MARKUP, MARKDOWN, SALES RETURNS, AND SALES TAXES

1. Goods carrying a gross cost of $248.20 and priced at $413.00 are marked down 15%. Calculate the markdown.

2. What is the markdown percent in problem A, above?

3. What is the maintained markon and maintained markon percent in problem A, above?

4. If the gross cost of merchandise is 65% of the original price and the markdown off percent amounts to 7%, what is the maintained markon percent?

5. A franchised hardware store finished the year with a maintained markon of $160,000, or 36%. What was its gross cost of goods sold?

6. Bradshaw's is featuring women's handbags at 20% off during their anniversary sale. If the original price of these handbags was $15, what is the markdown percent?

7. Fiberglas suitcases were marked down from $60 to $45 apiece. Calculate the markdown off percent.

8. Because of increased expenses, Art Johnson Travel Agency raised their commission from 15% to 18%. If a customer paid $920 for a packaged vacation trip last month, what would he have to pay if he took the same trip now?

9. The DayNite Drug Store raised its marking from 36% to 41% on the price of sunglasses. If the store pays $3.20 per pair, what markup did they apply?

10. The income statement of Flynn Bros., a small appliance store, reveals the following: net sales, $100,000; gross margin, $36,000; cash discounts earned, $4,480; net workroom costs, $1,200. What must be the maintained markon figure on their income statement?

11. The Paradise Community College Bookstore suffered markdowns last year of $12,260, or 8% of net sales. What were net sales for the year?

12. In Jack Fisher's children's wear shop, markon is calculated based on cost. Mr. Fisher's maintained markon based on cost last month was 67%. His gross cost of merchandise sold for the month was $8,900. What was his maintained markon, and what were net sales last month?

13. Calculate the sales tax on a sale of $64.40, using a tax rate of 4%.

14. The sales tax on a retail purchase is $9.26. Assuming a tax rate of 5%, what was the selling price of the goods bought?

15. Stores in a certain city must collect a $\frac{1}{2}$% city sales tax along with a 3% state sales tax on merchandise sold. How much will the city tax and the state tax be on a $74.00 sale?

16. Returns and allowances amounted to 6% of gross sales during the past year at the St. George Electric Co. If returns and allowances were $24,000, what were gross sales?

17. In the past two months, Karl's Men's Wear has made allowances totaling $100.00 on ten $62.50 topcoats due to poor workmanship. What percent of gross sales has Karl's lost on these topcoats?

18. If a customer received a 15% allowance on an electric skillet and ended up paying $17 for it, what was the original purchase price?

19. Calculate the percent of sales returns and allowances:

Gross sales	$68,000	
Less: sales returns and allowances	12,000	
Net sales		$56,000

20. If sales returns and allowances are 6% of gross sales and net sales are $47,000, what is the dollar amount of sales returns and allowances?

BUFFINGTON'S DEPARTMENT STORE INC.
INCOME STATEMENT
FOR THE YEAR ENDED JANUARY 31, 19XX

SALES				
Gross Sales			$2,120,000	
Less Sales Returns and Allowances			120,000	5.7%
Net Sales			$2,000,000	100.0%
COST OF SALES				
Beginning Inventory at Cost, February 1			$ 350,000	
Gross Purchases at Cost		$1,395,000		
Less Purchase Returns and Allowances		50,000		
Net Purchases			$1,345,000	
Transportation Charges on Purchases			25,000	
Total Merchandise Available for Sale			$1,720,000	
Less Ending Inventory at Cost, January 31			400,000	
Gross Cost of Goods Sold			$1,320,000	66.0%
Less Cash Discounts Earned			50,000	2.5%
Net Cost of Goods Sold			$1,270,000	63.5%
Net Alteration and Workroom Costs			10,000	.5%
Total Cost of Goods Sold			$1,280,000	64.0%
GROSS MARGIN OF PROFIT			$ 720,000	36.0%
OPERATING EXPENSES				
Payroll			$ 380,000	19.0%
Advertising			60,000	3.0%
Delivery			16,000	.8%
Supplies			24,000	1.2%
Depreciation			22,000	1.1%
Mortgage Expense			60,000	3.0%
Insurance			14,000	.7%
*Interest			20,000	1.0%
Taxes and Licenses			26,000	1.3%
Utilities			20,000	1.0%
Miscellaneous			28,000	1.4%
Total Operating Expenses			$ 670,000	33.5%
OPERATING PROFIT			$ 50,000	2.5%
OTHER INCOME			20,000	1.0%
NET PROFIT—BEFORE FEDERAL INCOME TAXES			$ 70,000	3.5%

*The concept of "imputed interest", found on actual store statements, is omitted for purposes of simplification.

THE INCOME STATEMENT

3

mathematics of
cost of sales

The sales and cost-of-sales portions of the income statement, sometimes referred to as the *trading section*, reflect how successfully a business has selected or manufactured items which satisfy its customers' wants. The net sales figure itself does not measure the degree of this success. The wants of customers must be satisfied at a profit or the company cannot stay in business. The costs of the goods which have been sold must be subtracted from the sales figure to obtain gross margin (gross profit), which is a better measure of successful buying and selling or trading. A term often used today in relation to business functions, purposes, or organization is "the marketing concept." In essence, this means satisfying customer wants at a profit. Sales volume alone is not the end goal. It is, rather, profitable sales volume which a firm seeks. The starting point in determining such profitability is *gross margin*.

SECTION 1—PURCHASE DISCOUNTS

A retailer must seek sources from which to buy his merchandise. He may buy from manufacturers or wholesalers, sources which are usually called *vendors*. In buying nonmerchandise items such as fixtures and equipment, the sources are usually called *suppliers*.

In determining the price which he must pay for merchandise, a retailer must consider three aspects of pricing by vendors: *trade discounts*, *cash discounts*, and *anticipation*. Each of these is a specific type of discount which may be granted by vendors. Collectively they are termed *purchase discounts* by a retailer.

Trade discounts

As an aid to their salesmen, many vendors publish expensive catalogs containing descriptions, illustrations, and prices of their products. The prices quoted in these catalogs are termed *catalog prices, list prices,* or *manufacturer's suggested retail prices.* Inexpensive price sheets are then supplied to customers indicating the discounts which they may take on the catalog prices when they order merchandise. These discounts are termed *trade discounts,* and the vendors can change their prices to any group of customers by simply sending out new trade discount lists rather then reprinting catalogs.

The term *trade discount* is used because it is granted to people engaged in trading activities—those buying for resale. The justification for such discounts is the marketing functions which these middlemen (wholesalers and retailers) perform. Making goods available to customers is just as productive a function as the initial manufacturing of the goods. A trade discount is a reduction of the list price expressed as a percent, such as 25%, or as a series of percents, such as 25%, 10%, and 5% (usually written 25/10/5 and termed *chain discounts*). When there is more than one discount, they are not added together and taken off of the list price. Rather, to arrive at the net price or the purchaser's cost, one of the series must be applied to the list price first and then each of the other discounts is applied to the result of the previous calculation. It makes no difference in what order the discounts are taken.

Example   An invoice for $1,000 bears a trade discount of 25/10/5. What is the net cost?

Three methods may be used for solution:

1. Converting the percents to either equivalent decimals or fractions and applying each of the discounts in series to a reduced balance:

$1,000.00
-250.00 ($1,000 $\times$ .25, or $1,000 $\times \frac{1}{4}$)
$ 750.00
$- 75.00$ ($750 $\times$ .10, or $750 $\times \frac{1}{10}$)
$ 675.00
$- 33.75$ ($675 $\times$ .05, or $675 $\times \frac{1}{20}$)
$ 641.25   Net cost

2. Applying the decimal or fractional complements of the discount rates in series to a reduced balance:

$1,000.00 $\times$ .75 = $750.00 $1,000.00 $\times \frac{3}{4}$ = $750.00

$750.00 $\times$ .90 = $675.00 $750.00 $\times \frac{9}{10}$ = $675.00

$675.00 $\times$ .95 = $641.25 Net cost $675.00 $\times \frac{19}{20}$ = $641.25 Net cost

3. Finding the complement of a single discount rate equivalent to the discount series and applying this rate to the list price. This complement of a single discount equivalence is the product of either the decimal or fractional complements of the individual rates in the series:

$$.75 \times .90 \times .95 = .64125, \quad \text{and } .64125$$
$$\times \$1,000.00 = \$641.25 \text{ (Net cost)}$$

$$\tfrac{3}{4} \times \tfrac{9}{10} \times \tfrac{19}{20} = \tfrac{513}{800}$$
$$= .64125, \quad \text{and } .64125 \times \$1,000.00 = \$641.25 \text{ (Net cost)}$$

Since the product $.75 \times .90 \times .95$ is the same as the product $.95 \times .90 \times .75$, it is apparent that the order in which these complements are multiplied is inconsequential. The single discount rate equivalent to the discount series would be

$$100 - .64125 = .35875 \quad \text{or} \quad 35.875\%$$

The individual rates in the series can neither be added nor multiplied together to find an equivalent rate. The product $.25 \times .10 \times .05$ is $.00125$ or $.125\%$, which is far removed from the correct single discount rate of 35.875%.

Cash discounts

After trade discounts are deducted from the list price, the net price is the legally enforceable amount which must be paid for the merchandise. However, some vendors will grant an additional discount for payment of the bill in advance of the due date. These additional discounts which are granted for strictly financial reasons are called *cash discounts* and are part of the terms of sale. The size of the discount allowed varies generally with the type of merchandise bought. Cash discounts on staple merchandise, such as hardware and textiles, may be from 1 to 5% and on style merchandise as much as 8%.

ordinary dating

Cash discount terms "2/10 net 30" (also written as 2/10 n/30) means that 2% of the net price may be deducted if the invoice is paid within 10 days of the date on the invoice. If not paid within that period, the entire net price must be paid not more than 30 days after the date on the invoice. After the 30-day period, the bill may become subject to interest charges. In counting days, the date of the invoice is omitted and the payment date is included. The discount may not be applied to transportation charges, display equipment, or other non-merchandise items.

Sometimes, more alternatives are given to the purchaser and terms such as 2/10, 1/30, n/60 may be used. In this case a discount of 2% may be taken if paid within 10 days, or 1% if paid between the 11th and 30th days. The net price must be paid if payment is made between the 31st and 60th days.

Example   How much must be paid on an invoice dated June 1 for $500 less 25% and 10% and terms of 5/10, 4/30, n/60, if payment is made on July 1?

Solution   Since the invoice was paid 30 days after the invoice date, the store is entitled to a 4% cash discount. The combination of the trade discounts and the cash discount results in a discount series of 25%, 10%, 4%:

$$\frac{\$.50}{\cancel{\$5.00}} \times \frac{3}{\cancel{4}} \times \frac{9}{\cancel{10}} \times \frac{\cancel{96}^{24}}{\cancel{100}} = \$324 \text{ Net payment}$$
$$\phantom{\cancel{\$500}} \quad 1 \quad\quad 1 \quad\quad 1$$

advance dating

Invoices are usually not enclosed with the merchandise, but are mailed separately to the retailer. The arrival of the merchandise at the store may be several days after the receipt of the invoice, and there is a natural reluctance to pay for something until it is received and checked against the purchase order. If all is in order, a retailer paying hundreds of invoices each week may still require a few days in order to process payment. Recognizing these problems, many vendors grant terms which have the discount period beginning on a date later than the invoice date.

1. *End-of-month (E.O.M.) dating* means that the discount period begins after the end of the month in which the invoice is dated. In practice, if the invoice is dated on or after the 26th of a month, the retailer may take the discount any time during the next month plus 10 days into the second month. Thus, an invoice dated March 12 with terms 2/10 E.O.M. means that a discount of 2% may be taken through April 10. If the invoice date were March 26, then the discount could be taken through May 10. Although the net period for making payment is usually not expressed with E.O.M. terms, it is generally considered to be 20 days after expiration of the discount period. Sometimes the term *proximo* (abbreviated "prox.") is used instead of the term E.O.M. It means the month following the current month.

2. *Receipt-of-goods (R.O.G.) dating* means that the discount period begins after the retailer receives the goods. When merchandise on an invoice dated March 12 with terms 3/10 R.O.G. is received on March 17, the 3% discount may be taken through March 27. The net due date would be 20 additional days or April 16.

3. *Extra ("extra," "ex," or "X") dating* means that the discount period is extended a certain specified number of days beyond the normal discount period. An invoice dated March 12 with terms 5/15–60X would allow the 5% discount until June 5, which is 75 days from March 12. These terms are most

often used on merchandise which has a strong seasonal sales pattern, and the vendor offers them as an inducement for early purchasing by the retailer.

partial payments

We found that the amount to be paid after deduction of the cash discount could be calculated by multiplying the invoice amount by the complement of the discount. If 2% cash discount is allowed on a $1,000 invoice, a single payment of $980 within the discount period would be given a credit of $1,000 (payment in full). This total payment is 98% (complement of the 2% cash discount) of the credit received. In like manner, any partial payments made during the discount period would be 98% of the credit received. *The credit received for each partial payment would be the amount of the payment divided by the complement of the cash discount.*

If a partial payment of $490 were made on the above invoice, the account would be credited as follows:

Percentage = Rate $\times$ Base $\therefore$ Base = Percentage $\div$ Rate

Payment   = Complement of discount $\times$ Credit to account
$490   = .98 $\times$ Credit to account

Credit to account = $\dfrac{\$490}{.98}$ = $500

Anticipation

Many vendors allow an extra discount in addition to the cash discount if the bill is paid prior to the expiration of the cash discount period. Such prepayment is termed *anticipation*, and the additional discount, typically computed at 6% of the amount owed, may be viewed as interest earned. The actual number of days prior to the end of the discount period are counted and a 360-day year is used in calculating the amount allowed for anticipation. The anticipation rate should be applied after the cash discount has been deducted as in a chain discount.

(*a*) An invoice for $1,000 with terms 2/10 n/30 is paid 5 days before the end of the discount period. If this invoice is anticipated, what payment should the retailer make?   *Example*

$1,000.00 $\times$ .02 = $20.00 Cash discount

$1,000.00 - $20.00 = $980.00 Amount of payment

$$\overset{\$9.80}{\cancel{\$980}} \times \frac{\overset{1}{\cancel{6}}}{\underset{1}{\cancel{100}}} \times \frac{\overset{1}{\cancel{5}}}{\underset{\underset{12}{\cancel{60}}}{\cancel{360}}} = \$.82 \text{ Amount allowed for anticipation}$$

$980.00 - $.82 = $979.18 Net payment

(*b*) If the invoice in (*a*), above, carried terms of 2/10–30 extra n/60, the discount period would be extended 30 days.* If payment is made 5 days after the invoice date as in (*a*), the calculation would be:

$1,000.00 × .02 = $20.00 Cash discount

$1,000.00 − $20.00 = $980.00 Amount of payment before anticipation

$$\$980 \times \frac{\overset{\$9.80}{\cancel{6}}}{\cancel{100}} \times \frac{\overset{1}{\underset{\cancel{60}}{\cancel{35}}}}{\underset{12}{\cancel{360}}} = \$5.72 \text{ Amount allowed for anticipation}$$

$980.00 − $5.72 = $974.28 Net payment

SECTION 2—GROSS COST OF GOODS SOLD

Purchase returns and allowances

Just as the sales of the retailer must be adjusted for returns by customers and allowances to customers, so must the retailer adjust his purchase figures for his returns to vendors and allowances from vendors. When a retailer is authorized by a vendor to return goods, he prepares an invoice (often called a *chargeback*) to the vendor charging him for the merchandise less any cash discount or anticipation originally accorded the retailer. In practice, this chargeback to the vendor is seldom paid in cash, but remains on the vendor's books as a credit to the retailer's account. When the retailer places another order and receives another invoice, the amount of the credit is deducted from the payment of the subsequent invoice. The difference between the total of all purchases from all vendors and the returns to and allowances from all vendors during the period is the amount for entry on the income statement as net purchases.

Example   (*a*) An invoice for $1,000 dated July 2 with terms 3/30 n/60 was paid July 12 and anticipated. The amount of the payment was calculated as follows:

$1,000.00 × .03 = $30.00 Cash discount

$1,000.00 − $30.00 = $970.00 Amount of payment before anticipation

$$\$970 \times \frac{\overset{\$9.70}{\cancel{6}}}{\underset{1}{\cancel{100}}} \times \frac{\overset{1}{\cancel{20}}}{\underset{\underset{3}{\cancel{60}}}{\cancel{360}}} = \frac{\$9.70}{3} = \$3.23 \text{ Amount for anticipation}$$

$970.00 − $3.23 = $966.77 Net payment

*Anticipation is seldom allowed on net invoices. Terms of 2/10 n/30 would ordinarily permit anticipation to the 10-day discount limit, not through the 30-day net payment period.

(b) Merchandise on the invoice in (a) with a cost of $200 was found to be defective and was returned to the vendor. The vendor was charged as follows:

$200.00 × .03 = $6.00 Cash discount

$200.00 − $6.00 = $194.00 Amount before anticipation

$$\$194 \times \frac{\cancel{6}}{\cancel{100}} \times \frac{\cancel{20}}{\cancel{360}} = \$1.94 = \$.65 \text{ Amount for anticipation}$$

$194.00 − $.65 = $193.35 Net chargeback

Total merchandise available for sale

The cost of goods includes not only the cost of the merchandise itself, but also the cost of getting the merchandise into the store. This shipping cost is termed *transportation-in* or *freight-in*. As explained in chapter 2, if the store is to pay for transportation, the terms would state F.O.B. at a point other than the store. The net purchase figure plus the transportation costs are added to the cost value of the inventory on hand at the beginning of the period to arrive at the cost of all merchandise available for sale during the period. Of course, not all of this merchandise is sold, and if the cost value of the inventory on hand at the end of the period is subtracted from the value of the merchandise available for sale, the difference is the *gross cost of goods sold*. This is the first of three cost-of-goods-sold figures appearing on the income statement.

Example

Beginning inventory at cost	$ 350,000
Net purchases	1,345,000
(this would include the $220 merchandise cost for each of the refrigerators referred to in chapter 2)	
Transportation charges on purchases	25,000
(this would include the $18 freight-in charge on each of the refrigerators)	
Total cost of merchandise available for sale	$1,720,000
Less: Ending inventory at cost	400,000
(this would include the $220 merchandise cost and the $18 freight-in charge on each of the refrigerators remaining unsold at the end of the period)	
Gross cost of goods sold	$1,320,000

EXERCISE 3-1 TRADE DISCOUNTS

A. Find the amount of trade discount and the net cost using method 1 of the example on p. 64—applying each discount in series to a reduced balance.

	List Price	Trade Discount Rate	Trade Discount Amount	Net Cost
1.	$ 70.00	40/10	_____	_____
2.	150.00	35/15	_____	_____
3.	200.00	30/20	_____	_____
4.	275.00	25/10	_____	_____
5.	360.00	28/12	_____	_____
6.	583.50	$37\frac{1}{2}/12\frac{1}{2}$	_____	_____
7.	615.40	$33\frac{1}{3}/16\frac{2}{3}$	_____	_____
8.	765.95	30/10/5	_____	_____
9.	987.67	$37\frac{1}{2}/25/12\frac{1}{2}$	_____	_____
10.	1,612.13	$33\frac{1}{3}/16\frac{2}{3}/8\frac{1}{3}$	_____	_____

B. Find the net cost and the amount of trade discount using method 2 of the example on p. 64—applying the decimal or fractional complements of the discount rates in series to a reduced balance.

	List Price	Trade Discount Rate	Net Cost	Trade Discount Amount
1.	$ 800.00	30/20	_____	_____
2.	1,200.00	35/15	_____	_____
3.	1,450.00	40/10	_____	_____
4.	975.00	25/20	_____	_____
5.	790.00	30/15/5	_____	_____
6.	1,550.50	$37\frac{1}{2}/25/12\frac{1}{2}$	_____	_____
7.	1,375.75	$33\frac{1}{3}/16\frac{2}{3}/8\frac{1}{3}$	_____	_____
8.	1,890.90	$27\frac{1}{2}/18\frac{1}{2}/15$	_____	_____
9.	2,345.15	$35/12\frac{1}{2}/5$	_____	_____
10.	1,730.45	$25/12\frac{1}{2}/10$	_____	_____

C. Find the single discount rate equivalent to a trade discount series, the amount of trade discount, and the net cost.

	List Price	Trade Discount Rate	Equivalent Single Rate	Trade Discount Amount	Net Cost
1.	$ 90.00	35/15	_____	_____	_____
2.	1,200.00	40/10	_____	_____	_____
3.	750.00	30/20	_____	_____	_____
4.	1,640.00	25/20/10	_____	_____	_____
5.	85.00	30/10/5	_____	_____	_____

	List Price	Trade Discount Rate	Equivalent Single Rate	Trade Discount Amount	Net Cost
6.	1,175.50	$15/8\frac{1}{3}/4$	_____	_____	_____
7.	416.75	$15/10/2\frac{1}{2}$	_____	_____	_____
8.	565.25	$25/16\frac{2}{3}/10$	_____	_____	_____
9.	789.12	$37\frac{1}{2}/25/5$	_____	_____	_____
10.	1,040.60	$33\frac{1}{3}/12\frac{1}{2}/10$	_____	_____	_____

EXERCISE 3-2 CASH DISCOUNTS

A. Find the amount of cash discount and the net cost.

	Invoice Amount	Cash Discount Rate	Cash Discount	Net Cost
1.	$ 695.00	2%	_____	_____
2.	1,613.00	5	_____	_____
3.	419.50	4	_____	_____
4.	1,114.15	$3\frac{1}{2}$	_____	_____
5.	28.50	8	_____	_____
6.	870.75	$2\frac{1}{2}$	_____	_____
7.	478.60	6	_____	_____
8.	1,574.63	$4\frac{1}{2}$	_____	_____
9.	1,918.10	7	_____	_____
10.	770.44	$2\frac{1}{2}$	_____	_____

B. Find the amount of cash discount and the net cost.

	Invoice Amount	Terms	Invoice Date	Receipt-of-Goods Date	Payment Date	Discount	Net Cost
1.	$ 312.14	2/10,n/30	1/15	1/17	1/25	___	___
2.	48.90	2/10,1/20,n/30	5/6	5/10	5/17	___	___
3.	112.25	3/10,2/15,n/30	3/8	3/9	3/12	___	___
4.	319.75	2/10 E.O.M.	3/13	3/16	4/10	___	___
5.	78.50	2/15–45 extra	1/19	1/26	3/20	___	___
6.	440.60	2/10 prox.	10/16	10/21	11/20	___	___
7.	1,760.00	4/20 R.O.G.	6/15	6/20	7/10	___	___
8.	930.17	3/15 E.O.M.	7/29	8/4	9/15	___	___
9.	650.00	5/10 R.O.G.	4/5	4/11	4/20	___	___
10.	225.50	2/10–40 extra	1/14	1/17	3/7	___	___

C. Find the amount of cash discounts earned for the following partial payments and the amounts still due on the invoices.

Invoice Amount	Terms	Invoice Date	Partial Payment Date	Partial Payment Amount	Discount	Balance Due
1. $1,000.00	2/10,n/30	9/5	9/12	$500.00	_____	_____
2. 800.00	4/10,n/20	2/8	2/15	200.00	_____	_____
3. 580.00	2/10 E.O.M.	3/15	4/9	280.00	_____	_____
4. 450.50	3/10 prox.	7/19	8/9	250.00	_____	_____
5. 125.73	3/10,2/15,n/30	4/3	4/15	75.00	_____	_____
6. 390.80	5/15,3/30,n/60	8/12	8/28	190.80	_____	_____
7. 220.60	3/15,2/20,n/30	12/8	12/29	120.60	_____	_____
8. 470.50	4/20 E.O.M.	6/28	8/15	200.00	_____	_____
9. 165.75	2/15–30 extra	9/16	10/31	100.00	_____	_____
10. 95.00	8/10,n/30	7/10	7/20	50.00	_____	_____

EXERCISE 3-3 PURCHASE DISCOUNTS

Find the total of the trade discounts and all earned cash discounts, the amount of anticipation possible, and the resultant net payment.

Invoice Amount	Trade Discount	Terms	Invoice Date	Payment Date	Total Discount	Anticipation	Net Payment
1. $ 350	25/10/10	2/30,n/60	7/16	7/21	_____	_____	_____
2. 500	30/10/5	4/20,2/30,n/60	9/4	9/25	_____	_____	_____
3. 800	35/15/5	3/15,n/30	4/6	4/7	_____	_____	_____
4. 1,000	20/20/10	8/10,n/30	1/8	1/9	_____	_____	_____
5. 1,600	$25/12\frac{1}{2}/10$	2/10 E.O.M.	3/2	3/5	_____	_____	_____
6. 2,000	40/5/5	5/10–30 ex	6/9	6/10	_____	_____	_____
7. 1,250	25/15/10	3/15 prox.	8/11	9/15	_____	_____	_____
8. 1,375	25/15/5	3/10 E.O.M.	5/30	7/10	_____	_____	_____
9. 750	35/10/5	2/10,1/20,n/30	3/3	3/24	_____	_____	_____
10. 1,800	25/20/5	2/15–45 ex	2/8	2/10	_____	_____	_____

EXERCISE 3-4 PURCHASE DISCOUNT PROBLEMS

1. Buffington's bought 12 dresser sets from a vendor at a list price of $19.95 each. They were granted a trade discount of 45%. What was the total net cost?

2. Raphael's Delicatessen was offered a gift box of seasonings by a vendor at $12.50 less a trade discount of $37\frac{1}{2}$%. What would be the total net cost of 4 dozen boxes?

3. A stationery distributor sold Compton's Stationery Store 12 dozen boxes of stationery at a catalog price of $1.95 a box with a trade discount of 40% and 6 dozen pens listing at $2.95 with a discount of 35%. What would be the total net cost of this merchandise.

4. The Fairview Hardware Store received an invoice for handtools totaling $1,214.00 subject to a trade discount of 25/10/5. What amount should be paid on this invoice?

5. A buyer for Buffington's was offered a discount of 40/10 on a $450 list price item by one vendor. Another vendor offered a discount of 20/10/5. Which is the better buy and by how much?

6. The purchasing agent for Buffington's was seeking filing cabinets for the offices. A suitable unit from Metal Masters, Inc. was priced at $49.50 with a trade discount of 30/10 with no charge for delivery. A similar unit from Safety File, Inc. was available at $44.00 with a trade discount of 10/10/5 and a transportation charge of $1.50 per unit. If 24 units were purchased, which would be the better buy and how much would be saved?

7. The Dalton Company grants a trade discount of $20/12\frac{1}{2}/10$ to retailers while the Besson Company offers 25/10/5. Which company offers the better discount?

8. A wholesaler received a trade discount of 30/10/5 from a manufacturer and sold this line of goods to retailers at the same list price less a discount of 20/10. What was his markon percent?

9. A line of merchandise was bought for $850 less 35/15/5. It was retailed at $37\frac{1}{2}$% more than cost. What was the retail price?

10. An invoice for $980 dated June 4 was paid June 14. It was subject to a trade discount of 25/15/10 and the terms were 3/15, 2/20, n/30. What was the net amount of the payment?

11. An invoice dated March 31 for $5,500 with a trade discount of 40/10/5 carried terms of 2/10-90 extra. The bill is paid April 26. Freight amounting to $50.60 was paid by the store. What was the net cost?

12. An invoice for $800 is subject to terms 2/10-30 extra, net 60. It is dated March 4, anticipated and paid March 14. How much was the net payment?

13. A retailer receives a shipment on March 14 and the covering invoice is dated March 9. The terms of sale are 3/10 R.O.G. and the invoice amount is $563.35 less a trade discount of 25/10/5. What should be the amount of the payment made on March 24?

14. A retailer received an invoice for $1,210 dated June 12. The vendor granted a trade discount of 35/15/5, terms of 3/15, 1/20, n/30, and allowed anticipation. How much should the retailer remit on June 27?

15. Buffington's received an invoice for $615 with terms 3/15, n/30. A portion of the goods was found to be defective and the vendor authorized a return of items with a cost value of $235. The invoice less the return credit was paid within the discount period. What was the amount of the net payment?

16. If identical merchandise with a list price of $1,250 may be purchased under either of the following conditions, which would be the better buy,

and by how much, if payment is made on the 10th day after the invoice date?

   a. trade discount 30/15/10 with terms 2/10, n/30, no anticipation, and a $22.50 freight charge.

   b. trade discount 20/10/10 with terms 3/10–30 ex, F.O.B. store, anticipation allowed.

17. On September 9, a retailer anticipated and paid for goods invoiced at $685.50 on August 31 with terms 2/10–30 extra. Subsequently, the vendor issued a credit to the retailer for returned goods with a cost value of $315. If the vendor should pay the retailer for this credit due him, what would be the net amount of payment?

18. A payment of $500 was made within the discount period on an invoice for $975.75 with terms 5/10, n/30. How much should be credited to the account for this payment and what would be the remaining balance due?

19. An invoice for $817.40 carried terms of 3/10, 2/20, 1/30, n/60. Payment was made in the following manner: $300.00—20 days after invoice date; $200.00—10 days after invoice date; and the balance on the last day of the net period. What should be the amount of the final payment?

20. A shipment was received July 18. The covering invoice dated July 14 granted a trade discount of 25/10/5 on merchandise with a list price of $225.60. In addition to this merchandise charge, the invoice also listed a display charge of $10.00 and a parcel post charge of $3.75. What should be the net payment on July 26 if the terms were 3/10, 2/20, n/30?

SECTION 3—NET AND TOTAL COST OF GOODS SOLD

Alternative methods of handling cash discounts

It was necessary to discuss cash discounts in arriving at the amount to be paid on invoices. However, there are three ways in which cash discounts may be shown on the income statement:

1. They may be shown as a reduction in the cost of purchases before arriving at net purchases.
2. They may be considered as strictly a financial matter, separate from the buying and selling operation of the retailer, and shown as other income after calculating the profit on merchandising operations.
3. The preferred treatment today is that followed by Buffington's, in which the cash discounts earned are deducted from the gross cost of goods sold to arrive at the net cost of goods sold. As explained in chapter 2, maintained markon is the difference between gross cost of goods sold and net sales.

Alteration and workroom costs

The costs considered up to this point apply to all merchandise purchased or in inventory. On certain items additional costs are incurred after the sale is made. These are the *alteration and workroom costs*. They do not apply to all items in the inventory and therefore are not included when calculating total merchandise available for sale. They are set out separately and added to net cost of goods sold to arrive at *total cost of goods sold*.

In many cases, a store will attempt to recover part of these costs by charging the customer for certain types of alterations or modifications of the merchandise. Competition takes place in this area as well as in pricing, so it would be a rare thing for all of these costs to be offset by charges to customers. They are usually reduced to a certain extent, and accordingly the term *net alteration and workroom costs* is used on the income statement, indicating that the amounts paid by customers for this service have been deducted from the total cost of providing the service.

Gross margin

The difference between net sales and total merchandise costs is called *gross margin* or *gross profit*. The term *gross* indicates that further refinement is necessary before a final or net figure is determined. In this case, as discussed in chapter 1, the subsequent refinement is the subtraction of expenses to arrive at *operating profit*. The term *gross margin* is preferable to *gross profit*, since most of it goes for expenses leaving very little for operating profit.

The relationship between sales, cost of sales, markon, and gross margin may be clarified by looking at aggregate costs and related aggregate retails. The following example is taken from the Buffington's operation:

	Cost	Retail
Net sales (and gross cost of sales)	$1,320,000	$2,000,000
Beginning inventory	350,000	550,000
Net purchases	1,370,000	2,265,000
Ending inventory	400,000	655,000
Cash discounts	50,000	
Alteration costs	10,000	
Original markon (on purchases for year)		
Net purchases at retail		$2,265,000
Net purchases at cost		−1,370,000
		$ 895,000 Original markon
$895,000 ÷ $2,265,000 =		39.3% Original markon percent
Initial markon (sometimes called *cumulative markon*)		
Beginning inventory	$ 350,000	$ 550,000
Purchases	+1,370,000	+2,265,000
Total merchandise available	$1,720,000	$2,815,000
Total merchandise available at retail		2,815,000
Total merchandise available at cost		−1,720,000
		$1,095,000 Initial markon
$1,095,000 ÷ $2,815,000 =		38.9% Initial markon percent

Maintained markon
   Net sales $2,000,000
   Gross cost of sales   -1,320,000
                         $ 680,000 Maintained markon

$680,000 \div $2,000,000 =   34% Maintained markon percent

Gross margin
   Maintained markon $ 680,000
   Cash discounts   +   50,000
                         $ 730,000
   Net alteration costs   -   10,000
                         $ 720,000 Gross margin

$720,000 \div $2,000,000 =   36% Gross margin percent

EXERCISE 3-5 COSTS OF GOODS SOLD AND GROSS MARGIN

Complete each of the five income statement trading sections:

	(1)	(2)	(3)	(4)	(5)
Net sales	3000	——	4800	7200	——
Gross cost of sales	1850	4500	——	4400	5900
Maintained markon	——	4000	1900	——	——
Cash discounts	100	——	225	——	630
Net cost of sales	——	4150	——	3890	——
Net alteration costs	250	——	315	——	——
Total cost of sales	——	4575	——	——	5680
Gross margin	——	——	——	3700	4120

EXERCISE 3-6 MARKON AND MARGIN PROBLEMS

1. A retailer's books show the following:

	Cost	Retail
Sales (and gross cost of sales)	$130,000	$200,000
Beginning inventory	40,000	65,000
Net purchases	140,000	240,000
Ending inventory	50,000	80,000
Cash discounts	5,000	
Net alteration costs	2,000	

Find the original markon, the initial markon, the maintained markon, and the gross margin.

2. A store had sales of $120,000, alteration costs of $1,200, and cash discounts of $3,100. Purchases were $75,000 at cost, the beginning inventory $25,000 at cost, and the ending inventory $30,000 at cost. Find the gross margin and the maintained markon.

3. The gross margin is $53,000, the cash discount earned $5,200, and the alteration costs $1,850. What is the maintained markon?

4. The maintained markon is $162,500, the cash discount $6,675, and workroom costs $4,213. What is the gross margin?

5. A department had an gross margin of 42%, cash discount earned of 3%, and alteration costs of 1%. What was the maintained markup?

SECTION 4—INVENTORY VALUATION

The differences between gross margin of profit, operating profit, and net profit were explained in chapter 1, section 2. By inspection of the income statement, it is seen that the value placed on inventory has a great effect upon gross margin and the ultimate operating profit. Buffington's ending inventory was valued at $400,000. If it had been $450,000, gross margin would have been $50,000 more and the operating profit would have been twice that which was reported. If the ending inventory had been valued at $350,000 the operating profit would have been completely eliminated.

The complications in inventory valuation arise first from the fact that certain items in the beginning inventory may or may not be in the ending inventory. If they are present, they may not be as salable as when first purchased. If sold, the cost of replacing them in inventory may be more or less than their original cost. A business firm concerned with continuing operations year after year does not want to overstate profits. This would result in higher income taxes and perhaps an excessive distribution of profits, which would impair future operations.

The most common methods of arriving at a value for inventories are:

1. the cost method using the specific invoice price of each item
2. the cost method with the assumption that the first items purchased during the period are the first items sold (first-in first-out or FIFO)
3. the cost-or-market-whichever-is-lower method
4. the retail method, which estimates inventory value approximating the cost or market method
5. the last-in-first-out (LIFO) method, with the assumption that the last items purchased are the first items sold, which may be used with either a cost or retail approach

To illustrate the different methods of inventory valuation, assume the following inventory and purchase figures for the Buffington refrigerator referred to in chapter 2:

		Cost
February 1, beginning inventory	10 units at $238 =	$2,380
March 23, purchased	20 units at $243 =	4,860
June 15, purchased	30 units at $248 =	7,440
December 5, purchased	10 units at $253 =	2,530
Units available for sale	70 units	$17,210
January 31, ending inventory	15 units	

Specific invoice price

Due to switching of inventory between warehouse, selling floor, and various display locations, the units were not sold in any specific order. Accordingly, the units left in the ending inventory had different age and cost codes:

```
Ending inventory
   2 units (March) at $243 = $  486
   5 units (June)  at $248 =  1,240
   8 units (Dec.)  at $253 =  2,024
  15 units                   $3,750
```

First-in first-out (FIFO)

Traditional store operations have always called for selling the oldest merchandise first. When shelves are replenished, the new stock is placed behind the old stock. When goods are not identified by cost codes, it is assumed that goods are rotated in this manner and, consequently, there is strong justification for using the first-in first-out method in valuing the ending inventory:

```
Ending inventory
  10 units (Dec.) at $253 = $2,530
   5 units (June) at $248 =  1,240
  15 units                  $3,770
```

Cost-or-market-whichever-is-lower

The justification for this method is that due to competition, most items which can be replaced for less than original cost usually must be marked down before they can be sold. Conversely, when the replacement price increases, it is seldom that the inventory is marked up until the store reorders at the higher price. Accountants have tended to be conservative in the values placed on the balance sheet, and this method is consistent with that approach:

```
Replacement or market price, January 31: $250
Ending inventory
   2 units (March)          at $243 = $  486
   5 units (June)           at $248 =  1,240
   8 units (at market price
     rather than at December
     cost of $253)          at $250 =  2,000
                                       $3,726
```

If the replacement price on January 31 were less than the $243 March cost, then the total ending inventory would be valued at replacement price. This is because market is lower than *any* of the cost prices.

Last-in first-out (LIFO)

Under the FIFO method, larger profits result during periods of rising prices because higher values are placed on ending inventories than on beginning inventories. To remedy this, the LIFO system was proposed. Because sales give rise to the need for replacement of inventory, it is held that the cost of inventory replacement should be matched against the sales necessitating such replacement. Therefore, ending inventory is valued at the cost of the items at the beginning of the period:

$$
\begin{array}{lll}
\text{Ending inventory} \\
\quad \text{10 units (February)} & \text{at \$238} = & \$2,380 \\
\quad \text{5 units (March)} & \text{at \$243} = & \underline{1,215} \\
& & \$3,595
\end{array}
$$

Retail method of inventory valuation

The retail method of inventory arrives at the cost value of inventory by applying a cost percent to the total retail value of the inventory. The aggregate retail value must be determined at least once a year by actually counting all items, extending and totaling their retail prices. Between these physical inventories, records are kept of all changes in retail value due primarily to sales, purchases, customer returns, markups, and markdowns. Thus, on the books of the company is a record, constantly maintained, of the ever-changing total retail value of its merchandise. This record is called the *book inventory*.

A key figure in the retail method is the total merchandise available for sale. The cost value of this merchandise is recorded from invoices and freight bills. The retail value is accumulated from the original markon and markups. Thus, the cost as a percent of retail (the complement of the initial markon) can readily be determined.

After finding this relationship between cost and retail on total merchandise handled, an assumption is made that this same relationship would apply to the items remaining in inventory. Hence, the cost percent is applied to the physical-inventory retail figure, and the result is the ending inventory at cost, which then enables the store to prepare an income statement.

One of the advantages of the retail method is that it permits determination of a cost value of the inventory at any time without taking an actual count. The retail value of the total merchandise available for sale is reduced by sales, markdowns, discounts to employees, and an estimated amount for shortages. All of these figures are kept on the company records, so the resultant book-inventory figure at retail can be converted to cost at any time, thus permitting the preparation of financial statements.

The retail method is an estimate, and is a good estimate only if it is applied to items with similar markon. This is why large stores are divided into departments each of which carries related merchandise with approximately the same marking. It also assumes that the retailer takes markups and markdowns in accordance with changes in market price. The result is an inventory valuation at cost or market value, whichever is lower. This is shown in the following example by the way markups and markdowns are handled. Markups are included in the total retail value of merchandise available for sale, reflecting an increase in the market value of the merchandise. At this point the cost as a percent of retail is calculated. This percent is subsequently applied to the retail value of the ending inventory to arrive at a cost value. The retail value added by markups carries through tending to increase the value of the ending inventory. On the other hand retail value deducted due to markdowns has a decreasing effect on the ending inventory. This happens because the cost percent applied to the retail ending inventory stays the same. The final cost value of the inventory has automatically been adjusted to a cost or market value whichever is lower.

	Cost	Retail
Beginning inventory	$ 350,000	$ 540,000
Net purchases	1,345,000	2,255,000
Transportation-in	25,000	
Net markups		20,000
Total merchandise available for sale	$1,720,000	$2,815,000
Cost as percent of retail		
($1,720,000 ÷ $2,815,000)	61.1%	
Deductions in retail value		
Sales $2,000,000		
Net markdowns 127,000		
Employee discounts 16,000		
Estimated shortages 17,000		
Total deductions		2,160,000
Estimated inventory	400,205	$ 655,000
(cost: $655,000 X .611)		
Actual physical inventory	400,000	654,665
Additional shortage over estimate	205	335

EXERCISE 3-7 COST METHOD OF INVENTORY VALUATION

A. The Koch Building Supply Co. wanted to compare the FIFO and LIFO methods of inventory valuation. From the following data find the total value of ending inventory by each of these methods for three stock items.

	Item A		Item B		Item C	
	Qty.	Unit Cost	Qty.	Unit Cost	Qty.	Unit Cost
Inventory, Feb. 1	300	$2.50	250	$4.75	150	$9.25
Purchases						
Mar. 25	300	2.60	750	4.60		
Apr. 9					200	9.35
June 27	350	2.60				
July 15			500	4.50	250	9.50
Sept. 21	275	2.70				
Oct. 14			425	4.50		
Nov. 20	225	2.75			500	9.75
Dec. 10			150	4.45		
Jan. 12	100	2.80				
Inventory, Jan. 31	270		225		165	
Total value						
Ending Inventory						
FIFO Method	_____		_____		_____	
LIFO Method	_____		_____		_____	

B. The Houseware Department of Buffington's had the following items in their ending inventory. Find the value of this inventory using the cost-or-market-whichever-is-lower method.

		Unit Price	
Item	Quantity	Cost	Market
A	415	$ .17	$ .19
B	312	.28	.31
C	178	.34	.38
D	62	4.20	4.35
E	78	9.75	10.15
F	23	225.00	237.00
G	8	410.00	375.00
H	16	125.00	110.00

C. A retailer had the following inventory and purchase figures at cost for the year:

February	1,	beginning inventory	10 units at $55.00
April	15	purchased	25 units at $50.00
July	20	purchased	12 units at $57.00
October	17	purchased	30 units at $60.00
December	1	purchased	8 units at $65.00
January	31	ending inventory	14 units

(Market value at ending inventory—$65.00)

Find the ending inventory valuation under each of the following assumptions:

1. The specific invoice price method was used. One of the units in the ending inventory was on hand at the beginning of the period; 2 were purchased on July 20, 4 on October 17, and 7 on December 1.
2. The first-in first-out method was used.
3. The cost-or-market-whichever-is-lower method was used and the units in the ending inventory were acquired as indicated in assumption 1, above.
4. The last-in first-out method was used.

SECTION 5—STOCK TURNOVER

The biggest investment of a retailer is in merchandise. The key to profitability is how effectively he uses his merchandise inventory. If he can generate more sales at the same initial markon with the same or even smaller inventory, he will realize a greater return on his investment. At even a lower markon, the sales increase with the same inventory could be great enough to result in more dollars of gross margin. One measure of the relationship between sales and stock is called *stock turnover*. It is the number of times that the average stock is sold during a period, and is found by dividing sales for a period by the average stock during that period.

The yearly rate of stock turnover varies by type of merchandise and type of store. In department stores it could well vary from about 1.5 for china and glassware, to 4.5 for major appliances, to 8 or 9 for millinery. In different kinds of businesses typical turnover rates could vary from approximately 1.5 for jewelry stores, to 3.5 for department stores, to 18 for supermarkets. Perishability and fashion will affect stock turnover, as will buying habits of customers and the extent of assortment a retailer offers his customers. A higher-than-average rate of stock turnover tends to increase profits, but does not insure higher profits. Too much restriction of inventories may result in loss of sales due to lack of suitable merchandise and out-of-stock conditions.

There are three ways to calculate stock turnover. These are illustrated using figures from Buffington's Department Store:

1. retail basis

$$\frac{\text{Net sales } \$2,000,000}{\text{Average stock at retail } \$615,000} = 3.25 \text{ Stock turnover at retail}$$

2. cost basis

$$\frac{\text{Cost of sales } \$1,320,000}{\text{Average stock at cost } \$375,000} = 3.52 \text{ Stock turnover at cost}$$

3. unit basis

$$\frac{\text{Units sold } 1,000}{\text{Average unit stock } 250} = 4.0 \text{ Stock turnover in units}$$

It is essential that these methods be used consistently; net sales, average stock at *retail*, and stock turnover at *retail*; or *cost* of sales, average stock at *cost*, and stock turnover at *cost*. Mixing retail and cost figures in the computation yields very misleading results. The relationship between sales or cost of sales, average stock, and stock turnover enables the retailer to find any one of these factors when the other two are known:

$$\frac{\text{Net sales } \$2,000,000}{\text{Stock turnover } 3.25} = \$615,000 \text{ Average stock at retail}$$

$$\frac{\text{Cost of sales } \$1,320,000}{\text{Stock turnover } 3.52} = \$375,000 \text{ Average stock at cost}$$

$$\frac{\text{Units sold } 1,000}{\text{Stock turnover } 4.0} = 250 \text{ Average unit stocks}$$

Average stock at retail $615,000 ×

Stock turnover 3.25 = $2,000,000 Net sales

Average stock at cost $375,000 ×

Stock turnover 3.52 = $1,320,000 Cost of sales

Average unit stock 250 × Stock turnover 4.0 = 1,000 Units sold

The retail basis is more often used because most departmentalized stores use the retail method of inventory and the retail figures are thus more readily available. It also results in a smaller, more conservative figure than when the corresponding cost figures are used. This is true because the amount of marking on sales is generally less than the amount of marking on stock. The unit method can only be used for identical units of merchandise within a particular department.

The average stock for a year could be the average of the beginning and ending inventories. However, this is usually not too realistic because there could be wide variance in the stock between these yearly inventories. A better average would be a total of the beginning inventories and the ending inventories for each of the 12 months divided by 13. Buffington's average stock at retail could be calculated as follows:

	Retail Stock
February 1	$ 540,000
February 28	570,000
March 31	600,000
April 30	630,000
May 31	585,000
June 30	560,000
July 31	570,000
August 31	600,000
September 30	630,000
October 31	660,000
November 30	720,000
December 31	675,000
January 31	655,000

$7,995,000 ÷ 13 = $615,000

Unless otherwise specified, store turnover reflects the retailer's performance over one year. However, it could be calculated for any period of time. It is common to calculate the turnover at the end of each month. If the turnover for a month is .5 (i.e., $\frac{1}{2}$), then the turnover for a 6-month season can be estimated as 6 X .5 or 3 and for a year it would be 12 X .5 or 6.

EXERCISE 3-8 RETAIL METHOD OF INVENTORY VALUATION

A. Find the cost value of the following ending book inventories:

Beginning Inventory		Purchases		Ending Inventory	
Cost	Retail	Cost	Retail	Cost	Retail
$ 6,000	$10,000	$ 21,000	$ 35,000	_____	$ 9,000
3,350	5,000	9,650	15,900	_____	5,500
8,400	12,000	22,500	33,600	_____	14,200
42,000	66,000	153,000	208,000	_____	73,500
16,820	22,300	67,200	89,600	_____	19,900

B. Find the ending book inventory at cost for each of the following:

| Beginning Inventory | | Purchases | | | | Ending Inventory |
Cost	Retail	Cost	Retail	Sales	Markdown	Costs
$ 250	$ 400	$ 750	$ 1,280	$ 1,100	$ 320	_____
425	800	1,225	2,400	1,800	875	_____
9,800	17,600	27,800	54,500	45,000	1,225	_____
850	1,220	2,550	3,900	2,600	550	_____
22,450	39,800	76,500	140,200	135,200	8,300	_____

C. Find the initial markon percent for each department:

	Dept. A	Dept. B	Dept. C
Beginning inventory at retail	$ 5,300	$23,000	$35,000
Beginning inventory at cost	2,700	13,000	21,000
Purchases at retail	21,500	31,000	84,000
Purchases at cost	11,800	17,000	52,000
Markup	200	500	1,200
Transportation-in	120	650	1,560
Initial markon percent	_____	_____	_____

D. Find the ending book inventory at cost and the gross margin in dollars and in percent for each department.

	Dept. A	Dept. B	Dept. C
Sales	$200,000	$300,000	$90,000
Beginning inventory at retail	32,000	44,000	25,000
Beginning inventory at cost	22,000	25,000	13,000
Purchases at retail	210,000	290,000	95,000
Purchases at cost	140,000	155,000	48,000
Transportation-in	8,000	9,000	1,200
Markups	2,000	3,000	700
Retail reductions	4,000	4,800	2,400
Ending book inventory	_____	_____	_____
Gross margin ($)	_____	_____	_____
Gross margin (%)	_____	_____	_____

E. Find the gross margin and maintained markon in dollars and in percent for each department.

	Dept. A		Dept. B		Dept. C	
	Cost	Retail	Cost	Retail	Cost	Retail
Cash discounts	$ 2,500		$ 525		$ 1,750	
Beginning inventory	$ 40,000	$ 65,000	$14,000	$20,000	$18,500	$33,000
Markdowns		9,700		1,800		3,500
Purchases	110,000	192,000	17,500	28,500	42,000	68,500
Markups		1,000		300		850
Sales		175,000		27,000		80,000
Employees discounts		1,700		750		1,250
Net alteration costs	1,800		550		1,400	
Estimated shortages		1,200		250		800
Gross margin ($)	____		____		____	
Gross margin (%)	____		____		____	
Maintained markon ($)	____		____		____	
Maintained markon (%)	____		____		____	

EXERCISE 3-9 STOCK TURNOVER

A. Find the missing elements in the basic stock turnover formula.

Sales	Average Stock	Stock Turnover
$ 1,260	$ 420	_____
_____	9,235	2.5
29,465	_____	1.7
52,810	_____	4.6
46,920	14,450	_____
_____	86,200	$3\frac{1}{4}$
_____	33,750	$4\frac{1}{3}$
212,600	_____	$7\frac{1}{6}$
419,500	7,600	_____
116,460	_____	6.4

B. Using the stock turnover for one period, find the estimated stock turnover for the two other indicated periods.

Monthly Turnover	Season (6-month) Turnover	Yearly Turnover
$\frac{1}{3}$	_____	_____
_____	$3\frac{3}{4}$	_____
_____	_____	$6\frac{1}{2}$
$\frac{1}{6}$	_____	_____
$\frac{7}{8}$	_____	_____
_____	4.5	_____
_____	_____	9.6
_____	_____	4.875
_____	3.4	_____
_____	_____	3.7

C. Find the book inventory and the stock turnover for each month and the stock turnover for the year to date at the end of each month.

	Beginning-of-Month Retail Inventory	Retail Purchases	Sales	Retail Reductions	Stock Turnover Monthly	Year to date
Feb.	$12,000	$ 9,000	$ 6,000	300		
Mar.		7,000	7,000	400		
Apr.		8,000	9,000	500		
May		6,000	8,000	500		
June		5,000	7,000	600		
July		4,000	6,500	900		
Aug.		7,000	8,000	500		
Sept.		9,000	8,000	400		
Oct.		10,000	9,000	400		
Nov.		14,000	10,000	500		
Dec.		9,000	12,000	600		
Jan.		7,000	5,000	1,200		
Feb.						

EXERCISE 3-10 PROBLEMS ON STOCK TURNOVER

1. From the following data, find the stock turnover on a cost basis and on a retail basis.

	Cost	Retail
Beginning inventory	$64,800	$108,000
Ending inventory	72,600	121,000
Sales		385,700
Cost of goods sold		229,100

2. A retailer had a beginning inventory at cost of $16,200 and an ending inventory of $19,800 at cost. What was his stock turnover on a cost basis if his cost of sales for the period was $96,400?

3. For the first month of the year a retailer had a beginning inventory of $8,500 at retail, which increased to $9,200 by the end of the month. His markdowns were $600 and his sales were $6,750. What was his stock turnover for the month and what would be his estimated turnover for the year?

4. A merchant planned sales of $124,600 and markdowns of $1,460 for 6 months. If his stock turnover goal for this period is 3.7 what should his average inventory be?

5. Upon receiving the results of the year-end physical inventory it was necessary for a buyer to revise his six-month plan. If his average stock is planned at $155,800 and management desired a season stock turnover of 1.8, what should his sales be for the 6 months?

6. A store had an average retail stock of $265,400 and a stock turnover of 4 during the past year. If a turnover of 4.5 is desired this year with the same average inventory, what percent increase in sales should be planned?

7. With increased competition, a merchant sees little chance of increasing his sales of $178,000 during the coming year. However, he does want to im-

prove his stock turnover from 2.8 to 3.2. By what percent will he have to reduce his average stock to achieve this goal?

8. A jeweler had sales for the year of $225,000 and a stock turnover of 1.5. He wants to increase sales by $12\frac{1}{2}$% next year. If he accomplishes this with the same average.stock, what will his stock turnover be? If he maintains the same stock turnover, by how much will he have to increase his average stock?

9. A merchandise plan calls for an increase in stock turnover from .62 to .78. The planned sales are $82,000 and the beginning inventory is $124,000. How much inventory should be planned for the end of the month?

10. A sporting goods store had sales of $315,000 for the year. The beginning inventory was $110,000 at cost and $180,000 at retail, the mid-year inventory was $134,000 at cost and $220,000 at retail, and the ending inventory was $105,000 at cost and $172,000 at retail. The net cost purchases were $215,000. Find the stock turnover on a cost basis and on a retail basis.

BUFFINGTON'S DEPARTMENT STORE INC.
INCOME STATEMENT
FOR THE YEAR ENDED JANUARY 31, 19XX

SALES			
Gross Sales		$2,120,000	
Less Sales Returns and Allowances		120,000	5.7%
Net Sales		$2,000,000	100.0%
COST OF SALES			
Beginning Inventory at Cost, February 1.....		$ 350,000	
Gross Purchases at Cost...............	$1,395,000		
Less Purchase Returns and Allowances	50,000		
Net Purchases..................		$1,345,000	
Transportation Charges on Purchases		25,000	
Total Merchandise Available for Sale		$1,720,000	
Less Ending Inventory at Cost, January 31...		400,000	
Gross Cost of Goods Sold.............		$1,320,000	66.0%
Less Cash Discounts Earned		50,000	2.5%
Net Cost of Goods Sold		$1,270,000	63.5%
Net Alteration and Workroom Costs		10,000	.5%
Total Cost of Goods Sold		$1,280,000	64.0%
GROSS MARGIN OF PROFIT		$ 720,000	36.0%
OPERATING EXPENSES			
Payroll............................	$ 380,000		19.0%
Advertising	60,000		3.0%
Delivery	16,000		.8%
Supplies	24,000		1.2%
Depreciation	22,000		1.1%
Mortgage Expense	60,000		3.0%
Insurance	14,000		.7%
* Interest	20,000		1.0%
Taxes and Licenses	26,000		1.3%
Utilities............................	20,000		1.0%
Miscellaneous	28,000		1.4%
Total Operating Expenses		$ 670,000	33.5%
OPERATING PROFIT....................		$ 50,000	2.5%
OTHER INCOME......................		20,000	1.0%
NET PROFIT—BEFORE FEDERAL INCOME TAXES......................		$ 70,000	3.5%

*The concept of "imputed interest", found on actual store statements, is omitted for purposes of simplification.

THE INCOME STATEMENT

4

mathematics of expenses

SECTION 1—NATURE OF EXPENSES

In this chapter we shall be concerned with the mathematics involved in calculating the various amounts that make up the expense section of the income statement. These amounts also have an important effect on the balance sheet.

Before learning how these expense items are calculated, we need to understand the meaning of the word *expense*. An *expense* is a disbursement or outlay of funds. Why does a business firm call some of its expenditures "costs" and others "expenses"? In the language of business the term *cost* is applied to any expenditure which is directly related to the merchandise produced or sold. In the income statement heading chapter 1, every expenditure item above gross margin is considered a "cost" because it is directly associated with the merchandise sold. Specifically, these costs include the cost of merchandise, the cost of transporting merchandise, and any net alteration or workroom costs incurred in making sales to customers. The term *expense* is applied to all other expenditures.

In this chapter, only those expense items whose calculation requires a significant degree of mathematics will be covered. For this reason, our attention will be given to the following types of expenses: interest, payroll, insurance, and property taxes. Depreciation expense will be taken up in chapter 5 as part of the mathematics of fixed assets.

SECTION 2—INTEREST EXPENSE

From time to time business firms, like individuals, find it necessary to borrow money. When a firm borrows, the loan may be either short-term (up to one year) or long-term. Short-term loans are usually working-capital loans—i.e., the money is used for paying current obligations such as payroll or for purchasing new inventory. Long-term loans ordinarily involve borrowing large sums of money for the purpose of buying new equipment, new buildings, or other costly assets.

There are a number of different kinds of lending institutions a firm may choose as a source of funds. Banks, finance companies, savings and loan associations, factoring companies, and the Small Business Administration are some of the possible borrowing sources. For long-term borrowing, many corporations issue bonds.

The Buffington Department Store income statement shows an interest expense of $20,000. Presumably, this indicates a certain amount of short-term borrowing during the year in addition to a sizeable interest payment on the building mortgage.

Greatest-common-divisor method

Simple interest is the "rent" paid for borrowed money. This rent is determined from the following calculation:

$$I = PRT$$

where I = interest
P = principal (amount borrowed)
R = rate of annual interest
T = time (length of the borrowing period in years or fractional parts of a year)

Example What is the interest on $400 for 1 year at 6%?

$$I = PRT$$
$$= \$400 \times 6\% \times 1 \text{ year}$$
$$= \$400(.06)(1)$$
$$= \$24$$

In figuring the length of the borrowing period, banks usually use a 360-day year, and count the exact number of days in the loan period beginning with the day after the loan is made and including the last day of the borrowing period. If the due date on a loan is not a business day, the loan period is extended to the first business day following, and interest is charged for the additional day or days. This set of rules is often called the *banker's method*. Occasionally, money is borrowed on the basis of what is called *ordinary time* or *30-day-month time*.

On this basis, each full month is counted as 30 days, regardless of its actual length. Any additional days are added to give the total number of days. This example contrasts the banker's method with the ordinary time method:

Loose Period is Sept. 20 to Nov. 10

Banker's		Ordinary Time	
Sept. 30-20	= 10	Sept. 30-20	= 10
October	= 31	October	= 30
November	= 10	November	= 10
Total	= 51 days	Total	= 50 days

Ordinary time will not be used for solving any interest problems in this chapter.

Find the interest due on a $1,000 loan at 4% for 45 days.   *Example 1*

$$I = PRT$$

$$= \$\overset{\$10}{\cancel{1,000}} \times \frac{\overset{1}{\cancel{4}}}{\underset{1}{\cancel{100}}} \times \frac{\overset{1}{\cancel{45}}}{\underset{2}{\cancel{\underset{90}{360}}}}$$

$$= \frac{\overset{\$5}{\cancel{\$10}}}{\cancel{2}} = \$5$$

What is the interest on a $1,200 bank loan at 6% interest made on April 4   *Example 2* and due July 15?

Here it is necessary to count the number of days beginning with the day after the loan is made, up to and including the due date. The following counting procedure is recommended:

April 30 − 4	= 26 days
May	31
June	30
July	15
Total	102 days

$$I = PRT$$

$$= \$\overset{\overset{\$1}{\cancel{\$12}}}{\cancel{1,200}} \times \frac{\overset{1}{\cancel{6}}}{\underset{1}{\cancel{100}}} \times \frac{102}{\underset{5}{\cancel{\underset{60}{360}}}}$$

$$= \frac{\$102}{5} = \$20.40$$

The total of principal ($1,200) and interest ($20.40) is called *maturity value*. This is the total amount that must be paid back to the lender on the due date. Maturity value is represented by the symbol S, so that $S = P + I$. In example 2, above,

$$S = \$1,200 + \$20.40$$

$$= \$1,220.40$$

Simple interest is sometimes calculated using the exact year of 365 days. Because this procedure is frequently followed by government agencies, this period is called the *government year* or *exact year*. When a 365-day base is used, interest expense will be slightly lower. Recalculating example 1, above, using the exact year,

$$I = PRT$$

$$= \cancel{\$1,000} \times \frac{\overset{\$10}{4}}{\underset{1}{\cancel{100}}} \times \frac{\overset{9}{\cancel{45}}}{\underset{73}{\cancel{365}}}$$

$$= \frac{\$360}{73} = \$4.93 \text{ (7 cents less)}$$

The solutions to the simple-interest problems presented so far have been obtained by the *greatest-common-divisor method* (sometimes called the *cancellation method*), wherein the principal, rate, and time were multiplied together and the process simplified by finding the greatest common divisors for the factors represented. This is exactly like reducing a fraction to its lowest terms, as explained in appendix I.

Percent—day method

The *percent-day method* is based on 360 days' time and 1% interest. The product 360 days $\times$ 1% is 360%-days ("percent-days"). Thus, any interest rate multiplied by any number of days is equal to so many %-days. For example, 60 days at 6% = 360%-days; 90 days at 4% = 360%-days; 82 days at 5% = 410%-days; and so on. The rest of the calculation to find interest using this method involves multiplying the amount of interest at 1% by the ratio of %-days to 360. This is easier to demonstrate than to explain.

Example 1   What is the interest on $720 at 7% for 92 days?

$$7\% \times 92 \text{ days} = 644\%\text{-days}$$

$$\begin{matrix} & & \$.10 \\ & & \$.80 \\ I = & \dfrac{644}{360} & \times \ \$7.20 \ (1\% \text{ for } 360 \text{ days}) \\ & 40 & \\ & 5 & \end{matrix}$$

$$= \frac{\$64.40}{5}$$

$$= \$12.88$$

Find the interest on \$2,600 at $4\frac{1}{2}\%$ for 120 days.

Example 2

$$4\tfrac{1}{2}\% \times 120 \text{ days} = 540\%\text{-days}$$

$$I = \frac{540}{360} \times 26 \ (1\% \text{ for } 360 \text{ days})$$

$$I = \$39$$

One popular version of the %-day method of computing simple interest is the so-called *6%, 60-day method*. This method makes use of the fact that interest for 60 days at 6% is $\frac{1}{6}$ of the interest for 360 days at 6%. Consequently, the interest for 60 days will always be equal to 1% of the principal ($\frac{1}{6} \times 6\% = 1\%$). The interest on \$380 at 6% for 60 days is obtained by finding 1% of \$380. The answer (\$3.80) is found quickly by moving the decimal point two places to the left (\$3.80 $\times$ .01). From this point on, the method involves finding the interest for fractional parts or multiples of 60 days.

Find the interest on \$840 at 6% for 90 days.

Example 1

Interest on \$840 for 60 days at 6% = \$8.40
+Interest on \$840 for 30 days at 6% = 4.20 ($\frac{1}{2}$ of int. for 60 days)
Interest on \$840 for 90 days at 6% =\$12.60

Find the interest on \$1,800 at 6% for 53 days.

Example 2

Interest on \$1,800 at 6% for 60 days = \$18.00
−Interest on \$1,800 at 6% for 6 days = 1.80 ($\frac{1}{10}$ of int. for 60 days)
−Interest on \$1,800 at 6% for 1 day = .30 ($\frac{1}{6}$ of int. for 6 days)
Interest on \$1,800 at 6% for 53 days = \$15.90 (60 days − 7 days)

Example
  3

Find the interest on $540 at 8% and at 5% for 92 days.

At interest rates other than 6% it is best first to find the answer using 6%, then to adjust that answer to the rate given.

Interest on $540 at 6% for 60 days = $ 5.40
Interest on $540 at 6% for 30 days =   2.70
+Interest on $540 at 6% for   2 days =   .18 $\left(\frac{1}{15}\ \text{of int. for 30 days}\right)$
Interest on $540 at 6% for 92 days = $ 8.28
+Interest on $540 at 2% for 92 days =   2.76 $\left(2\% = \frac{1}{3}\ \text{of int. at 6\%}\right)$
Interest on $540 at 8% for 92 days = $11.04

Interest on $540 at 5% for 92 days = $ 6.90 $\left(5\% = \frac{5}{6}\ \text{of int. at 6\%}\right)$

Reverse operations in simple interest

Using the basic formula for finding interest $(I = PRT)$ we should be able to calculate any one of the other values which may be missing. The principal, rate, or time can be computed using variations of the basic interest formula. These variations are often referred to collectively as *reverse operations in simple interest*.

Example

Consider a $1,800 loan at 4% for 30 days (banker's method).

$$I = PRT$$

$$\$6 = \$1{,}800 \times \frac{4}{100} \times \frac{30}{360}$$

A. To find principal:

$$P = \frac{I}{RT}$$

$$= \frac{\$6}{\frac{4}{100} \times \frac{30}{360}}$$

$$= \frac{\$6}{\frac{1}{300}}$$

$$= \$6 \times \$300 = \$1{,}800$$

or

$$P = \frac{S \, (\text{maturity value})}{1 + RT}$$

$$= \frac{\$1,806}{1 + \frac{4}{100} \times \frac{30}{360}}$$

$$= \frac{\$1,806}{1 + \frac{1}{300}}$$

$$= \frac{\$1,806}{1\frac{1}{300}}$$

$$= \frac{\$1,806}{\frac{301}{300}}$$

$$= \$1,806 \times \frac{300}{301}$$

$$= \frac{\$541,800}{301} = \$1,800$$

B. To find the annual interest rate:

$$R = \frac{I}{PT}$$

$$= \frac{\$6}{\$1,800 \times \frac{30}{360}}$$

$$= \frac{\$6}{\$150} = .04 = 4\%$$

C. To find the time in years:

$$T = \frac{I}{PR}$$

$$= \frac{\$6}{\$1,800 \times \frac{4}{100}}$$

$$= \frac{\$6}{\$72} = \frac{1}{12} \text{ year}$$

Then,

$$\frac{1}{12} \times 360 \text{ days} = 30 \text{ days}$$

Note: In performing reverse operations in simple interest, the rate and time may be expressed in fractional or decimal equivalents.

EXERCISE 4-1 SIMPLE INTEREST

A. Using the greatest-common-divisor method, calculate the simple interest on the following short-term loans using the banker's method.

	Principal	Annual Interest Rate	Borrowing Period	Interest
1.	$ 600	5%	90 days	_____
2.	385	6	45 days	_____
3.	1,200	7	200 days	_____
4.	500	$8\frac{1}{2}$	165 days	_____
5.	940	$5\frac{3}{4}$	67 days	_____
6.	450	9	52 days	_____
7.	150	$7\frac{1}{2}$	30 days	_____
8.	10,000	$8\frac{1}{4}$	3 years	_____
9.	780	$4\frac{1}{4}$	2 years	_____
10.	2,600	5	$1\frac{1}{2}$ years	_____

B. Using the greatest-common divisor method, calculate the exact interest on the following loans.

	Principal	Annual Interest Rate	Borrowing Period	Interest
1.	$ 600	5%	90 days	_____
2.	800	6	45 days	_____
3.	250	$5\frac{1}{2}$	70 days	_____
4.	1,000	8	83 days	_____
5.	2,500	$7\frac{3}{4}$	150 days	_____
6.	6,000	$5\frac{3}{4}$	240 days	_____
7.	7,500	9	430 days	_____
8.	10,000	6	2 years	_____
9.	15,500	7	3 years	_____
10.	12,600	$8\frac{1}{2}$	6 years	_____

C. Using the 6%, 60-day method, calculate the interest due on these loans.

	Principal	Borrowing Period	Annual Interest Rate	Interest
1.	$ 1,400	120 days	6%	_____
2.	725	80	6	_____

	Principal	Borrowing Period	Annual Interest Rate	Interest
3.	930	33	6	————
4.	1,375	200	6	————
5.	12,400	51	6	————
6.	8,250	60	5	————
7.	2,145	57	5	————
8.	6,000	88	4	————
9.	1,680	49	7	————
10.	22,500	570	8	————

EXERCISE 4-2 REVERSE OPERATIONS IN SIMPLE INTEREST

A. Using the banker's year and the greatest-common-divisor method, calculate the time and the interest due on these loans. Note: A leap year is any year divisible evenly by 4, such as 1972. In a leap year, February has 29 days.

	Principal	Annual Interest Rate	Borrowing Period	Time (days)	Interest
1.	$ 490	7%	June 14 to Oct. 12	——	——
2.	600	5	Apr. 5 to Oct. 8	——	——
3.	1,400	6	Nov. 9 to Feb. 20	——	——
4.	2,225	8	Feb. 4 to July 19	——	——
5.	5,500	$5\frac{1}{2}$	Jan. 2 to Dec. 4	——	——
6.	725	$7\frac{3}{4}$	Aug. 18 to Oct. 10	——	——
7.	4,750	9	June 11, 1970, to Apr. 8, 1971	——	——
8.	12,250	$8\frac{1}{2}$	Sept. 5, 1971, to Sept. 5, 1975	——	——
9.	500	$6\frac{1}{4}$	Mar. 14, 1968, to Aug. 22, 1971	——	——
10.	1,840	3	May 7, 1969, to Feb. 2, 1970	——	——

B. Find the principal, and the maturity value (where indicated), in each of the following simple-interest problems. Use the banker's year.

	Interest	Maturity Value	Time	Annual Interest Rate	Principal
1.	$ 10.00	————	60 days	6%	————
2.	24.00	————	54 days	5	————
3.	3.07	$ 309.40	90 days	4	————
4.	26.50	————	45 days	$7\frac{1}{2}$	————
5.	113.33	6,913.33	200 days	3	————
6.	5.95	430.95	84 days	6	————

	Interest	Maturity Value	Time	Annual Interest Rate	Principal
7.	120.17	_____	247 days	8	_____
8.	14.09	476.06	122 days	9	_____
9.	15.04	_____	83 days	$7\frac{3}{4}$	_____
10.	5.39	_____	2 years	$5\frac{1}{2}$	_____

C. Find the annual rate of interest in each of these problems. Use the banker's year.

	Interest	Principal	Time	Annual Interest Rate
1.	$ 24.00	$ 400	1 year	_____
2.	21.60	360	$1\frac{1}{2}$ years	_____
3.	20.00	1,000	90 days	_____
4.	14.78	2,150	45 days	_____
5.	4.84	215	180 days	_____
6.	75.44	1,736	202 days	_____
7.	84.34	4,325	78 days	_____
8.	270.83	7,500	400 days	_____
9.	.24	62.50	21 days	_____
10.	961.80	9,618	4 years	_____

D. Find the time to the nearest day in these problems.

	Interest	Principal	Annual Interest Rate	Time in days
1.	$ 7.50	$ 300	5%	_____
2.	12.20	660	6	_____
3.	46.30	1,270	$4\frac{1}{2}$	_____
4.	2.45	78	8	_____
5.	200.00	12,800	7	_____
6.	2.00	100	$1\frac{1}{2}$	_____
7.	482.00	7,500	5	_____
8.	1,570.00	22,000	$6\frac{1}{2}$	_____
9.	23.60	900	$8\frac{1}{2}$	_____
10.	5.88	1,650	3	_____

SECTION 3—PAYROLL EXPENSE

Payroll is generally the largest single expense item in a business operation. A glance at the income statement heading chapter 1 shows this to be the case for Buffington's Department Store. Because of its tremendous effect on profits, payroll expense should receive careful attention in every firm. Proper recruiting, training, and supervision of personnel is often thought to be the most important function of company management.

When measuring the productivity of workers, management looks for an acceptable relationship between value produced (measured in terms of sales) and value received (measured in terms of wages). This value could be measured in terms of net sales per employee or by the ratio of net sales to payroll expense. Using Buffington's income statement and assuming a work force of 78 full-time equivalent employees, these figures for one year are computed as follows:

$$\text{Net sales per employee} = \frac{\$2,000,000}{78} = \$25,641$$

$$\text{Ratio of net sales to payroll expense} = \frac{\$2,000,000}{\$380,000} = 5.26 \text{ times}$$

In Buffington's store, the net-sales-to-payroll-expense ratio means that store personnel produced value (sales) more than five times greater than the value paid to them (payroll expense).

Another important measure of employee productivity is based on a comparison of sales volume with the earnings of salespeople. If, in order to achieve a net profit of 3.5%, Buffington's must limit direct selling expenses (salespeoples' wages) to 8% of net sales, the allowable payroll expense for salespeople can be computed as follows:

$$\text{Salespeoples' wages} = \text{Net sales} \times 8\%$$
$$= \$2,000,000 \times .08$$
$$= \$160,000$$

Obviously, the 8% sales expense figure could be automatically controlled if all salespeople worked on a straight commission of 8%. However, in most department stores, many of the salespeople are paid a fixed hourly wage regardless of the sales volume they produce.

To fall within the 8% sales expense limit, a salaried salesworker earning $3.00 per hour should produce an average of at least $300 in sales for every 8 hours of work ($3.00 $\times$ 8 hours = $24.00 $\div$ .08 = $300.00).

Compensation by salary and wages

The majority of American employees are paid on a straight salary basis. Salaries and wages are stated as a definite amount of money to be paid per unit of time, i.e., hourly, weekly, monthly, etc. Businesses usually make a distinction between "salaries" and "wages." The term *salary* is used in reference to the compensation of company executives, while *wages* refers to the compensation of all other employees. Total compensation is termed *payroll expense*.

In many cases, employees paid on an hourly basis are only paid for the actual number of hours worked, while employees who are paid weekly, biweekly, or monthly receive their full salaries even when they have been absent from work during some portion of the pay period. This occurs when a paid-sick-leave provision is part of the employment agreement.

Overtime pay is most frequently associated with hourly workers. Typically, this is a 50% or 100% or in some cases a 200% increase in the hourly rate of pay for each hour spent on the job beyond the customary number of hours required per day or per week. The familiar terms *time-and-a-half*, *doubletime*, and *triple-time* describe these three overtime pay conditions, respectively.

Example   George Dudley is paid a base wage of $3.40 per hour and works a 5-day, 40-hour week. Overtime pay is calculated as follows:

Over 8 hours, Monday–Friday	Time-and-a-half
First 8 hours on Saturday	Time-and-a-half
Over 8 hours on Saturday	Doubletime
Any hours on Sunday or holidays	Tripletime

What will be Mr. Dudley's compensation for a week during which he puts in 2 extra hours on Tuesday, 4 hours on Saturday, and 4 hours on Sunday in addition to his basic 40-hour work week?

40 hours, Monday–Friday	@$ 3.40 =	$136.00
2 hours on Tuesday	@ 5.10 =	10.20
4 hours on Saturday	@ 5.10 =	20.40
4 hours on Sunday	@ 10.20 =	40.80
Total wages		$207.40

Compensation by commission

Industrial salesmen, wholesale salesmen, stockbrokers, door-to-door salesmen, agent middlemen, some retail salesmen, and even lawyers are likely to earn a major part of their compensation on a commission basis.* Simply stated, a *commission* is calculated as some percentage of a base figure. Most often this base is gross or net sales.

Commissions offer management a flexible device for compensating sales-people. They may be based on gross sales, net sales, or gross margin; they may entail fixed, variable, progressive, or regressive rates. They may be applied to all sales, to sales above a certain quota, to sales by product group, or to sales by department. At Buffington's, salesmen of major appliances are paid a straight commission of 8% based on gross sales. Thus, one appliance salesman selling $3,000 worth of goods in a given week would earn a commission of $240 ($3,000 × .08). Other salespeople at Buffington's working on an hourly wage plan may also qualify for a 3% commission on all sales above their personal quotas. If quotas were based on monthly sales performance, the earnings of a salesperson could be calculated as follows:

February, actual sales	$9,200	
February, sales quota	8,000	
3% commission on excess	$1,200 =	$ 36.00
Regular wages for Feb. ($3 × 160 hours)	=	480.00
Total compensation for Feb.		$516.00

*Currently, the favorite plan for compensating outside salesmen includes both salary and commission. Direct salesmen calling on consumers at home are still almost always paid on a straight commission basis.

The 3% commission in this example could just as easily have been based on total departmental sales over a quota, and the earned commission divided among the employees of that department on some fair basis.

In cases where variable rates of commission are used, more calculations are required.

Example

```
2 $100 items @  8%   = $  200 × .08  = $ 16.00
5 $400 items @ 10%   =   2,000 × .10  =  200.00
8 $325 items @ 9½%   =   2,600 × .095 =  247.00
              Total compensation      $463.00
```

Guarantee and drawing account

Some salesmen paid on a commission basis may work under an agreement called a *guarantee*, or under a different agreement called a *draw against commission*. These two arrangements differ in one very important way, as shown below for a salesman who earns a 20% commission on all sales:

	$600 Guarantee		$600 Draw Against Commission	
	Earnings	Pay	Earnings	Pay
Month 1 Sales:				
$2,500	$500	$600	$500	$600
Salesman owes Co.	0	....	100	....
Month 2 Sales:				
$4,000	$800	$800	$800	$700
Salesman owes Co.	0	....	0	....

Guarantee: Salesman is paid his actual earnings or a guaranteed minimum, whichever is greater.

Draw: Salesman may draw more pay than he has actually earned, but this extra pay represents a personal loan which must be paid back out of future commissions. In the example above, $100 was deducted from the salesman's earnings to pay back his $100 loan from the previous month.

Compensation by piece rate

Piece-rate wage plans were developed to provide a reward for fast, efficient work. These plans are all based on an employee's productivity: the greater his output, the greater his pay.

A piece-rate wage plan for production or office workers is similar to a commission plan for salesworkers. For a piece-rate plan to be successful, management must make sure that pay rates per unit of work accomplished are based on a scientific job analysis which is updated regularly.

The simplest type of piece-rate plan is one which pays a fixed amount per item produced. A worker who produces 80 units or pieces in a given day at the rate of $.32 per unit will earn $25.60 for the day.

To give employees an incentive for achieving higher output, a standard piece-rate plan may have a bonus feature added to it. The bonus rate is paid for each unit produced in excess of a specified minimum. If, in the previous example, a rate of $.40 per piece were paid for all production over 70 units, the day's pay would have been:

Base pay:	70 units @ $.32	= $25.60
Bonus pay:	10 units @ $.40	= 4.00
Earnings		$29.60

A third piece-rate plan makes use of two rates of pay—one for production below the established minimum, the other for production above the minimum. Under this plan, only one rate of pay is applied to all items produced, depending on whether the entire output is above or below the standard. Using the same example as before and given a rate of $.32 below and $.40 above 70 units, the day's pay is found to be $32.00 (80 units X $.40).

Many other piece-rate plans exist in American industry, and these usually involve additional rates per piece or some combination of piece-rate and time wages. In order to provide a genuine incentive to workers, every piece-rate plan (indeed, any compensation plan) must be based on measurable, objective factors which have a direct bearing on the employee's output. Only when the plan is considered a fair one will it have any real chance to achieve its objectives.

Payroll deductions

Although the wages and salaries earned by employees and managers in a firm show up on the income statement as payroll expense, not all of this money is actually paid out as wages and salaries. A significant portion is deducted from gross wages for various purposes before paychecks are made out. Before explaining various deductions from gross wages, one point should be made clear. Although the contributions made by the employers to federal Social Security and unemployment funds are discussed here in connection with payroll expense, these expenditures are properly considered to be taxes. As such, they are recorded as part of tax expense on the company's income statement.

social security tax

The Federal Insurance Contributions Act (FICA) provides for retirement funds (federal old-age, disability, and survivors insurance, plus hospital benefits under Medicare) which are paid for by equal contributions from employer and employee (or entirely by the individual if self-employed). For employees, the required amount is deducted from each paycheck until the maximum amount for the year has been deposited. After matching employees' deductions, employers forward the total amounts due to the Internal Revenue Service on a quarterly basis. Table 4-1 indicates the rate of FICA tax each employee must pay currently, plus scheduled future increases.

Determining the FICA contribution owed by an employee is a problem in percentage. For example, what would be withheld from the gross wages of an employee who earned $740 in February of 1971?

$$\text{FICA tax} = \text{Earnings} \times \text{Rate}$$
$$= \$740 \times .049$$
$$= \$36.26$$

TABLE 4-1 FICA tax rates based on first $7,800 of annual income

	Rate		
	Employer	Employee	Self-Employed
1969–70	4.8%	4.8%	6.9%
1971–72	5.2	5.2	7.5
1973–75	5.65	5.65	7.65
1976–79	5.7	5.7	7.7
1980–86	5.8	5.8	7.8
1987 and after	5.9	5.9	7.9

Note: These rates are subject to change at any time by act of Congress.

Employees who work for more than one employer in a year will have FICA tax withheld by each employer. Should this result in his paying more tax than required for the year, he may apply that overpayment to reduce his federal income tax for the same year.

What would be the excess FICA tax withheld for an employee who earned   *Example*
$3,200, $4,600, and $5,800 on three different jobs in 1970?

FICA tax employer #1	$3,200 × .048 = $153.60
FICA tax employer #2	4,600 × .048 = 220.80
FICA tax employer #3	5,800 × .048 = 278.40
Total FICA tax withheld	= $652.80
Maximum FICA tax ($7,800 × .048)	= 374.40
Excess FICA tax withheld	= $278.40

People who work part of the year as employees and another part in a self-employed status make FICA contributions out of their wages as employees and on only that portion of their self-employment earnings required to bring their total earnings up to the $7,800 maximum.

What would be the FICA tax of an employee who grossed $5,700 in   *Example*
salary and an additional $4,500 as a self-employed businessman in 1972?

FICA tax	$5,700 × .052 = $296.40
	$2,100 × .075 = 157.50
Total FICA tax	= $453.90

unemployment and disability insurance

Federal law has created unemployment funds which are administered by the states. These funds, provided for solely by employers' contributions, are made available to unemployed workers who meet the eligibility requirements of their state. Benefits typically provide $15 to $75 per week for a maximum of 39 weeks. In California, benefits range from $25 to $65 weekly.

Currently, California, Rhode Island, New York, and New Jersey require employees to contribute to a disability insurance fund. These funds make available weekly benefits for disability and some related hospital costs. In California, for example, a 1% disability fund deduction is made on the first $7,800 of gross wages. Disability benefits and the maximum benefit period tend to be the same as for unemployment benefits.

Example   What would be the disability fund contribution of a California employee who earns $242 per week? What would be his total contribution for the year?

Weekly disability contribution = .01 × $242 = $2.42
Yearly disability contribution = .01 × $7,800 = $78.00

federal income tax

Employers are responsible for withholding a certain portion of the gross wages of employees in payment of their federal income taxes. This "pay-as-you-go" procedure keeps many employees from having to come up with a big income tax payment at the end of the year.

The amount of income tax withheld depends primarily on the number of exemptions (dependents) claimed by the employee and the level of his gross earnings. In 1971 taxpayers could claim a $650 exemption ($700 in 1972, $750 in 1973) for every individual who

1. receives over half of his or her support from the taxpayer;
2. is closely related and does not have $650 gross income during the tax year (1971)—unless he or she is under 19 years of age or, if over 19 years, is a full-time student of a recognized school for at least 5 months of the tax year; and
3. if married and employed, does not already claim a personal exemption.

A taxpayer may claim fewer exemptions for purposes of withholding than he is entitled to claim on his tax return. This has the effect of withholding more out of gross wages than required, usually resulting in a refund for the taxpayer. The Bureau of Internal Revenue supplies withholding tax tables covering various pay periods, some of which are reproduced here as tables 4-2, 4-3, and 4-4.

As shown in tables 4-2, 4-3, and 4-4, the tax withheld depends not only on the level of earnings and the number of exemptions claimed, but also on the employee's marital status and the length of the pay period.

Example
1   What is the income tax withheld from an employee's weekly pay if he is single, claims one exemption, and has earnings of $215?

Tax from tax table = $35.20

Example
2   What is the tax withheld from the paycheck of a married employee with 4 exemptions for a week in which he worked 40 hours at $4.25 per hour?

Tax on $170 from tax table = $16.70

TABLE 4-2 federal withholding tax (married persons—weekly payroll period)

And the wages are—		And the number of withholding exemptions claimed is—										
At least	But less than	0	1	2	3	4	5	6	7	8	9	10 or more
		The amount of income tax to be withheld shall be—										
70	72	8.00	5.80	3.70	1.90	.10	0	0	0	0	0	0
72	74	8.30	6.20	4.10	2.10	.40	0	0	0	0	0	0
74	76	8.70	6.50	4.40	2.40	.70	0	0	0	0	0	0
76	78	9.00	6.90	4.70	2.70	1.00	0	0	0	0	0	0
78	80	9.30	7.20	5.10	3.00	1.20	0	0	0	0	0	0
80	82	9.60	7.50	5.40	3.30	1.50	0	0	0	0	0	0
82	84	10.00	7.90	5.80	3.60	1.80	0	0	0	0	0	0
84	86	10.30	8.20	6.10	4.00	2.10	.30	0	0	0	0	0
86	88	10.60	8.60	6.40	4.30	2.40	.60	0	0	0	0	0
88	90	10.90	8.90	6.80	4.70	2.60	.90	0	0	0	0	0
90	92	11.20	9.20	7.10	5.00	2.90	1.20	0	0	0	0	0
92	94	11.60	9.60	7.50	5.30	3.20	1.40	0	0	0	0	0
94	96	11.90	9.90	7.80	5.70	3.60	1.70	0	0	0	0	0
96	98	12.20	10.20	8.10	6.00	3.90	2.00	.30	0	0	0	0
98	100	12.50	10.50	8.50	6.40	4.20	2.30	.50	0	0	0	0
$100	$105	$13.10	$11.10	$9.10	$7.00	$4.80	$2.80	$1.00	$0	$0	$0	$0
105	110	13.90	11.90	9.90	7.80	5.70	3.60	1.70	0	0	0	0
110	115	14.70	12.70	10.70	8.70	6.50	4.40	2.40	.70	0	0	0
115	120	15.50	13.50	11.50	9.50	7.40	5.30	3.10	1.40	0	0	0
120	125	16.30	14.30	12.30	10.30	8.20	6.10	4.00	2.10	.30	0	0
125	130	17.10	15.10	13.10	11.10	9.10	7.00	4.80	2.80	1.00	0	0
130	135	17.90	15.90	13.90	11.90	9.90	7.80	5.70	3.60	1.70	0	0
135	140	18.70	16.70	14.70	12.70	10.70	8.70	6.50	4.40	2.40	.70	0
140	145	19.50	17.50	15.50	13.50	11.50	9.50	7.40	5.30	3.10	1.40	0
145	150	20.30	18.30	16.30	14.30	12.30	10.30	8.20	6.10	4.00	2.10	.30
150	160	21.50	19.50	17.50	15.50	13.50	11.50	9.50	7.40	5.30	3.10	1.40
160	170	23.10	21.10	19.10	17.10	15.10	13.10	11.10	9.10	7.00	4.80	2.80
170	180	25.00	22.70	20.70	18.70	16.70	14.70	12.70	10.70	8.70	6.50	4.40
180	190	26.90	24.50	22.30	20.30	18.30	16.30	14.30	12.30	10.30	8.20	6.10
190	200	28.80	26.40	24.10	21.90	19.90	17.90	15.90	13.90	11.90	9.90	7.80
200	210	30.70	28.30	26.00	23.60	21.50	19.50	17.50	15.50	13.50	11.50	9.50
210	220	32.60	30.20	27.90	25.50	23.10	21.10	19.10	17.10	15.10	13.10	11.10
220	230	34.50	32.10	29.80	27.40	25.00	22.70	20.70	18.70	16.70	14.70	12.70
230	240	36.40	34.00	31.70	29.30	26.90	24.50	22.30	20.30	18.30	16.30	14.30
240	250	38.30	35.90	33.60	31.20	28.80	26.40	24.10	21.90	19.90	17.90	15.90
250	260	40.20	37.80	35.50	33.10	30.70	28.30	26.00	23.60	21.50	19.50	17.50
260	270	42.10	39.70	37.40	35.00	32.60	30.20	27.90	25.50	23.10	21.10	19.10
270	280	44.10	41.60	39.30	36.90	34.50	32.10	29.80	27.40	25.00	22.70	20.70
280	290	46.20	43.60	41.20	38.80	36.40	34.00	31.70	29.30	26.90	24.50	22.30
290	300	48.30	45.70	43.10	40.70	38.30	35.90	33.60	31.20	28.80	26.40	24.10
300	310	50.40	47.80	45.20	42.60	40.20	37.80	35.50	33.10	30.70	28.30	26.00
310	320	52.50	49.90	47.30	44.70	42.10	39.70	37.40	35.00	32.60	30.20	27.90
320	330	54.60	52.00	49.40	46.80	44.10	41.60	39.30	36.90	34.50	32.10	29.80
330	340	56.70	54.10	51.50	48.90	46.20	43.60	41.20	38.80	36.40	34.00	31.70
340	350	58.80	56.20	53.60	51.00	48.30	45.70	43.10	40.70	38.30	35.90	33.60
350	360	60.90	58.30	55.70	53.10	50.40	47.80	45.20	42.60	40.20	37.80	35.50
360	370	63.00	60.40	57.80	55.20	52.50	49.90	47.30	44.70	42.10	39.70	37.40
370	380	65.10	62.50	59.90	57.30	54.60	52.00	49.40	46.80	44.10	41.60	39.30
380	390	67.30	64.60	62.00	59.40	56.70	54.10	51.50	48.90	46.20	43.60	41.20
390	400	69.80	66.70	64.10	61.50	58.80	56.20	53.60	51.00	48.30	45.70	43.10
400	410	72.30	69.10	66.20	63.60	60.90	58.30	55.70	53.10	50.40	47.80	45.20
410	420	74.80	71.60	68.50	65.70	63.00	60.40	57.80	55.20	52.50	49.90	47.30
420	430	77.30	74.10	71.00	67.90	65.10	62.50	59.90	57.30	54.60	52.00	49.40
430	440	79.80	76.60	73.50	70.40	67.30	64.60	62.00	59.40	56.70	54.10	51.50
440	450	82.30	79.10	76.00	72.90	69.80	66.70	64.10	61.50	58.80	56.20	53.60
450	460	84.80	81.60	78.50	75.40	72.30	69.10	66.20	63.60	60.90	58.30	55.70
460	470	87.30	84.10	81.00	77.90	74.80	71.60	68.50	65.70	63.00	60.40	57.80
470	480	89.80	86.60	83.50	80.40	77.30	74.10	71.00	67.90	65.10	62.50	59.90
480	490	92.30	89.10	86.00	82.90	79.80	76.60	73.50	70.40	67.30	64.60	62.00
490	500	94.80	91.60	88.50	85.40	82.30	79.10	76.00	72.90	69.80	66.70	64.10
500	510	97.30	94.10	91.00	87.90	84.80	81.60	78.50	75.40	72.30	69.10	66.20
510	520	99.80	96.60	93.50	90.40	87.30	84.10	81.00	77.90	74.80	71.60	68.50
520	530	102.30	99.10	96.00	92.90	89.80	86.60	83.50	80.40	77.30	74.10	71.00
		25 percent of the excess over $530 plus—										
$530 and over		103.50	100.40	97.30	94.10	91.00	87.90	84.80	81.60	78.50	75.40	72.30

TABLE 4-3 federal withholding tax (single persons—weekly payroll period)

And the wages are—		And the number of withholding exemptions claimed is—										
At least	But less than	0	1	2	3	4	5	6	7	8	9	10 or more
		The amount of income tax to be withheld shall be—										
$80	$82	$11.00	$8.50	$6.00	$3.60	$1.50	$0	$0	$0	$0	$0	$0
82	84	11.40	8.90	6.40	4.00	1.90	0	0	0	0	0	0
84	86	11.80	9.30	6.80	4.30	2.20	.30	0	0	0	0	0
86	88	12.20	9.70	7.20	4.70	2.50	.60	0	0	0	0	0
88	90	12.60	10.10	7.60	5.10	2.90	.90	0	0	0	0	0
90	92	13.00	10.50	8.00	5.50	3.20	1.20	0	0	0	0	0
92	94	13.40	10.90	8.40	5.90	3.60	1.40	0	0	0	0	0
94	96	13.80	11.30	8.80	6.30	3.90	1.80	0	0	0	0	0
96	98	14.20	11.70	9.20	6.70	4.20	2.10	.30	0	0	0	0
98	100	14.60	12.10	9.60	7.10	4.60	2.50	.50	0	0	0	0
100	105	15.20	12.80	10.30	7.80	5.30	3.10	1.00	0	0	0	0
105	110	16.10	13.80	11.30	8.80	6.30	3.90	1.80	0	0	0	0
110	115	17.00	14.80	12.30	9.80	7.30	4.80	2.60	.70	0	0	0
115	120	17.90	15.70	13.30	10.80	8.30	5.80	3.50	1.40	0	0	0
120	125	18.80	16.60	14.30	11.80	9.30	6.80	4.30	2.20	.30	0	0
125	130	19.70	17.50	15.20	12.80	10.30	7.80	5.30	3.10	1.00	0	0
130	135	20.60	18.40	16.10	13.80	11.30	8.80	6.30	3.90	1.80	0	0
135	140	21.60	19.30	17.00	14.80	12.30	9.80	7.30	4.80	2.60	.70	0
140	145	22.60	20.20	17.90	15.70	13.30	10.80	8.30	5.80	3.50	1.40	0
145	150	23.70	21.10	18.80	16.60	14.30	11.80	9.30	6.80	4.30	2.20	.30
150	160	25.30	22.60	20.20	17.90	15.70	13.30	10.80	8.30	5.80	3.50	1.40
160	170	27.40	24.70	22.10	19.70	17.50	15.20	12.80	10.30	7.80	5.30	3.10
170	180	29.50	26.80	24.20	21.60	19.30	17.00	14.80	12.30	9.80	7.30	4.80
180	190	31.60	28.90	26.30	23.70	21.10	18.80	16.60	14.30	11.80	9.30	6.80
190	200	33.70	31.00	28.40	25.80	23.20	20.60	18.40	16.10	13.80	11.30	8.80
200	210	35.80	33.10	30.50	27.90	25.30	22.60	20.20	17.90	15.70	13.30	10.80
210	220	38.00	35.20	32.60	30.00	27.40	24.70	22.10	19.70	17.50	15.20	12.80
220	230	40.40	37.40	34.70	32.10	29.50	26.80	24.20	21.60	19.30	17.00	14.80
230	240	42.80	39.80	36.80	34.20	31.60	28.90	26.30	23.70	21.10	18.80	16.60
240	250	45.20	42.20	39.20	36.30	33.70	31.00	28.40	25.80	23.20	20.60	18.40
250	260	47.60	44.60	41.60	38.60	35.80	33.10	30.50	27.90	25.30	22.60	20.20
260	270	50.00	47.00	44.00	41.00	38.00	35.20	32.60	30.00	27.40	24.70	22.10
270	280	52.40	49.40	46.40	43.40	40.40	37.40	34.70	32.10	29.50	26.80	24.20
280	290	54.80	51.80	48.80	45.80	42.80	39.80	36.80	34.20	31.60	28.90	26.30
290	300	57.20	54.20	51.20	48.20	45.20	42.20	39.20	36.30	33.70	31.00	28.40
300	310	59.60	56.60	53.60	50.60	47.60	44.60	41.60	38.60	35.80	33.10	30.50
310	320	62.00	59.00	56.00	53.00	50.00	47.00	44.00	41.00	38.00	35.20	32.60
320	330	64.40	61.40	58.40	55.40	52.40	49.40	46.40	43.40	40.40	37.40	34.70
330	340	66.80	63.80	60.80	57.80	54.80	51.80	48.80	45.80	42.80	39.80	36.80
340	350	69.20	66.20	63.20	60.20	57.20	54.20	51.20	48.20	45.20	42.20	39.20
350	360	71.60	68.60	65.60	62.60	59.60	56.60	53.60	50.60	47.60	44.60	41.60
		24 percent of the excess over $360 plus—										
$360 and over		72.80	69.80	66.80	63.80	60.80	57.80	54.80	51.80	48.80	45.80	42.80

TABLE 4-4 federal withholding tax (married persons—monthly payroll period)

And the wages are—		0	1	2	3	4	5	6	7	8	9	10 or more
At least	But less than											

At least	But less than	0	1	2	3	4	5	6	7	8	9	10 or more
		The amount of income tax to be withheld shall be—										
$420	$440	$54.40	$45.70	$36.90	$27.70	$18.50	$10.00	$2.50	$0	$0	$0	$0
440	460	57.60	48.90	40.30	31.10	21.90	12.80	5.30	0	0	0	0
460	480	60.80	52.10	43.50	34.50	25.30	16.10	8.10	.50	0	0	0
480	500	64.00	55.30	46.70	37.90	28.70	19.50	10.90	3.30	0	0	0
500	520	67.20	58.50	49.90	41.20	32.10	22.90	13.70	6.10	0	0	0
520	540	70.40	61.70	53.10	44.40	35.50	26.30	17.10	8.90	1.30	0	0
540	560	73.60	64.90	56.30	47.60	38.90	29.70	20.50	11.70	4.10	0	0
560	580	76.80	68.10	59.50	50.80	42.10	33.10	23.90	14.70	6.90	0	0
580	600	80.00	71.30	62.70	54.00	45.30	36.50	27.30	18.10	9.70	2.10	0
600	640	84.80	76.10	67.50	58.80	50.10	41.50	32.40	23.20	14.00	6.30	0
640	680	91.20	82.50	73.90	65.20	56.50	47.90	39.20	30.00	20.80	11.90	4.30
680	720	97.60	88.90	80.30	71.60	62.90	54.30	45.60	36.80	27.60	18.40	9.90
720	760	104.90	95.30	86.70	78.00	69.30	60.70	52.00	43.30	34.40	25.20	16.00
760	800	112.50	102.20	93.10	84.40	75.70	67.10	58.40	49.70	41.10	32.00	22.80
800	840	120.10	109.80	99.60	90.80	82.10	73.50	64.80	56.10	47.50	38.80	29.60
840	880	127.70	117.40	107.20	97.20	88.50	79.90	71.20	62.50	53.90	45.20	36.40
880	920	135.30	125.00	114.80	104.50	94.90	86.30	77.60	68.90	60.30	51.60	42.90
920	960	142.90	132.60	122.40	112.10	101.80	92.70	84.00	75.30	66.70	58.00	49.30
960	1,000	150.50	140.20	130.00	119.70	109.40	99.10	90.40	81.70	73.10	64.40	55.70
1,000	1,040	158.10	147.80	137.60	127.30	117.00	106.70	96.80	88.10	79.50	70.80	62.10
1,040	1,080	165.70	155.40	145.20	134.90	124.60	114.30	104.00	94.50	85.90	77.20	68.50
1,080	1,120	173.30	163.00	152.80	142.50	132.20	121.90	111.60	101.30	92.30	83.60	74.90
1,120	1,160	180.90	170.60	160.40	150.10	139.80	129.50	119.20	108.90	98.70	90.00	81.30
1,160	1,200	188.80	178.20	168.00	157.70	147.40	137.10	126.80	116.50	106.20	96.40	87.70
1,200	1,240	197.20	185.80	175.60	165.30	155.00	144.70	134.40	124.10	113.80	103.50	94.10
1,240	1,280	205.60	194.20	183.20	172.90	162.60	152.30	142.00	131.70	121.40	111.10	100.80
1,280	1,320	214.00	202.60	191.30	180.50	170.20	159.90	149.60	139.30	129.00	118.70	108.40
1,320	1,360	222.40	211.00	199.70	188.30	177.80	167.50	157.20	146.90	136.60	126.30	116.00
1,360	1,400	230.80	219.40	208.10	196.70	185.40	175.10	164.80	154.50	144.20	133.90	123.60
1,400	1,440	239.20	227.80	216.50	205.10	193.70	182.70	172.40	162.10	151.80	141.50	131.20
1,440	1,480	247.60	236.20	224.90	213.50	202.10	190.70	180.00	169.70	159.40	149.10	138.80
1,480	1,520	256.00	244.60	233.30	221.90	210.50	199.10	187.80	177.30	167.00	156.70	146.40
1,520	1,560	264.40	253.00	241.70	230.30	218.90	207.50	196.20	184.90	174.60	164.30	154.00
1,560	1,600	272.80	261.40	250.10	238.70	227.30	215.90	204.60	193.20	182.20	171.90	161.60
1,600	1,640	281.20	269.80	258.50	247.10	235.70	224.30	213.00	201.60	190.20	179.50	169.20
1,640	1,680	289.60	278.20	266.90	255.50	244.10	232.70	221.40	210.00	198.60	187.20	176.80
1,680	1,720	299.30	286.60	275.30	263.90	252.50	241.10	229.80	218.40	207.00	195.60	184.40
1,720	1,760	309.30	295.80	283.70	272.30	260.90	249.50	238.20	226.80	215.40	204.00	192.70
1,760	1,800	319.30	305.80	292.30	280.70	269.30	257.90	246.60	235.20	223.80	212.40	201.10
1,800	1,840	329.30	315.80	302.30	289.10	277.70	266.30	255.00	243.60	232.20	220.80	209.50
1,840	1,880	339.30	325.80	312.30	298.70	286.10	274.70	263.40	252.00	240.60	229.20	217.90
1,880	1,920	349.30	335.80	322.30	308.70	295.20	283.10	271.80	260.40	249.00	237.60	226.30
1,920	1,960	359.30	345.80	332.30	318.70	305.20	291.60	280.20	268.80	257.40	246.00	234.70
1,960	2,000	369.30	355.80	342.30	328.70	315.20	301.60	288.60	277.20	265.80	254.40	243.10
2,000	2,040	379.30	365.80	352.30	338.70	325.20	311.60	298.10	285.60	274.20	262.80	251.50
2,040	2,080	389.30	375.80	362.30	348.70	335.20	321.60	308.10	294.50	282.60	271.20	259.90
2,080	2,120	399.30	385.80	372.30	358.70	345.20	331.60	318.10	304.50	291.00	279.60	268.30
2,120	2,160	409.30	395.80	382.30	368.70	355.20	341.60	328.10	314.50	301.00	288.00	276.70
2,160	2,200	419.30	405.80	392.30	378.70	365.20	351.60	338.10	324.50	311.00	297.50	285.10
2,200	2,240	429.30	415.80	402.30	388.70	375.20	361.60	348.10	334.50	321.00	307.50	293.90
2,240	2,280	439.30	425.80	412.30	398.70	385.20	371.60	358.10	344.50	331.00	317.50	303.90
		25 percent of the excess over $2,280 plus—										
$2,280 and over		444.30	430.80	417.30	403.70	390.20	376.60	363.10	349.50	336.00	322.50	308.90

EXERCISE 4-3 PAYROLL EXPENSE

A. Calculate the net sales per employee and the ratio of net sales to payroll expense.

Net Sales	Payroll Expense	No. of Employees	Net Sales per Employee	Ratio of Net Sales to Payroll Expense
$ 30,000	$ 6,000	10	_____	_____
84,000	12,600	20	_____	_____
94,500	8,250	12	_____	_____
147,250	7,645	16	_____	_____
68,780	10,000	8	_____	_____
12,800	3,200	3	_____	_____
16,990	1,680	2	_____	_____
57,345	2,875	13	_____	_____
202,940	18,420	25	_____	_____
4,662,528	516,514	80	_____	_____

B. Calculate the week's payroll for hourly workers of the Beckley Co. Use the overtime schedule of the example on p. 100.

Employee	M	T	W	Th	F	S	Sun.	Base Rate	Total Reg. Hrs.	Total Hours, Time-and-a-Half, at $____	Total Hours, Double time, at $____	Total Hours, Triple time, at $____	Reg. Pay	Over-time Pay	Total Pay
Atkins, J.	8	8	8	9	8	10	0	$3.10	___	___	___	___	___	___	___
Avilar, S.	8	8	8	9	8	10	4	$3.10	___	___	___	___	___	___	___
Calkins, R.	8	8	10	9	9	0	0	$2.25	___	___	___	___	___	___	___
Darrow, T.	8	8	0	8	8	4	4	$2.40	___	___	___	___	___	___	___
Gerard, L.	8	8	10	8	8	0	8	$2.65	___	___	___	___	___	___	___
Hartwell, R.	8	8	8	8	8	0	0	$3.00	___	___	___	___	___	___	___
Mancuso, R.	8	8	7	8	8	0	4	$2.15	___	___	___	___	___	___	___
Stanley, J.	0	8	8	8	8	8	0	$2.75	___	___	___	___	___	___	___
Tolbert, L.	8	8	8	8	8	8	4	$2.88	___	___	___	___	___	___	___
Wagner, W.	8	8	8	0	8	4	4	$1.95	___	___	___	___	___	___	___

Total Week's Payroll _____

C. Calculate the commission earnings of the following salespeople. Weekly commission rates are 8% on the first $2,000 sales, 9% on sales $2,001 to $3,000, and 10% on all sales over $3,000.

Salesman	Sales	Sales at 8%	Comm.	Sales at 9%	Comm.	Sales at 10%	Comm.	Gross Earnings
Boitano, R.	$1,868.00	___	___	___	___	___	___	___
Crema, A.	2,492.00	___	___	___	___	___	___	___
Ellington, M.	2,180.00	___	___	___	___	___	___	___
Iannacone, J.	3,147.00	___	___	___	___	___	___	___
Kenneally, J.	4,256.00	___	___	___	___	___	___	___
Miner, J.	3,495.50	___	___	___	___	___	___	___
Parker, S.	2,885.25	___	___	___	___	___	___	___
Rice, E.	1,298.00	___	___	___	___	___	___	___
Saso, T.	3,226.75	___	___	___	___	___	___	___
Yarrington, R.	2,080.50	___	___	___	___	___	___	___

D. Calculate the wages earned by these salesmen working under a guarantee plan.

Salesman	Sales	Commission	Weekly Guarantee	Gross Wages
Briscoe, M.	$1,600.00	10%	$175	_____
Dooley, B.	2,450.00	15	200	_____
Fragger, R.	1,990.00	8	150	_____
Hines, W.	3,100.00	8	200	_____
Komes, M.	1,562.00	12	160	_____
Nuñez, R.	3,000.00	10	200	_____
Rowlands, G.	1,285.50	20	180	_____
Sotter, K.	3,000.00	5	200	_____
Timmons, J.	2,642.50	$7\frac{1}{2}$	150	_____
Valdez, D.	900.00	30	125	_____

E. Calculate the wages due the following workers under a piece-rate plan which pays these piece rates:

$.37 for each unit up to 60 units
$.42 for each unit when total is more than 60 units
$.20 bonus on each unit over 75 units

Employee	Pieces	Wages	Bonus Wages	Total Wages
Adams, R.	58	_____	_____	_____
Clark, R.	64	_____	_____	_____
Dubrowski, K.	73	_____	_____	_____
Eaton, D.	81	_____	_____	_____
Hudson, B.	68	_____	_____	_____
Jordan, G.	75	_____	_____	_____
Langer, W.	47	_____	_____	_____
Nance, P.	60	_____	_____	_____
Overmeyer, H.	79	_____	_____	_____
Snider, S.	85	_____	_____	_____
Williams, W.	52	_____	_____	_____

F. Complete the payroll record below using tables 4-2, 4-3, and 4-4 for income tax, 4.9% as the current FICA tax rate, and 1% as the rate for unemployment insurance.

Employee	Exemptions	Marital Status	Weekly Earnings	FICA Tax	Fed. Inc. Tax	Unemp. Ins.	Total Ded.	Net Pay
Armstrong, G.	2	M	$225.00	___	___	___	___	___
Belzer, R.	4	M	210.00	___	___	___	___	___
Dierro, J.	3	M	195.00	___	___	___	___	___
Farmer, H.	3	M	175.00	___	___	___	___	___
Harvey, J.	5	M	200.00	___	___	___	___	___
Klaus, H.	2	S	215.00	___	___	___	___	___
Mancini, H.	1	S	165.00	___	___	___	___	___
Palmer, S.	4	M	175.00	___	___	___	___	___
Roland, V.	6	M	285.00	___	___	___	___	___
Schmidt, K.	2	S	312.50	___	___	___	___	___

EXERCISE 4-4 PAYROLL PROBLEMS

1. A company had net sales of $87,646 for the first quarter of the year. The payroll expense for 26 employees amounted to $13,650. Find (a) net sales per employee, and (b) ratio of net sales to payroll expense.

2. A retail salesperson is paid $2.50 per hour. What volume of sales must she produce in a 40-hour week if her wages are to be held to 7% of sales?

3. The partial sales record of a salesman is as follows:

Monday	$ 800	Thursday	$940
Tuesday	750	Friday	—
Wednesday	1,025		

If he is paid a commission of 6% of sales, what must his sales be for Friday in order for him to earn $258 for the 5-day week?

4. If a salesman on a drawing account is paid $250 for the week, how much was loaned to him that week if his sales were $2,000 and he earns a commission of 10%?

5. An employee is paid a salary of $2.45 per hour. During one week he worked 40 hours of straight time and 8 hours at time-and-a-half. What was his pay for the week?

6. During the work week, an employee earned $165. If his regular pay is $3 per hour for 40 hours and his overtime pay is at time-and-a-half, how many overtime hours did he work?

7. Salesmen in the Cascade Co. earn a bonus of 2% for all sales over quota. If one salesman earns $80 in bonus pay for the month, what were his sales over quota?

8. Route salesmen for a wholesale bakery earn wages of $200 per week, plus a commission of 5% for sales over $1,600. What would be the earnings for a salesman who sells $2,000 worth of goods in a week?

9. If an employee has a $36.20 FICA deduction for the month of March, 1971, what was his gross pay that month?

10. What is the federal income tax deduction for a married person claiming 4 exemptions and earning $926.25 per month?

11. The weekly wages paid by a firm are determined as follows:

Sales of $1,500–2,000: 5% commission
Sales of   2,001–3,000: 6
Sales of   3,001–3,500: 7
Sales of   3,600 and over: 8

What are monthly earnings of a salesman who produces these sales results: week 1, $2,200; week 2, $3,000; week 3, $3,750; week 4, $1,990.

12. Employees in a clothing factory are paid on this daily piece-rate schedule:

Up to 20 pieces per hour: $.12 per piece
21 to 30 pieces per hour: $.15
31 to 40 pieces per hour: $.18

What is the gross pay of an employee who produces 162 pieces in a 6-hour shift?

13. Tom Sutherland earned $8,056 in 1972 from operating his own collection agency. He also earned another $4,190 working part time as a retail sales-man. What will be Tom's FICA contribution deducted from his self-em-ployment income?

14. Hal Richards worked on three different jobs in 1969. His earnings were $2,756.50, $3,742.65, and $2,941.16 on these jobs. What was the amount of his FICA overpayment?

15. If Mr. Richards in problem 14, above, had been a California worker paying 1% of gross wages to a disability insurance fund, what would have been his overpayment to that fund?

16. How much less federal income tax would a married man with 2 exemptions earning $235 a week have withheld per week than a single person with 1 exemption earning the same wage?

17. James Bently, a married man claiming 2 exemptions, had monthly wages for 1971 as follows:

Jan.	$ 987.62	July	$ 802.23
Feb.	844.50	Aug.	619.38
Mar.	1,061.19	Sept.	856.11
Apr.	683.50	Oct.	983.74
May	671.95	Nov.	1,006.21
June	817.48	Dec.	714.88

a. How much in federal income tax was withheld from his earnings for the year?

b. What was his FICA contribution for the year?

c. What was his net pay for the year?

18. Two separate but similar manufacturing firms have distinctly different com-pensation plans for their assembly workers. Company A pays drill press operators a salary of $4.22 per hour, while Company B pays their press operators the following piece rates:

60 to 75 pieces per hour: $3.87 per hour
76 to 85 pieces per hour: $.055 per piece per hour
86 to 100 pieces per hour: $.06 per piece per hour

What will be the pay for an 8-hour day for

a. Company A salaried press operators?

b. A Company B press operator who produces 624 pieces?

c. A Company B press operator who produces an average of 90 pieces per hour?

19. Calculate the gross pay and FICA contribution for the year of a married salesman with 3 dependents who claims only 2 exemptions and earned a 10% commission on sales of $147,365 in 1970.

20. In 1971, the firm of Slater and Son had a first-quarter payroll of $18,511.50. Employee federal income tax of $2,596 was withheld during this period. On February 10, Slater and Son deposited $2,748.50 in the bank for pay-ment of all FICA and federal income taxes. Use the form below to deter-

mine the amount of tax which Slater and Son must remit with their quarterly tax return in April.

FICA tax	_____
Federal income tax withheld	_____
Total taxes	_____
Less: Deposits	
(bank receipts attached)	_____
Balance of tax remitted	_____

SECTION 4—INSURANCE EXPENSE

The business firm is subject to a large number of risks. Losses due to fire, theft, explosion, riot, and even shifts in customer demand are some of the perils that could befall a business organization. In particular, the retail firm runs the heavy risk of personal injury to customers who may suffer physical harm from an accident on the premises. All of these risks and the loss of income which is almost always associated with physical loss of any kind deserve the careful attention of company management.

Although a retail firm like Buffington's may in effect transfer some of the risk of loss of merchandise to its vendors by buying small quantities of goods more frequently, there is a practical limit to this strategy. No retailer can really afford to be out of stock on salable merchandise. Sales come first, and assortments must be complete if rising sales volume is to be obtained.

Some risks can be minimized by careful management and diligent housekeeping. The installation of a sprinkler system, the use of fireproof building materials and metal fixtures, and frequent inspections of the wiring and heating systems in the building are all examples of minimizing the risks of loss by fire.

Most of the serious risks faced by business firms are transferred to insurance companies. In this way, potentially large losses are exchanged for definitely smaller insurance premiums. The income statement heading chapter 1 shows an expenditure by Buffington's of $14,000 in insurance premiums. The merchandise inventory alone on January 31 was worth $400,000 and, as we shall see, the $14,000 insurance expense covers much more than the loss of inventory.

The two major categories of risk which Buffington's has insured against are (1) losses of property, and (2) liability for injury to customers and employees.

Property insurance

It is possible for a business firm to purchase a single-package policy which covers losses of property due to fire and a variety of other events and liability losses resulting from injury to customers. When protection against more than the usual or ordinary kinds of risk is desired, it may be added to the basic policy. Added perils are included under a supplementary agreement called an *extended coverage endorsement*. One example might be paying a higher premium to cover window glass under a basic fire insurance policy. Because this kind of all-risk policy is more convenient and costs less than purchasing separate policies to cover the same risks, this is the type of all-inclusive policy Buffington's has purchased.

As part of its all-risk policy, for which it pays an annual premium of $8,442, Buffington's has obtained property insurance which will reimburse it up to $840,000 for damage to the building, and maximum coverage of $820,000 for loss of merchandise, furniture, fixtures, or equipment. The policy covers loss caused by any of the following perils: fire; lightning; windstorm; hail; riot; civil commotion; explosion; falling aircraft; falling objects other than aircraft; smoke; building collapse; weight of ice, snow, or sleet; sprinkler leakage; and in the case of movable property, burglary and theft.

In determining the fire insurance premium for a building and its contents, a number of factors are taken into account by the insurance carrier. The location of the building, its type of construction, and the activity it is used for are three of the most important factors. These factors are shown in the following tables.

TABLE 4-5 fire ratings—or risk zone I

Location	Class	Occupancy	Building	Equipment	Stock
Maple and Baldwin					
1006	D	Office	.62	.62	. . . .
1012	All-steel	Gas. sta.*	.286	.464	.58
Baldwin and Castle					
1102, Sec					
Baldwin	All-steel	Gas. sta.*	(.286)	.464	.58
1108–20	D	One- and two-story			
		frame & reconc.	.66	.93	.116
		Pharmacy	. . . .	.85	.118
		Groc. store	. . . .	(.93)	(116)
		Offices	. . . .	.66	. . . .

*Apply class C Average Clause credits.

TABLE 4-6 fire rating protection classes

Local Zone	National Rating Board Protection Class
Zone 1	(3)
Zone 2	8
	3 (dwellings)
Zone 3	9

TABLE 4-7 tables for unsprinkled risks

Unless otherwise provided, the applicable Average Clause Table shall be determined in accordance with the Protection Class, as follows:

Prot. Class:	2	3	4	5	6	7	8	9	9b	10 & Unpro.
Av. Cl. Table:	I	I	I	II	II	III	IV	V	V	VI

Table	Amount of Average Clause (Coinsurance)	PERCENTAGE CREDITS FOR USE OF AVERAGE CLAUSE					
		Class A or B Risks		Class C Risks		Class D Risks	
		Bldgs.	Conts.	Bldgs.	Conts.	Bldgs.	Conts.
	100%	70%	40%	54%	40%	30%	30%
	90	67	35	50	35	(25)	(25)
I	80	64	30	45	30	15	20
	70	59	25	40	25	10	10
	60	53	15	35	15	. . . .	. . . .

TABLE 4-7 (continued)

Table	Amount of Average Clause (Coinsurance)	PERCENTAGE CREDITS FOR USE OF AVERAGE CLAUSE					
		Class A or B Risks		Class C Risks		Class D Risks	
		Bldgs.	Conts.	Bldgs.	Conts.	Bldgs.	Conts.
II	100%	65%	35%	50%	35%	20%	20%
	90	62	30	45	30	15	15
	80	60	25	40	25	10	10
	70	55	20	35	20	5	5
	60	49	10	25	10	....	....
III	100%	63%	30%	45%	30%	15%	15%
	90	60	25	40	25	10	10
	80	56	20	35	20	5	5
	70	50	15	30	15	....	....
	60	45	5	20	5	....	....

TABLE 4-8 rate adjustments

Rate Adj. Guide No.	Subject of Ins.	Class D and All-Steel		Class C		Class A and B	
		Prot. Cl. 1–8 Incl.	Prot. Cl. 9, 10, & Unprot.	Prot. Cl. 1–8 Incl.	Prot. Cl. 9, 10, & Unprot.	Prot. Cl. 1–8 Incl.	Prot. Cl. 9, 10, & Unprot.
1	B	−10%	−10%	+40%	+40%	−20%	−20%
	E&S	−10	−10	....	....	−20	−20
2	B	−10%	−10%	+40%	+40%	−20%	−20%
	E&S	+60	+60	+60	+60	−20	−20
3	B	+60%	+60%	+60%	+60%	−20%	−20%
	E&S	+60	+60	+60	+60	−20	−20
4	B&E&S	−70%	−50%	−50%	−50%	−20%	−20%
5	B&E&S	+40%	+40%	+60%	+60%	−20%	−20%
6	B&E&S	+25%	+25%	+50%	+50%	+25%	+25%
7	B&E&S	+25%	+25%	+50%	+50%	−20%	−20%
8	B&E&S	−70%	−70%	−70%	−70%	−40%	−40%
9	B&E&S	(−50%)	−10%	−30%	−10%	−20%	−20%
10	B&E&S	....	....	....	....	−20%	−20%
11	B&E&S	−20%	−20%	−20%	−20%	−20%	−20%

TABLE 4-9 extended coverage endorsement general rates

Class A, B, and All-Steel Construction—All States

% AVERAGE CLAUSE IN FIRE POLICY					
100%	90%	80%	70%	0 to 70%	
				Bldgs.	Conts.
.016	.017	.018	.019	.072	.036

TABLE 4-9 (continued)

Class C and D Construction, Unsprinklered Risks

District	% AVERAGE CLAUSE IN FIRE POLICY				
	100%	90%	80%	70%	0 to 70%
State A	.144	.152	.160	.168	.320
State B	.045	(.048)	.050	.053	.100

Using tables 4-5 through 4-9, we shall see how a building and its contents are rated for insurance purposes. Insurance companies use the term *debit* to indicate an increase over regular rates due to factors that increase the risk of loss. Likewise, they use the term *credit* to denote discounts from regular rates based on those factors that reduce the underwriter's risk. In the following example, showing how insurance tables are used to help calculate a premium, much of the terminology will be unfamiliar. But this should be no cause for worry; the most important terms will be explained later on in this section.

Calculate the insurance premium for the grocery store located at 1118 Baldwin St. Coverage is a 3-year fire policy on building and contents with an extended coverage endorsement and a 90% average (coinsurance) clause. Building is valued at $120,000, equipment at $60,000, and stock at $400,000. (In the tables used in determining the premium, all of the figures required for this example have been circled to make the process easier to follow.)   *Example*

Step 1: Because it is located at 1118 Baldwin St., this building falls into zone 1 of the Fire Rating Table (table 4-5). Basic rates for a class D risk are .66 building, .93 equipment and .116 stock.   *Solution*

Step 2: According to table 4-6, local zone 1 is converted to National Rating Board protection class 3.

Step 3: At the top of table 4-7 we find that protection class 3 calls for the use of "Average Clause Table I." In "Table I," a class D risk coinsured at 90% carries a 25% credit on both the building rate and contents rate.

Step 4: Having determined elsewhere that this kind of activity (retail grocery merchandising) carries the rate adjustment guide number 9, then we find that the rate adjustment credit is 50% (table 4-8, Rate Adjustments, under class D, protection classes 1–8, opposite rate adjustment guide no. 9). At this point we can make the following calculations:

	(Step 1) Basic rate		(Step 3) Coins		(Step 4) Bldg. use credit				
(Fire) Bldg.	.66	−	25%	−	50%	= .247 ×	2.7* (3 years)	=	.667†
	$\left(.66\right.$	×	$\dfrac{3}{4}$	×	$\left.\dfrac{1}{2}\right)$				

*Insurance companies grant a discount on policies taken out for more than 1 year. In this case, the premium on a 3-year policy is not 3 times the 1-year premium, but only 2.7 times. This represents a 10% discount. For example, a 1-year $100 premium would be $270 for 3 years, rather than $300; so $300 − $270 = $30 or 10% discount.

†In these calculations, the result of each operation of multiplication and division is rounded to the nearest thousandth.

	(Step 1) Basic rate		(Step 3) Coins		(Step 4) Bldg. use credit						
(Fire) Equip.	.93	–	25%	–	50%	=	.349	X	2.7	(3 years)	= .942
	(.93	X	$\frac{3}{4}$	X	$\frac{1}{2}$)						
(Fire) Stock	.116	–	25%	–	50%	=	.043	X	2.7	(3 years)	= .116
	(.116	X	$\frac{3}{4}$	X	$\frac{1}{2}$)						

Step 5: From table 4-9, the extended-coverage rate on a class D risk with a 90% coinsurance clause in state B is .048 X 2.7 (3-year policy) = .130.

Step 6: The 3-year fire insurance premium for $120,000 coverage on the building, $60,000 on the equipment, and $400,000 on the stock can now be calculated as follows:

Building
Fire:	$.667 per $100 X 1,200	=	$ 800.40
Ex. cov.:	$.130 per $100 X 1,200	=	156.00

Equipment
Fire:	$.942 per $100 X 600	=	565.20
Ex. cov.:	$.130 per $100 X 600	=	78.00

Stock
Fire:	$.116 per $100 X 4,000	=	464.00
Ex. cov.:	$.130 per $100 X 4,000	=	520.00

Total 3-year premium = $2,583.60

In developing a fire insurance premium, discounts from regular rates are given for fire-resistant building construction, less hazardous building use, and a high percentage of coinsurance. Naturally, it would be logical to conclude that a company manufacturing explosives in a frame building insured for only 70% of its value would pay a much higher premium for the same dollar coverage as the grocery store in our example.

coinsurance

The insurance contract covering Buffington's property contains a *coinsurance* clause—an agreement whereby Buffington's, in return for a lower premium, agrees to carry insurance coverage equal to 90% of the actual value of the property insured. If at the time of loss, the face value of the policy is less than 90% of the value of the property, the store becomes in effect a coinsurer and does not recover the full amount of the loss. If the coverage meets or exceeds the coinsurance requirement, the full amount of the loss is paid. Of course, under no circumstances can the payment to the insured be larger than the amount of insurance he carries. The amount received from the insurance company is called the *indemnity*. In coinsurance cases, the indemnity is that percentage of the loss represented by the ratio of the coverage in force to the coverage required.

Example
1

What will be the indemnity paid as a result of a fire in which $24,000 worth of merchandise is destroyed if, at the time of the fire, Buffington's had property valued at $800,000 and property insurance coverage of $690,000 with a 90% coinsurance clause in the contract?

Actual property value	$800,000
Coinsurance requirement	× .90
Required coverage	$720,000

$$\text{Indemnity} = \text{Loss} \times \frac{\text{Actual coverage}}{\text{Required coverage}}$$

$$= \$24,000 \times \frac{\$690,000}{\$720,000}$$

$$= \$23,000$$

Full $24,000 is not reimbursed because the face value of the policy did not equal 90% of the actual property value.

What will be the indemnity paid as a result of $50,000 fire loss on prop- *Example* erty valued at $300,000 if the property was insured for $280,000 and an 80% *2* coinsurance clause was in effect?

Actual property value	$300,000
Coinsurance requirement	× .80
Required coverage	$240,000
Actual coverage	$280,000

Indemnity = $50,000 (full amount of the loss)

Full $50,000 is reimbursed because the face value of the policy exceeded 80% of the actual property value.

In example 2, above, if the loss were $50,000 and the actual coverage only *Example* $200,000, what would be the indemnity? *3*

Actual property value	$300,000
Coinsurance requirement	× .80
Required coverage	$240,000

$$\text{Indemnity} = \$50,000 \times \frac{\$200,000}{\$240,000}$$

$$= \$41,667$$

Full $50,000 is not reimbursed because the face value of the policy did not equal 80% of the actual property value.

business interruption insurance

Included in the package policy covering Buffington's Department Store for property losses is coverage for the loss of the use of property. If business were interrupted by fire or other causes, earnings would certainly be curtailed. If the loss or damage were serious enough, the firm might not be able to continue operating. However, many expenses would continue despite a shutdown. Because of this risk, Buffington's has purchased business interruption insurance as part of its overall coverage. This coverage has been designed to pay the store enough to meet its expenses and earn a modest profit for a specified period of time until it can resume full activities.

For the sake of simplicity, let us assume that Buffington's most recent quarterly profit figures are exactly one-fourth of the year-end profit figures shown in their income statement. To cover all expenses and provide a net profit, Buffington's will need $180,000 coverage. This is found by dividing gross margin by 4: $720,000 ÷ 4 = $180,000. This amount would probably be sufficient to pay all expenses and a net profit for three months until business could be resumed.

cancellation and short-term rates

There are times when a firm or individual may want insurance coverage for less than one year. At other times, the insured may have reason to cancel his policy before it expires. In both cases, the insurance company will refer to a short-rate cancellation table such as table 4-10. The rates in this table are set to exceed exact pro rata rates. For example, the premium on a 182-day (half-year) policy is 60% (100% − 40%) of the full-year premium.

Example 1   What portion of a $2,400 1-year premium would be charged for 80 days of insurance coverage? From the table, 80 days = 68% unearned premium. Thus,

$$\text{Short rate} = 32\% \times \$2,400 = \$768$$

Example 2   What portion of the $248 premium would be refunded on a 3-year policy, canceled after being in force for 239 days? From the table, 239 days = 73% unearned premium. Thus,

$$\text{Refund} = \$248 \times .73 = \$181.04$$

fidelity bond

A final form of property insurance required by a business firm is protection against the risk of loss due to employee dishonesty. There are two basic approaches which can be taken to provide this kind of coverage: (1) A bond covering named individuals, or (2) a blanket position bond covering all job positions in the firm regardless of what individuals occupy them at any given time.

Buffington's has decided on the latter approach, in order to have complete long-run coverage. The cost of the blanket fidelity bond is obviously greater than a bond specifying named individuals.

Liability insurance

In addition to insurance covering the loss of property and the loss of the use of property, Buffington's has purchased liability coverage to protect the business

TABLE 4-10 short-rate cancellation table

1-Year Policies

Days in Force	Unearned Prem. %	Days in Force	Unearned Prem. %	Days in Force	Unearned Prem. %	Days in Force	Unearned Prem. %
1	95	66-69	71	154-156	47	256-260	23
2	94	70-73	70	157-160	46	261-264	22
3-4	93	74-76	69	161-164	45	265-269	21
5-6	92	77-80	68	165-167	44	270-273	20
7-8	91	81-83	67	168-171	43	274-278	19
9-10	90	84-87	66	172-175	42	279-282	18
11-12	89	88-91	65	176-178	41	283-287	17
13-14	88	92-94	64	179-182	40	288-291	16
15-16	87	95-98	63	183-187	39	292-296	15
17-18	86	99-102	62	188-191	38	297-301	14
19-20	85	103-105	61	192-196	37	302-305	13
21-22	84	106-109	60	197-200	36	306-310	12
23-25	83	110-113	59	201-205	35	311-314	11
26-29	82	114-116	58	206-209	34	315-319	10
30-32	81	117-120	57	210-214	33	320-323	9
33-36	80	121-124	56	215-218	32	324-328	8
37-40	79	125-127	55	219-223	31	329-332	7
41-43	78	128-131	54	224-228	30	333-337	6
44-47	77	132-135	53	229-232	29	338-342	5
48-51	76	136-138	52	233-237	28	343-346	4
52-54	75	139-142	51	238-241	27	347-351	3
55-58	74	143-146	50	242-246	26	352-355	2
59-62	73	147-149	49	247-250	25	356-360	1
63-65	72	150-153	48	251-255	24	361-365	0

TABLE 4-10 (continued)

3-Year Policies, First Year (Term Multiple: 2.7*)

Days in Force	Unearned Prem. %	Days in Force	Unearned Prem. %	Days in Force	Unearned Prem. %	Days in Force	Unearned Prem. %
1	98.1	66-69	89.3	154-156	80.4	256-260	71.5
2	97.8	70-73	88.9	157-160	80.0	261-264	71.1
3-4	97.4	74-76	88.5	161-164	79.6	265-269	70.7
5-6	97.0	77-80	88.1	165-167	79.3	270-273	70.4
7-8	96.7	81-83	87.8	168-171	78.9	274-278	70.0
9-10	96.3	84-87	87.4	172-175	78.5	279-282	69.6
11-12	95.9	88-91	87.0	176-178	78.1	283-287	69.3
13-14	95.6	92-94	86.7	179-182	77.8	288-291	68.9
15-16	95.2	95-98	86.3	183-187	77.4	292-296	68.5
17-18	94.8	99-102	85.9	188-191	77.0	297-301	68.1
19-20	94.4	103-105	85.6	192-196	76.7	302-305	67.8
21-22	94.1	106-109	85.2	197-200	76.3	306-310	67.4
23-25	93.7	110-113	84.8	201-205	75.9	311-314	67.0
26-29	93.3	114-116	84.4	206-209	75.6	315-319	66.7
30-32	93.0	117-120	84.1	210-214	75.2	320-323	66.3
33-36	92.6	121-124	83.7	215-218	74.8	324-328	65.9
37-40	92.2	125-127	83.3	219-223	74.4	329-332	65.6
41-43	91.9	128-131	83.0	224-228	74.1	333-337	65.2
44-47	91.5	132-135	82.6	229-232	73.7	338-342	64.8
48-51	91.1	136-138	82.2	233-237	73.3	343-346	64.4
52-54	90.7	139-142	81.9	238-241	73.0	347-351	64.1
55-58	90.4	143-146	81.5	242-246	72.6	352-355	63.7
59-62	90.0	147-149	81.1	247-250	72.2	356-360	63.3
63-65	89.6	150-153	80.7	251-255	71.9	361-365	63.0

*The 2.7 term multiple means that a 3-year policy costs 2.7 times the premium for a 1-year policy. This results in a 10% discount.

3-Year Policies, Second Year (Term Multiple: 2.7*)

In Force Yrs.	Days	Unearned Prem. %	In Force Yrs.	Days	Unearned Prem. %	In Force Yrs.	Days	Unearned Prem. %	In Force Yrs.	Days	Unearned Prem. %
1	1-5	62.5	1	96-100	54.3	1	191-195	46.1	1	286-290	38.0
1	6-10	62.1	1	101-105	53.9	1	196-200	45.7	1	291-295	37.5
1	11-15	61.7	1	106-110	53.5	1	201-205	45.3	1	296-300	37.1
1	16-20	61.2	1	111-115	53.0	1	206-210	44.9	1	301-305	36.7
1	21-25	60.8	1	116-120	52.6	1	211-215	44.4	1	306-310	36.2
1	26-30	60.4	1	121-125	52.2	1	216-220	44.0	1	311-315	35.8
1	31-35	59.9	1	126-130	51.8	1	221-225	43.6	1	316-320	35.4
1	36-40	59.5	1	131-135	51.3	1	226-230	43.1	1	321-325	34.9
1	41-45	59.1	1	136-140	50.9	1	231-235	42.7	1	326-330	34.5
1	46-50	58.7	1	141-145	50.5	1	236-240	42.3	1	331-335	34.1
1	51-55	58.2	1	146-150	50.0	1	241-245	41.8	1	336-340	33.6
1	56-60	57.8	1	151-155	49.6	1	246-250	41.4	1	341-345	33.2
1	61-65	57.4	1	156-160	49.2	1	251-255	41.0	1	346-350	32.8
1	66-70	56.9	1	161-165	48.7	1	256-260	40.5	1	351-355	32.3
1	71-75	56.5	1	166-170	48.3	1	261-265	40.1	1	356-360	31.9
1	76-80	56.1	1	171-175	47.9	1	266-270	39.7	1	361-365	31.5
1	81-85	55.6	1	176-180	47.4	1	271-275	39.2			
1	86-90	55.2	1	181-185	47.0	1	276-280	38.8			
1	91-95	54.8	1	186-190	46.6	1	281-285	38.4			

*The 2.7 term multiple means that a 3-year policy costs 2.7 times the premium for a 1-year policy. This results in a 10% discount.

TABLE 4-10 (continued)

3-Year Policies, Third Year (Term Multiple: 2.7*)

In Force Yrs.	Days	Unearned Prem. %	In Force Yrs.	Days	Unearned Prem. %	In Force Yrs.	Days	Unearned Prem. %	In Force Yrs.	Days	Unearned Prem. %
2	1-5	31.1	2	96-100	22.9	2	191-195	14.7	2	286-290	6.5
2	6-10	30.6	2	101-105	22.4	2	196-200	14.2	2	291-295	6.0
2	11-15	30.2	2	106-110	22.0	2	201-205	13.8	2	296-300	5.6
2	16-20	29.8	2	111-115	21.6	2	206-210	13.4	2	301-305	5.2
2	21-25	29.3	2	116-120	21.1	2	211-215	12.9	2	306-310	4.7
2	26-30	28.9	2	121-125	20.7	2	216-220	12.5	2	311-315	4.3
2	31-35	28.5	2	126-130	20.3	2	221-225	12.1	2	316-320	3.9
2	36-40	28.0	2	131-135	19.8	2	226-230	11.6	2	321-325	3.5
2	41-45	27.6	2	136-140	19.4	2	231-235	11.2	2	326-330	3.0
2	46-50	27.2	2	141-145	19.0	2	236-240	10.8	2	331-335	2.6
2	51-55	26.7	2	146-150	18.5	2	241-245	10.4	2	336-340	2.2
2	56-60	26.3	2	151-155	18.1	2	246-250	9.9	2	341-345	1.7
2	61-65	25.9	2	156-160	17.7	2	251-255	9.5	2	346-350	1.3
2	66-70	25.4	2	161-165	17.3	2	256-260	9.1	2	351-355	0.9
2	71-75	25.0	2	166-170	16.8	2	261-265	8.6	2	356-360	0.4
2	76-80	24.6	2	171-175	16.4	2	266-270	8.2	2	361-365	0.0
2	81-85	24.2	2	176-180	16.0	2	271-275	7.8			
2	86-90	23.7	2	181-185	15.5	2	276-280	7.3			
2	91-95	23.3	2	186-190	15.1	2	281-285	6.9			

*The 2.7 term multiple means that a 3-year policy costs 2.7 times the premium for a 1-year policy. This results in a 10% discount.

against financial losses arising from injury to customers or employees. The liability protection against customer injury is a part of Buffington's all risk package policy which we have been discussing thus far.

The liability insurance which indemnifies the store for injury to employees is provided for in a separate liability policy, called *workmen's compensation insurance*, which will be explained later in this section. Employers are required by law to provide workmen's compensation insurance.

Buffington's customer liability insurance covers injury to customers due to accidents in the store, defective merchandise, and the operation of Buffington's five delivery trucks, and includes indemnity not only for actual bodily injury and property damage, but also personal injury arising from judgments awarded for false arrest, libel, or slander. The liability limits for this coverage are $250,000/500,000 (often written 250/500) for bodily injury and $100,000 property damage. The two bodily-injury figures refer to the maximum indemnity for any one person injured in an accident ($250,000) and the maximum indemnity the insurance company will pay for two or more persons injured in the same accident ($500,000).

To determine the insurance premium for liability and property damage coverage on Buffington's delivery vehicles, a number of factors were considered: age, weight, original cost, and type of vehicle; area of operation; previous operating record, type of use; and, of course, the length and amount of coverage desired. Let us assume for purposes of illustration that Buffington's delivery vehicles are listed as class 4A, territory 80. From this point, the premium is determined as follows:

Basic Limits	Annual Premium (per Vehicle)
$10,000/$20,000 bodily injury	$64
$5,000 property damage	$43

Increased Limits (in $1,000^S)

Bodily Injury	Factor	Property Damage	Factor
20/20	1.08	$10,000	1.10
15/30	1.09	$15,000	1.15
20/40	1.15	$25,000	1.20
25/50	1.19	$50,000	1.25
50/100	1.30	$100,000	1.30
100/300	1.41		
250/500	1.57		

Since Buffington's chose the maximum protection in each category, the premium is found to be as follows:

Bodily injury = Base rate × Factor
= $64 × 1.57 = $100.48
Property damage = base rate × factor
= $43 × 1.30 = $55.90
Premium per vehicle = $100.48 + $55.90 = $156.38

The premium for Buffington's five delivery trucks might be less than 5 times the per-vehicle premium if fleet discount rates apply.

Workmen's compensation insurance

Financial protection for the loss of earnings by employees caused by job-connected accidents or sickness is the aim of workmen's compensation insurance.

The cost of this insurance varies according to the rates of pay in the firm and the number of employees at each earnings level. At Buffington's, five levels of earnings are distinguishable: executives, commission salespeople, hourly-wage salespeople, delivery drivers, and office personnel. Calculating the required insurance premiums involves multiplying the appropriate premium rate by the total earnings for each employee category.

Example   What workmen's compensation premium would Buffington's pay for five delivery drivers who collectively earned $4,886.22 last month, if the premium rate is $1.08 per $100 of wages paid?

$$\text{Premium} = \frac{\$4,886.22}{\$100} \times \$1.08$$
$$= 48.8622 \times \$1.08 = \$52.77$$

Group insurance

Many businesses provide life insurance and/or health insurance for their employees. In some cases the cost of this coverage is shared by the firm and the employee, but just as often it is borne solely by the employer. Sometimes the life insurance is term insurance (no cash value), while the health insurance frequently takes the form of a major-medical policy.

At Buffington's, every employee starts with a $5,000 permanent life insurance policy, which is increased each time the employee is promoted up to a maximum of $20,000 for top management personnel.

Buffington's pays the cost of a health insurance plan for each employee. Coverage of employees' dependents is not included, but can be purchased by the insured. This plan provides for payment by the insurance company of 80% of the hospital costs incurred by the employee after the first $50. This combination group life and health insurance costs Buffington's about $12.50 per employee per month.

Key man insurance

The management of any business firm will establish a number of company objectives. The most familiar ones are couched in terms of profit, growth, service to customers, and return on investment. Another objective might be called survival. A firm is more likely to survive and grow if its key executives are able to direct that growth. In other words, the death of a key executive is a serious risk faced by every business firm. Many business firms have thus adopted the practice of insuring the life of the chief executive by purchasing *key man insurance.* The company pays the annual premiums and is the policy benefi- ciary. Although the firm is not allowed to deduct the premiums as a business expense, it is not taxed on the proceeds of the policy when the insured dies.

The alternatives available to a firm which is buying insurance on the life of its top executive are in essence the same alternatives faced by an individual who must decide on the type of life insurance policy he should purchase for the financial benefit of his wife and family.

types of life insurance

There are many variations in life insurance policies. A comparison of one kind of policy with the same kind offered by a competing insurance company is difficult to make because of all the variables involved. Still, it is possible to dis- tinguish some basic policy types, which from company to company are more similar than dissimilar.

TABLE 4-11 comparative features of life insurance policies (per $10,000 of coverage)

Type of Policy	Premium	Length of Time Premium is Paid	Protection	Cash Value and Borrowing Privileges
Term insurance	lowest	contract period	$10,000	no
Permanent insurance				
Whole life	low	lifetime	10,000	yes
Life-paid-up-at-65	medium	until age 65	10,000	yes
20-pay life	high	20 years	10,000	yes
Endowment	highest	contract period	10,000	yes

As table 4-11 indicates, term insurance provides protection only. Since there is no savings feature in a term insurance policy, there is no cash value and therefore no borrowing privilege. Each kind of permanent life insurance calls for a larger premium than term insurance. The excess premium payment beyond the cost of the risk itself builds for the insured or his survivors cash values or savings. These savings usually earn interest at a guaranteed rate of $2\frac{1}{2}$ to 3% and, at the discretion of the insured, may be borrowed or (if the policy is canceled or converted) taken in cash or used to buy extended term insurance.

The life–paid-up-at-65 and the 20-pay life policies are simply whole life policies which are paid up faster. To do this, of course, premiums must be higher than when the policy is paid on over a lifetime. The endowment policy builds up larger cash values over the contract period, and this can only be done by paying larger premiums. A close look at tables 4-12 through 4-16 will permit a more exact comparison of annual premiums and cash surrender values for dif- ferent types of life insurance policies.

types of life insurance companies

Life insurance companies can be separated into two major types: stock companies and mutual companies. The stock company is owned by stockholders

TABLE 4-12 annual premium rates per $1,000 of life insurance, companies A and B

Age at Issue	10-Year Renewable Term	Whole Life Co. A (particp.)	Whole Life Co. B (nonparticp.)	20-Pay Life Co. A	20-Pay Life Co. B	Life-Paid-Up-at-65 Co. A	Life-Paid-Up-at-65 Co. B	20-Year Endowment Co. A	20-Year Endowment Co. B
17	$ 3.81	$12.84	$ 8.91	$22.77	$17.81	$14.84	$11.56	$45.89	$42.26
18	3.82	13.30	9.83	23.29	18.21	15.10	12.26	45.98	42.26
19	3.86	13.77	10.04	23.85	18.63	15.75	12.81	46.03	42.26
20	3.90	14.88	12.16	24.48	19.04	16.61	13.21	46.19	42.26
21	3.94	15.21	12.48	24.94	19.51	17.07	13.63	46.24	42.26
22	3.98	15.58	12.82	25.41	19.98	17.54	14.07	46.28	42.27
23	4.03	15.99	13.17	25.90	20.46	18.03	14.54	46.31	42.29
24	4.08	16.40	13.55	26.38	20.96	19.05	15.04	46.36	42.32
25	4.13	16.82	13.95	26.92	21.48	19.09	15.57	46.41	42.58
30	4.41	19.30	16.30	29.80	24.33	22.36	18.71	46.82	43.21
35	5.13	22.48	19.21	33.28	27.62	26.84	23.01	47.62	44.40
40	6.65	26.67	23.29	37.49	31.58	33.19	29.01	49.05	46.06
45	8.93	32.09	28.37	42.61	36.33	42.61	38.01	51.37	48.99
50	12.61	39.22	34.71	48.99	41.60	57.85	54.01	55.09	53.57
55	18.90	48.69	42.86	57.26	48.51	87.04	84.21	61.01	60.79
60	28.11	61.47	53.26	68.47	57.96	.....	.....	70.26	

Notes: Rates given are for males. Female rates tend to be the same as the rates for males 3 years younger.
Semiannual rate is .51 times annual rate; quarterly, .26; monthly, .09.

TABLE 4-13   cash surrender values, whole life policies
per $1,000, companies A and B

Age at Issue	Company A (participating) End of Policy Year				Company B (nonparticipating) End of Policy Year			
	5	10	15	20	5	10	15	20
20	$31	$85	$146	$216	$26	$80	$142	$212
25	39	103	175	255	33	98	170	250
30	48	124	207	297	43	119	202	291
35	59	148	242	342	54	142	236	335
40	70	173	280	390	65	166	272	380

Note: All or part of cash value may be borrowed at 5% simple annual interest.

TABLE 4-14 cash surrender values, 20-pay life policies
per $1,000, companies A and B

Age at Issue	Company A (participating) End of Policy Year				Company B (nonparticipating) End of Policy Year			
	5	10	15	20	5	10	15	20
20	$69	$172	$286	$413	$58	$159	$277	$413
25	79	196	324	466	68	183	315	466
30	92	223	366	523	80	209	356	523
35	105	251	409	582	93	236	398	582
40	118	280	452	642	105	264	441	642

Note: All or part of cash value may be borrowed at 5% simple annual interest.

TABLE 4-15   cash surrender values, 20-year endowment policies
per $1,000, companies A and B

Age at Issue	Company A (participating) End of Policy Year				Company B (nonparticipating) End of Policy Year			
	5	10	15	20	5	10	15	20
20	$179	$418	$689	$1000	$164	$401	$677	$1000
25	179	418	689	1000	164	401	677	1000
30	179	419	689	1000	165	401	677	1000
35	180	419	688	1000	165	401	677	1000
40	180	418	686	1000	165	399	669	1000

Note: All or part of cash value may be borrowed at 5% simple annual interest.

TABLE 4-16 20-year dividends on company A participating policies for selected ages, per $1,000, coverage policies issued in 1948

Age at issue	Whole Life					20-Pay Life		20-Year Endowment	
	20	25	30	35	40	25	35	25	35
Annual premium:*	$17.16	$19.20	$22.56	$26.44	$30.18	$31.64	$38.92	$47.53	$50.18
1949 1	$ 2.94	$ 3.27	$ 3.72	$ 4.38	$ 5.35	$ 3.65	$ 4.75	$ 4.12	$ 5.08
1950 2	3.10	3.45	3.95	4.67	5.65	3.95	5.14	4.56	5.55
1951 3	3.25	3.63	4.18	4.96	5.95	4.25	5.53	5.00	6.03
1952 4	3.41	3.83	4.42	5.26	6.25	4.56	5.92	5.46	6.52
1953 5	3.69	4.31	5.29	6.28	7.01	4.88	6.60	5.92	7.31
1954 6	4.06	4.85	5.79	6.78	7.58	5.29	7.09	6.59	7.91
1955 7	4.57	5.30	6.16	7.36	8.72	6.21	8.11	7.40	8.74
1956 8	4.89	5.63	6.56	7.80	9.21	6.73	8.69	8.14	9.46
1957 9	5.76	6.49	7.47	8.75	10.22	7.83	9.85	9.73	11.02
1958 10	6.12	6.96	8.03	9.36	10.99	8.71	10.83	10.98	12.23
1959 11	6.45	7.35	8.48	9.82	11.54	9.33	11.53	11.89	13.09
1960 12	6.88	7.85	9.05	10.52	12.23	10.16	12.45	13.11	14.26
1961 13	7.26	8.28	9.55	11.09	12.82	10.86	13.23	14.15	15.23
1962 14	7.71	8.81	10.12	11.67	13.48	11.78	14.16	15.54	16.48
1963 15	8.05	9.18	10.53	12.13	13.97	12.35	14.77	16.36	17.21
1964 16	9.20	10.47	11.96	13.61	15.55	14.43	17.00	19.41	20.12
1965 17	9.59	10.89	12.42	14.09	16.10	15.10	17.67	20.38	20.96
1966 18	10.54	12.03	13.76	15.59	17.71	16.95	19.75	23.09	23.56
1967 19	10.96	12.51	14.25	16.12	18.28	17.69	20.48	24.16	24.46
1968 20	12.56	14.31	16.25	18.39	20.86	20.73	23.91	28.58	28.84

*Premiums were higher in 1948 than they are today for comparable policies.

who have purchased shares in the company. This is precisely the ownership arrangement that exists in all corporations. All profits belong to the stockholders, who receive dividends when management elects to pay them. In some cases, stock insurance companies may sell participating policies which entitle the policyholder to a limited share in company dividends.

The policyholders of a mutual insurance company own the company—there are no stockholders as such. The dividends received by these policyholders are legally considered to be refunds on excess premium charges. At the discretion of the policyholder, his annual dividends (refund) may be withdrawn in cash or left with the company to prepay future premiums, purchase additional insurance, or accumulate at a minimum guaranteed rate of interest. When dividends are left to accumulate, they serve to increase the death benefit—or the cash value if the policy is surrendered during the lifetime of the insured. The data for the participating policies of Company A referred to in tables 4-12 through 4-16 are representative of mutual insurance companies. The data for the non-participating policies of Company B in the same tables is typical of stock insurance companies.

calculating life insurance premiums

Determining the annual premium for a life insurance policy involves multiplying the rate per $1,000 for the appropriate age of the insured by the number of $1,000s purchased. (The rates in the following examples are found in table 4-12.)

If Buffington's purchased a $50,000 Company B nonparticipating 20-pay life policy on a key executive, age 35, what would be the annual premium?   *Example 1*

$$\text{Annual premium} = \$27.62 \text{ per } \$1,000$$
$$= \$27.62 \times 50 = \$1,381$$

If Buffington's purchased a $50,000 whole life participating policy from Company A for the executive in example 1, above, what would be the annual premium?   *Example 2*

$$\text{Annual premium} = \$22.48 \text{ per } \$1,000$$
$$= \$22.48 \times 50 = \$1,124$$

or

$$\text{Semiannual premium} = \$1,124 \times 51 = \$573.24$$

Savings on annual
over semiannual
premium $= \$573.24 \times 2 - \$1,146.48$
                $= \$1,146.48 - \$1,124 = \$22.48$

figuring the net cost or return on a life insurance policy

Before Buffington's makes a decision on the type of life insurance policy it should buy to insure against the loss of a key executive, the cash surrender value and any expected dividends from the policy should be taken into account. Although future dividends can never be known for certain, they can be realistically forecasted by investigating the dividend history of the insurance company in question. The analysis which follows takes into account premium costs, cash values, and expected dividends (calculated using tables 4-12, 4-14, and 4-16), but no consideration is given to interest which may be earned from dividend accumulation. Neither is any consideration given to the interest that might be earned by investing the difference in annual premium between the stock company and mutual company policies.

TABLE 4-17   probable net cost or return on $50,000 life insurance policies (age at issue: 35)

Policy	Annual Premiums (20 yrs)		Guaranteed Cash Value		Expected Dividends		Net Cost (+) or Net Return (−)
20-pay life, Co. A (participating)	$33,280 ($1,664 × 20)	−	$29,100	+	$11,873	=	−$7,693 net return
20-pay life, Co. B (nonparticipating)	$27,620 ($1,381 × 20)	−	$29,100	+	0	=	−$1,480 net return

In table 4-17, it was assumed that dividends to be paid by Company A over the next 20 years would be neither more nor less than the total dividends they paid from 1949 to 1968. That is why this analysis has used the total actual dividends paid from 1948 to 1968 on a 20-pay life policy issued at age 35, as shown in table 4-16. Total dividends were found by summing the 20-year series and multiplying the result by 50. It should also be pointed out that the insurance purchaser might well be able to invest the difference in premiums between the two policies ($5,660 over 20 years or $283 per year) and earn a return as good as or better than the dividend return shown here on the participating policy.

EXERCISE 4-5 COINSURANCE

Solve the following problems in coinsurance.

	Property Value	Amount of Loss	Insurance Coverage	Coinsurance Requirement	Indemnity
1.	$ 16,000	$ 12,000	$ 14,000	90%	_____
2.	40,000	8,000	30,000	90	_____
3.	168,400	24,600	156,200	80	_____
4.	214,750	38,550	200,000	80	_____
5.	78,875	78,875	60,000	90	_____
6.	64,320	4,200	64,320	90	_____
7.	344,225	100,000	325,000	90	_____
8.	1,721,548	64,500	1,500,000	80	_____
9.	32,500	9,600	24,600	90	_____
10.	81,312	22,000	63,700	90	_____

EXERCISE 4-6 FIRE INSURANCE

Using tables 4-5 through 4-9, calculate the fire insurance premium on each of these buildings, including extended-coverage endorsements. All buildings are located in zone 1, and carry a basic rate of .66.

	Coverage Building	Policy Years	Risk Class	Coinsurance (Avg. Clause)	Rate Adj. Guide No.	Premium
1.	$ 60,000	1	B	90%	5	_____
2.	280,000	1	D (state A)	80	4	_____
3.	96,500	3	C (state A)	90	9	_____
4.	127,750	3	A	70	3	_____
5.	54,520	1	C (state B)	80	8	_____
6.	350,000	3	D (state B)	90	7	_____
7.	820,000	1	B	80	2	_____
8.	45,950	3	A	70	6	_____
9.	138,500	1	C (state A)	60	6	_____
10.	2,285,000	3	D (state B)	90	9	_____

EXERCISE 4-7 SHORT-RATE AND CANCELLED POLICIES

A. Using table 4-10, calculate the short-rate premium on the fire insurance policies in Exercise 4-6.

	Full Premium (from Exercise 4-6)	Policy Period	Days in Force	Short-Rate Premium
1.	_____	1	60	_____
2.	_____	1	125	_____
3.	_____	3	426	_____
4.	_____	3	844	_____
5.	_____	1	228	_____
6.	_____	3	572	_____
7.	_____	1	30	_____
8.	_____	3	396	_____
9.	_____	1	108	_____
10.	_____	3	910	_____

B. Using table 4-10, calculate the refunds on these canceled policies.

	Full Premium	Policy Period	Days in Force	Refund
1.	$ 110.00	3	65	_____
2.	87.00	1	40	_____
3.	296.00	1	288	_____
4.	312.00	3	457	_____
5.	68.50	3	97	_____
6.	872.00	3	591	_____
7.	1,256.00	3	843	_____
8.	75.00	1	133	_____
9.	648.75	1	312	_____
10.	8,440.00	3	903	_____

EXERCISE 4-8 LIFE INSURANCE

Using table 4-12, calculate the premiums on the following policies from Companies A and B.

Policy	Coverage	(Male) Age at Issue	Annual Premium Company A	Company B
Whole life	$10,000	17	_____	_____
Life–paid-up-at-65	25,000	21	_____	_____
Life–paid-up-at-65	38,000	30	_____	_____

| | | (Male) | Annual Premium | |
Policy	Coverage	Age at Issue	Company A	Company B
Whole life	$60,000	25	_____	_____
Whole life	45,000	23	_____	_____
10-year term	25,000	24	_____	_____
20-pay life	52,000	30	_____	_____
20-year endowment	40,000	23	_____	_____
20-pay life	30,000	18	_____	_____
Whole life	50,000	40	_____	_____

EXERCISE 4-9   NET COST OF LIFE INSURANCE

A. Using tables 4-12 through 4-16, calculate the net cost or net return on these permanent life insurance policies. Indicate net cost by circling your answer. Assume that premiums are paid annually.

Company	Policy Type	Coverage	(Male) Age at Issue	Premiums	Cash Value	Estimated Dividends	Net Cost or Net Return
A	Whole life	$20,000	20	_____	____	_____	_____after 5 yrs.
B	Whole life	20,000	20	_____	____	_____	_____after 5 yrs.
A	Whole life	35,000	30	_____	____	_____	_____after 5 yrs.
B	Whole life	35,000	30	_____	____	_____	_____after 5 yrs.
A	20-pay life	5,000	35	_____	____	_____	_____after 5 yrs.
B	20-pay life	5,000	35	_____	____	_____	_____after 5 yrs.
A	20-year end.	25,000	25	_____	____	_____	_____after 5 yrs.
B	20-year end.	25,000	25	_____	____	_____	_____after 5 yrs.
A	20-pay life	15,000	35	_____	____	_____	_____after 15 yrs.
B	20-pay life	15,000	35	_____	____	_____	_____after 15 yrs.

B. Convert the following annual premium payments to the indicated modes of paymen

Annual Premium	Semiannual Premium (.51)	Quarterly Premium (.26)	Monthly Premium (.09)
$ 200	_____	_____	_____
165	_____	_____	_____
302	_____	_____	_____
87	_____	_____	_____
98	_____	_____	_____
475	_____	_____	_____
60	_____	_____	_____
88	_____	_____	_____
187	_____	_____	_____
2,848	_____	_____	_____

EXERCISE 4-10 INSURANCE PROBLEMS

1. What is the 3-year premium on a fire insurance policy with an extended-coverage endorsement for a building in zone 1 (State A) with these coverages: $240,000 on building, $40,000 on equipment, and $160,000 on merchandise? Assume class C risk, rate adjustment guide no. 8, average clause of 80%, and basic rates of .62 for the building, .46 for the equipment, and .342 for the stock.

2. For the policy in problem 1 above, what would be the indemnity paid after a $20,000 equipment loss if the value of equipment at the time of fire was $50,000?

3. What per-vehicle premium would Buffington's have paid for delivery-vehicle insurance with bodily-injury limits of 100/300 ($100,000/-$300,000) and property damage of $25,000?

4. The court awarded judgments of $14,000, $10,000, $6,000, and $5,000 respectively to four persons injured in an automobile accident. If the insurance contract calls for bodily-injury coverage of 15/30, what portion of the judgment will not be paid by the insurance company?

5. If Buffington's were to cancel its 1-year auto insurance policy on July 8, what refund would they receive? Assume an issue date of February 1 and no fleet discount.

6. What is the premium for a 1-year $10,000 fire insurance policy with an extended-coverage endorsement on the stock of the gas station located at 1102 Baldwin Avenue in zone 1? Assume that the rate adjustment guide number is 9 and that an 80% coinsurance clause is in the contract.

7. If the policy in problem 6, above, were canceled after 200 days in force, what portion of the premium would be retained by the insurance company?

8. What would have been the difference in premium in problem 6 if a 90% clause had been included instead of the 80% clause?

9. What is the difference in the annual premium charge for a $20,000 whole life, issued at age 18, from Company A and from Company B?

10. Find the net cost or return after 15 years on a Company A $10,000 whole life policy issued when the insured was 20 years of age.

11. If a person buys a $15,000 10-year term insurance policy at the age of 24, how much can he save by paying premiums annually instead of monthly?

12. Find the 1-year premium for fire and extended coverage on a class A, $600,000 building in National Rating Board, protection class 5, state B, with equipment worth $240,000 and stock worth $300,000, if each coverage is purchased at 90% of the values shown. Assume rate adjustment guide no. 4, a 90% average clause, and basic rates of .77 for building, .424 for equipment, and .58 for stock.

13. What indemnity would an insurance company pay on a fire loss of $30,000 for a building worth $380,000 and covered for $200,000 under a 70% coinsurance clause?

14. On April 5, 1971, Ralph Osborn purchased a 1-year fire policy for an annual premium of $316. He canceled the policy on September 22 of that year. What refund should he receive? What was his per diem cost of fire insurance? If refunds were made on a pro rata basis, what amount would he have received?
15. An employer made a $350 deposit on his workmen's compensation insurance premium for the current quarter. If the premium rate covering his employees was $3.10 per $100 of wages, and quarterly wages totaled $12,980, what premium does he still owe for the quarter?

SECTION 5—TAXES

Every business firm has certain local, state, and federal taxes it is required to pay in addition to federal and state income taxes. While income taxes are calculated as some percentage of the firm's net income, the taxes shown in the expense section of the income statement are primarily based on the value of certain property owned by the firm. Our discussion here will be limited to these taxes.

Property tax

A tax on the property of a business firm is commonly imposed by county and municipal governments to help pay the cost of public works such as parks, streets, hospitals, and schools. Real property taxes are levied on land and its fixed improvements, while personal property taxes are levied on all other property such as inventory, fixtures, and equipment. For example, the state of California has for some time levied a separate tax on the value of business inventory. Not all city and county governments tax the personal property of business firms or individuals. Whether tax is based on real property or on a combination of real and personal property, the method of calculating property tax is the same.

Once a city has prepared an expense budget which has been approved by the city council or other authorized body, the city's property tax can be determined. The city and county tax is usually combined, so that each property owner receives one bill for his share of both taxes.

The value of real property used for tax purposes is called its *assessed value*. This differs from the *market value*, which is the price at which the property could be expected to sell on the open market. Property values are usually determined by a county assessor, who has the responsibility of ascertaining the market value of all property in the county. Once the market value is determined, some legally approved percent of that value is applied to arrive at assessed value. For example, if the market value of a piece of property is $40,000 and the assessed-value percent is 25%, the property would be assessed at $10,000 for tax purposes.

Finding the tax, tax rate, or assessed value of a community or any single piece of property in it is a problem in percentage, where

$$\text{Tax rate} = \text{Rate}$$

$$\text{Assessed value} = \text{Base}$$

$$\text{Tax} = \text{Percentage}$$

What is the tax rate in a community where the year's budget is $2,200,000 *Example* and the assessed value is $32,000,000? *1*

$$\text{Tax rate} = \frac{\text{Tax}}{\text{Assessed value}}$$

$$= \frac{\$2,200,000}{\$32,000,000} = \$.06875 = \$6.88 \text{ per } \$100$$

Note: Tax rates are typically stated in dollars per $100 of assessed value. The practice is to raise the last digit to the next highest number no matter how small the remainder. Here $6.875 was raised to $6.88; an answer of $8.4111 would be raised to $8.42 per $100.

What is the tax to be collected by a city with an assessed value of *Example* $84,220,000 and a tax rate of $10.20 per $100 of assessed value? *2*

$$\text{Tax} = \text{Tax rate} \times \text{Assessed value}$$

$$= .1020 \times \$84,220,000$$
$$\text{or } 10.20 \times \$842,200 \text{ (per } \$100 \text{ of assessed value)}$$

$$= \$8,590,440$$

When solving for the assessed value, it is important to make sure to do one of two things, either (A) divide the tax rate, expressed in cents per dollar into the total dollars of tax or (B) divide the tax rate expressed in dollars per $100, into the tax expressed in hundreds of dollars. Failure to be consistent here will result in gross errors.

What is the assessed value of a municipality where the tax rate is $.1174 *Example* and the budget for the year is $12,346,000?

$$\text{Assessed value} = \frac{\text{Tax}}{\text{Tax rate}}$$

Using cents per dollar,

$$\frac{\$12,346,000}{\$.1174} = \$105,161,839.86$$

Using dollars per $100,

$$\frac{\$123.460}{\$11.74} = \$105,161,839.86$$

Market value

Finding the market value of property is a simple matter when its assessed value and the rate of assessed value are known.

Example　　What is the market value of property assessed at $8,200 if property is assessed at 25% of market value?

$$\text{Base (Market value)} = \frac{\text{(Percentage)}}{\text{Rate}}\text{Assessed value}$$

$$\text{Market value} = \frac{\$8,200}{.25} = \$32,800$$

In this example, it is even easier to think of market value as being 4 times greater than assessed value ($8,200 × 4 = $32,800).

When the assessed value is not known, but the tax and tax rate are known, market value can still be determined by first finding the assessed value and then dividing it by the assessed value rate:

$$\text{Assessed value} = \frac{\text{Tax}}{\text{Tax rate}}$$

$$\text{Market value} = \frac{\text{Assessed value}}{\text{Assessed value } \% \text{ of Market value}}$$

Example　　What is the market value of property where the tax rate is $.0600, the tax paid is $540, and assessed value is 25% of market value?

$$\text{Assessed value} = \frac{\$540}{.06} = \$9,000$$

$$\text{Market value} = \frac{\$9,000}{.25} = \$36,000$$

Other taxes

Like all business firms, Buffington's has to purchase and renew a city business license. The cost of a license sometimes depends on the size of the firm measured by the number of employees, net sales, or some other base. Since Buffington's maintains a small fleet of delivery trucks, the vehicle license fees on these trucks represent another tax. The proceeds of this tax are very often divided between the county and state governments and usually earmarked for road construction and maintenance. The federal Social Security and unemployment taxes paid by employers were discussed earlier in this chapter in connection with payroll deductions. However, it should be remembered that according to recommended accounting procedure, these expenses are properly shown as taxes in Buffington's income statement.

EXERCISE 4-11 PROPERTY TAX

A. Express the following tax rates in terms of dollars per $100 assessed value.

	Tax Rate	Tax Rate per $100 of Assessed Value
1.	$.0472	_____
2.	.1113	_____
3.	.07514	_____
4.	.09332	_____
5.	.00821	_____
6.	52.50 per $1,000	_____
7.	87.92 per $1,000	_____
8.	.05003	_____
9.	.2184	_____
10.	23.36 per $1,000	_____

B. Find the tax rate per $100 of assessed value given the following information. Note: Remember to raise the tax rate 1 cent whenever there is a remainder.

	Assessed Value	Tax	Tax Rate
1.	$ 8,000,000	$ 400,000	_____
2.	16,400,000	1,312,000	_____
3.	27,385,000	2,800,000	_____
4.	41,762,350	3,562,316	_____
5.	158,932,000	7,415,286	_____
6.	262,822,900	13,141,145	_____
7.	76,438,244	8,152,116	_____
8.	26,000	2,340	_____
9.	6,000	752.40	_____
10.	8,887,360	1,452,725	_____

C. Find the tax to be collected given the following information. Raise remainders to the next highest cent, and when necessary, raise the tax rate to the next highest cent per $100.

	Tax Rate	Assessed Value	Tax
1.	$.0800	$ 16,000,000	_____
2.	.0745	38,280,000	_____
3.	.0988	27,342,800	_____
4.	.11622	9,684	_____
5.	.12263	164,577,385	_____
6.	8.42 per $100	232,881,927	_____
7.	5.84 per $100	12,865	_____
8.	10.25 per $100	32,658	_____

	Tax Rate	Assessed Value	Tax
9.	9.93 per $100	92,814,626	_____
10.	4.87 per $1,000	254,166,312	_____

D. Find the assessed value given the following information. Raise all remainders to the next highest dollar.

	Tax Rate	Tax	Assessed Value
1.	$.0300	$ 6,000,000	_____
2.	.0840	12,250,000	_____
3.	.1153	4,816,400	_____
4.	.1256	8,792,000	_____
5.	6.00 per $100	521.28	_____
6.	8.65 per $100	640.10	_____
7.	5.22 per $100	439,002	_____
8.	12.18 per $100	2,186,324	_____
9.	7.77 per $100	1,533,707	_____
10.	31.50 per $1,000	945	_____

E. Find the market value of property given the following information. Raise all remainders to the next highest dollar.

	Assessed Value	Assessed Value (% of Market Value)	Tax Rate	Tax	Market Value
1.	$ 10,000	20%			_____
2.	8,800	25			_____
3.	5,250	$33\frac{1}{3}$			_____
4.		20	$5.60 per $100	$ 560	_____
5.		25	6.72 per $100	336	_____
6.	138,656	28			_____
7.	68,875	$23\frac{3}{4}$			_____
8.		23	12.40 per $100	$2,852	_____
9.		27	9.75 per $100	616.59	_____
10.		32	.1140	450	_____

EXERCISE 4-12 PROPERTY TAX PROBLEMS

When solving for assessed value or market value, raise all remainders to the next highest dollar; when solving for the property tax or the tax rate, solve to the next highest cent. Remember to raise the tax rate per $100 by 1 cent whenever there is a remainder.

1. Find the real property tax paid by Buffington's Department Store if the rate of assessed value is 25% and the tax rate is $10.96 per $100. Assume the land and building has a market value of $375,000.

2. George Finch has an apartment house assessed at $60,000. If the tax rate is $86.40 per $1,000 of assessed value, what tax will Mr. Finch pay this year?

3. The budget for a community is $2,622,000 for the current tax year. If assessed value amounts to $146,960,000, what will be the property tax rate this year in dollars per $100 of assessed value?

4. The assessed valuation on the home of Lawrence Shepherd is $8,200. If the city tax rate is $6.58 per $100 and the county rate is $2.17 per $100 of assessed value, find Mr. Shepherd's combined property tax.

5. Stanton Melton paid property tax of $432 last year. If his property was assessed at 20% of market value, and the tax rate was $8.00 per $100, what was the market value of his property last year?

6. In problem 5, above, if the cost of supporting local schools accounted for $3.25 per $100 out of the tax rate, how much of Mr. Melton's tax went for school support?

7. What is the assessed value in a community where the expenses for the year are budgeted at $950,000 and the tax rate is $.1692?

8. Arthur Papke's property tax bill is $531.76. If the market value of his house is $28,950 and the tax rate is $7.82 per $100 of assessed value, find (a) the assessed value of his home in dollars, and (b) the assessed value as a percent of market value.

9. If the property tax on a piece of property worth $62,000 is $2,400, find the property tax rate per $100 of assessed value. Note: Property is assessed at 28% of market value.

10. What is the market value of property in a community where the tax rate is $9.66 per $100, the tax collected is $4,391,685, and the property is assessed at 20% of market value?

BUFFINGTON'S DEPARTMENT STORE INC.
BALANCE SHEET
AS OF JANUARY 31, 19XX

ASSETS

CURRENT ASSETS:			
Cash on Hand and in Bank		$180,000	15.0%
Notes Receivable.........................		5,000	.4%
Accounts Receivable	$310,000		
Less: Estimated Bad Debts	10,000	300,000	25.0%
Merchandise Inventory (at cost)		400,000	33.3%
Supplies		10,000	.9%
Prepaid Expenses		5,000	.4%
Total Current Assets		$ 900,000	75.0%
FIXED ASSETS:			
Furniture, Fixtures and Equipment	$125,000		
Less: Accumulated Depreciation	45,000	$ 80,000	6.7%
Delivery Equipment	$ 50,000		
Less: Accumulated Depreciation	30,000	20,000	1.7%
Building	$250,000		
Less: Accumulated Depreciation...........	50,000	200,000	16.6%
Total Fixed Assets		300,000	25.0%
TOTAL ASSETS		$1,200,000	100.0%

LIABILITIES AND PROPRIETORSHIP

CURRENT LIABILITIES:			
Notes Payable		$ 50,000	4.2%
Accounts Payable		220,000	18.3%
Expenses Payable		5,000	.4%
Total Current Liabilities................		$ 275,000	22.9%
LONG-TERM LIABILITIES:			
Mortgage Payable		125,000	10.4%
Total Liabilities		$ 400,000	33.3%
PROPRIETORSHIP:			
Preferred Stock........................	$100,000		
Common Stock	500,000		
Retained Earnings	200,000		
Total Proprietorship (net worth)..........		800,000	66.7%
TOTAL LIABILITIES AND			
PROPRIETORSHIP		$1,200,000	100.0%

THE BALANCE SHEET

5

mathematics of
assets

In chapter 1 we likened the balance sheet to a photo of a business on a particular day. It is a picture of all those things of value, called *assets*, which the company possesses. Possession does not always mean ownership, so the balance sheet also shows the ownership rights to the assets, and these are termed *equities*. In this chapter we are concerned with the calculations related to the characteristics and use of the major types of assets. The mathematics of creditor equities will be discussed in chapter 6 and those of proprietorship equities in chapter 7.

SECTION 1—CASH

The assets are listed on a balance sheet in accordance with their *liquidity*, or ease with which they may be converted into cash. It has been pointed out that one of the measures of the health of a business is the adequacy of its working capital. In addition to the adequacy of cash, the control of cash funds demands the closest of management attention. These funds may be maintained within the business as *change funds* or as *petty cash funds*. They may also be on deposit in a bank or savings and loan company in the form of checking or savings accounts.

Petty cash fund

The best practice in control of cash and that followed by most businesses is to deposit all receipts in a bank account. Likewise, all disbursements would be made by check. This minimizes the opportunities for theft and uses the bank's records as proof of payments and validation of the company's record of receipts. However, there are continual needs for small expenditures which would be not only costly but a nuisance to pay by check. A *petty cash fund* is used to provide for these small payments. This is a type of *imprest fund*, so called because it might be considered as an imprest (advance or loan) from the amounts which would normally be on deposit in a bank.

The fund is established by writing a check for the estimated total of small expenditures which are likely to be made during a short period. The check is cashed and the money turned over to the *petty cashier*, who is responsible for the fund, for making disbursements from it, and for seeing that it is replenished by the company cashier.

As each disbursement is made, a *petty cash voucher*, as in figure 5-1, is

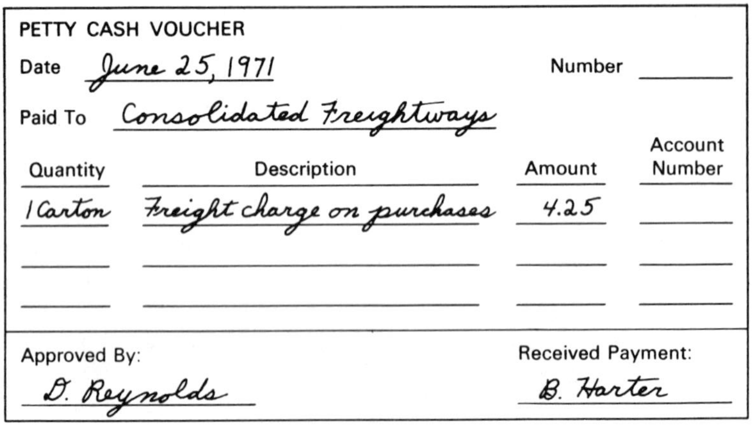

PETTY CASH VOUCHER

Date June 25, 1971 Number ______

Paid To Consolidated Freightways

Quantity	Description	Amount	Account Number
1 Carton	Freight charge on purchases	4.25	

Approved By: D. Reynolds

Received Payment: B. Harter

FIGURE 5-1

prepared and signed by the person receiving the money. The paid voucher replaces the money in the fund. Usually, each paid voucher is entered in a *petty cash record* or *book* as in figure 5-2. Under this system the fund always contains paid vouchers and money equal to the amount of the cash fund. When the fund needs replenishing, the petty cashier submits the paid vouchers to the company cashier, who writes a reimbursing check for the total of the voucher. Thus, the money in the petty cash fund is restored to its original amount, and the vouchers support entries to the proper expense accounts for the amounts previously paid from the fund.

EXERCISE 5-1 PETTY CASH RECORDS

Prepare a separate petty cash record for each of the following months. Enter each of the disbursements, the balance of the fund at the end of the month, and the amount of the replenishing check.

						Distribution of Expense			
Date	Voucher Number	Explanation	Receipt	Payment	Postage	Freight In	Office Exp.	Amt.	Acct.
6/1		Established Fund (ck #93)	50.00						
4	312	Rubber cement		2.50				2.50	
8	313	Stamps (6¢)		10.00	10.00				
12	314	Telegram		1.50				1.50	
15	315	Newspapers		.60				.60	
15	316	Special Delivery		5.00				5.00	
21	317	Calculator repair		8.50			8.50		
22	318	Air Express (Purchase)		7.25		7.25			
23	319	Notary Fee		1.00				1.00	
24	320	Special Del. stamps		1.80	1.80				
25	321	Freight chg. (Purchase)				4.25			
		Totals	50.00	42.40	11.80	11.50	11.00	8.10	
		Balance		7.60					
			50.00	50.00					
6/27		Cash on hand	7.60						
		Replenishing check	42.40						

(Table title: PETTY CASH RECORD)

FIGURE 5-2

A. January 2 Cashed a $50.00 check to start a petty cash fund
3 Purchased 100 eight-cent stamps
5 Paid 89 cents for Band-Aids
6 Paid $1.50 for telegram
9 Paid $2.50 for messenger service
11 Paid $1.75 dinner money to custodian
14 Paid $3.75 freight charges on purchases
17 Donated $2.00 to high school trophy fund
19 Purchased file folders for $5.35
22 Paid $5.50 express charges on purchases
24 Paid $11.75 for business cards
25 Received replenishing check from company cashier

B. March 1 Cashed a $75.00 check to start a petty cash fund
4 Paid $9.25 for advertising material
5 Paid $7.50 for distribution of advertising material
6 Paid five employees $1.50 each for dinner money
7 Purchased Girl Scout cookies: $2.00
9 Paid $9.50 for desk drawer repairs
11 Purchased 200 eight-cent stamps
12 Paid $2.00 to customer for hosiery torn on store chair
13 Purchased ditto typewriter ribbon: $3.25
14 Reimbursed employee for parking fee: $1.25
15 Paid $4.35 express fee on purchases
17 Received replenishing check from company cashier

C. October 1 Cashed a $20 check to start petty cash fund
2 Paid $1.50 for collect telegram
3 Paid $7.50 for window washing
4 Purchased 50 eight-cent stamps
5 Purchased ditto masters: $2.50
6 Paid $4.60 express charges on purchases
7 Received a check from the company cashier to replenish the fund and to increase the size of the fund to $50.00
9 Paid six employees $1.75 each for dinner money
11 Paid $7.50 for flowers for hospitalized employee
12 Donated $5.00 to Policemen's Widows and Orphans Fund
14 Paid $3.16 freight charges on purchases
15 Received replenishing check from cashier

Bank reconciliation

Except for petty cash payments, a business will pay all of its bills by check. Some form of *check register* or checkbook record of checks issued and deposits made, and a running balance of the checking account, must be maintained by the business. Once a month a description of the state of the account is received from the bank. This *bank statement* lists chronologically all checks, deposits, and any special charges or credits recorded by the bank during the month. All entries on the statement are supported by canceled checks, and copies of deposit slips or special charge or credit memoranda, which are enclosed with the statement. The balance shown on the bank statement, except in exceedingly rare instances, differs from the balance shown on the company's check record. Immediately upon receipt of the statement it is necessary to reconcile this difference. *Reconciling* the bank statement involves adjustment of the bank statement balance and the check record balance to arrive at the *true balance*, which is the amount available to the company at the time of reconciliation.

This difference between the balances does not mean that an error has been made. It means that the company has made deposits or written checks that the bank had not yet recorded at the time the statement was prepared. Likewise, the bank has made certain charges to the account, the exact amount of which the company would not be aware until receiving the statement. Typical charges are service charges for checks written and for printing new checks, and authorized payments on behalf of the depositor such as Christmas fund allotments, insurance premiums, or loan payments. However, the reconciliation process does disclose errors which may have been made by either the company or the bank.

To reconcile the bank statement, the following steps are taken:

1. Check off each check listed on the statement against the check record. Any checks which have been written but do not appear on the statement are termed *outstanding checks* (checks which have not been cashed and returned to the bank for payment)
2. Check off each deposit listed on the statement against the check record.
3. Enter the new bank statement balance on a reconciliation form.
   a. Add any deposits shown on the check record which are not shown on the statement.
   b. Subtract the total of the outstanding checks to give the *true balance* as recorded by the bank.
4. Enter the check record balance.
   a. Add any deposits shown on the statement which were not entered in the check record.
   b. Subtract any checks shown on the statement which were not entered in the check record.
   c. Subtract any bank charges shown on the statement to give the *true balance* as recorded in the check record.

A company received their bank statement showing a balance of $6,932.20 *Example* as of June 30, while their check register balance was $6,757.75. In comparing

TABLE 5-1

Bank statement balance	$6,932.20	Check record balance	$6,757.75
Deposits not recorded by bank (1)*	+ 375.00	Deposit not entered in record (3)	+ 116.50
	$7,307.20	Check not entered in record (3)	$6,874.25
Outstanding checks (2)	− 749.50		− 78.50
True bank balance	$6,557.70		$6,795.75
		Service charges (4)	− 6.25
			$6,789.50
		Check from previous deposit returned due to insufficient funds by maker (5)	− 224.60
			$6,564.90
		Printing of checks (4)	− 7.20
		True check record balance	$6,557.70

*Numbers in parentheses refer to the items in the example.

the statement with the check record, the following discrepancies were noted (see table 5-1): (1) deposits of $200 and $175 were made after the statement was prepared; (2) there were outstanding checks for $149, $213, $365, and $22.50; (3) there were no entries in the check record for a $116.50 deposit and a $78.50 check; (4) service charges totaled $6.25, and there was an additional charge of $7.20 for printing checks; (5) a customer's check for $224.60, which had been deposited, was returned due to insufficient funds.

EXERCISE 5-2 BANK STATEMENT RECONCILIATION

1. On January 31, the bank statement balance was $914.22 while the check record balance was $796.92. There were outstanding checks for $15.75, $28.40, and $76.30. The bank had assessed a service charge of $3.15. What was the true balance?
2. The September bank statement for the Beckwith Company showed a balance of $1,245.20. The company's check record balance was $960.14. In reconciling the bank statement it was discovered that a check for $180.00 was entered in the check record as $150.00. Also, a deposit receipt for $130.00 had not been entered. Another deposit of $64.80 did not appear on the bank statement. Checks for $116.12, $54.20, and $83.14 had not been paid by the bank. The service charge on the account for the month was $3.60. Prepare the bank reconciliation.
3. When the Dixon Company received their bank statement, they found that their last deposit included customer checks for $64.50 and $18.90 which were returned due to insufficient funds. The ending balance on the statement was $2,728.81 and their check record had a balance of $3,020.80. There were outstanding checks of $32.75, $52.20, $118.36, and $220.50. Deposits of $100.00 and $150.00 were made too late to be recorded on the statement. A deposit receipt for $300.00 had been entered on the check record as $500.00. The bank statement showed a transfer of $100.00 from their checking account to their savings account. The bank had also made an authorized loan payment of $75.00. Service charges were $7.40. Prepare the reconciliation.

Compound interest

In chapter 4 interest was discussed as a business expense. For most businesses, a common type of interest payment is for short-term loans. Such interest is termed simple interest and as explained in the previous chapter is calculated by using the basic interest formula:

$$I = PRT$$

where I = dollar amount of interest
         P = principal or amount borrowed

R = rate of interest per year

T = time in years for which principal is borrowed

In the mathematics of assets, interest is of great importance in conserving and effectively using current assets. The funds of the business may be invested at simple interest, but the return is greater if they are invested at compound interest. Deposits in savings accounts in banks and in savings and loans companies draw interest on a compound basis. *Compound interest* is the amount of interest on an investment when the interest for one period is added to the principal to arrive at a higher amount on which interest is calculated for the succeeding period. The length of the *compounding period*—at the end of which interest is calculated and added to the principal—need not be a year, but must be constant. Interest is commonly compounded annually, semiannually, quarterly, or monthly, but could be compounded daily or weekly—although this is rarely the case.

The difference between simple interest and compound interest may be demonstrated by comparing, in table 5-2, the growth of $1,000 invested at 8% simple interest for 4 years and of $1,000 invested at 8% interest compounded annually for 4 years.

At the end of 1 year (the first compounding period), there is no difference

TABLE 5-2

		Maturity value = Principal + Interest	Differ- ence
1st Year			
At compound interest:	$\dfrac{\$10}{\$1{,}000} \times \dfrac{8}{\dfrac{100}{1}} \times 1 = \$80 + \$1{,}000$ =	$1,080.00	
At simple interest:	$\dfrac{\$10}{\$1{,}000} \times \dfrac{8}{\dfrac{100}{1}} \times 1 = \$80 + \$1{,}000$ =	1,080.00	0
2nd Year			
At compound interest:	$\dfrac{\$10.80}{\$1{,}080} \times \dfrac{8}{\dfrac{100}{1}} \times 1 = \$86.40 + \$1{,}080$ =	$1,166.40	
At simple interest:	$\dfrac{\$10}{\$1{,}000} \times \dfrac{8}{\dfrac{100}{1}} \times 1 = \$80.00 + \$1{,}080$ =	1,160.00	$6.40
3rd Year			
At compound interest:	$\dfrac{\$11.664}{\$1{,}166.40} \times \dfrac{8}{\dfrac{100}{1}} \times 1 = \$93.31 + \$1{,}166.40$ =	$1,259.71	
At simple interest:	$\dfrac{\$10}{\$1{,}000} \times \dfrac{8}{\dfrac{100}{1}} \times 1 = \$80.00 + \$1{,}160.00$ =	1,240.00	$19.71
4th Year			
At compound interest:	$\dfrac{\$12.5971}{\$1{,}259.71} \times \dfrac{8}{\dfrac{100}{1}} \times 1 = \$100.78 + \$1{,}259.71$ =	$1,360.49	
At simple interest:	$\dfrac{\$10}{\$1{,}000} \times \dfrac{8}{\dfrac{100}{1}} \times 1 = \$80.00 + \$1{,}240.00$ =	1,320.00	$40.49

between simple interest and compound interest. For subsequent periods, compound interest is always greater than simple interest and the difference between the two increases with each period. This difference is, of course, the interest earned on the interest portion of the accumulated funds.

If the compounding period is less than 1 year, the annual rate is designated first and then the number of compounding periods in a year. The derived rate for each compounding period is termed the *periodic rate*:

Annual Rate	Periodic Rate
8% compounded annually ÷ 2 =	4% compounded semiannually
8% compounded annually ÷ 4 =	2% compounded quarterly
8% compounded annually ÷ 12 =	$\frac{2}{3}$% compounded monthly

For instance, using the basic interest formula,

$$I = PRT$$

we calculate 8% interest on $1,000 compounded annually as follows:

$$\overset{\$10.00}{\cancel{\$1,000}} \times \frac{\overset{8}{\cancel{8}}}{\underset{1}{\cancel{100}}} \times 1 = \$80$$

whereas $\frac{2}{3}$% interest on $1,000 compounded monthly for 1 year is

$$\overset{\$10.00}{\cancel{\$1,000}} \times \frac{\overset{2}{\cancel{2}}}{\underset{\underset{1}{\cancel{3}}}{\cancel{300}}} \times \overset{4}{\cancel{12}} = \$80$$

calculation of maturity value

The formula for calculating the amount of any investment at compound interest is

$$S = P(1 + i)^n$$

where S = maturity value
         P = principal
         i = periodic rate
         n = number of compounding periods

Example: What is the maturity value of $1,000 invested at 8% compounded semiannually for 2 years?

$$S = P(1 + i)^n$$
$$= \$1,000 \, (1 + .04)^4$$
$$= \$1,000 \times (1.04)(1.04)(1.04)(1.04)$$
$$= \$1,000 \times 1.16985856$$
$$= \$1,169.86$$

In this calculation, the amount invested is always multiplied by an *accumulation factor*, represented by $(1 + i)^n$. Since the rate of increase is always constant, it has been possible to compile tables of accumulation-factor values for various periodic rates and compounding periods. Factor column 1 in the compound interest tables in appendix IV, showing the growth of $1.00 at various rates of compound interest, makes the above calculation less difficult. By simply consulting the 4% table and reading across, we find that the accumulation factor for the fourth period is 1.16985856, which we then multiply by the principal:

$$\$1,000 \times 1.16985856 = \$1,169.86$$

calculation of compound interest

Either of two formulas may be used to find the amount of the compound interest alone.

First:

$$I = S - P$$

Using the above example,

$$I = \$1,169.86 - \$1,000.00$$
$$= \$169.86$$

Second:

$$I = P[(1 + i)^n - 1]$$
$$= \$1,000 \,[1.16985856 - 1]$$
$$= \$1,000 \times .16986$$
$$= \$169.86$$

Note: In using accumulation factors from a table, the values may be rounded to the decimal digit corresponding to the number of significant digits required in the answer.

extension of compound interest tables

In the tables in appendix IV, the "Amount of 1" column (factor column 2) gives the values of the accumulation factor $(1 + i)^n$ Although values are given only through 60 periods ($n = 60$), it is possible to extend the table for any desired number of periods. This is done by multiplying the accumulation factors of any component periods whose sum is equal to the desired number of periods.

Example   What is the maturity value of $500 at 6% interest compounded monthly for 8 years?

$$S = P(1 + i)^n$$
$$= \$500 \left(1 + \tfrac{1}{2}\%\right)^{96}$$
$$= \$500 \left[\left(1 + \tfrac{1}{2}\%\right)^{60} \left(1 + \tfrac{1}{2}\%\right)^{36}\right]$$
$$= \$500(1.34885 \times 1.19668)$$
$$= \$500 \times 1.61414 = \$807.07$$

If the desired number of periods were greater than 120—for example, 196—the multiplication would be

$$(1 + i)^{60}(1 + i)^{60}(1 + i)^{60}(1 + i)^{16} = (1 + i)^{196}$$
$$1.34885 \times 1.34885 \times 1.34885 \times 1.08371 = 2.66016$$

calculation of compound rate of interest

There are occasions when the compound *rate* of interest is desired when the principal and the maturity value are known. The rate may be determined by transposing the basic compound interest formula to solve for the accumulation factor,

$$S = P(1 + i)^n$$
$$P(1 + i)^n = S$$
$$(1 + i)^n = \frac{S}{P}$$

and then using the compound interest tables.

Example   If an investment of $5,200 will have a maturity value of $7,800 in 5 years, what rate of interest compounded quarterly would be received?

$$(1 + i)^n = \frac{S}{P}$$
$$(1 + i)^{20} = \frac{\$7,800}{\$5,200}$$
$$= 1.50$$

Since this means that $1.00 will grow to $1.50 at a certain rate in 20 periods, we look in each of the compound interest tables, reading across on line 20 in the "Periods" column, until we find the value closest to 1.50 in the first factor column. In the 2% table the value is 1.485947, and in the $2\tfrac{1}{2}\%$ table it is 1.638616. Therefore, the rate would be between 2 and $2\tfrac{1}{2}\%$. The exact rate may be obtained by interpolation—the development of a ratio between the rate difference and the value difference. The lower of the known rates is, in a sense, the base:

$$\frac{\text{Unknown rate} - \text{lower known rate}}{\text{Higher known rate} - \text{lower known rate}} =$$

$$\frac{\text{Value at unknown rate} - \text{value at lower known rate}}{\text{Value at higher known rate} - \text{value at lower known rate}}$$

Let X = the unknown rate. Then

$$\frac{X - .02}{.025 - .02} = \frac{1.50 - 1.485947}{1.638616 - 1.485947}$$

$$\frac{X - .02}{.005} = \frac{.014053}{.152669}$$

Multiplying both sides by .005

$$X - .02 = \frac{.000070265}{.152669}$$

$$X - .02 = .00046$$

$$X = .02046 \text{ or } 2.046\%$$

Since the interest is compounded quarterly, the yearly rate would be

$$4 \times 2.046 = 8.18\%$$

calculation of time at compound interest

A similar procedure to that for finding the rate is used to find the time when the compound rate of interest, the principal, and the maturity value are known. The necessary transposition of the basic compound interest formula is

$$S = P(1 + i)^n$$
$$P(1 + i)^n = S$$
$$(1 + i)^n = \frac{S}{P}$$

If $1,200 is invested at 6% interest compounded semiannually, how long *Example* will it take for the investment to reach a value of $2,400?

$$(1 + i)^n = \frac{S}{P}$$

$$(1 + .03)^n = \frac{\$2,400}{\$1,200} = 2.00$$

Since 6% interest compounded semiannually is equivalent to a 3% annual rate, we first turn to the 3% compound interest table. We find that the 2.00 value falls between the 23rd period value (1.973587) and the 24th period value (2.032794). The actual time must be found by again using the interpolation process, this time with the formula:

$$\frac{\text{Unknown period } - \text{ lower known period}}{\text{Higher known period } - \text{ lower known period}} =$$

$$\frac{\text{Value at unknown period } - \text{ value at lower known period}}{\text{Value at higher known period } - \text{ value at lower known period}}$$

Let X = unknown time in periods then:

$$\frac{X - 23}{24 - 23} = \frac{\$2.00 - \$1.973587}{\$2.032794 - \$1.973587}$$

$$X - 23 = \frac{.026413}{.059207}$$

$$X - 23 = .446112$$

$$X = 23.446112 \text{ Periods}$$

Since each period has 6 months,

$$23.446112 + 6 = 140.676672 \text{ or } 140.7 \text{ months}$$
$$\text{Actual Time} = 11 \text{ years } 8.7 \text{ months}$$

calculation of present value at compound interest

The remaining term in the compound interest formula which we must consider is the amount invested P. It is often necessary to find out how much must be invested in order to obtain a specified financial goal in the future. This requires another transposition of the basic compound interest formula.

$$S = P(1 + i)^n$$
$$P(1 + i)^n = S$$

Dividing both sides by $(1 + i)^n$ gives

$$P = \frac{S}{(1 + i)^n}$$

The known maturity value is inserted for S. The value of the accumulation faction $(1 + i)^n$ is found in the compound interest tables. It is then possible to solve for P.

Example   If a maturity value of $4,000 is desired in 10 years, how much must be invested now at 4% compounded semiannually? Using factor column 1 (amount of 1.00) of the compound interest tables in appendix IV:

$$P = \frac{S}{(1 + i)^n}$$

$$P = \frac{\$4,000}{(1 + .02)^{20}}$$

$$P = \frac{\$4,000}{1.485947} = \$2,691.88$$

However, present-value tables have been prepared which simplify procedures. Factor column 4 of Appendix IV gives the present value of $1.00 at compound interest. The symbol V^n is used for the present worth (or present value) of 1.00. In other words, V^n is equivalent to $\frac{S}{(1 + i)^n}$ when the value of S is $1.00. To find the present value P of maturity values larger than $1.00 it is necessary only to multiply the V^n value by the larger amount.

If a maturity value of $4,000 is desired in 10 years, how much must be invested now at 4% compounded semiannually? Using factor column 4 ("Present worth of 1") in the compound interest table in appendix IV: *Example*

$$V^n = \frac{1}{(1 + .02)^{20}}$$

$$= .672971$$

$$P = S V^n$$

$$= \$4,000 \times .672971 = \$2,691.88$$

EXERCISE 5-3 COMPOUND INTEREST PERIODS

Determine the number of periods and the periodic rate.

	Annual Rate	Compounding Period	Time	Number of Periods	Periodic Rate
1.	6%	annual	11 years	_____	_____
2.	4	monthly	4 years	_____	_____
3.	5	quarterly	8 years	_____	_____
4.	3	semiannual	3 years, 6 months	_____	_____
5.	8	monthly	7 years, 5 months	_____	_____
6.	$8\frac{1}{2}$	monthly	2 years, 10 months	_____	_____
7.	$6\frac{1}{2}$	quarterly	5 years, 3 months	_____	_____
8.	$10\frac{1}{4}$	semiannual	6 years, 9 months	_____	_____
9.	$12\frac{1}{8}$	annual	14 years	_____	_____
10.	$9\frac{1}{2}$	quarterly	4 years, 6 months	_____	_____

EXERCISE 5-4 MATURITY VALUE

A. Without the use of tables, determine the maturity value at simple interest and at compound interest.

	Initial Investment	Annual Rate	Time	Maturity Value Compounded at Simple Interest	Compounding Period	Maturity Value at Compound Interest
1.	$ 100	9%	3 years	_____	annual	_____
2.	900	4	2 years	_____	semiannual	_____
3.	300	12	1 year	_____	quarterly	_____
4.	400	6	3 months	_____	monthly	_____
5.	800	5	1 year	_____	annual	_____
6.	800	5	1 year	_____	quarterly	_____
7.	1,000	$7\frac{1}{2}$	4 months	_____	monthly	_____
8.	600	$6\frac{3}{4}$	2 years	_____	semiannual	_____
9.	700	$5\frac{1}{2}$	1 year, 6 months	_____	annual	_____
10.	1,000	$4\frac{1}{2}$	2 years, 6 months	_____	semiannual	_____

B. Determine the accumulation factor from appendix IV and the maturity value.

	Initial Investment	Rate	Time	Compounding Period	Accumulation Factor	Maturity Value
1.	$2,400	5%	10 years	semiannual	_____	_____
2.	1,400	8	8 years	quarterly	_____	_____
3.	3,200	6	5 years	monthly	_____	_____
4.	900	$4\frac{1}{2}$	13 years	annual	_____	_____
5.	1,800	7	22 years	semiannual	_____	_____
6.	2,600	7	14 years, 6 months	semiannual	_____	_____
7.	9,300	$3\frac{1}{2}$	24 years	annual	_____	_____
8.	7,200	8	7 years, 3 months	quarterly	_____	_____
9.	5,500	6	5 years, 1 month	monthly	_____	_____
10.	6,800	8	20 years, 9 months	quarterly	_____	_____

EXERCISE 5-5 COMPOUND INTEREST

Determine the accumulation factor from appendix IV and the compound interest.

	Initial Investment	Rate	Time	Compounding Period	Accumulation Factor	Compound Interest
1.	$9,400	4%	28 years	annual	_____	_____
2.	1,700	6	19 years	semiannual	_____	_____
3.	5,300	$2\frac{1}{2}$	13 years	annual	_____	_____
4.	750	8	4 years	quarterly	_____	_____
5.	6,300	6	5 years	monthly	_____	_____
6.	4,200	$4\frac{1}{2}$	12 years	annual	_____	_____
7.	9,600	5	15 years, 6 months	semiannual	_____	_____
8.	7,700	8	7 years, 9 months	quarterly	_____	_____
9.	3,800	7	6 years, 6 months	semiannual	_____	_____
10.	2,600	18	8 years, 2 months	monthly	_____	_____

EXERCISE 5-6 COMPOUND INTEREST PROBLEMS

In solving these problems use the compound interest tables in appendix IV.

1. On August 7, 1970, Redman Brothers deposited $5,000 in a savings and loan company at an annual rate of 5% compounded quarterly. When they closed the account on February 7, 1972, what was the maturity value of their original investment?

2. James August invested $3,300 at 7% compounded semiannually. How long did it take for the investment to double itself?

3. Frilly Frocks deposited $2,600 in a bank at 4% compounded quarterly. How much was on deposit at the end of 4 years? How much interest was earned?

4. Johnson & Co. had a choice of depositing $8,500 for 6 years at 8% interest compounded semiannually or at 7% compounded quarterly. Which investment would provide the greater amount of interest and by how much?

5. What is the difference in $6,800 compounded quarterly at 6% and $6,800 compounded monthly at 6% for 4 years?

6. A company deposited $4,800 in a bank paying interest at $4\frac{1}{2}$% per year. How much more interest would the company receive if interest were paid every 6 months?

7. The Guardian Company had a credit union paying 6% interest compounded semiannually. How much would an employee receive in interest if he had $1,200 on deposit for 2 years?

8. A deposit of $2,000 was made 8 years ago; $3,000 was deposited in the same account 6 years ago; and $4,000 was deposited 4 years ago. At an annual interest rate of 4% compounded semiannually, what is the value of the total deposits today?

9. An investor with $2,500 wanted his money to grow to $7,500. At 8% compounded quarterly, how long would this take?

10. If an investment of $24,000 will have a maturity value of $62,089.68 in 12 years, what rate of interest compounded quarterly would be received?

11. If $5,000 is invested at 12% interest compounded quarterly, how long will it take for the investment to achieve a value of $12,500?

12. If $4,800 is invested at 9% compounded semiannually, how long will it take to reach a value of $14,400?

13. What is the maturity value of 4% compounded quarterly for 18 years?

14. An investment of $1,800 will have a maturity value of $3,960 in 7 years. What rate of interest compounded monthly would be received?

15. If a maturity value of $5,000 is desired in 5 years, how much must be invested at 4% compounded quarterly?

16. An investment goal is $10,000 in 8 years. How much must be invested now at 8% compounded semiannually?

17. A company bought a piece of property for $10,000, held it for 10 years, and then sold it for $18,000. What rate of return on an annual basis was received on the investment?

18. How long will it take $3,200 at 7% compounded semiannually to grow to $12,400?

19. How much must be invested at 4% compounded quarterly to accumulate to $5,000 at the end of 5 years?

SECTION 2—NOTES RECEIVABLE

A *promissory note* (or simply *note*) is an unconditional written promise to pay a certain sum of money on a definite date to a specified person or to the bearer (the person in possession of the note). This document is a contract which formalizes a debt, represents credit, and acts as a substitute for money. As such, it can be transferred from person to person and is thus a *negotiable instrument* or a type of *commercial paper*. Other types of negotiable instruments are checks, certificates of deposit, and drafts (bills of exchange). Because notes are more readily convertible into cash than are accounts receivable, (the subject of the following section), they should be the first receivable listed on the balance sheet. Likewise, when a company has borrowed money by giving notes to creditors, the first liability listed would be notes payable.

In some cases a note may require the repayment of the principal of the debt with no mention of interest. In other cases a note may require that the principal be repaid at a designated rate of interest for the life of the note. Figure 5-3 is an example of a promissory note. In terms of this note, the following definitions can be made:

Maker: The party who promises to pay the obligation: Everett Rice.

Payee: The party to whom the obligation is owed: Buffington's Department Store Inc.

Note date: Date when promise was made: November 1, 1971.

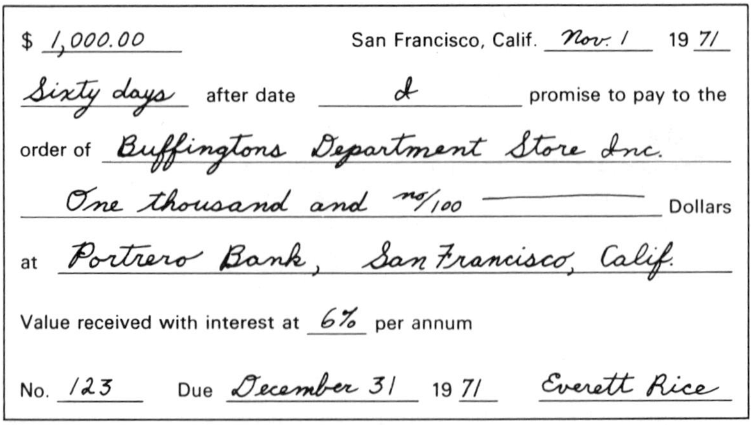

$ *1,000.00*   San Francisco, Calif. *Nov. 1*   19 *71*

Sixty days after date _____*I*_____ promise to pay to the

order of *Buffingtons Department Store Inc.*

One thousand and no/100 ———————— Dollars

at *Portrero Bank, San Francisco, Calif.*

Value received with interest at *6%* per annum

No. *123*   Due *December 31* 19 *71*   *Everett Rice*

FIGURE 5-3

Maturity date: Date when payment must be made: December 31, 1971.

Term of note: The time between the note date and maturity date: 60 days.

Face value: The dollar amount shown on the note: $1,000.

Maturity value: The amount that must be paid on the maturity date—the face value plus interest: $1,000 + \left(\$1,000 \times \frac{6}{100} \times \frac{60}{360}\right) = \$1,010.$

Discounting notes

A note may be held until the maturity date, at which time payment of the maturity value is received. However, it is possible to convert the note into a certain amount of cash at any time by taking it to a bank and *discounting* it. The bank charges a fee for this service. This fee is called a *bank discount*. It is calculated by applying a certain discount rate to the maturity value for the *term of discount*—the number of days between the discount date and the maturity date. The difference between the maturity value of the note and the discount, called the *proceeds*, is the net amount paid for the note by the bank. On the maturity date, the maker of the note pays the maturity value to the bank rather than to the original holder of the note.

discounting non-interest-bearing notes

Non-interest-bearing notes usually originate when money is borrowed from a bank. However, this does not mean that there is no charge for the use of this money. In such cases, the bank immediately deducts the bank discount from the maturity value of the note, giving the borrower the proceeds. Upon maturity, the note is paid at the maturity value—which is the same as the face value, since the charge for the use of the money was deducted in advance as discount rather than added to the principal at maturity as interest.

The formula for calculating discount is very similar to the basic interest formula ($I = PRT$):

$$D = Sdt$$

where D = amount of discount
 S = maturity value: face value for a non-interest-bearing note, face value plus interest for an interest-bearing note
 d = rate of discount
 t = term of discount (small t used to distinguish it from time in interest formula or from term of a note)

The formula for the proceeds would be

$$p = S - D$$

Example
1

(*a*) On November 1, Buffington's borrowed $10,000 from the bank for 60 days at an interest rate of 8%. What is the amount of the interest and the maturity value?

Note Date	Term of Note	Maturity Date
Nov. 1 ←	—— 60 days —— →	Dec. 31

Face Value	Interest Rate	Interest	Maturity Value
$10,000	8%	$133.33	$10,133.33

$$ I = P \times R \times T $$

$$ = \$10{,}000 \times \frac{\overset{4}{\cancel{8}}}{\underset{1}{\cancel{100}}} \times \frac{\overset{1}{\cancel{60}}}{\underset{\underset{3}{\cancel{6}}}{\cancel{360}}} = \frac{400}{3} = \$\ \ 133.33 \ \text{Interest} $$

$$\begin{array}{r} \$\ \ 133.33 \ \text{Interest} \\ +10{,}000.00 \ \text{Face value} \\ \hline \$10{,}133.33 \ \text{Maturity value} \end{array}$$

(*b*) If the loan had been made on a bank-discount basis rather than on an interest basis, Buffington's would not have had use of the full face value for the term of the note. In this case, what would be the amount of discount and the proceeds if the discount rate were 9%?

Note Date and Discount Date	Term of Note and Term of Discount	Maturity Date
Nov. 1 ←	—— 60 days —— →	Dec. 31

Proceeds	Discount Rate	Discount	Maturity Value
$9,850	9%	$150	$10,000

$$ D = S \times d \times t $$

$$ = \$10{,}000 \times \frac{\overset{3}{\cancel{9}}}{\underset{1}{\cancel{100}}} \times \frac{\overset{1}{\cancel{60}}}{\underset{\underset{2}{\cancel{6}}}{\cancel{360}}} = \frac{300}{2} = \$150 \ \text{Discount} $$

$$ p = S - D $$

$$ = \$10{,}000 - \$150 = \$9{,}850 \ \text{Proceeds} $$

(*c*) If the loan had been made on a discount basis, but a full $10,000 rather than $9,850 were required, the maturity value of the note would have to be higher. To find the maturity value in such cases requires derivation of an additional formula. This is sometimes referred to as a reverse operation similar to that discussed in chapter 4 section 2 under interest expense. In part (*b*), above, we found that

$$p = S - D$$
$$= \$10,000 - \$150 = \$9,850$$

Likewise,

$$p = S(1 - dt)$$
$$= \$10,000 \left[1 - \left(\tfrac{9}{100} \times \tfrac{60}{360} \right) \right]$$
$$= \$10,000 (1 - .015)$$
$$= \$10,000 \times .985 = \$9,850$$

This formula will work for all values, since the 1 stands for 100% of the maturity value. It is simply multiplying the maturity value by the complement of the discount rate times the term of discount. Dividing both sides of this equation by $(1 - dt)$, we have

$$p = S(1 - dt)$$

$$S = \frac{p}{1 - dt}$$

$$= \frac{\$10,000}{1 - \left(\tfrac{9}{100} \times \tfrac{60}{360} \right)} = \frac{\$10,000}{1 - .015} = \frac{\$10,000}{.985} = \$10,152.28$$

which is the required maturity value to make $10,000 immediately available.

$$D = S \times d \times t \qquad\qquad \textit{Proof}$$

$$= \$10,152.28 \times \tfrac{9}{100} \times \tfrac{60}{360} = \$152.28$$

$$p = S - D$$
$$= \$10,152.28 - \$152.28 = \$10,000.00$$

(*d*) To find the discount rate when other values are known, we would use another variation of the basic discount formula:

$$D = Sdt$$

Dividing both sides by St, we have

$$d = \frac{D}{St}$$

If we let $D = \$150$, $S = \$10,000$, and $t = 60$ days, then

$$d = \frac{\$150}{\$10,000 \times \frac{60}{360}}$$

$$= \frac{\$150}{\$10,000/6} = \$150 \times \frac{6}{\$10,000} = \frac{900}{\$10,000} = .09 \text{ or } 9\%$$

(e) To find the term of discount when the other values are known, the basic discount formula would be varied by dividing both sides of

$$D = Sdt$$

by Sd, giving

$$t = \frac{D}{Sd}$$

Letting $D = \$150$, $S = \$10,000$, and $d = 9\%$, then

$$t = \frac{\$150}{\$10,000 \times \frac{9}{100}} = \frac{\$150}{\$10,000/100} = \frac{\$150}{\$900}$$

$$= .16\tfrac{2}{3} \text{ or } \tfrac{1}{6} \times 360 \text{ days} = 60 \text{ days}$$

Example 2 Buffington's held a $1,000, 60-day, non-interest-bearing note dated November 1. On December 1 they discounted it at the bank at 9%. What was the amount of discount and the proceeds?

Note Date	Term of Note		Maturity Date
Nov. 1 ←	— 60 days	→	Dec. 31

	Discount Date	Term of Discount	
	Dec. 1 ←	— 30 days —	→

Face Value	Proceeds	Discount Rate	Discount	Maturity Value
$1,000	$992.50	9%	$7.50	$1,000

$$D = S \times d \times t$$

$$= \cancel{\$1,000} \times \dfrac{\overset{3}{\cancel{9}}}{\underset{1}{\cancel{100}}} \times \dfrac{\overset{1}{\cancel{30}}}{\underset{\underset{4}{\cancel{12}}}{\cancel{360}}} = \dfrac{30}{4} = \$7.50 \text{ Discount}$$

with $\$10$ above.

$$p = S - D$$
$$= \$1,000 - \$7.50 = \$992.50 \text{ Proceeds}$$

Discounting interest-bearing notes

In developing a formula for bank discount, it was necessary to substitute maturity value for principal or face value of the note. In discounting an interest-bearing note, there must first be the calculation of the maturity value by means of the basic interest formula and then the calculation of the discount using the bank-discount formula.

Buffington's held the $1,000, 60-day, 6% interest bearing note dated November 1 which is illustrated in figure 5-3. They discounted it on December 1 at a 9% discount rate. What was the amount of discount and the proceeds?   *Example*

Step 1:

Note Date	Term of Note	Maturity Date
Nov. 1	←——— 60 days ———→	Dec. 31

Step 2:

Face Value	Interest Rate	Interest	Maturity Value
$1,000	6%	$10	$1,010

$$I = P \times R \times T$$

$$= \cancel{\$1,000} \times \dfrac{\overset{1}{\cancel{6}}}{\underset{1}{\cancel{100}}} \times \dfrac{\overset{1}{\cancel{60}}}{\underset{\underset{1}{\cancel{6}}}{\cancel{360}}} = \$10.00$$

with $\$10$ above.

Step 3:

Discount Date	Term of Discount	Maturity Date
Dec. 1	←——— 30 days ———→	Dec. 31

Step 4:

Proceeds	Discount Rate	Discount
$1,002.42	9%	$7.58

$$D = S \times d \times t$$

$$= \cancel{\$1,010} \times \frac{\cancel{9}}{\cancel{100}} \times \frac{\cancel{30}}{\cancel{360}} = \frac{\$30.30}{4} = \$7.575 \text{ or } \$7.58$$

(with intermediate values: $\$10.10$ over $\cancel{1}$; and $\frac{\cancel{30}}{\cancel{12}}$ over 4)

$$p = S - D$$

$$= \$1,010 - \$7.58 = \$1,002.42 \text{ Proceeds}$$

Determination of Term of Discount

The procedure discussed in chapter 4 section 2 in calculating the number of days for which interest is calculated is applicable to discount problems. The term of a note may be expressed in months or in days. If in months, the due date or maturity date falls a designated number of months after the note date. Thus, a 2-month note dated April 1 would be due June 1; if the note were for a 60-day period, then the maturity date would be May 31. In the latter case (using days), each day must be counted with the date of origin excluded, but the date of payment included.

The term of discount is always figured in days. A 2-month note dated April 1 and discounted April 30 would have 32 days in the term of discount:

Days in April	30
Discount date, April	−30
	0
Days in May	+31
	31
Due date, June 1	+ 1
	32 Days in term of discount

A 60-day note dated April 1 and discounted April 30 would have 31 days in the term of discount:

Days in April	30
Discount date, April	−30
	0
Days in May including due date (May 31)	+31
	31 Days in term of discount

When the term of the note is expressed in days, it may be easier to find the term of discount by subtracting the number of days the note has been held from the term of the note. The term of discount for a 90-day note dated July 21 and discounted on August 14 could be found in the following manner:

Note Date	Term of Note	Maturity Date
July 21 ←————————— 90 days —————————————→		

Note Held	Discount Date	Term of Discount
←——— 24 days ———→ August 14 ←————— 66 Days —————→		

Days in July	31		Term of note	90
Date of origin, July	−21		Days held	−24
Days held in July	10		Term of discount	66
Days held in August	+14			
Total days held	24			

Discounting drafts

A *draft* differs from a promissory note in that it is an order for payment rather than a promise to pay. A creditor, who is called the *maker* or *drawer*, originates the document, demanding that payment be made by a debtor, who is called the *drawee*. The person who is to receive the payment is called the *payee*, who may be the drawer himself or a creditor of the drawer. The document has no validity until the drawee writes "accepted" and the date of acceptance across the face of the draft.

Drafts may be bank drafts, banker's acceptances, or trade acceptances. A *bank draft* is a check drawn on one bank by another bank. It is most often used by travelers, since a check drawn by a bank is more acceptable in a distant city than an individual's personal check. A *banker's acceptance* is often used by the seller of goods who obtains acceptance of the draft by the buyer's bank. This would entail less risk than carrying an account receivable, receiving the buyer's personal check, or having the buyer accept the draft.

A *trade acceptance*, illustrated in figure 5-4, is a type of draft demanding payment at a future date, and is commonly used in commercial transactions. The seller draws the draft on the buyer, designating himself as payee. When accepted, the debt is acknowledged, and the draft becomes negotiable in the same manner as a note.

A *sight draft* is one which calls for payment immediately—"upon sight," which constitutes acceptance. Payment is usually made to the seller's bank, which then authorizes the freight carrier to release the goods to the buyer. A *time draft* calls for payment at a future time. This may be designated as so many days "after date," (meaning the date of the draft) or "after sight" (meaning on date of acceptance). However, the seller may receive payment, less discount, at any time by discounting the draft at a bank.

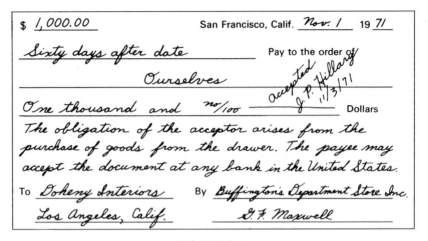

FIGURE 5-4

Example   Buffington's provided interior decorating service and imported fabrics to Doheny Interiors. Credit was arranged by means of a 60-day after-date trade acceptance drawn up on November 1. On November 16, Buffington's discounted the draft at a 7% discount rate. How much did they receive from the bank?

$$p = S(1 - dt)$$

$$= \$1,000 \left[1 - \left(\frac{7}{100} \times \frac{45}{360} \right) \right]$$

$$= \$1,000(1 - .00875)$$

$$= \$1,000 \times .99125 = \$991.25 \text{ Proceeds}$$

or

$$D = S \times d \times t$$

$$= \$\overset{\$10}{\underset{1}{\cancel{1,000}}} \times \frac{7}{\underset{1}{\cancel{100}}} \times \frac{\overset{45}{\cancel{1}}}{\underset{8}{\cancel{360}}} = \frac{\$70}{8} = \$8.75$$

$$p = S - D$$

$$= \$1,000 - \$8.75 = \$991.25$$

Note: If the draft had designated a due date 60 days after sight and it was accepted on November 3, then the maturity date would have been January 2 and the term of discount 47 days.

EXERCISE 5-7 MATURITY DATE

Determine the maturity date of each of the following notes:

Date of Note	Term of Note	Maturity Date
1. August 9	1 month	_____
2. August 9	30 days	_____
3. February 3	60 days	_____
4. September 18	90 days	_____
5. October 23	3 months	_____
6. March 14	48 days	_____
7. December 8	75 days	_____
8. October 30	180 days	_____
9. May 17	90 days	_____
10. December 20	120 days	_____

EXERCISE 5-8 TERM OF DISCOUNT

Determine the maturity date and the term of discount for each of the following notes.

Date of Note	Term of Note	Discount Date	Maturity Date	Term of Discount
1. July 5	3 months	August 15	_____	_____
2. September 17	30 days	September 21	_____	_____
3. March 13	6 months	July 5	_____	_____
4. December 22	60 days	December 28	_____	_____
5. February 3	2 months	March 5	_____	_____
6. October 28	120 days	December 7	_____	_____
7. January 7	90 days	March 17	_____	_____
8. May 15	4 months	September 1	_____	_____
9. October 17	75 days	October 19	_____	_____
10. November 25	120 days	February 28	_____	_____

EXERCISE 5-9 PROCEEDS

Determine the term of discount and the proceeds of each of the following non-interest-bearing notes.

	Maturity Value	Note Date	Term of Note	Discount Date	Discount Rate	Term of Discount	Proceeds
1.	$1,000	4/3	1 month	4/4	6%	_____	_____
2.	540	7/17	30 days	7/26	6	_____	_____
3.	450	1/8	3 months	3/12	8	_____	_____
4.	800	5/12	60 days	5/14	8	_____	_____
5.	720	4/30	90 days	6/1	4	_____	_____
6.	900	3/16	3 months	4/16	7	_____	_____
7.	300	6/10	90 days	7/31	5	_____	_____
8.	600	8/24	120 days	8/31	$4\frac{1}{2}$	_____	_____
9.	660	12/7	60 days	12/9	$6\frac{1}{2}$	_____	_____
10.	750	10/14	6 months	11/14	$8\frac{1}{2}$	_____	_____

EXERCISE 5-10 PROCEEDS

Determine the proceeds of each of the following notes.

	Face Value	Note Date	Term of Note	Interest Rate	Discount Date	Discount Date	Proceeds
1.	$1,000	3/1	3 months	6%	4/1	6%	_____
2.	800	10/4	60 days	4	10/14	6	_____
3.	600	1/5	75 days	7	1/10	8	_____
4.	500	7/15	30 days	5	7/16	7	_____
5.	750	4/20	2 months	8	5/1	7	_____
6.	840	11/6	30 days	7	11/10	9	_____
7.	920	2/15	90 days	5	2/17	6	_____
8.	360	6/20	4 months	$6\frac{3}{4}$	7/20	$7\frac{1}{2}$	_____
9.	480	9/10	60 days	$4\frac{1}{4}$	10/1	$6\frac{1}{2}$	_____
10.	675	12/14	120 days	$7\frac{1}{2}$	12/28	$8\frac{1}{2}$	_____

EXERCISE 5-11 PROBLEMS ON NOTES

1. The owner of Harvey Food Store borrowed $1,000 from his uncle, giving him a 60-day non-interest-bearing note. Thirty days after receipt of the note, his uncle discounted it at a bank at an 8% rate. How much did his uncle receive from the bank?
2. On March 13, the Belmont Tool & Die Works discounted a $4,800, 7%, 60-day note dated March 1. The bank's discount rate was 8%. What were the proceeds of the note?

3. The Puma Supply Company wanted to borrow $3,000 for 3 months. They could obtain the loan from the Third National Bank at a 7% interest rate or from the Fourth National Bank at a $6\frac{1}{2}$% discount rate. What would be the difference in cost of the loan?

4. Buffington's accepted an 8%, 90-day, $1,200 note from the sale of used office equipment. The note was dated December 28, but they discounted it at $7\frac{1}{2}$% on February 2. What were the proceeds of the note?

5. The Bruce Company shipped $1,800 of merchandise to Erin Brothers. They gave the carrier an order bill of lading and sent a 30-day sight draft to a bank located in the same city as Erin Brothers. Erin accepted the draft on April 7 and the Bruce Company discounted it on April 13 at $6\frac{1}{2}$%. What were the proceeds of the draft?

6. On September 3, the Marcia Manufacturing Company accepted a 60-day, $3,600 time draft dated August 28. The Martion Company, which was the drawer of the draft, discounted it on September 15 at 7%. What were the proceeds of the draft?

7. On January 7, the Marston Company received an $1,800 draft from Langley Enterprises. The draft was payable 4 months after date. How much would the bank pay Langley if they discounted the note on February 4 at 6%?

8. How much will a bank pay on a $1,450 draft dated August 9, due 90 days after date, accepted September 3, and discounted October 5?

9. A 7% interest-bearing note for $880, dated April 10 and due in 60 days, is discounted on May 5 at 6%. What are the proceeds?

10. The P. E. Joyce Company received a 3-month $5\frac{1}{2}$% interest-bearing note for $8,970 on August 14. They discounted it on August 16 at 7%. What were the proceeds?

11. If a loan were to be made on an 8% discount basis, what maturity value would be required to make $5,400 immediately available?

12. When a note with a $6,800 maturity value was discounted 90 days before maturity, the amount of discount was $110.50. What was the rate of discount?

13. A note with a $1,600 maturity value was discounted at $8\frac{1}{2}$%, the discount amounting to $17.00. What was the term of discount?

14. The Warren Jackson Company discounted their personal, 60-day, non-interest-bearing note at a bank. If the proceeds were $2,800 and the discount rate was $6\frac{1}{2}$%, what was the face value of the note?

15. The proceeds of a 7% non-interest-bearing note were $1,491.25 when a $1,500 note was discounted. What was the term of discount?

Present value at true discount

non-interest-bearing notes

We have found that *bank discount* is interest paid in advance on the maturity value of a note. This is calculated by use of the formula $D = Sdt$. By deducting the bank discount from the maturity value, we arrive at the proceeds; in terms of a formula,

$$p = S - D$$

The amount or principal which must be invested to obtain a given maturity value is termed *present value*. The difference between the maturity value of a note and its present value is called *true discount*. While bank discount is interest paid in advance on the maturity value, true discount is interest paid at maturity on a principal.

Present value is calculated by use of the formula:

$$P = \frac{S}{1 + \gamma t}$$

where P = present value   5
S = maturity value
1 = 100% of the present value
γ = rate of true discount
t = term of note in years

Accordingly true discount (T.D.) is:

$$T.D. = S - P$$

Referring to example 1, (part *b*), on p. 158, we found that $10,000 borrowed on a bank-discount basis at 9% for 60 days resulted in proceeds of $9,850. If true discount were applied, the present value and the amount of true discount of the note would be found as follows:

$$P = \frac{S}{1 + rt}$$

$$= \frac{\$10,000}{1 + \left(\frac{9}{100} \times \frac{60}{360}\right)}$$

$$= \frac{\$10,000}{1 + .015} = \frac{\$10,000}{1.015} = \$9,852.22 \text{ Present value}$$

$$T.D. = \qquad S - P$$

$$= \$10,000 - \$9,842.22 = \$147.78$$

Thus, $9,852.22 would mature to $10,000 in 60 days at 9% interest. The difference of $2.22 between proceeds ($9,850) and present value ($9,852.22) is the 9% interest for 60 days on the $147.78 of true discount. In other words, bank discount includes an interest charge on interest.

interest-bearing notes

The procedure for finding the present value of an interest-bearing note differs from the procedure for a non-interest-bearing note only in the necessity of calculating the maturity value, which differs from the face value by the amount of interest. Referring to the example in our discussion of discounting interest-bearing notes (p. 162), proceeds of $1,002.42 resulted when a $1,000, 60-day, 6% note was discounted at 9%, 30 days before the maturity date. The present value and the true discount on the discount date would be calculated as follows:

$$P = \frac{S}{1 + rt}$$

$$= \frac{\$1,010}{1 + \left(\frac{9}{100} \times \frac{30}{360}\right)}$$

$$= \frac{\$1,010}{1 + (.0075)} = \frac{\$1,010}{1.0075} = \$1,002.48 \text{ Present value}$$

$$\text{T.D.} = S - P$$

$$= \$1,010 - \$1,002.48 = \$7.52 \text{ True discount}$$

Again, the 6¢ difference between proceeds ($1,002.42) and present value ($1,002.48) represents 9% on the true discount of $7.52 for 30 days.

A more common application of the present-value concept, pertaining to annuities, is discussed in chapter 6.

EXERCISE 5-12 PRESENT VALUE AND TRUE DISCOUNT

A. Determine the present value and true discount of each of the following non-interest-bearing notes:

	Maturity Value	Note Date	Term of Note	Discount Date	Discount Rate	Present Value	True Discount
1.	$1,000	3/12	60 days	4/11	6%	_____	_____
2.	450	8/8	30 days	8/10	7	_____	_____
3.	940	4/17	2 months	5/1	8	_____	_____
4.	850	1/15	45 days	2/15	5	_____	_____
5.	680	9/22	1 month	9/24	9	_____	_____
6.	750	12/10	90 days	12/20	8	_____	_____
7.	350	7/18	3 months	7/20	$5\frac{1}{2}$	_____	_____
8.	400	4/28	60 days	5/1	$6\frac{1}{2}$	_____	_____

	Maturity Value	Note Date	Term of Note	Discount Date	Discount Rate	Present Value	True Discount
9.	600	5/30	60 days	6/29	$8\frac{1}{4}$	_____	_____
10.	500	10/14	30 days	10/16	$7\frac{3}{4}$	_____	_____

B. Determine the present value and true discount of each of the following interest-bearing notes:

	Face Value	Note Date	Term of Note	Interest Rate	Discount Date	Discount Rate	Present Value	True Discount
1.	$1,000	6/1	60 days	6%	7/1	8%	_____	_____
2.	500	4/23	1 month	8	4/25	9	_____	_____
3.	800	10/14	30 days	6	10/24	7	_____	_____
4.	400	1/2	2 months	9	1/12	8	_____	_____
5.	600	3/16	90 days	7	3/20	8	_____	_____
6.	950	9/8	3 months	8	10/1	$8\frac{1}{2}$	_____	_____
7.	450	7/15	45 days	$6\frac{1}{2}$	7/30	$7\frac{1}{2}$	_____	_____
8.	875	8/9	90 days	$8\frac{1}{4}$	8/19	8	_____	_____
9.	675	11/5	30 days	$7\frac{3}{4}$	11/7	8	_____	_____
10.	550	5/1	60 days	$5\frac{1}{2}$	6/1	$6\frac{1}{2}$	_____	_____

EXERCISE 5-13 PROBLEMS ON NOTES

1. Buffington's held a $6,000, non-interest-bearing 6-month note dated April 15. They discounted it on July 15 at 6%. What were the proceeds at bank discount?

2. In problem 1, above, what was the present value at July 15, and what would have been the amount of true discount on that date?

3. A 90-day non-interest-bearing note for $2,860, dated March 18 was discounted on April 1 at 8%. What were the present value and true discount at the time of discount?

4. What are the present value and true discount at a 7% rate, on September 21, of a $3,500, 60-day non-interest-bearing note dated September 1?

5. What is the present value of $6\frac{1}{2}$% true discount on February 12 of a 90-day non-interest-bearing note for $1,250, dated February 4?

6. A non-interest-bearing 60-day note which had been held for 30 days was discounted at 7% true discount. At the time of discount, what were the present value and the true discount?

7. Buffington's held a $1,840, 9%, 40-day note dated March 18 and dis-

counted on March 28 at 8% true discount. What was the present value and the true discount on March 28?

8. On July 5, Barber Bros. discounted a $2,100, 6%, 60-day note dated June 15. At $6\frac{1}{2}$% true discount, what was the present value and true discount on the day of discount?

9. Miss Pat Fashions discounted at $7\frac{1}{2}$% true discount a 3-month $4,500 note on April 2. The note was dated May 16 and specified interest at $5\frac{1}{2}$%. What were the present value and true discount?

10. Sparks & Sons gave the Hurley Hoist Co. a $2,600, 90-day, 7% note dated May 1. Hurley Hoist Co. discounted the note on May 15 at 6%. At that time what would have been (a) the proceeds at bank discount? (b) the present value? (c) the true discount?

SECTION 3—ACCOUNTS RECEIVABLE

Accounts receivable are classified as current assets because they are continually being converted to cash as customers pay on their accounts. They may also be used as collateral for bank loans during periods when there is a drain on working capital. Buffington's usually experiences their greatest financial requirements of the year during the early fall, when inventories have been peaked but the crest of the Christmas sales volume has not yet arrived.

Since a company offering credit must replace the merchandise sold before receiving full payment for it, a greater amount of capital is required to finance credit sales. For this reason, some companies may offer credit terms to be competitive, but immediately sell their accounts receivable to financial institutions. In such cases, the amount of discount they must grant in selling the accounts is considered to be less than the cost of maintaining credit and collective operations plus the cost of the additional capital required in the business.

Financial firms performing the credit function for industrial companies are called *factors*. In financing a business through *factoring*, the accounts are sold "without recourse" to the seller (i.e., the seller is not responsible for bad debts), and the customers make payment directly to the factor. In retailing, the accounts are often pledged or assigned to a financial institution as collateral for loans. In such cases, the store's customers are unaware of the assignment and make their payments directly to the retailer. In contrast to outright sale of the accounts, the retailer is responsible for any bad debts.

types of credit

Terms of sale or the types of credit granted to retailers were discussed in chapter 3. The types of credit granted by retailers to customers are varied, but may be generally classified as open-account, installment credit, or revolving credit. In all types, the decision to extend credit to a customer is based on an assessment of the individual's character, capacity, and capital. *Character* refers to the individual's willingness to pay; *capacity* means ability to pay out of current income; and *capital* is his assets, to which the retailer might lay claim to force payment.

In *open-account credit*, the customer receives the merchandise and agrees to pay within a certain period of time—usually, 30 days. The customer pays no more than the cash price when this type of credit is extended. However, if payment is not paid within the specified time, a service charge is assessed. This charge is customarily 1 to $1\frac{1}{2}$% of the unpaid balance each month.

Installment credit usually requires (1) a written contract; (2) a down payment; (3) additional payments predetermined as to size and kind; (4) a separate charge for the credit extended; (5) some security. The finance charge may be assessed monthly on the unpaid balance as of the beginning of the month. It may also be assessed on the original balance and divided evenly among the required number of payments. There are three basic types of installment contracts; the conditional sales contract, the chattel mortgage, and the bailment lease (leasing with option to buy).

The *conditional sales contract* leaves title to the merchandise in the retailer's hands until full payment has been made. It provides for repossession if full payment is not made. Upon repossession, the buyer is still liable for the difference between the resale value of the merchandise and the balance (including accumulated service charges) owed at the time of repossession.

The *chattel-mortgage-type contract* transfers title to the buyer at the time of sale and the seller receives a mortgage on the merchandise. If payment is not made as agreed, the seller may foreclose on his mortgage and repossess the goods.

The *bailment lease* or *leasing with option to buy* is quite similar to the conditional sales contract. Title remains with the retailer, who is considered to be merely leasing the merchandise to the customer. However, after a specified number of payments, title is transferred to the buyer for a nominal sum—such as $1.00.

Revolving credit (frequently referred to as revolving accounts) lies between open-account credit and installment credit. It may require a certain fixed payment each month with a maximum-charge limit equivalent to the total of a certain number of payments—such as 6 or 12. It may be offered to open-account customers as an option if they decide not to pay the balance within the open-account period. In either case, it grants full use of a certain amount of credit at all times. It also requires a service charge after a period of time equivalent to the open-account period. The customary service charge is 1 to $1\frac{1}{2}$% of the unpaid balance each month.

FINANCE CHARGES

Retailers usually refer to the charge assessed on any credit purchase as a *service charge* rather than a "carrying charge" or "interest." The distinction between these terms has been vague and confusing, as have other credit terms and practices. The federal Truth-in-Lending Law (Consumer Credit Protection Act) of

1969 requires that all costs, terms, and conditions of credit transactions to be expressed in the same terms by everybody extending credit to consumers. The two most important items of required information are the finance charge and the annual percentage rate. The *finance charge* is the total of all charges to be paid for credit. Although it includes not only interest but also all service charges or carrying charges such as loan fees, investigation fees, and premiums for required insurance, in calculating the finance charge we shall refer to it as *interest*. The annual *percentage rate* is simply the finance charge expressed as an annual rate. This rate must be accurate to the nearest one-quarter of 1%. It is often referred to as the *nominal rate*. The federal act does not fix maximum rates; these are set by state law and vary from state to state. Retailers may charge what they please under this act and use any method of assessing charges. The main point is that there must be full disclosure of all costs and conditions of the credit in standard terms.

declining-balance method of financing

Typical of the revolving-credit plans, and a feature of some installment contracts, is the assessment of a service charge on the unpaid balance each month. If the charge is 1%, the annual rate would be 12 times larger or 12%; for $1\frac{1}{2}\%$ the annual equivalent would be 18%. The amount of the payments would be less each month as the balance declined. However, payments of the same amount are sometimes deemed to be more practical. This can be accomplished by dividing the total amount of interest plus the principal by the number of payments. The following example demonstrates these two ways of using the declining-balance method.

(a) The total cash price and tax on a television was $450. A down pay-   *Example*
ment of $50 was made, leaving $400 to be financed over an 8-month period. If there were no finance charges, this would require 8 monthly payments of $50 each to retire the debt. With financing terms of 1% a month, the total of the payments would be greater by the amount paid for the credit service (see table 5-3).

TABLE 5-3   schedule for part (a) of example

Payment	Unpaid Balance, Beginning of Month	Payment on Principal	Payment of Interest	Total Payment
1	$ 400	$ 50	$ 4.00	$ 54.00
2	350	50	3.50	53.50
3	300	50	3.00	53.00
4	250	50	2.50	52.50
5	200	50	2.00	52.00
6	150	50	1.50	51.50
7	100	50	1.00	51.00
8	50	50	.50	50.50
	$1,800	$400	$18.00	$418.00

(b) To arrive at the same totals with equal payments, the $400 principal would be added to the $18.00 total interest and the sum divided by the 8 payments. The payment of the total interest is thus spread evenly over the eight months (see table 5-4).

TABLE 5-4   schedule for part (b) of example

Payment	Unpaid Balance, Beginning of Month	Payment on Principal	Payment of Interest	Total Payment
1	$ 400	$ 50	$ 2.25	$ 52.25
2	350	50	2.25	52.25
3	300	50	2.25	52.25
4	250	50	2.25	52.25
5	200	50	2.25	52.25
6	150	50	2.25	52.25
7	100	50	2.25	52.25
8	50	50	2.25	52.25
	$1,800	$400	$18.00	$418.00

A common problem is the determination of the total interest and the uniform monthly payment under the declining-balance method. In schedule (a) (table 5-3), the payments of monthly interest constitute an arithmetic progression, since there is a constant difference of 50¢ between each interest amount. The sum of any arithmetic progression can be approximated by multiplying the sum of the highest and lowest values by the number of items in the series divided by two.

Example

First-month interest = $400 × $\frac{1}{100}$ = $4.00

Last-month interest = $50 × $\frac{1}{100}$ = $.50

$$\text{Total interest} = (\text{First-month interest} + \text{Last-month interest}) \times \frac{\text{Number of payments}}{2}$$

$$= (\$4.00 + \$.50) \times \frac{8}{2}$$

$$= \$4.50 \times 4 = \$18.00$$

$$\text{Monthly payment} = \frac{\text{Principal} + \text{Total interest}}{\text{Number of payments}}$$

$$= \frac{\$400 + \$18.00}{8} = \frac{\$418}{8} = \$52.25$$

Another arithmetic approach to determining the interest charge on the declining-balance method is to use the formula

$$I = \frac{RP(n + 1)}{2M}$$

where

I = total interest
R = equivalent annual rate
P = principal or original balance
n = number of payments
M = number of payment periods in year

Thus,

$$\frac{.12 \times \$400 \times (8 + 1)}{2 \times 12} = \frac{\$432}{24} = \$18.00$$

$$\text{Monthly payment} = \frac{\$400 + \$18}{8} = \frac{\$418}{8} = \$52.25$$

Note: The value of M would vary with the payment plan. Our example is based on monthly payments, so M = 12. If payments had been weekly, then M = 52; if quarterly, M = 4; if semiannually, M = 2.

It is also possible to find the total interest and the amount of the periodic payment by use of the "Partial Payment" column (the sixth column of factors) in the appendix IV tables. This column gives the amount of the periodic payment necessary to pay off a loan of $1.00 in from 1 to 60 periods. Using these tables for the preceding example,

$$\text{Monthly payment} = \$400 \times .13069 \ (1\% \text{ periodic rate for 8 periods})$$
$$= \$52.28$$
$$\text{Interest} = \text{Total payments} - \text{Principal}$$
$$= (52.28 \times 8) - \$400$$
$$= \$418.24 - \$400 = \$18.24$$

Note: The use of these tables gives the most accurate answer because values are carried out to the tenth place.

Original-balance method of financing

In retail credit, the declining-balance method is most often used for revolving accounts. If a big-ticket item such as a stove or refrigerator is purchased on the installment basis, a special *contract account* may be opened for this particular purchase. The contract usually provides for a fixed rate of interest on the original balance, which is then added to the original balance and the total divided by the number of payments to arrive at the uniform amount of the installment payments. In the next section, we shall find that this nominal rate is less than the true or effective rate, since the full amount on which the interest is based is not available to the purchaser during the repayment period.

Example   If the preceding television sale (described on p. 173) was financed for 8 months at 6% of the original balance, the amount of interest and payments would be calculated as follows:

Cash price	$450.00
Down payment	− 50.00
Original balance	$400.00

$$\text{Interest} = \overset{\$4}{\cancel{\$400}} \times \frac{\overset{1}{\cancel{6}}}{\underset{1}{\cancel{100}}} \times \frac{\overset{4}{\cancel{8}}}{\underset{\underset{1}{\cancel{2}}}{\cancel{12}}} = \$16.00$$

Total payment	$416.00

Monthly payments = $416.00 ÷ 8 = $52.00

true rate of interest

The finance charge is the difference between the cash price and the installment price (any down payment plus all installment payments) regardless of the method used in installment financing. In table 5-4, the periodic rate of 1% per month is equivalent to an effective rate of 12% per year. This can also be shown by transposing the basic interest formula:

$$I = PRT$$

$$\$18 = \$1,800 \times R \times \tfrac{1}{12}$$

$$\frac{\$18}{\$1,800} = R \times \tfrac{1}{12}$$

$$\frac{\$18}{\$1,800} \div \tfrac{1}{12} = R$$

$$R = 12 \times \frac{\$18}{\$1,800}$$

$$= \frac{12 \times \$18}{\$1,800} = \frac{\$216}{\$1,800} = .12 \text{ or } 12\%$$

We shall henceforth identify this effective rate with the symbol r rather than the R which is normally used to express a nominal annual rate.

Using table 5-4 and the arithmetic progression principal, a formula may be developed which can be used to find the *true rate of interest* in all types of installment loans or purchases:

1. Using the "Unpaid Balance" column of table 5-4 as an arithmetic

progression,

$$\text{Sum} = \text{Largest value} \times \frac{\text{Number of payments} + 1}{2}$$

$$= \$400 \times \frac{8 + 1}{2} = \$400 \times 4.5 = \$1,800$$

2. We found previously that

$$r = \frac{12 \times \$18}{\$1,800} = 12\%$$

or

$$r = \frac{\text{Number of payments periods in year} \times \text{Interest}}{\text{Original balance} \times \dfrac{\text{Number of payments} + 1}{2}}$$

3. The formula may be more easily used if both numerator and denominator are multiplied by 2:

$$r = \frac{2 \times \text{Payment periods in year} \times \text{Interest}}{\text{Original balance} \times (\text{Number of payments} + 1)}$$

Thus, if M = payment periods in year, I = interest, P = original balance, and n = number of payments, then

$$r = \frac{2MI}{P(n + 1)}$$

4. Applying this new formula to our example,

$$r = \frac{2 \times 12 \times \$18}{\$400(8 + 1)} = \frac{24 \times \$18}{\$400 \times 9} = \frac{\$432}{\$3,600} = .12 \text{ or } 12\%$$

Note: It should again be recognized that the value of M will change with the payment plan—i.e., for weekly payments, M = 52; for quarterly payments, M = 4; for semiannual payments, M = 2.

application to original-balance method

Using the example under the explanation of the original-balance method on p. 176, the following steps are taken in calculating the effective annual rate. In this case, the balance was financed for 8 months at 6% of the original balance.

1. Calculate the original balance or the amount being financed:

Cash price	$450
Down payment	50
Original balance	$400

2. Calculate the installment price:

Down payment	$ 50
Installment payments: $52.00 × 8 =	416
Installment price	$466

3. Compare cash price with installment price to find total installment cost:

Installment price	$466
Less: Cash price	450
	$ 16

4. Apply true-interest formula:

$$r = \frac{2MI}{P(n + 1)}$$

$$= \frac{2 \times 12 \times \$16}{\$400(8 + 1)} = \frac{\overset{1}{\cancel{24}} \times \$16}{\underset{\substack{\$50 \\ 3}}{\cancel{\$400} \times \cancel{9}}} = \frac{\$16}{\$150} = .1067 \text{ or } 10.67\%$$

The reason that the effective annual rate is higher than the nominal annual rate lies in the fact that the original balance is not available to the buyer during the entire repayment period. The $400 principal was repaid by $50 from each of the 8 payments. The balance of the payments covered the finance charge. The use period for each $50 part of the $400 principal is shown in diagram form in table 5-5.

TABLE 5-5

Use of $400 Principal	8-Month Repayment Period	Use Period
1st $50		1 month
2nd 50		2 months
3rd 50		3
4th 50		4
5th 50		5
6th 50		6
7th 50		7
8th 50		8
		36 months

The interest was calculated on the $400 original balance, but only $50 of this amount was available to the buyer for the full 8-month period. In reality, $50 was loaned for 36 months or the total of the use periods for each $50 payment. Using our basic interest formula, we find that

$$I = PRT$$

$$\$16 = \$50 \times R \times \frac{36}{12}$$

$$\frac{\$16}{R} = \$50 \times \frac{\overset{3}{\cancel{36}}}{\underset{1}{\cancel{12}}}$$

$$= \$150$$

$$R = \frac{\$16}{\$150} = .1067 \text{ or } 10.67\%$$

effective rate equivalent to nominal rate

It is often helpful to determine directly the effective rate equivalent to a certain *nominal rate*. This can be done by use of the following formula:

$$r = \frac{2nR}{n + 1}$$

where r = effective interest
   n = number of payments
   R = nominal interest rate

We found above that payment of the original balance of $400 in 8 payments at 6% resulted in a true rate of 10.67%. Using the above formula, the equivalence may be found directly.

$$r = \frac{2 \times 8 \times 6\%}{8 + 1}$$

$$= \frac{96\%}{9} = 10.67\%$$

EXERCISE 5-14 DECLINING BALANCE METHOD

A. Determine the total interest and the periodic payment for each of the following original balances financed under the declining-balance method. Use one of the arithmetic methods.

Original Balance	Periodic Rate	Payment Plan	Total Interest	Periodic Payment
1. $1,000	1%	12 monthly	———	———
2. 500	$1\frac{1}{2}$	8 monthly	———	———
3. 750	2	8 quarterly	———	———
4. 640	$\frac{3}{4}$	24 monthly	———	———
5. 980	5	4 semiannual	———	———
6. 360	3	4 quarterly	———	———
7. 880	$1\frac{1}{4}$	18 monthly	———	———
8. 250	$\frac{1}{4}$	26 weekly	———	———
9. 300	$\frac{1}{2}$	12 weekly	———	———
10. 775	$1\frac{1}{2}$	24 monthly	———	———

B. Determine the total interest and the periodic payment for each of the following original balances, financed under the declining-balance method. Use the "Partial payment column," (the last column of factors) in the appendix IV tables.

Original Balance	Periodic Rate	Payment Plan	Total Interest	Periodic Payment
1. $1,000	$1\frac{1}{2}$	12 monthly	———	———
2. 360	1	18 monthly	———	———
3. 720	$\frac{1}{2}$	24 monthly	———	———
4. 440	$1\frac{1}{2}$	9 monthly	———	———
5. 950	$2\frac{1}{2}$	9 quarterly	———	———
6. 225	$\frac{1}{2}$	12 weekly	———	———
7. 890	5%	4 semiannual	———	———
8. 980	$1\frac{1}{2}$	36 monthly	———	———
9. 750	$3\frac{1}{2}$	8 quarterly	———	———
10. 630	$4\frac{1}{2}$	6 quarterly	———	———

EXERCISE 5-15 ORIGINAL BALANCE METHOD

Determine the original balance, the total interest, and the periodic payment for each of the following purchases financed under the original-balance method.

Cash Price	Down Payment	Annual Rate	Payment Plan	Original Balance	Total Interest	Periodic Payment
1. $1,000	$200	6%	12 monthly	———	———	———
2. 2,400	$500	8	24 monthly	———	———	———
3. 3,200	$320	9	18 monthly	———	———	———

	Cash Price	Down Payment	Annual Rate	Payment Plan	Original Balance	Total Interest	Periodic Payment
4.	4,850	10%	7	36 monthly	——	——	——
5.	1,750	20%	$4\frac{1}{2}$	9 monthly	——	——	——
6.	760	$80	24	24 weekly	——	——	——
7.	1,440	$240	10	8 quarterly	——	——	——
8.	2,600	$400	8	4 semiannual	——	——	——
9.	2,900	$300	$7\frac{1}{2}$	9 monthly	——	——	——
10.	1,800	30%	$6\frac{1}{2}$	6 monthly	——	——	——

EXERCISE 5-16 TRUE ANNUAL RATE OF INTEREST

Determine the periodic payment and the true annual rate of interest for each of the following purchases financed under the original-balance method.

	Cash Price	Down Payment	Annual Rate	Payment Plan	Periodic Payment	True Annual Rate
1.	$1,100	$100	8%	12 monthly	——	——
2.	760	$160	6	9 monthly	——	——
3.	340	0	$6\frac{1}{2}$	12 monthly	——	——
4.	3,850	$400	7	24 monthly	——	——
5.	5,450	10%	$7\frac{1}{2}$	36 monthly	——	——
6.	2,600	15%	$5\frac{1}{2}$	9 monthly	——	——
7.	950	20%	$6\frac{1}{2}$	12 monthly	——	——
8.	85	$15	12	24 weekly	——	——
9.	1,480	$200	8	8 quarterly	——	——
10.	1,750	$250	$6\frac{1}{2}$	4 semiannual	——	——

EXERCISE 5-17 PROBLEMS ON FINANCE CHARGES

Use an arithmetic method in solving the following problems.

1. Buffington's sold a $250 set of china on a revolving account which required the payment of $1\frac{1}{2}$% a month on the declining balance. The set was paid off in 10 months. What was the monthly payment and how much total interest was paid?

2. Buffington's opened a contract account for one of their revolving-account customers when he purchased a boat and motor. The cash price was $1,850; after a down payment of $250, the balance was financed over 18 months at 6% a year. What was the monthly payment and how much total interest did Buffington's receive?

3. A finance company loaned $400 to Arthur Strickler. It was to be repaid in 12 equal monthly payments at an annual interest rate of 18% on the declining balance. How much was each of the monthly payments?

4. John Chapin borrowed $750, agreeing to pay the interest on the declining balance at an annual rate of 8% in 4 quarterly payments. How much was each payment?

5. A television was purchased for $550 plus tax of 5%. A down payment of $57.50 was made and the balance was financed at 1% a month on the declining balance. Total payment was made in 14 months. How much was the periodic payment and how much total interest was paid?

6. Barrows Furniture extended credit on a $1,200 dining room set. The terms were 10% down, the balance to be paid in 15 months with interest at 2% a month on the declining balance. How much was the total interest paid on this contract and how much was the monthly payment?

7. The House of Mark advertised a bedroom set for $695.00. Credit terms were offered which required no down payment and 24 monthly payments of $34.50. How much interest would be paid if a customer accepted these credit terms?

8. The Straight Line Office Supply Co. sold a safe for $1,850. After a down payment of $500, the customer paid 7% interest on the original balance and a carrying charge of $25.00. The purchase was paid off in 12 equal monthly payments. How much were the payments?

9. A customer bought carpeting for $950, paying 20% down and agreeing to pay the balance in 12 months at $\frac{3}{4}$% a month on the declining balance plus $24.00 carrying charge on which no interest was to be paid. How large was each payment?

10. A used-car dealer offered a customer a $300 trade-in allowance on his old car as a down payment on a newer car. The cash price of the car was $2,150 and the unpaid balance was to be financed over a 24-month period at $1\frac{1}{2}$% a month on the declining balance. How much were the monthly payments and what would be the amount of the total interest?

11. John Hartley purchased a set of golf clubs for $165. He paid $25 down and agreed to pay the balance in 8 monthly payments of $19.50 each. What rate of interest did he pay?

12. James Brooks bought a tape recorder for $175.95. After a down payment of $25.95, he agreed to pay the balance in 18 monthly payments of $9.05 each. What yearly rate of interest was he paying?

13. A lamp was purchased for $40. The tax was 5% and a down payment of $12 was made. The balance was paid in 4 monthly payments of $8.00 each. What was the annual rate of interest?

14. A 15% down payment requirement on a $2,600 car was fulfilled by a trade-in allowance on a customer's old car. The balance was financed over 24 monthly payments at $6\frac{1}{2}$% interest. How much was the monthly payment and what was the true annual rate of interest?

15. Some kitchen remodeling cost $2,100. The contractor required $300 down

and the balance paid in 24 months at $90 a month. What is the true rate of interest?

16. An allowance of $550 was given on a car traded in on a $2,400 truck. The payments were $92 a month for 24 months. How much was the total interest paid? What was the nominal rate of interest? What was the effective rate of interest?

17. The finance charge for a loan of $900 included interest at 12%, a carrying charge of $24, and an insurance charge of $6. Repayment was to be made in 12 monthly payments. What was the total finance charge? What was the nominal rate of this charge? What was the effective rate?

18. Monthly payments of $46 are required for 1 year to repay a $460 loan. What is the nominal interest rate? What is the effective interest rate?

19. A loan of $560 was repaid in weekly payments of $19 for 32 weeks. What is the effective rate of interest that was being charged?

20. What is the effective rate of interest comparable to a nominal rate of 14% on the original balance for 26 weekly payments?

Aging of accounts receivable

Unfortunately, practice shows that all of the accounts receivable representing claims against customers for sales on credit will not be collected. At the end of each accounting period, an estimate must be made of the amount of *bad debts*. This estimate is shown on the balance sheet as a reduction of accounts receivable. If the receivables were shown at their gross amount, it would be an overstatement of assets and of stockholders' equity. It would also fail to recognize bad debts as one of the expenses of credit sales and the need to take this into account when pricing merchandise.

The estimate of bad debts may be made in one of three ways:

1. by using a percent of credit sales based on the company's past bad debt loss expenses
2. by using a percent of current accounts receivable
3. by aging the accounts receivable to arrive at an estimate of uncollectibility.

The third method involves analyzing the accounts to determine which portions are current and the extent to which the other portions are past due.

Although a 100% aging of accounts is most time-consuming and costly, it is the most reliable method because it studies the individual accounts. This permits a review of collection efforts and may result in action that could salvage some accounts rather than letting them automatically slip into the write-off category. Rather than aging each account, a sample of the accounts may be aged, and this experience projected to all other accounts.

Table 5-6 shows Buffington's analysis of accounts receivable by age.   *Example*

TABLE 5-6 accounts receivable January 31, 19XX

Customer	Total Balance	Current	Days Past Due 1–30	31–60	61–90	Over 90
John Abbott	$ 588	$ 478	$ 22	$ 50	$......	$ 38
Mary Adams	273	244	29	......	......	......
James Clark	362	50	156	150	6	......
Alan Dane	593	313	150	130	......	......
Jay Sims	960	......	......	......	900	60
Roy Smith	320	100	200	20	......	......
All others	306,904	166,215	83,143	24,450	14,594	18,502
Totals	$310,000	$167,400	$83,700	$24,800	$15,500	$18,600
% of Total	100%	54%	27%	8%	5%	6%

Table 5-6 shows the current status of the accounts receivable. A dollar amount has been determined for accounts falling in the current category and in each of the four past due categories. Buffington's must now determine what percent of each category is likely to become uncollectible. The primary basis for this determination is their past collection experience. In this manner the estimated bad debts is calculated. The total amount, $10,000, becomes the reduction in accounts receivable as shown on Buffington's balance sheet. This procedure is illustrated as follows:

Classification	Amount	Percent Estimated to be Uncollectible	Estimated Bad Debts
Current	$167,400	1%	$ 1,675
1–30 days past due	83,700	3	2,510
31–60	24,800	5	1,240
61–90	15,500	7.9	1,225
Over 90	18,600	18	3,350
	$310,000		$10,000

EXERCISE 5-18 ACCOUNTS RECEIVABLE

An aging of the Maxwell Co. accounts receivable showed the following:

Current	$120,000
1–30 days past due	58,000
31–60	24,000
61–90	11,000
Over 90	4,000

The estimate of bad debts was based on the following percents:

Current accounts	.5%
1–30 days past due	2
31–60	4
61–90	10
Over 90	25

Prepare the accounts receivable portion of the income statement.

EXERCISE 5-19 AGING ACCOUNTS RECEIVABLE

On January 31, 1971, the accounts receivable of J. Costro Distributing Co. showed the following data. Since the company's terms of sale were net 30, any amount unpaid after 30 days of the invoice date was listed as past due. The following percents were used in estimating uncollectible accounts: current, .75%; 1–30 days past due, 3.5%; 31–60 days past due, 8.5%; 61–90 days past due, 15%; over 90 days past due, 25%.

Customer	Invoice Date	Amount
Fiesta Market	January 5, 1971	$ 1,150.25
Granada Stores Inc.	November 18, 1970	675.50
Holverson Co.	September 15, 1970	410.10
Jordan Bros.	October 3, 1970	290.00
Kahl & Kahl	December 13, 1970	1,725.50
Lester & Sons	January 15, 1971	890.50
Others	January, 1971	15,435.25
Others	December, 1970	8,875.75
Others	November, 1970	3,300.00
Others	October, 1970	2,000.00
Others	September, 1970	1,560.50
Others	Prior to September, 1970	850.75

a. Prepare an age analysis of the accounts receivable.

b. Compute the estimate of bad-debt losses.

SECTION 4—INVENTORIES

In chapter 1, we showed the position of merchandise inventory on the balance sheet. In the case of merchandising businesses, this item has a higher value than any other asset. In chapter 3, the procedures for valuation of merchandise inventories and the effect of such valuation on profits were discussed. In the case of manufacturing businesses, the subject of inventories is more complex. They must control the inventory of raw materials, the inventory of goods in process, and the inventory of finished goods ready for sale.

Inventory in the cost-of-sales section of Buffington's income statement could be contrasted with that of a manufacturing business as follows:

Buffington's		A Manufacturing Business	
Cost of Sales		Cost of Sales	
Beginning inventory	$ 350,000	Beginning inventory of	
Net purchases	1,345,000	finished goods	$ 50,000
Transportation-in	25,000	Goods manufactured	1,090,000
Merchandise available		Finished goods avail-	
for sale	$1,720,000	able for sale	$1,140,000
Ending inventory	400,000	Ending inventory of	
Gross cost of goods		finished goods	75,000
sold	$1,320,000	Cost of goods sold	$1,065,000

TABLE 5-7 schedule of cost of goods manufactured

Raw materials used		
Raw materials beginning inventory		$ 50,000
Raw material purchased	$450,000	
Freight-in on raw materials	12,000	
Gross cost of raw materials purchased	$462,000	
Less: Purchase returns and allowances	18,000	
Net cost of purchases		444,000
Cost of raw materials available for use		$ 494,000
Less: Raw materials ending inventory		55,500
Cost of raw materials used		$ 438,500
Direct labor		400,000
Manufacturing overhead		
Depreciation—Machinery and equipment	$ 20,000	
Factory rent	15,000	
Factory utilities	75,000	
Factory maintenance	22,000	
Factory insurance	6,000	
Indirect labor	55,000	
Miscellaneous factory costs	27,000	
Total manufacturing overhead		220,000
Total manufacturing costs for period		$1,058,500
Plus: Work-in-process beginning inventory	$ 61,000	
Less: Work-in-process ending inventory	29,500	
Work-in-process difference		31,500
Cost of goods manufactured		$1,090,000

The $1,090,000 cost of goods manufactured in the manufacturing business must be developed from a schedule of the costs of raw materials, of direct labor performed on the product, and of all factory costs (manufacturing overhead) incurred in the manufacturing process. However, since manufacturing is a continuing process, there are always some goods in an incomplete state whenever financial statements are prepared. Therefore, an estimate must be made of the costs incurred to date for each item in production. This valuation of the *work-in-process inventory* is deducted from the total manufacturing costs to arrive at the cost of goods manufactured, as shown in table 5-7.

Inventory in the asset section of Buffington's balance sheet could be contrasted with that of a manufacturing business as follows:

Buffington's		A Manufacturing Business	
Merchandise inventory	$400,000	Raw material inventory	$ 55,500
		Work-in-process inventory	29,500
		Finished goods inventory	75,000
		Total inventories	$160,000

EXERCISE 5-20 COST OF RAW MATERIALS

Calculate the missing amounts below.

	1	2	3	4	5
Raw materials					
Beginning inventory	$_____	$ 500	$ 2,000	$_____	$ 5,650

	1	2	3	4	5
Raw màterial purchased	82,000	55,000	_____	64,000	72,840
Raw material freight-in	_____	1,500	1,000	3,600	_____
Gross cost of raw material purchases	84,400	_____	41,000	67,600	76,270
Purchase returns & allowances	_____	500	400	_____	2,482
Net cost of purchases	83,200	_____	40,600	66,700	73,788
Cost of raw materials available	84,200	56,500	_____	77,700	_____
Raw materials ending inventory	1,200	_____	12,800	6,500	_____
Cost of raw materials	83,000	54,000	_____	_____	74,576

EXERCISE 5-21   COST OF GOODS MANUFACTURED

Calculate the missing amounts below.

		1	2	3	4	5
Cost of raw materials used						
Direct labor	45%	$_____	$20,000	$25,400	$ 9,900	$16,300
Manufacturing overhead	40	4,000	_____	15,600	12,200	13,900
Total manufacturing cost for period	20	2,000	25,400	_____	7,600	5,800
Work-in-process beginning inventory	95–105	10,500	93,900	61,300	_____	_____
Work-in-process ending inventory	3–10	_____	5,600	_____	4,300	2,700
Cost of goods manufactured	3–10	500	_____	6,200	2,500	_____
	100	11,000	94,700	58,800	_____	28,870

EXERCISE 5-22   COST OF GOODS MANUFACTURED

The following information was developed for the controller of a manufacturing business. Prepare a schedule of cost of goods manufactured.

Depreciation—Machinery and equipment	$ 8,600
Factory rent	7,400
Factory utilities	28,700
Factory maintenance	9,500
Factory insurance	2,800
Indirect labor	19,500
Miscellaneous factory costs	15,600
Raw material beginning inventory	25,600
Work-in-process beginning inventory	28,700
Raw material ending inventory	27,800
Work-in-process ending inventory	16,300
Direct labor	173,400
Freight-in on raw materials	5,500
Raw material purchase returns & allowances	4,800
Raw material purchases	225,800

SECTION 5 – DEPRECIATION OF FIXED ASSETS

The fixed assets of a business have a predictable useful life. The length of life for various assets depends upon such factors as wear and tear and obsolescence. It is necessary to allocate the costs of these assets to their serviceable years, when they are contributing to the revenue of the business. This yearly allocation of cost is termed *depreciation expense*. If the useful life of an item is less than 1 year, then the entire cost would be an expense chargeable to that year. In this case, an expense term such as "supplies" could be used rather than "depreciation." A business may own land, but that does not have a limited life and consequently cannot be depreciated. The Internal Revenue Service has established guidelines for the acceptable number of years over which to depreciate about 75 different classes of assets.

The valuation of an asset on the "books" of a business is termed its *book value*. The cost of the asset and all expenditures necessary to make it operationally useful is its original book value. Consequently, the balance sheet shows the book value of assets at the end of a particular accounting period.

The income statement shows the depreciation expense charged to the period. Accordingly, the book value of an asset would decline each year until the end of its estimated useful life. From then on, it would be carried at a *residual value* until the asset is disposed of. This residual value may be termed *salvage value*, *scrap value*, or *trade-in value*.

Methods of computing depreciation

We have discussed the effect of various expenses upon operating profit in chapter 4. Since depreciation is an expense against operations, the Internal Revenue Service must be concerned about the method used in calculating depreciation. The amount charged to each period varies greatly in accordance with the method used. Care must be taken in selecting the method most appropriate for a particular asset of a particular business. Once a method has been adopted, IRS regulations outline the requirements for change to another method; certain changes are even prohibited.

straight-line method

Under the straight-line method, depreciation is related only to the period of serviceable life, with the assumption that the asset is continuously available for use during this period. Consequently, the same amount is charged each year, resulting in the name *straight-line*. The frequent use of the straight-line method is probably attributable more to its ease of calculation than to the logic of matching costs to revenues.

Example   On January 2, a machine with an estimated useful life of 5 years was purchased for $10,000. The residual (or trade-in) value was estimated at $1,000. Prepare a depreciation schedule for this asset.

Step 1: Determine total depreciation:

$$\text{Cost} - \text{Residual value} = \text{Total depreciation}$$
$$\$10,000 - \quad \$1,000 \quad = \quad \$9,000$$

Step 2: Determine annual depreciation:

$$\text{Total depreciation} \div \text{Years in estimated useful life} = \text{Annual depreciation}$$
$$\$9,000 \quad \div \quad\quad 5 \quad\quad = \quad \$1,800$$

Step 3: Determine rate of depreciation:

$$\text{Rate of depreciation} = \frac{\text{Annual depreciation}}{\text{Cost}} \quad \text{or} \quad \frac{\$1,800}{\$10,000} = .18 \text{ or } 18\%$$

Step 4: Prepare a schedule as shown in table 5-8.

TABLE 5-8   depreciation schedule—straight-line method

Year	Book Value	Annual Depreciation	Accumulated Depreciation	End-of-Year Balance Sheet Value
1	$10,000	$1,800	$1,800	$8,200
2	8,200	1,800	3,600	6,400
3	6,400	1,800	5,400	4,600
4	4,600	1,800	7,200	2,800
5	2,800	1,800	9,000	1,000*

* Residual value.

declining-depreciation methods

In contrast to the constant amount of annual depreciation under the straight-line method, other methods yield decreasing amounts of annual depreciation as the useful life of the asset progresses. Many hold that these *declining-depreciation methods* are more realistic since maintenance and repair expenses increase with the age of the asset and, consequently, total costs are more evenly spread over the useful life. Also, a new machine may be more productive than an older machine, a greater portion of its original cost is thus allocated to the most productive portion of its useful life. Obsolescence occurs very fast in the case of such assets as electronic equipment and computer systems, so that trade-in values drop rapidly. Finally, every consumer is aware of the rapid decrease in the trade-in value of his personal car—regardless of how few miles it has been driven or how much care it has been given.

1. *Sum-of-the-Years'-Digits Method.* Under this method, the annual depreciation is calculated by multiplying the total depreciation (cost less residual value) by a fraction which is reduced in value each year. The constant denominator of this fraction is the sum of the number of years in the estimated useful life of the asset. The numerator is the position of each year in the estimated use-

ful life taken in reverse order. The contrast with the straight-line method can be seen by using the same example:

Step 1: Determine total depreciation:

$$\text{Cost} - \text{Residual value} = \text{Total depreciation}$$
$$\$10,000 - \$1,000 = \$9,000$$

Step 2: Total (sum) the years in the estimated useful life:

1st year
2nd year
3rd year
4th year
5th year
‾‾‾‾‾‾‾‾
15 years

Note: The sum of any arithmetic progression of this type may be found by the following formula, where n = highest number in progression:

$$\frac{n(n + 1)}{2} = \text{Sum}$$

$$\frac{5(5 + 1)}{2} = \frac{5 \times 6}{2} = \frac{30}{2} = 15$$

Step 3: Apply the position/sum fraction to the total depreciation to calculate the annual depreciation, which declines each year:

$$\frac{5}{15} \times \$9,000 = \$3,000 \text{ First-year depreciation}$$
$$\frac{4}{15} \times \$9,000 = \$2,400 \text{ Second-year depreciation}$$
$$\frac{3}{15} \times \$9,000 = \$1,800 \text{ Third-year depreciation}$$
$$\frac{2}{15} \times \$9,000 = \$1,200 \text{ Fourth-year depreciation}$$
$$\frac{1}{15} \times \$9,000 = \$600 \text{ Fifth-year depreciation}$$

Step 4: Prepare the schedule as in table 5-9.

TABLE 5-9 depreciation schedule—sum-of-the-years'-digits method

Year	Book Value	Annual Depreciation	Accumulated Depreciation	End-of-Year Balance Sheet Value
1	$10,000	$3,000	$3,000	$7,000
2	7,000	2,400	5,400	4,600
3	4,600	1,800	7,200	2,800
4	2,800	1,200	8,400	1,600
5	1,600	600	9,000	1,000*

*Residual value.

2. *Declining-Balance Method.* The calculation of annual depreciation under the declining-balance method is based on book value alone, without adjustment for residual value. When the book value is reduced to the residual value, the calculation of depreciation on the asset is stopped. A fixed rate of depreciation is applied each year to the declining book value; hence the name *declining-balance method.* Under current regulations, the rate for new asset items must not be more than twice the rate which would apply if the straight-line method were used. If this allowable maximum rate is used, the depreciation method is referred to as the *double-declining-balance method.* Because residual value is not considered in this calculation, the straight-line rate is 100% divided by the number of years in the estimated useful life. Using the 5-year life in our extended example, the straight-line rate would be 20% and a depreciation schedule would be developed as follows:

Step 1: Determine annual rate of depreciation: we shall use the 20% rate in our straight-line example.

Step 2: Calculate annual depreciation and develop the schedule as in table 5-10.

TABLE 5-10 depreciation schedule—declining-balance method

Year	Book Value	X	20% Rate	=	Annual Depreciation	Accumulated Depreciation	End-of-Year Balance Sheet Value
1	$10,000	X	.20	=	$2,000	$2,000	$8,000
2	8,000	X	.20	=	1,600	3,600	6,400
3	6,400	X	.20	=	1,280	4,880	5,120
4	5,120	X	.20	=	1,024	5,904	4,096
5	4,096	X	.20	=	819	6,723	3,277
6	3,277	X	.20	=	655	7,378	2,622
7	2,622	X	.20	=	524	7,902	2,098
8	2,098	X	.20	=	420	8,322	1,678
9	1,678	X	.20	=	336	8,658	1,342
10	1,342	X	.20	=	268	8,926	1,074
11	1,074	....		=	74*	9,000	1,000†

*Only $74 depreciation may be taken in the 11th year, since book value can not be reduced below the $1,000 residual value.
†Residual value.

If the maximum rate or double-declining balance were used, the schedule would be determined as follows:

Step 1: Determine annual rate of depreciation:

$$\frac{100\%}{\text{Years in estimated useful life}} = \frac{100\%}{5} = 20\% \text{ Straight-line rate}$$

2 X Straight-line rate = Double-declining-balance rate

2 X   20%   =   40%

Step 2: Calculate annual depreciation and develop the schedule as in table 5-11.

TABLE 5-11   depreciation schedule—double-declining-balance method

Year	Book Value X	40% Rate =	Annual Depreciation	Accumulated Depreciation	End-of-Year Balance Sheet Value
1	$10,000 X	.40 =	$4,000	$4,000	$6,000
2	6,000 X	.40 =	2,400	6,400	3,600
3	3,600 X	.40 =	1,440	7,840	2,160
4	2,160 X	.40 =	864	8,704	1,296
5	1,296	.... =	296	9,000	1,000*

* Residual value.

asset-usage methods

With a concern for matching the costs for a given period with revenues for the same period, there is much justification for using a method of depreciation which is related to use or productivity of the asset. This has particular application to machinery which may not be in continual use. The basis of depreciation may be either number of hours in use or number of units produced.

1. *Hours in Use.* We can tailor our basic example to this method by assuming an estimated useful life of 25,000 hours.

Step 1: Determine total depreciation:

$$\text{Cost} \quad - \quad \text{Residual value} = \text{Total depreciation}$$

$$\$10,000 - \quad \$1,000 \quad = \quad \$9,000$$

Step 2: Determine hourly depreciation:

$$\frac{\text{Total depreciation}}{\text{Estimated useful life in hours}} = \text{Hourly depreciation}$$

$$\frac{\$9,000}{25,000} = \$.36 \text{ per hour}$$

Step 3: Determine annual depreciation on basis of hours used and prepare a schedule as in table 5-12.

TABLE 5-12   depreciation schedule based on hours in use

Year	Book Value	Hours Used X	Depreciation per Hour =	Annual Depreciation	Accumulated Depreciation	End-of-Year Balance Sheet Value
1	$10,000	6,000 X	.36 =	$2,160	$2,160	$7,840
2	7,840	6,000 X	.36 =	2,460	4,320	5,680
3	5,680	5,000 X	.36 =	1,800	6,120	3,880
4	3,880	5,000 X	.36 =	1,800	7,920	2,080
5	2,080	3,000 X	.36 =	1,080	9,000	1,000*

* Residual value.

2. *Units Produced.* If the estimated useful life of the asset is set at 15,000 units of production, then the following steps would be followed:

Step 1: Determine total depreciation:

$$\text{Cost} \quad - \quad \text{Residual value} \quad = \quad \text{Total depreciation}$$
$$\$10,000 \quad - \quad \$1,000 \quad = \quad \$9,000$$

Step 2: Determine depreciation per unit:

$$\frac{\text{Total depreciation}}{\text{Estimated useful life in product units}} = \text{Depreciation per unit}$$

$$\frac{\$9,000}{15,000} = \$.60 \text{ per unit}$$

Step 3: Determine annual depreciation on basis of units produced and prepare the schedule as in table 5-13.

TABLE 5-13 depreciation schedule based on units produced

Year	Book Value	Units Produced X	Depreciation per unit	=	Annual Depreciation	Accumulated Depreciation	End-of-Year Balance Sheet Value
1	$10,000	5,500 X	.60	=	$3,300	$3,300	$6,700
2	6,700	4,200 X	.60	=	2,520	5,820	4,180
3	4,180	2,700 X	.60	=	1,620	7,440	2,560
4	2,560	1,600 X	.60	=	960	8,400	1,600
5	1,600	1,000 X	.60	=	600	9,000	1,000*

*Residual value.

Other considerations

In our extended example, we have used January 2 as the date when the asset was purchased. This permitted a full year's depreciation during the first calendar year. In practice, however, assets are bought and disposed of at different times in the yearly accounting period. Procedures vary from company to company as to the amount of depreciation to be charged to these partial periods. The easiest approach is to charge an amount which is in the same proportion to the annual depreciation as the number of months the asset is held to the 12 months in the accounting period. If the asset was purchased on or before the 15th day of a month, that month is used in the calculation. If it was purchased on the 16th day or later, then that month is excluded from the calculation.

Assuming an asset was purchased on September 12 (instead of January 2), *Example* then for depreciation purposes September 1 would be considered the purchase date. If the accounting period corresponds to the calendar year, then the asset would have been held 4 months at the end of the period. If the annual depreciation charge were \$1,800, then the amount charged to this first period would be:

$$\frac{4}{12} \times \text{Annual depreciation} = \text{Depreciation charge}$$

$$\frac{4}{12} \times \qquad \$1,800 \qquad = \qquad \$600$$

Consistency is most important in depreciation practices; such is the thrust of most of the guidelines and regulations of the Internal Revenue Service. Current laws and regulations should always be reviewed before making depreciation decisions. At times, special allowances may be permitted during the first year of asset ownership. The relationship between the straight-line rate and the maximum declining-balance rate may be changed depending upon whether the purchased asset is new or used. Changing from one method of depreciation to another is a particularly exacting move in the eyes of the law.

EXERCISE 5-23   DEPRECIATION, DATE OF DEPRECIATION, AND BOOK VALUE

A. Determine the annual depreciation and the rate of depreciation for each of the following using the straight-line method.

	Cost	Residual Value	Estimated Life (Years)	Annual Depreciation	Annual Rate
1.	\$ 5,300	\$ 600	6	_____	_____
2.	2,800	500	7	_____	_____
3.	6,200	800	5	_____	_____
4.	850	75	12	_____	_____
5.	8,600	400	15	_____	_____
6.	1,550	100	8	_____	_____
7.	42,450	2,000	16	_____	_____
8.	16,480	500	14	_____	_____
9.	125,000	7,500	25	_____	_____
10.	150,000	12,000	20	_____	_____

B. Determine the annual depreciation for the first and third years using the sum-of-the-years'-digits method.

	Cost	Residual Value	Estimated Life (Years)	Depreciation 1st Year	Depreciation 3rd Year
1.	\$ 3,000	\$300	5	_____	_____
2.	2,450	470	6	_____	_____

	Cost	Residual Value	Estimated Life (Years)	Depreciation 1st Year	3rd Year
3.	1,100	110	9	_____	_____
4.	5,900	500	8	_____	_____
5.	7,814	450	4	_____	_____
6.	4,500	500	5	_____	_____
7.	7,250	250	10	_____	_____
8.	7,300	300	7	_____	_____
9.	10,000	640	12	_____	_____
10.	9,964	100	8	_____	_____

C. Determine the annual depreciation and the book value for each of the following using the double-declining-balance method.

	Estimated Life (Years)	Cost	1st Year Depreciation	2nd Year Book Value	Depreciation
1.	4	$1,600	_____	_____	_____
2.	6	2,800	_____	_____	_____
3.	10	3,600	_____	_____	_____
4.	8	5,500	_____	_____	_____
5.	5	6,450	_____	_____	_____
6.	7	4,428	_____	_____	_____
7.	9	5,416	_____	_____	_____
8.	6	3,225	_____	_____	_____
9.	8	7,850	_____	_____	_____
10.	12	9,675	_____	_____	_____

EXERCISE 5-24 PROBLEMS ON DEPRECIATION

1. On February 1, the first day of their fiscal year, Buffington's purchased a display case for $1,100. It was to be depreciated over 8 years and the residual value was established at $200. Prepare a depreciation schedule for the asset using the straight-line method.

2. A calculator was purchased for $1,600 on the first day of the annual accounting period. The serviceable life was set at 6 years, at the end of which time the trade-in value was estimated at $340. Prepare a depreciation schedule using the sum-of-the-years'-digits method.

3. A baler was acquired for $8,600 and was to be depreciated at a fixed rate of 30% a year. The residual value was estimated to be $1,200. Prepare a depreciation schedule.

4. A delivery truck was bought for $3,400. The estimated useful life was 6

years and the residual value was $400. Prepare a depreciation schedule using the double-declining-balance method.

5. A lathe for a cabinet shop was purchased for $2,900. Its useful life was set at 20,000 hours and its residual value was $300. Prepare a depreciation schedule using the following record of yearly usage:

Year	Usage (Hours)
1	3,800
2	4,400
3	3,600
4	2,600
5	2,800
6	1,600
7	1,200

6. A stamping machine cost $12,400 and was to have an estimated useful life of 18,000 units of production. Its scrap value was $400. Prepare a depreciation schedule using the following record of yearly output:

Year	Units Produced
1	3,200
2	3,900
3	3,800
4	2,800
5	2,500
6	1,800

7. A delivery truck was purchased for $4,800 and had an estimated useful life of 4 years and a trade-in value of $600. What would be the first-year depreciation using each of the following methods: (a) straight-line? (b) sum-of-the-years'-digits? (c) double-declining-balance? (d) usage method, assuming 80,000 miles of useful life and 22,500 miles of use in the first year?

8. A machine was purchased for $36,000. Its estimated useful life was 6 years and its residual value was to be $2,000. Prepare depreciation schedules for the first 4 years using each of the following methods: (a) straight-line; (b) sum-of-the-years'-digits; (c) double-declining-balance; (d) usage method, assuming a life of 12,000 hours and actual usage hours for each of the first 4 years of 2,600, 2,800, 1,900, and 1,600, respectively.

9. A company purchased a $16,000 machine on March 17. It had an estimated life of 5 years and a trade-in value of $2,000. How much depreciation was charged December 31 of the first and second year of ownership using each of the following methods: (a) straight-line? (b) sum-of-the-years'-digits? (c) double-declining-balance method?

10. The accounting year for the Hanson Co. is from July 1 through June 30. On October 6, 1969, they bought a bookkeeping machine for $2,750 with an

estimated useful life of 8 years and a trade-in value of $350. How much depreciation would have been recorded on June 30, 1970, and how much on June 30, 1971, under each of the following methods: (*a*) straight-line? (*b*) sum-of-the-years'-digits? (*c*) double-declining-balance?

BUFFINGTON'S DEPARTMENT STORE INC.
BALANCE SHEET
AS OF JANUARY 31, 19XX

<u>ASSETS</u>

CURRENT ASSETS:

Cash on Hand and in Bank		$180,000	15.0%
Notes Receivable		5,000	.4%
Accounts Receivable	$310,000		
Less: Estimated Bad Debts	10,000	300,000	25.0%
Merchandise Inventory (at cost)		400,000	33.3%
Supplies		10,000	.9%
Prepaid Expenses		5,000	.4%
Total Current Assets		$ 900,000	75.0%

FIXED ASSETS:

Furniture, Fixtures and Equipment	$125,000		
Less: Accumulated Depreciation	45,000	$ 80,000	6.7%
Delivery Equipment	$ 50,000		
Less: Accumulated Depreciation	30,000	20,000	1.7%
Building	$250,000		
Less: Accumulated Depreciation	50,000	200,000	16.6%
Total Fixed Assets		300,000	25.0%
TOTAL ASSETS		$1,200,000	100.0%

- -

LIABILITIES AND PROPRIETORSHIP

CURRENT LIABILITIES:

Notes Payable		$ 50,000	4.2%
Accounts Payable		220,000	18.3%
Expenses Payable		5,000	.4%
Total Current Liabilities		$ 275,000	22.9%

LONG-TERM LIABILITIES:

Mortgage Payable		125,000	10.4%
Total Liabilities		$ 400,000	33.3%

PROPRIETORSHIP:

Preferred Stock	$100,000		
Common Stock	500,000		
Retained Earnings	200,000		
Total Proprietorship (net worth)		800,000	66.7%
TOTAL LIABILITIES AND PROPRIETORSHIP		$1,200,000	100.0%

THE BALANCE SHEET

6

mathematics of creditor equities

This chapter will explain the mathematics required for all of the items in the liabilities section of the balance sheet. In the case of Buffington's Department Store, the liabilities are notes payable, accounts payable, expenses payable, and mortage payable.

Although Buffington's has not issued any bonds, this chapter will also explain the calculations involved in bond transactions.

SECTION I—ACCOUNTS PAYABLE AND NOTES PAYABLE

Notes Payable may result when the debtor company borrows money from a bank or when it needs more time to pay one of its suppliers or perhaps when expensive equipment is purchased and financed for a year or longer. The mathematics of notes payable are the same as for notes receivable, since the debtor's note payable is the creditor's note receivable (see chapter 5). Should the debtor wish to borrow money secured by a note, he may be asked to pay interest in advance (bank discount) or he may pay the interest when the note comes due.

Accounts Payable usually include all of those debts that are due within a year of the balance sheet date. These are the current obligations that will be paid out of operating revenue. Accounts payable can be separated into two classifications based on what was purchased by the company. One category includes those payables owed to creditors from whom Buffington's bought merchandise for resale; the remainder are those debts owed for any other goods or services used in the operation of the business. Merchandise purchases, whether paid for or not, are shown in the cost-of-sales section of the income statement and as current assets on the balance sheet, whereas debts owed to creditors outside the company are detailed under operating expenses in the income statement. The notation *expenses payable* as a current liability represents money owed to employees in the form of salaries, wages, bonuses, etc.

SECTION 2—MORTGAGE PAYABLE

Buffington's balance sheet lists a mortgage payable of $125,000 as its only long-term liability, and their income statement shows $60,000 to be the annual payment on the mortgage. Mortgage loans are usually set up so that interest is paid on the declining (unpaid) balance. Payments are equal in size and each payment covers the current interest due and partly reduces the outstanding principal. This method of retiring an interest-bearing loan is called *amortization*, and loans paid back in this way are referred to as *amortized* or *direct-reduction loans*. Payments may be scheduled semiannually, monthly, weekly, or for any other time period.

When Buffington's purchased its store property for $888,195, a down payment of $200,000 was made, leaving a balance of $688,195. This money was borrowed from a bank and secured by a mortgage note calling for year-end payments at the rate of 6% per year on the declining balance for 20 years. At that time the problem was to set up a payment schedule which would retire the loan (principal plus interest) in 20 years. This is a problem which can best be solved by referring to a partial-payment table, such as the tables in appendix IV (last column of factors). This table gives the periodic payment necessary to pay off a loan of $1. After locating the appropriate periodic interest rate [i] at the top of the page, the periodic payment necessary to pay off a loan of $1 can be found. Mathematically the table gives the value of $\dfrac{1}{a_{\overline{n}|}}$ which means "1 divided by a [present worth of $1 per period] sub n [number of payments]" at the given periodic rate of interest [i]. The formula for finding the equal payment is

$$R\,(\text{Rent}) = A \left(\begin{array}{c}\text{Present value of the debt}\\ \text{or}\\ \text{Beginning loan balance}\end{array}\right) \times \frac{1}{a_{\overline{n}|}} \text{ at the periodic rate } (i)$$

Example   As an example of amortization, find the equal annual payment required to retire Buffington's $688,195 mortgage if payments are made at the end of each year for the next 20 years and the interest charge is 6%.

$$R = \$688,195 \times .0871846 \quad (20 \text{ periods at } 6\%)$$
$$= \$60,000$$

Note: Had this loan called for quarterly payments, we would have used $n = 80\,(4 \times 20$ years) and $i = 1\frac{1}{2}\%$ ($6\% \div 4$ quarters).

Now that the equal annual rent payment is known, it is possible to construct an amortization schedule for Buffington's showing the annual reduction of interest and principal over the life of the loan. This is shown in table 6-1.

TABLE 6-1   schedule of direct-reduction loan (loan: $688,195; rate: 6%; term: 20 years; annual payment $60,000*)

Payment Number	Net Interest	Principal Payment	Balance of Loan
1	41,291.70	18,708.30	669,486.70
2	40,169.20	19,830.80	649,655.90
3	38,979.35	21,020.65	628,635.25
4	37,718.12	22,281.88	606,353.37
5	36,381.20	23,618.80	582.734.57
6	34,964.07	25,035.93	557,698.64
7	33,461.92	26,538.08	531,160.56
8	31,869.63	28,130.37	503,030.19
9	30,181.81	29,818.19	473.212.00
10	28,392.72	31,607.28	441,604.72
11	26,496.28	33,503.72	408,101.00
12	24,486.06	35,513.94	372,587.06
13	22,355.22	37,644.78	334,942.28
14	20,096.54	39,903.46	295,038.82
15	17,702.33	42,297.67	252,741.15
16	15,164.47	44,835.53	207,905.62
17	12,474.34	47,525.66	160,379.96
18	9,622.80	50,377.20	110,002.76
19	6,600.17	53,399.83	56,602.93
20	3,396.18	56,602.93	59,999.11*

*The final payment is usually somewhat different from the regular payment, and is shown starred on the last line.

Source: Prepared by Financial Publishing Company, Boston

For purposes of comparison, another amortization schedule is shown in table 6-2 for a smaller loan having a different interest rate and duration.

EXERCISE 6-1 PROBLEMS ON AMORTIZATION

Find the equal rent payment required to amortize the following loans:

1. The Ajax Trucking Company has contracted to pay off a loan of $360,000 by making semiannual payments at 4% annual interest for the next 30 years. What will be the size of each payment?

2. Paying back a loan of $4,275 at 6% compounded monthly over a 2-year period requires equal payments of what size?

3. Had Buffington's mortgage been for 25 years, what would the equal annual payment have been?

TABLE 6-2 schedule of direct-reduction loan (loan: $6,400.00; rate: 7%; term: 60 months; monthly payment: $126.73*)

Payment Number	Net Interest	Principal Payment	Balance of Loan
1	37.33	89.40	6,310.60
2	36.81	89.92	6,220.68
3	36.29	90.44	6,130.24
4	35.76	90.97	6,039.27
5	35.23	91.50	5,947.77
6	34.70	92.03	5,855.74
7	34.16	92.57	5,763.17
8	33.62	93.11	5,670.06
9	33.08	93.65	5,576.41
10	32.53	94.20	5,482.21
11	31.98	94.75	5,387.46
12	31.43	95.30	5,292.16
13	30.87	95.86	5,196.30
14	30.31	96.42	5,099.88
15	29.75	96.98	5,002.90
16	29.18	97.55	4,905.35
17	28.61	98.12	4,807.23
18	28.04	98.69	4,708.54
19	27.47	99.26	4,609.28
20	26.89	99.84	4,509.44
21	26.31	100.42	4,409.02
22	25.72	101.01	4,308.01
23	25.13	101.60	4,206.41
24	24.54	102.19	4,104.22
25	23.94	102.79	4,001.43
26	23.34	103.39	3,898.04
27	22.74	103.99	3,794.05
28	22.13	104.60	3,689.45
29	21.52	105.21	3,584.24
30	20.91	105.82	3,478.42
31	20.29	106.44	3,371.98
32	19.67	107.06	3,264.92
33	19.05	107.68	3,157.24
34	18.42	108.31	3,048.93
35	17.79	108.94	2,939.99
36	17.15	109.58	2,830.41
37	16.51	110.22	2,720.19
38	15.87	110.86	2,609.33
39	15.22	111.51	2,497.82
40	14.57	112.16	2,385.66
41	13.92	112.81	2,272.85
42	13.26	113.47	2,159.38
43	12.60	114.13	2,045.25
44	11.93	114.80	1,930.45
45	11.26	115.47	1,814.98
46	10.59	116.14	1,698.84
47	9.91	116.82	1,582.02
48	9.23	117.50	1,464.52
49	8.54	118.19	1,346.33
50	7.85	118.88	1,227.45
51	7.16	119.57	1,107.88
52	6.46	120.27	987.61
53	5.76	120.97	866.64
54	5.06	121.67	744.97
55	4.35	122.38	622.59
56	3.63	123.10	499.49
57	2.91	123.82	375.67
58	2.19	124.54	251.13
59	1.46	125.27	125.86
60	.73	125.86	126.59*

*The final payment is usually somewhat different from the regular payment, and is shown starred on the last line.

Source: Prepared by Financial Publishing Company, Boston

SECTION 3—CORPORATE BONDS

Bonds represent another type of long-term liability incurred by a company when it borrows money from the general public. Bonds carry a specified rate of interest which the borrowing firm promises to pay on the bond *interest dates* (usually semiannually) along with the *face value* of the bond, which comes due on the *maturity date*. Corporate bonds are of various types, depending upon whether or not they are secured by certain assets of the issuing company. Mortgage bonds and equipment bonds are examples of bonds secured by certain company assets; debenture bonds are those having no specific corporate assets pledged as security for the payment of bond interest or the repayment of the face value. Bonds may also be *callable*, which gives the company the right to repurchase (buy back) existing bonds prior to their maturity date; or they may be *convertible*, which gives the bondholder the right to exchange his bonds for common stock at an agreed-upon price per share. Bonds come in two basic formats: *registered bonds* are listed by the company in the name of each bondholder and interest checks are mailed directly to the bondholder, while *coupon bonds* have a series of promissory notes attached to them. In the latter case, the bondholder presents a coupon to his bank to collect the interest when it is due.

Bond prices

Bond prices are quoted at a percent of par (face) value. Table 6-3 shows some bond quotations for May 20, 1970. Although bonds normally do not fluctuate in price as much as do stocks, one can see that in less than 5 months during 1970 these bond prices changed considerably. It is important to remember that the bonds shown here have been sold by the issuing corporations, and are now being bought and sold in the marketplace. We cannot determine from this list what price the issuing company received when the bonds were first offered to the public. The first bond on the list is one issued by the Airlift Co., paying $6\frac{1}{2}\%$ interest and due in 1986. A notation such as 05 would indicate

TABLE 6-3

AMERICAN STOCK EXCHANGE BONDS May 20, 1970, volume, $2,150,000

	1970 (Jan. 1 to May 20) $239,279,000	1969 (full year) $394,245,000	1968 (full year) $400,520,000	
	Tues. (5/20)	Mon. (5/19)	Fri. (5/16)	Thur. (5/15)
Issues traded	84	82	89	91
Advances	19	27	43	18
Declines	46	27	28	61
Unchanged	19	28	18	12
New highs, 1970	0	0	0	0
New lows, 1970	11	13	17	27

1970 High	1970 Low	Bonds	Sales in $1,000	High	Low	Close	Net Chg.
$102\frac{1}{2}$	78	Airlift $6\frac{1}{2}$s86	3	$74\frac{3}{4}$	$72\frac{5}{8}$	$72\frac{5}{8}$	$-5\frac{3}{8}$
$48\frac{3}{4}$	32	Airlift $5\frac{3}{4}$s87	64	$32\frac{1}{4}$	30	$31\frac{1}{2}$	$-\frac{5}{8}$
114	83	Alask $6\frac{7}{8}$s87	1	82	82	82	-2
$132\frac{7}{8}$	92	Alaska $6\frac{1}{2}$s86	1	100	100	100	$+5$
56	46	AllegA $5\frac{1}{2}$s87	10	46	46	46	$-\frac{1}{4}$

the bonds mature in the year 2005, 10 would be 2010, and so on. The interest rate is expressed in plural form (s) since it applies to every bond in this bond issue.

So far since January 1, 1970, $3,000 of Airlift $6\frac{1}{2}$s bonds have been sold. The highest price was $102\frac{1}{2}$% and the lowest has been 78% of the face value. For a $100 bond this represents a high of $102.50 ($100 × 1.025) and a low of $78 ($100 × .78). For a $1,000 bond, the high would be $1,025 and the low $780. The sales of the day show a high price of $74\frac{3}{4}$ and a low—and closing—price of $72\frac{5}{8}$. The change for the day was $2\frac{1}{8}$, which is a decrease of $2.125 per $100 bond.

When a bond sells for more than its face value, it is said to be selling at a *premium* (see example 1, below); when the price is less than the face value, the bond is sold at a *discount* (see example 2).

Example 1 The Owens Corp. sold 6,000 bonds in $1,000 denominations at a price of 102. What amount did they receive and what was the total premium?

Bonds Face value Price
6,000 × $1,000 × 102% = $6,000,000 × 1.02

= $6,120,000 Amt. rec'd.

= 6,000,000 Face value

= $ 120,000 Premium

The Owens Corp. has the use of the $6,120,000. The $120,000 premium, in effect, reduces their interest cost over the life of the bonds.

Example 2 The Alucard Corp. sold 2,500 bonds of $100 denomination at a price of 95. What amount did they receive and what was the total discount?

Bonds Face value Price
2,500 × $100 × 95% = $250,000 × .95

= $237,500 Amt. rec'd.

= 250,000 Face value

= $ 12,500 Discount

The Alucard Corp. has the use of $237,500. The $12,500 discount, in effect, represents an added interest cost over the life of the bonds.

Commissions and taxes on bond transactions

Bonds are bought and sold through brokerage firms. These firms charge a commission for the service they perform. The schedule in table 6-4 is representative of the brokerage charges for most bond transactions.

TABLE 6-4 brokerage charges for bond transactions

Selling Price per $1,000 of Face Value	Commission per $1,000 of Face Value
(a) less than $10.00	
(1% of face value)	$ .75
(b) $10.00–$99.99	
(1% and over, but less than 10%)	1.25
(c) $100 and over	
(10% and above)	2.50

Find the brokerage commission on the exchange of 25 bonds of $1,000 *Example* face value sold at $62\frac{1}{2}$.

Since the selling price per bond is $625, it falls under category (c) in the schedule in table 6-4, and the commission is $2.50 per $1,000 for a total of $62.50 ($2.50 × 25 bonds).

The federal government's Securities and Exchange Commission imposes a charge on the seller of bonds at the rate of 1¢ for each $500 or portion thereof of the price paid. For convenience, the brokerage firm remits this charge to the SEC and deducts it (along with its commission) from the price received.

Find the proceeds to the seller of 12 bonds at $8\frac{3}{4}$. Assume a face value of *Example* $1,000 per bond.

$$\$1,000 \times 8\tfrac{3}{4} = \$87.50 \text{ Price per bond}$$

$$\$87.50 \times 12 = \$1,050 \text{ Total price}$$

Proceeds   = Total price − Commission

= $1,050 − 9.00 [i.e., 12 × $.75] = $1,041.00

SEC charge = 3 × 1¢   = −   .03

Proceeds to the seller   = $1,040.97

EXERCISE 6-2 PROBLEMS ON BOND TRANSACTIONS

1. Using the bond quotations in table 6-3, find the dollar difference per $1,000 bond between the high and low price for the year for each corporation listed.

2. For the bonds in problem 1, above, find the net proceeds after commissions and fees to the seller of eight $1,000 Alask $6\frac{7}{8}$s87 at the day's closing price.

3. Find the brokerage commission charge on each of these bond transactions. Assume $1,000 denominations.

   a. one bond at $10\frac{1}{4}$

   b. 3 bonds at $105\frac{3}{8}$

   c. 15 bonds at 75

   d. 4 bonds at $\frac{5}{6}$

   e. 26 bonds at $5\frac{1}{2}$

4. Find the proceeds to the issuing company. Assume all are $1,000 bonds.

   a. 500 XYZ $4\frac{1}{2}$s95 at 86

   b. 150 ABC $7\frac{1}{4}$s05 at 103

   c. 2,000 GHI $6\frac{5}{8}$s10 at $98\frac{1}{2}$

5. Find the net proceeds after commissions and fees to the bond seller.

   a. 62 bonds, face value $1,000, at $87\frac{1}{2}$

   b. 13 bonds, face value $1,000, at 96

   c. 20 bonds, face value $1,000, at $19\frac{3}{4}$

Interest on bond sales

Every corporate bond carries a stipulated rate of interest based on the face value and payable (most often semiannually) on the listed interest dates. The calculation of bond interest is exactly like that for any other simple-interest problem.

Example   An invester has 6 Ajax Corp. 6s95 $1,000 bonds, with interest due on March 1 and September 1 of each year. What is the semiannual interest payment?

$$\frac{\overset{\$60}{\cancel{\$6,000}}}{1} \times \frac{\overset{3}{\cancel{6}}}{\underset{1}{\cancel{100}}} \times \frac{1}{\underset{1}{\cancel{2}}} = \$180 \text{ Total}$$

or

$$\frac{\$180}{6} = \$30 \text{ per bond}$$

When a bondholder sells his bonds through a brokerage firm to another investor, the transaction may very likely take place between bond interest dates. The question arises as to who is entitled to the interest or how much of the semiannual interest should go to each party. The problem is precluded by a standard procedure followed in all corporate bond transactions. This procedure calls for the purchaser of bonds to pay the interest which has accrued between the date of the last interest payment and the day before the *settlement date*.

Brokerage firms universally make the settlement date 4 business days after the date of sale. This means, for example, that a sale made on Wednesday, November 4, would have a settlement date of Tuesday, November 10. In addition, 30-day-month time is used when calculating the interest on bonds sold between interest dates. This of course means that every month is considered to have 30 days, no more and no less. If we assume that interest was last paid on September 1, then interest for 69 days (using 30-day-month time) must be paid as part of the purchase price. This was determined as follows:

Last interest date: Sept. 1 to 30th = 30 days
　　　　　　　　　　 October　　　　 = 30 days
　　　　　　　　　　 November　　　 = 9 days (1 day before settlement date)

The problem of calculating accumulated bond interest is shown graphically in figure 6-1 using another set of dates.

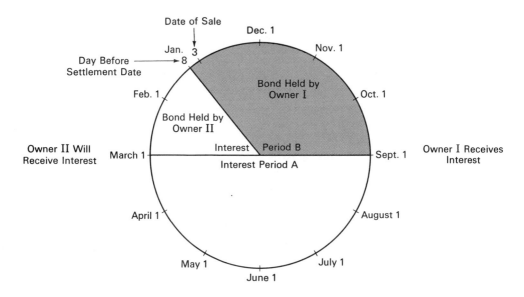

Read Counterclockwise

FIGURE 6-1

1. Owner I received the last interest payment on his Empire Corp. 6½s05 on September 1.
2. Owner I sold bond to Owner II on Thursday, January 3.
3. Owner II will receive semiannual interest for period B from the Empire Corp. on March 1.
4. Owner I held the bond for 128 days in period B (Sept. = 30 + Oct. 30 + Nov. 30 + Dec. 30 + Jan. 8) and is entitled to the interest for that many days. He will not receive it from the Empire Corp. because all of the interest for period B will be paid to Owner II on March 1.
5. Therefore, Owner I must charge Owner II the interest for 128 days when he sells the bond to him.

calculating the current yield on bond investments

The *current yield* on bonds is a measure of the percent of return on a bond investment assuming no change in the *current* market price. It is found by dividing the interest earned (or to be earned) by the market price.

Example

What is the current yield on an Apex Corp. $5\frac{1}{2}$s90 selling at 104?

$$\text{Current yield} = \$1{,}000 \times .055 = \$55$$

$$\text{Yield \%} = \frac{\$55}{\$1{,}040} = .0528 = 5.3\%$$

calculating the yield to maturity on bond investments

The investor who expects to hold a bond until it matures is interested in the rate of return he will receive over the life of the bond. In this case, since the bond pays a specific rate of interest based on its face (maturity) value, the *yield to maturity* will be increased when the bond is bought at discount, and decreased when bought at a premium.

The formula for finding the rate of yield to maturity is simply a matter of comparing the average interest received over the bond's life to the average yearly investment:

$$\text{Rate} = \frac{\text{Annual interest} + (\text{Discount/years remaining until maturity})}{\text{Average yearly investment}}$$

> NOTE: Average yearly investment is found by adding bond cost to face value at maturity, then dividing the sum by 2.

or

$$\text{Rate} = \frac{\text{Annual interest} - (\text{Premium/years remaining until maturity})}{\text{Average yearly investment}}$$

What is the yield to maturity of a Harry Patrick 6% bond that matures in 20 years, purchased for 86?

$$\frac{\$60 \text{ Annual interest} + (\$140 \text{ Discount}/20)}{(\$860 \text{ Bond cost} + \$1,000 \text{ Face value})/2} = \frac{\$67}{\$930}$$

$$= .072 = 7.2\%$$

What is the yield to maturity of a Waco Plastic Corp. 8% bond maturing in $15\frac{1}{2}$ years purchased for $106\frac{1}{2}$?

$$\frac{\$80 \text{ Annual interest} - (\$65 \text{ Premium}/15.5)}{(\$1,065 \text{ Bond cost} + \$1,000 \text{ Face value})/2} = \frac{\$80 - \$4.19}{\$1,032.50}$$

$$= \frac{\$75.81}{\$1,032.50}$$

$$= .0734 = 7.34\%$$

EXERCISE 6-3 PROBLEMS ON BOND PRICES AND YIELD

A. Find the selling price of these bonds sold between interest dates. Assume all are $1,000 bonds.
1. Warren Co. 6s85, one bond selling at 92, with interest payable on January 1 and July 1, sold on Tuesday, March 8
2. Pierson Corp. $4\frac{1}{2}$s99, 5 bonds selling at 68, with interest payable on October 1 and April 1, sold on Friday, January 6
3. Watanabe Corp. $7\frac{1}{4}$s10, 8 bonds selling at 101 with interest payable on November 1 and May 1, sold on Thursday, May 18
4. Bermuda Ltd. $5\frac{1}{2}$s88, 20 bonds selling at par (face value), with interest payable on February 1 and August 1, sold on Wednesday, June 10
5. Kent-Clark Corp. $6\frac{3}{4}$s95, 3 bonds selling at $98\frac{1}{2}$, with interest payable on January 1 and July 1, sold on Monday, April 2

B. Calculate the current yield (to the nearest tenth) on these prospective bond purchases. Ignore commission charges.

	Bond Face Value	Price	Rate of Interest	Current Yield
1.	$1,000	88	5%	_____
2.	500	$91\frac{1}{4}$	$6\frac{1}{4}$	_____
3.	500	112	$8\frac{5}{8}$	_____
4.	100	$62\frac{1}{2}$	4	_____
5.	1,000	$105\frac{3}{8}$	$7\frac{3}{4}$	_____

C. Calculate the years to maturity, annual interest, and the yield to maturity on these bond purchases. Ignore commission charges and assume interest is paid semiannually.

Face Value	Bond	Final Interest Date	Date of Purchase	Price Paid	Years to Maturity	Annual Interest	Yield to Maturity
$1,000	6s95	July 1	1/2/72	par	———	———	———
1,000	7s05	May 1	5/2/75	103	———	———	———
500	$5\frac{1}{2}$s85	Aug. 1	8/2/68	90	———	———	———
1,000	8s90	Apr. 1	4/2/71	$105\frac{1}{2}$	———	———	———
100	$5\frac{1}{4}$s78	July 1	1/2/69	$83\frac{1}{4}$	———	———	———
1,000	$8\frac{1}{8}$s82	Nov. 1	11/2/70	111	———	———	———

SECTION 4—ANNUITIES

In its broadest meaning, any series of more or less equal payments made over a period of time constitutes an *annuity*. The series of monthly payments millions of Americans make on their homes, automobiles, life insurance policies, and department store charge accounts all represent annuities. For Buffington's Department Store, the payments made to amortize their real estate mortgage represents an annuity, as does the series of salary payments paid by them to any one of their employees. When an annuity is paid for a definite period of time and the date of termination is fixed, it is called an *annuity certain*. An example would be the series of payments required to pay back a bank loan. When the continuation of payments depends upon some uncontrollable event, the term used is *contingent annuity*. For example, the salary payments made by Buffington's to an employee will continue only as long as he remains employed there.

In addition, annuities may be further classified based on the purpose for which they are created. In business, two kinds of annuities are common. One, called a *sinking fund*, is an annuity accumulated to meet a non-interest-bearing debt coming due on some future date (e.g., the planned purchase of equipment at some future date). The other, called *amortization*, is an annuity created to retire both the principal and interest of an interest-bearing debt. Buffington's mortgage payments are an example of amortization.

Calculating the amount of an annuity

In order to calculate the amount of an annuity, the nomenclature of annuities must be understood. The following are the concepts involved:

Rent (abbreviated R). The value of a periodic payment.

Ordinary annuity. An annuity wherein rent is paid at the end of each rent period.

Annuity due. An annuity wherein rent is paid at the beginning of each rent period.

Term. The duration of the annuity measured from the beginning of the initial rent period to the end of the last rent period.

Amount (abbreviated *S*). The term-end value of all the rent payments, including the compound interest earned on each one.

Present value (abbreviated *A*). The value today of the annuity amount, or the principal of the loan at the beginning of the first rent period.

The amount of an annuity may be found by use of column 1 of the tables in appendix IV, which shows how $1 left at compound interest will grow. In using this column it is necessary to compute the term-end value of each rent payment and then add these values to arrive at the annuity amount. Instead of this elongated procedure, it is simpler and faster to find the appropriate periodic interest rate at the top of the page and then use column 2, which gives the amount per period of $1 left at compound interest. After locating this figure we have only to multiply it by the rent to get the annuity amount. Example 1, below, demonstrates this procedure for an ordinary annuity.

To create a sum sufficient to purchase some new assets in the future, Buffington's deposits $6,000 at the end of each quarter, starting in March of this year, with a savings and loan company which pays 6% interest compounded quarterly. How much will this account be worth at the end of 4 years?   *Example 1*

Since the rent is paid at the end of each rent period, this is an ordinary annuity. *S* (the term end value) will equal *R* (the value of each periodic payment) times *s* (the amount of an ordinary annuity of $1 per year) payable for *n* periods at *i* (the periodic rate of interest). So:

$$S = Rs_{\overline{n}|i}$$
$$= \$6,000 \, (s_{\overline{16}|.015})$$
$$= \$6,000 \, (17.9323698)$$
$$= \$107,594.22$$

Notice that since interest is paid quarterly, we used the quarterly deposit at the rate per period of $1\frac{1}{2}\%$ (6% ÷ 4 quarters) for 16 periods (4 quarters × 4 years).

The same example with regard to an annuity due (example 2, below) would mean that the first $6,000 rent payment will be made on the beginning of the first quarter rather than at the end.

$$S = R(s_{\overline{n+1}|\,i} - 1)$$ *Example 2*
$$= \$6,000 \, (s_{\overline{16+1}|\,.015} - 1)$$

$$= \$6,000\,(19.2013554 - 1)$$
$$= \$6,000\,(18.2013554)$$
$$= \$109,208.13$$

The difference of $1,613.91 between the amount of the ordinary annuity and that of the annuity due is the additional compound interest for the term of the annuity on the first $6,000 quarterly payment made at the *beginning* of the first year. In other words, the first-quarter interest on this $6,000 compounded 16 times over the term of the annuity accumulates an additional $1,613.91. Checking the compound interest table for 16 periods at $1\frac{1}{2}\%$ shows

$$1.26899 \times \$6,000 = \$7,613.94$$

and

$$\$7,613.94 - \$6,000 = \$1,613.94$$

Calculating the present value of an annuity

The *present value* (or *present worth*) of an annuity is the value today of a series of future rent payments. In the case of a loan, the present value is, of course, the principal of the loan. To find the present value of an annuity, we need to determine the discounted value of the payments at the specified interest rate (i) for the given number of interest periods (n). Although column 4 in appendix IV tables could be used, column 5 ("Present Worth of $1 per period") makes the calculation simpler. Notice that this column differs from column 4 in that the latter shows the present value of only one payment or sum, while column 5 gives the present value of a series of payments.

Example (Present Value of Ordinary Annuity)

What is the present value of a series of annual rents of $800 paid at the end of the next 12 years if they will be earning 6% interest compounded annually? Use column 5 in the appendix IV tables.

$$A = R\overline{\underset{\overline{n}|i}{a}}$$
$$= \$800\left(\overline{\underset{\overline{12}|.06}{a}}\right)$$
$$= \$800(8.38384394)$$
$$= \$6,707.08$$

Example (Present Value of Annuity Due)

What is the present value of a $225 annual insurance premium paid each January 1 for 25 years if interest of 4% is compounded semiannually?

$$A = R(1 + \overline{\underset{\overline{n-1}|i}{a}})$$
$$= \$225(1 + \overline{\underset{\overline{50-1}|.02}{a}})$$
$$= \$225(1 + 31.05207801)$$
$$= \$225(32.05207801)$$
$$= \$7,311.72$$

SECTION 5—SINKING FUNDS

Sinking funds are taken up separately in this section in order to achieve more clarity of explanation and not because they are essentially different from the annuities already covered. Remember that a sinking fund *is* an annuity. Mathematically, the amount and present value of a sinking fund is found in exactly the same manner as explained for those annuities in the preceding section.

In this section we shall be concerned with calculating the rent required to accumulate a *sinking fund* (annuity) at some future date. This is similar to the process of finding the rent required to pay back both principal and interest on a loan in equal periodic payments. This procedure, called *amortization*, was explained in Section 2 of this chapter.

The difference between finding rent in amortization and rent in a sinking fund is that in the latter case we are looking for a rent that, when paid at regular intervals, will accumulate with interest to create a fund sufficient in size to pay off the principal of a non-interest-bearing obligation on its due date. In amortization, on the other hand, we were looking for a periodic rent which would reduce the principal and interest of an interest-bearing obligation so that its balance would be zero after the last payment was made.

Calculating rent in a sinking fund

Just as there are special tables for finding the amount or present value of an annuity, there are tables (column 3, appendix IV) to help simplify calculation of rent in a sinking fund. The following example illustrates the use of column 3 (subtitled "Periodic deposit that will grow to $1 at future date").

Buffington's wants to accumulate a fund of $40,000 at the end of 6 years   *Example*
to be used for the replacement of fixed assets. What yearly contribution must they make to a fund which will earn 6% interest compounded semiannually?

$$R = A \times \frac{1}{s_{\overline{n}|i}}$$

$$= \$40,000 \times \frac{1}{s_{\overline{12}|.03}}$$

$$= \$40,000(.07046209)$$

$$= \$2,818.48 \text{ Semiannual deposit to sinking fund}$$

Then,

$$\$2,818.48 \times 2 = \$5,636.96 \text{ Yearly rent}$$

Notice that the rent arrived at from the use of the table is the rent for 6 months, since interest is compounded semiannually and we used 12 semiannual periods at 3% per period in the formula.

EXERCISE 6-4 PROBLEMS ON ANNUITIES AND SINKING FUNDS

A. Calculate the amount of the following annuities:

1. Arthur Ashton signed an insurance contract calling for annual premium payments of $400 each year, paid semiannually. Interest of 5% compounded semiannually is the guaranteed rate. If the first payment is made on March 1, the day the contract was signed, find the amount after 30 years.

2. Al and John Paige want to start a partnership in 3 years. They plan to make deposits of $150 each at the end of every quarter for the next 3 years. What will be the value of their annuity after the 3-year period if their deposit earns 6% compounded quarterly?

3. To create a fund large enough to replace some capital equipment, the Ennis Bearing Co. started making monthly deposits of $500 on March 1, 1967. With interest at 8% compounded semiannually, how much will this fund amount to by March 2, 1972?

4. Mr. George Braun decided to establish a college fund for his son Bill. Beginning on the boy's first birthday and on every birthday thereafter, he deposited $200 in a savings account earning interest of $5\frac{1}{2}$% per year compounded annually. What will the fund be worth on the day before Bill's 17th birthday?

5. Beginning on January 1, 1972, if you consistently invested $12 a week at 6% interest compounded monthly, how much would you have 4 years from now? Use a rent payment of $52 per month.

6. Hugh Corcoran has received an inheritance of $6,000 per year for 10 years to be paid at the end of each quarter. If he began receiving these payments on July 1 of 1947, how much will his annuity be worth at the end of June in 1953? Assume he invests the money at 5% compounded quarterly.

B. Calculate the present value of the following annuities.

1. What is the present value of $400 per year received at year's end for 10 years if money is worth 5% compounded annually?

2. Mr. and Mrs. John Gravendyk are considering selling their house. One offer they received calls for $7,000 down today (September 1, 1971) and $1,200 every three months up to and including September 1, 1977. If money is worth 8% compounded quarterly, what would be the present cash value of this offer today?

3. John Kennealy has calculated a likely annual return of $18,000 on an apartment house he is thinking of buying. Assuming the $18,000 net income could be earned at the end of each of the next 12 years, and that Mr. Kennealy wants to earn 8% interest compounded annually on his investment, what is the apartment house worth today?

4. Romeo Gigilone is about to buy a set of wedding rings on credit. The terms call for payments of $28 now and on the 1st of each month for the next 24 months. What is the present value (cash value) of these rings today if money is worth 6% compounded monthly?

5. A boy received an inheritance which paid him $50 on the first of each month beginning on his 18th birthday and ending after his 30th birthday. Assuming that his payments could earn an average of 6% compounded monthly, what would be the present value of his inheritance the day before he turns 27?

6. In problem #5, what is the present value of the inheritance the day before his 29th birthday?

7. Buffington's Department Store is considering the establishment of a branch store. One location available can be obtained on a 20 year lease calling for $60,000 to be paid at the end of each six month period. If money is worth 8% compounded semiannually, what is the present value of this lease?

C. Calculate the rent in these sinking funds.

1. A man desires to open his own men's wear store. He figures he will need $30,000 of his own capital to start. If he wants to accumulate the necessary capital in 10 years, how much must he deposit annually, if his deposits will earn 7% compounded annually?

2. On his 21st birthday a man begins making equal annual contributions to an endownment insurance fund. If the fund will earn 6% interest compounded annually, how much will he need to deposit each year in order to have a fund of $50,000 on his 55th birthday?

3. If in problem 2, above, interest at the rate of 6% is compounded semi-annually and the man was 40 years old when he started, what would the semiannual deposit have to be to accumulate $50,000 by age 55?

4. Mr. and Mrs. Woodson have purchased a home on which there is a second mortgage of $5,000. This mortgage was obtained from the seller and provides that the Woodson's will repay the loan with simple annual interest of 8% in one lump payment made at the end of a 5-year period. How much should be deposited each quarter to pay off this mortgage if the Woodson's can earn 6% interest compounded quarterly?

5. The Walcott Electronics Corp. is required to establish a bond sinking fund in order to be able to redeem a $220,000 bond issue which matures in 30 years. How much will the company need to deposit to this sinking fund each year if the deposits are expected to earn 5% interest compounded semiannually?

BUFFINGTON'S DEPARTMENT STORE INC.
BALANCE SHEET
AS OF JANUARY 31, 19XX

ASSETS

CURRENT ASSETS:			
Cash on Hand and in Bank		$180,000	15.0%
Notes Receivable		5,000	.4%
Accounts Receivable	$310,000		
Less: Estimated Bad Debts	10,000	300,000	25.0%
Merchandise Inventory (at cost)		400,000	33.3%
Supplies		10,000	.9%
Prepaid Expenses		5,000	.4%
Total Current Assets		$ 900,000	75.0%
FIXED ASSETS:			
Furniture, Fixtures and Equipment	$125,000		
Less: Accumulated Depreciation	45,000	$ 80,000	6.7%
Delivery Equipment	$ 50,000		
Less: Accumulated Depreciation	30,000	20,000	1.7%
Building	$250,000		
Less: Accumulated Depreciation	50,000	200,000	16.6%
Total Fixed Assets		300,000	25.0%
TOTAL ASSETS		$1,200,000	100.0%

LIABILITIES AND PROPRIETORSHIP

CURRENT LIABILITIES:			
Notes Payable		$ 50,000	4.2%
Accounts Payable		220,000	18.3%
Expenses Payable		5,000	.4%
Total Current Liabilities		$ 275,000	22.9%
LONG-TERM LIABILITIES:			
Mortgage Payable		125,000	10.4%
Total Liabilities		$ 400,000	33.3%
PROPRIETORSHIP:			
Preferred Stock	$100,000		
Common Stock	500,000		
Retained Earnings	200,000		
Total Proprietorship (net worth)		800,000	66.7%
TOTAL LIABILITIES AND PROPRIETORSHIP		$1,200,000	100.0%

THE BALANCE SHEET

7

mathematics
of proprietorship
equities

In chapter 1, a distinction was made between possession and ownership. A business possesses many things of value, called assets, but seldom do the owners of the business have full ownership rights to those assets. The creditors of the business have ownership rights to the assets which precede those of the owners. The mathematics of creditor rights or equities, termed the *liabilities of the business*, were discussed in chapter 6. To conclude the balance sheet, this chapter is concerned with the mathematics of proprietorship equities.

The types of proprietorship or business ownership were explained in chapter 1. The *single proprietorship* is the oldest and simplest type of business organization. Although it is the most common type when numbers of businesses are concerned, it is rarely used for larger businesses with 100 or more employees. The *corporation* is symbolic of modern business because it permits the raising of the great amounts of capital required by large-scale business activities. Since it brings many people into the role of ownership through different types of stock, the distribution of profits become more complex. For this reason, we shall concentrate on the corporate type of proprietorship typified by our example of Buffington's Department Store. The *partnership* type of ownership lies between the single proprietorship and the corporation.

SECTION I—CORPORATE STOCKS

Nature of a corporation

A corporation is an artificial person or legal entity created according to the corporation laws of a particular state. The extent of its operations, its rights, and privileges are set out in a *charter*, granted by the state in which it is incorporated. It has several owners called *stockholders*, since each holds *stock certificates* (also called *securities* or simply *stocks*) as evidence of their ownership of a portion of the corporation. The primary advantage of the corporation as a business organization is the more ready accumulation of capital. Its primary advantage to the owners is that a stockholder's property cannot be taken to satisfy the debts of the business. Owners under single proprietorship and partnerships do not have such *limited liability*.

The stockholders' investment in the corporation is termed its *capital stock*. A certain portion—sometimes all—of the profits of the corporation may be retained to assure continuous operation despite any adverse conditions as well as to permit growth or expansion. Any amount of profits kept by the corporation is termed *retained earnings* on the balance sheet. It is part of the total stockholders' equity—but not a part of capital stock, which is the actual investment or contribution of the stockholders. Profits may also be distributed to the stockholders in the form of *dividends*. In Buffington's case, the capital stock is $600,000 and the retained earnings are $200,000.

The state charter authorizes the corporation to issue a certain number of shares of capital stock, although seldom is the maximum amount issued. A specific dollar amount termed *par value* may be shown on the stock certificates. This is the minimum amount which the investor must pay the corporation for each share of stock. If he pays less than par then he is contingently liable to creditors for the amount of discount in case of business failure. Some stock is issued at *no par value* (usually called *no-par* stock) in which case the board of directors gives it a *stated value* for accounting purposes. In actuality, par value and stated value have little significance today. The value of stock—the market price—is dependent upon the corporation's assets and its present or anticipated earnings as well as the demand for stock and general business conditions. Two kinds of stock are usually issued, *preferred* and *common*. Buffington's balance sheet shows $100,000 of preferred stock and $500,000 of common stock.

Preferred stock

Preferred stock has certain features which make it more salable to a certain portion of the market. Usually the preference relates to dividends, which means that dividends at a specified rate or amount must be paid to preferred stockholders before any dividends can be paid to common stockholders. *Cumulative preferred stock* accumulates dividends for years in which dividends are not paid, requiring that the corporation pay all back dividends before any payments can be paid to holders of noncumulative preferred stock or common stock. Holders of *participating preferred stock* receive dividends up to the specified amount, but after common stockholders receive a like amount they share any additional dividends with the common stockholders.

Preferred stock also has preference as to assets if the corporation is dissolved. After creditors are satisfied, remaining assets must satisfy the claims of preferred stockholders before common stockholders receive any payment. A corporation may also distinguish classes of preferred stock such as *1st preferred* and *2nd preferred*, each with different types of preferences. An added attraction to an issue may be a conversion right, in which case the stock is called *convertible preferred*. Such stock may be exchanged for common stock, within a certain time period, at a price designated at time of issuance.

Ownership of preferred stock generally does not confer voting rights, as does that of common stock. Thus, control or management of a company is seldom a motive when investment is made in preferred stock.

Common stock

If only one type of stock is issued, then there is no preference between shares all of which are known as common stocks. However, there may be voting stock designated *class A common* and nonvoting stock designated *class B common*, the only distinction between the two classes being the voting privilege. Thus, class B stock can be used to raise additional capital without sacrificing the control of the existing stockholders.

Common stockholders may receive no return on their investment when earnings are low, due to the prior claims of preferred stockholders. However, when earnings are high, the return may be much greater than the fixed returns for creditors or preferred stockholders. Continued high earnings or increase in assets tend to increase the market price, so that gains may then be made by sale of the stock.

Corporations often "split" their common stock, particularly following a great advance in market price. A *stock split* is simply the division of the outstanding shares into a greater number of shares. Thus, a 2-for-1 split would double the shares outstanding and a person owning 100 shares would receive an additional 100 shares. At the same time, the par value of each share would be cut in half. (Approximately the same thing would happen to the market value.) The purpose of a split is to lower the per-share market price in order to make it easier for more people to buy the stock.

Issuing and selling stock

A company may sell its stock directly to individuals, which is usually the case with small and closely held or "family" corporations such as Buffington's. However, a broader market can be obtained if the shares are sold to the general public. *Going public* customarily means outright sale of the entire issue to an investment banker, who makes a middleman's profit for his services in marketing the securities.

Maintaining a market for the securities is important, as many would hesitate to buy the shares if there would be difficulty in selling them. A market may be established *over-the-counter*, which means that security dealers will buy and sell the stocks in their offices or by telephone rather than on a stock exchange.

Stocks (and bonds) may be offered for sale on a *stock exchange*. To have its securities listed on an exchange, the corporation must meet certain requirements of the Securities and Exchange Commission and of the stock exchange as to capitalization, sales, number of stockholders, shares issued, and so forth. The exchange is a nonprofit association of dealers or brokers in securities. Stock exchanges are located in many of the larger cities, but the New York Stock Exchange is the most important. "Seats" on the New York exchange—i.e., membership in the exchange—is limited to 1,375 brokers, and the great demand for membership has resulted in raising the cost of seats to over $200,000. Only members are permitted to buy and sell stock in an exchange. The public must therefore use the services of a *broker* and pay him a commission for buying or selling securities on their behalf.

A stock exchange is not a source of capital for the corporation. The corporation sells its securities *on* the exchange through investment bankers. The transactions in a stock exchange are between individuals, companies, or various types of fund organizations seeking profits on their investments in various types of securities.

Stock quotations

After each day of trading, a summary of transactions on the New York Stock Exchange (and sometimes other exchanges) is carried in the financial section of most newspapers. A highly abbreviated version of such a summary is shown in table 7-1. The line for each stock, called a *quotation*, contains the following information: highest price and lowest price paid for the stock in the current year; the name of the issuing corporation (in abbreviated form); designation of pre-

TABLE 7-1 selected daily stock quotations

Year's High	Year's Low	Stocks	Div.	Sales in 100s	Open	High	Low	Close	Net Change
$53\frac{7}{8}$	$40\frac{3}{8}$	Am T&T	2.60	429	$43\frac{1}{4}$	$43\frac{3}{4}$	$43\frac{1}{8}$	$43\frac{5}{8}$	$+\frac{3}{8}$
78	$60\frac{1}{4}$	Gen Elec	2.60	159	$73\frac{3}{4}$	74	$73\frac{1}{2}$	74	$+\frac{1}{4}$
$76\frac{1}{4}$	$59\frac{1}{2}$	Gen Mot	2.55[a]	366	$67\frac{1}{2}$	$67\frac{3}{4}$	$67\frac{3}{8}$	$67\frac{3}{4}$	$-\frac{1}{4}$
$76\frac{1}{2}$	$67\frac{1}{2}$	Gen Mot 5pf	5	6	71	$71\frac{1}{4}$	$70\frac{3}{8}$	$70\frac{7}{8}$	$-\frac{1}{8}$
387	$218\frac{3}{4}$	IBM	4.80	385	$230\frac{3}{4}$	$235\frac{1}{4}$	$227\frac{1}{2}$	$235\frac{1}{4}$	$+5\frac{3}{8}$
$29\frac{1}{2}$	$22\frac{1}{8}$	Safeway	1.10	84	$29\frac{3}{8}$	$29\frac{1}{2}$	$29\frac{1}{4}$	$29\frac{1}{4}$	$+\frac{1}{8}$
$69\frac{3}{8}$	51	SearsR	1.20	107	60	$60\frac{1}{4}$	$59\frac{7}{8}$	$60\frac{1}{4}$	$+\frac{1}{4}$
$64\frac{1}{4}$	$49\frac{7}{8}$	StOilNJ	2.70	240	$62\frac{1}{8}$	$62\frac{5}{8}$	$62\frac{1}{8}$	$62\frac{1}{2}$	$+\frac{3}{8}$
$115\frac{3}{4}$	$65\frac{1}{4}$	Xerox Cp	.60	443	$67\frac{3}{8}$	$67\frac{7}{8}$	67	$67\frac{3}{4}$	$+\frac{5}{8}$

[a]Declared or paid so far this year.

ferred issues with "pf"; the annual dividend rate per share and other dividend information; sales for the day in hundreds of shares; the price per share of the first transaction after opening of the market; the highest and lowest price for the day; the closing price; and the net change between the closing price for the day and that of the previous day on which the stock was traded. Price figures are given in dollars and fractions of dollars, and are sometimes referred to as "points." Thus, a net change of $\frac{3}{8}$ of a point would mean $\frac{3}{8}$ of a dollar or $.375; $\frac{1}{8}$ of a point or $.125 is the smallest measurement of price changes.

EXERCISE 7-1 PROBLEMS BASED ON STOCK QUOTATIONS

Solve the following problems using the stock quotations in table 7-1.

1. If 100 shares of American Telephone and Telegraph were purchased at the day's lowest price, how much money would be involved?
2. Roy Edwards purchased 50 shares of General Electric at the lowest price for the current year. As of the end of trading today, what was the value of his stock? What has been the dollar gain in value and the rate of gain?
3. Charles Lacey purchased 160 shares of General Motors common stock at the year's high. As of the end of trading today, has he a gain or loss on his investment? What has been the amount and rate of gain or loss?
4. If no additional dividends are paid this year on the General Motors common stock, how much greater in amount and rate would be the return on 75 shares of preferred stock over 75 shares of common stock?
5. What is the day's change in total value on 150 shares of IBM?
6. What has been the amount and rate of increase in value on 75 shares of Safeway stock from its year's low to its closing price today?
7. Richard Fremont bought 100 shares of Sears Roebuck stock at its year's low. If he holds it for a year, how much will he receive in dividends and what would be the rate of return on his investment?
8. What would be the rate of return on an investment in 100 shares of Standard Oil (New Jersey) if it were purchased at the year's high? At the year's low?
9. What rate of decrease has there been in the price of one share of Xerox from its year's high to today's closing?
10. What would be the total value of today's trading in Xerox stock figured at the closing price per share?

SECTION 2—COSTS OF TRADING

Brokerage commissions

Transactions on an exchange are made either in round or odd lots. A *round lot*, unless otherwise specified, is 100 shares; an *odd lot* is any portion of 100 shares.

An exception is when a few stocks are traded in "round lots" of 10 shares, in which case an "odd lot" is any portion of 10 shares.

When shares of listed stock are bought or sold, a commission must be paid to the stockbroker. The New York Stock Exchange specifies the minimum commission rates which all member organizations must charge customers. This is done to insure a professional relationship between broker and client and between brokers. The emphasis then is on minimum rather than maximum rates. Commissions on stocks selling at $1.00 or more per share are computed on the basis of the amount of money involved in a *single transaction*, which is the purchase or sale of a single round lot or odd lot.

The minimum commission charge per transaction involving $100 or more is $1.50 per share. The total commission must be at least $6.00, but should not exceed $75.00. When the amount involved in a transaction is less than $100, the minimum commission shall be as mutually agreed. An *order* is defined as all purchases or sales for one account on the same day, and may involve several round lots and an odd lot.

Table 7-2 gives the New York Stock Exchange minimum commission charges for the first 1,000 shares of an order and for any portion in excess of 1,000 shares.

TABLE 7-2 brokerage commissions for transactions on the New York Stock Exchange

First 1,000 Shares of an Order Selling at $1.00 or More per Share

Total Money Involved	Round-lot Commission	Odd-lot Commission
Under $100.00	As mutually agreed	As mutually agreed
$100.00–399.99	2% plus $3.00	2% plus $1.00
$400.00–2,399.99	1% plus $7.00	1% plus $5.00
$2,400.00–4,999.99	$\frac{1}{2}$% plus $19.00	$\frac{1}{2}$% plus $17.00
$5,000 and over	$\frac{1}{10}$% plus $39.00	$\frac{1}{10}$% plus $37.00
Compute the commission for 1 round lot and multiply by the number of lots traded.		Any odd lot is deemed to be a separate transaction.

Portion of Order in Excess of 1,000 Shares— for Each 100 Shares or Less

Total Money Involved (per 100 Shares or Less)	Commission (per 100 Shares or Less)
$100.00–2,800.00	$\frac{1}{2}$% of money involved plus $4.00
$2,800.01–3,000.00	compute as for $2,800.00
$3,000.01–9,000.00	$\frac{1}{2}$% of money involved plus $3.00
over $9,000.00	$\frac{1}{10}$% of money involved plus $39.00

Note: The great amount of paperwork resulting from increased volume on the exchanges has posed a major problem. On April 6, 1970, the Securities and Exchange Commission imposed a surcharge of $15.00, or 50% of the current commissions, whichever is lesser. The 90-day effective period was extended twice; but since it is still a temporary measure, the surcharge will not be considered in any calculations in this text.

For transactions of less than round lots, brokers on the floor specializing in odd lots must be used. When sales involve less than the 100 share round lot, they receive a commission of $12\frac{1}{2}$ cents a share on stocks selling below \$55 and 25 cents a share on stocks selling at \$55 or above. This commission is termed an *odd-lot differential*, and is either added to the effective round-lot price when purchasing or subtracted when selling.

calculation of brokerage commissions on New York Stock Exchange
(based on Table 7-2)

Purchased: 100 shares @\$48—money involved, \$4,800   *Example 1*

$\frac{1}{2}$% of \$4,800 = \$24.00
Plus   19.00
Commission   \$43.00

Purchased: 400 shares @\$52—money involved, \$20,800   *Example 2*

Money involved per 100 shares = \$20,800 ÷ 4 = \$5,200
$\frac{1}{10}$% of \$5,200   = \$ 5.20
Plus   39.00
Commission per 100 shares   \$44.20
Number of round lots   ×   5
Commission on 400 shares   \$221.00

Purchased: 100 shares @\$$1\frac{1}{8}$—money involved, \$112.50   *Example 3*

2% of \$112.50   \$2.25
Plus   3.00
Calculated commission   \$5.25
Actual commission   \$6.00 Minimum requirement for
                               single transaction

Purchased: 100 shares @\$375—money involved, \$37,500   *Example 4*

$\frac{1}{10}$% of \$37,500 = \$37.50
Plus   39.00
Commission   \$76.50

When the calculated commission is greater than \$75, the broker may charge the full amount. However, \$75 is generally considered to be the maximum charge.

Example 5

Purchased: 1,500 shares @$23—money involved, $34,500

First 1,000 shares: money involved, $23,000

Money involved per 100 shares	= $23,000 ÷ 10 = $2,300	
1% of $2,300	$23.00	
Plus	7.00	
Commission per 100 shares	$30.00	
Number of round lots	× 10	
Commission on first 1,000 shares	$300.00:	$300.00

Balance of 500 shares: money involved, $11,500

Money involved per 100 shares	= $11,500 ÷ 5 = $2,300	
$\frac{1}{2}$% of $2,300	$ 11.50	
Plus	4.00	
Commission per 100 shares	$ 15.50	
Number of round lots	× 5	
Commission on balance (500 shares)	$ 77.50:	77.50
Total commission		$377.50

Example 6

Purchased: 75 shares @$40

	$40.00
Odd-lot differential, $\frac{1}{8}$ point	.125
Adjusted price per share	$40.125 (money involved, $3,093.75)
$\frac{1}{2}$% of $3,093.75	= $15.47
Plus	17.00
Commission	$32.47

Example 7

Purchased: 90 shares @$60

	$60.00
Odd-lot differential, $\frac{1}{4}$ point	.25
Adjusted price per share	$60.25 (money involved, $5,422.50)
$\frac{1}{10}$% of $5,422.50	$ 5.42
Plus	37.00
Commission	$42.42

Example 8

Purchased: 1,090 shares @$59.75

First 1,000 shares: money involved, $59,750
Money involved per 100 shares = $59,750 ÷ 10 = $5,975

$\frac{1}{10}$% of $5,975	= $ 5.98	
Plus	39.00	
Commission per 100 shares	$ 44.98	
	× 10	
	$449.80:	$449.80
Balance of 90 shares @	$ 59.75	
Odd-lot differential, $\frac{1}{4}$ point	.25	
Adjusted price per share	$ 60.00; money involved, $5,400	
$\frac{1}{2}$% of $5,400	= $ 27.00	
Plus	3.00	
Commission on balance (90 shares) $30.00:		30.00
Total commission		$479.80

Taxes and fees

A *stock transfer tax* is a tax imposed on a securities transaction. Prior to 1966 a transfer tax was assessed by the federal government as well as by a few states. Currently there is no federal transfer tax, and the only states levying such a tax are New York and Florida; New York's rates are shown in table 7-3.

TABLE 7-3   New York State Stock Transfer Tax

Selling Price per Share	Rate of Tax per Share*
less than $5.00	$1\frac{1}{4}$¢
$5.00–9.99	$2\frac{1}{2}$¢
$10.00–19.99	$3\frac{3}{4}$¢
$20.00 or over	5

*Sales by nonresidents are taxed at a reduced rate.

In addition, the New York Stock Exchange imposes a fee for each transaction on the exchange. This fee, called the "Securities and Exchange Commission's fee" because it is used to pay the exchange's annual registration fee assessed by the SEC, is 1¢ for each $500 or fraction thereof of money involved in a transaction, excluding commissions and taxes. Both taxes and fees are paid by the seller or transferrer of stock.

calculation of New York State Stock Transfer Tax and SEC Fees
(based on Table 7-3)

Sold: 100 shares @$33—money involved, $3,300   *Example*
N. Y. State tax: .05 × 100 = $5.00   *1*
SEC fee: .01 × 7   =   .07
   Total taxes and fees $5.07

Sold: 35 shares @$300—money involved, $10,500   *Example*
N. Y. State tax: .05 × 35 = $1.75   *2*
SEC fee: .01 × 21   =   .21
   Total taxes and fees $1.96

Sold: 750 shares @$2.00—money involved, $1,500   *Example*
N. Y. State tax: .0125 × 750 = $9.38   *3*
SEC fee: .01 × 3   .03
   Total taxes and fees $9.41

calculation of commissions, taxes, and fees

Sold: 100 shares @$42—money involved, $4,200   *Example*
Commission   *1*

$\frac{1}{2}$% of $4,200	$21.00
Plus	19.00
Commission	$40.00
N.Y. State tax: .05 × 100	5.00
SEC Fee: .01 × 9	.09
Total cost of trading	$45.09

Example
2

Sold: 1,250 shares @$60—money involved, $75,000
Commission
  First 1,000 shares—money involved, $60,000
    Money involved per 100 shares = $60,000 ÷ 10 = $6,000

$\frac{1}{10}$% of $6,000	$ 6.00	
Plus	39.00	
Commission per 100 shares	$45.00	
Number of round lots	× 10	
Commission on first 1,000 shares $450.00:		$450.00

200 shares over 1,000 shares—money involved, $12,000
  Money involved per 100 shares = $12,000 ÷ 2 = $6,000

$\frac{1}{2}$% of $6,000	$30.00	
Plus	3.00	
Commission per 100 shares	$33.00	
Number of round lots	× 2	
Commission on 200 shares over 1,000 shares	$66.00:	66.00
Balance of 50 shares@	$60.00	
Odd-lot differential, $\frac{1}{4}$ point	.25	
Adjusted price per share	$60.25:	money involved, $3,012.50

$\frac{1}{2}$% of $3,012.50 = $15.06		
Plus	3.00	
Commission on 50 shares	$18.06:	$18.06
Total commission		$534.06
N.Y. State tax: .05 × 1,250		62.50
SEC fee: .01 × 150		1.50
Total cost of trading		$598.06

EXERCISE 7-2 PROBLEMS ON COST OF TRADING—ROUND LOTS

Using tables 7-2 and 7-3, calculate the minimum New York Stock Exchange brokerage commission, the New York State stock transfer tax, and the exchange's SEC fee on the following round-lot transactions:

1. 100 shares American Telephone & Telegraph at $50 per share.
2. 300 shares American Telephone & Telegraph at $50 per share.
3. 100 shares Safeway at 29\frac{1}{4}$ per share.
4. 500 shares General Electric at $74 per share.
5. 100 shares IBM at $387 per share.
6. 100 shares United Park City Miner at $1.00 per share.
7. 200 shares Ogden Corp. at 7\frac{3}{8}$ per share.
8. 400 shares Clark Equipment at 28\frac{1}{2}$ per share.
9. 200 shares Sears Roebuck at 60\frac{1}{4}$ per share.
10. 800 shares Standard Oil (New Jersey) at 62\frac{5}{8}$ per share.

EXERCISE 7-3 PROBLEMS ON COST OF TRADING—ODD LOTS

Calculate the minimum New York Stock Exchange brokerage commission, the New York state stock transfer tax, and the exchange's SEC fee on the following odd-lot transactions: Include odd-lot differentials in your calculations.

1. Sold 25 shares Xerox at $66\frac{3}{4}$ per share.
2. Sold 10 shares IBM at $234\frac{3}{4}$ per share.
3. Sold 1 share Burroughs at $121\frac{3}{4}$ per share.
4. Sold 8 shares American Express at $16\frac{3}{8}$ per share.
5. Sold 35 shares General Electric at $74\frac{1}{8}$ per share.
6. Sold 50 shares Caterpillar Tractor at $33\frac{5}{8}$ per share.
7. Sold 80 shares Memorex at $110 per share.
8. Sold 40 shares General Motors at $65\frac{3}{4}$ per share.
9. Sold 14 shares Federated Department Stores at $30\frac{1}{2}$ per share.
10. Sold 90 shares Macy's at $27\frac{1}{4}$ per share.

EXERCISE 7-4 PROBLEMS ON COST OF TRADING—ROUND LOTS AND ODD LOTS

Calculate the minimum New York Stock Exchange brokerage commission, the New York State stock transfer tax, and the exchange's SEC fee on the following orders.   When applicable, include odd-lot differentials in your calculations.

1. 2,000 shares Ampex at $20 per share.
2. 2,000 shares Disney at $100 per share.
3. 2,000 shares Safeway at $29 per share.
4. 1,050 shares General Electric at $75 per share.
5. 1,100 shares Admiral at $7 per share.
6. 1,250 shares Marshall Field at $22 per share.
7. 1,075 shares Gimbel Bros. at $30 per share.
8. 1,200 shares Broadway Hale at $35 per share.
9. 1,100 shares Grand Union at $25 per share.
10. 1,090 shares J. C. Penney at $40 per share.

SECTION 3—DIVIDENDS ON STOCK

Cash dividends

The board of directors of a corporation determines at least once a year how much of the company's earnings will be distributed to its owners·as dividends on the stock which they hold. As previously stated, preferred stockholders have first rights to any such distribution of profits. The amount of the dividend to be paid on preferred stock, when declared, is specified on the stock certificate. If the preferred issue has a par value, the dividend is stated as a percent of that value. Thus, "5% preferred stock" means that each dividend will equal 5% of its par value: if the par value is $100, the annual dividend will be $5. If the issue has no par value, the dividend is indicated as a dollar amount, as in "$5 preferred stock."

In the case of cumulative preferred stock, unpaid dividends from previous years (i.e., those in which no dividends were declared) must first be paid before any profits may be distributed. Thus, if dividends are declared after passing them for two years, holders of $5 cumulative preferred stock will receive $10 in back dividends plus $5 in dividends for the year of declaration. If this preferred issue were also participating, its holders might receive an additional amount. The amount of participation, just as the dividend, is specified by the company at the time the stock is issued. *Full or 100% participation* means that, in terms of our current example, after common stockholders each receive a $5-per-share dividend for a given year (if they receive dividends at all that year), any additional distribution will be shared equally by preferred and common stockholders.

Example 1   Buffington's has 1,000 shares of 5% $100 par-value preferred stock and 5,000 shares of $100 par-value common stock outstanding. They declared a dividend of $25,000. How much will be paid on each class of stock?

Dividend declared	$25,000
Preferred stockholders' portion	
5% X $100 par value = $5.00 per share	
1,000 shares X $5.00 =	5,000
Amount available for common stockholders	$20,000

$20,000 ÷ 5,000 shares = $4.00 per share

Example 2   The capital of the Broadmore Company consisted of 5,000 shares of $4 no-par cumulative preferred stock and 20,000 shares of no-par common stock. No dividends were declared in 1969, 1970, and 1971. In 1972 the directors declared a dividend of $100,000. How much will be paid on each class of stock?

Dividend declared	$100,000
Cumulative preferred stockholders' portion	
Annual dividend:	
5,000 shares X $4.00 = $20,000	
Accumulated dividends:	
4 years X $20,000 =	80,000
Amount available for common stockholders	$20,000

Example 3   J. W. Thompson Co. declared a dividend of $128,000. Their capitalization was 2,000 shares of 8%, $50 par-value cumulative 2% participating preferred stock (2% of par value or $1.00 per share maximum participation) and 20,000 shares of $100 par-value common stock. No dividend has been declared in the prior year. How much will be paid on each class of stock?

Dividend declared	$128,000

Cumulative 2% participating preferred stockholders' portion
Annual dividend:
    8% × $50 = $4.00 per share
    2,000 shares × $4.00 = $8,000
Accumulated dividends:
    2 years × $8,000 =   16,000
Amount remaining for distribution $112,000
Common stockholders' portion at equivalent rate
    20,000 shares × $4.00   80,000
Available for participation $32,000
    Preferred stock, 2,000 shares (at 2% of $50.00 par value
    or $1.00 per share)   2,000
    Common stock, 20,000 shares $30,000

$$\$30,000 \div 20,000 \text{ shares} = \$1.50 \text{ per share}$$

Total distribution to preferred stockholders
    Accumulated dividends $8.00 per share
    Participating dividends   1.00 per share
                           $9.00 × 2,000 shares = $ 18,000
Total distribution to common stockholders
    Equivalent dividends $4.00 per share
    Participating dividends   1.50 per share
                           $5.50 × 20,000 shares = 110,000
Total distribution to stockholders $128,000

EXERCISE 7-5 DIVIDEND DISTRIBUTION

Complete the following table.

	Dividend Declared	Total Preferred Shares	Par Value per Share	Total Par Value	Dividend Rate per Share	Dividend per Share (Preferred)	Total Dividend (Preferred)	Available for Common
A.	$50,000	1,000	$100	$100,000	5%	_____	_____	_____
B.	10,000	500	none	none	$5½	_____	_____	_____
C.	60,000	2,000		$100,000	8%	_____	_____	_____
D.	8,000		$ 25	$ 10,000	10%	_____	_____	_____
E.	20,000	1,250	none	none	$4.25	_____	_____	_____
F.	90,000	9,000	$100		6%	_____	_____	_____
G.	8,000		$ 50	$ 75,000	6½%	_____	_____	_____
H.	18,000	6,000		$450,000	4%	_____	_____	_____
I.	9,000	1,200	$ 80	$112,500	4½%	_____	_____	_____
J.	12,500	1,500			7½%	_____	_____	_____

EXERCISE 7-6 PROBLEMS ON DIVIDEND DISTRIBUTION

1. The Tom Watkins Corporation has a capitalization of 1,000 shares of 4% $100 par-value preferred stock and 4,000 shares of $100 par-value common stock. They declared a dividend of $12,000. How much will be paid per share and in total on each class of stock?

2. Amalgamated Mines have 10,000 shares of $5 no-par cumulative preferred

stock and 50,000 shares of no-par common stock. Dividends were omitted the past two years. This year the directors declared a dividend of $225,000. How much will be paid per share and in total on each class of stock?

3. A dividend of $150,000 was declared by the Angel Seed Company this year after passing the dividend last year. Their stock issues consisted of 3,000 shares of $5\frac{1}{2}$% $100 par-value cumulative participating preferred stock and 30,000 shares of no-par common stock. How much in total will the company pay in dividends on each class of stock? How much per share will preferred stockholders receive? How much per share will common stock-holders receive?

4. The capital of Fairfield Magnetics consisted of 1,000 shares $4\frac{1}{2}$% $75 par-value cumulative fully participating preferred stock and 15,000 shares of no-par common stock. They declared a dividend of $74,375 after skipping it the prior year. How much will be paid per share and in total on each class of stock?

5. The J & J Toy Company's proprietorship consisted of 50,000 shares of no-par common and 10,000 shares of 6% $100 par-value preferred. A dividend of $420,000 was declared. How would this be divided between the two classes of stock and what would be the payment per share?

6. The outstanding stock of Rapid Freight, Inc. was 400,000 shares of $10 par-value common and 10,000 shares 6% $100 par-value preferred cumulative for 2 years. What will be the payment per share and in total for each class of stock if a dividend of $380,000 is declared?

7. Rebera Reapers had issued 10,000 shares of 6% $50 par-value cumulative preferred stock and 50,000 shares of no-par common stock. A dividend of $225,000 was declared. During the previous two years no dividend had been paid. How much will be paid on each share of stock?

8. The Wayne Company has 10,000 shares of $10 par-value common stock and 2,000 shares of 6% $80 par-value cumulative preferred stock. Last year no dividend was paid. This year a dividend of $15,000 was declared. How much will be paid on each share of stock?

9. After skipping dividends last year, Raley Laboratories declared a dividend of $54,000. How much will be paid on each share of stock? The capitalization is 10,000 shares no-par common stock and 1,000 shares 8% $100 par-value cumulative preferred stock.

10. Prentice & Goodrich Co. had stockholders equity represented by 2,000 shares $6\frac{1}{2}$% $75 par-value fully participating cumulative preferred stock and 10,000 shares of no-par common stock. Dividends were passed for two years, and in the third year a dividend of $45,000 was declared. How much will now be paid on each share of stock?

Stock dividends

A corporation may pay dividends in the form of additional shares of its autho-rized stock rather than in cash. A new corporation may issue stock dividends to conserve cash. In the case of very large corporations, the issuance of the additional stock would tend to reduce the market price and encourage a more widespread ownership. Sometimes, a combination cash and stock dividend may be declared.

When a stock dividend is declared, a portion of retained earnings is transferred to capital stock. Thus, the stockholders' equity in the corporation is not altered, because the change is entirely within the proprietorship section of the balance sheet, with no change in assets or liabilities. Stock dividends seldom apply to preferred stockholders, but a preferred stock dividend payment may be made to common stockholders.

Buffington's declared a 12% stock dividend on its 5,000 shares of $100 *Example* par-value common stock. This would call for a distribution of 600 shares (12% × *1* 5,000) to the owners of common stock. The total par-value of the common stock is now $560,000 ($500,000 + 600 shares at $100 per share). The transfer from retained earnings to capital would be at market value, with any amount over par value being reflected as a premium on common stock in the proprietorship section of the balance sheet. Assuming a market value of $120 per share of common stock, the excess over par-value is $20 per share ($120 – $100) and the total premium is $12,000 (600 shares at $20 per share). The reduction in retained earnings, the last item in the proprietorship section, is $72,000 (600 shares at $120).

	Before Stock Dividend	After Stock Dividend
Proprietorship		
Preferred stock, 5%, $100 par value	$100,000	$100,000
Common stock, $100 par value	500,000	560,000
Premium on common stock		12,000
Retained earnings	200,000	128,000
Total proprietorship	$800,000	$800,000
Preferred shares outstanding	1,000	1,000
Preferred stockholders' equity per share:		
$100,000 ÷ 1,000	$100	$100
Common shares outstanding	5,000	5,600
Common stockholders' equity per share:		
$500,000 Common stock capital		
200,000 Retained earnings		
$700,000 Total equity ÷ 5,000 shares	$140	
$560,000 Common stock capital		
12,000 Premium on common stock		
128,000 Retained earnings		
$700,000 Total equity ÷ 5,600 shares		$125
Effect on owner of 100 shares:		
100 × $140	$14,000	
112 × $125		$14,000
Ownership as percent of total proprietorship	$1\frac{3}{4}$%	$1\frac{3}{4}$%

The increase in number of shares (5000 to 5600) is exactly offset by the decrease in the value of each share ($140 to $125). The owner of 100 common shares has the same equity ($14,000) after the stock dividend as he had before.

EXERCISE 7-7 PROBLEMS ON STOCK DIVIDENDS

1. The Gibbard Corp. declared a 5% stock dividend on its 8,000 shares of $100 par-value common stock, which had a current market value of $110. It had $120,000 in retained earnings. What effect would the issuance of this stock have on the proprietorship section of its balance sheet?

2. The owner of 150 shares of $50 par-value common stock of Clinton Mills noted the declaration of a 6% stock dividend. The market value of the stock was $62.50 a share. What would be the total market value of his holdings after receiving the dividend? What would be the effect on the book value of his holdings or his equity in the corporation?

3. The Boydsden Corp. had 10,000 shares of $10 par-value common stock outstanding.   It had unrestricted retained earnings of $100,000 a portion of which they wanted to "plow back" into the business. They declared a stock dividend of 20% at a time when the market value was $22 a share. Complete the following analysis of the effect of this dividend.

BOYDSDEN CORPORATION

	Before Dividend	After Dividend
Common stock	$ _____	$ _____
Premium on common stock	_____	_____
Retained earnings	_____	_____
Total proprietorship	_____	_____
Number of shares outstanding	_____	_____
Equity per share	_____	_____

A STOCKHOLDER'S INVESTMENT

Shares owned	100	_____
Total equity	_____	_____
Equity as % of total proprietorship	_____	_____

4. The Reardon Corporation had retained earnings of $75,000. It declared a 10% dividend on its 25,000 shares of $15 par-value common stock, which was selling at $17.50 a share. What was the effect on the capital accounts of the company?

5. The owner of 250 shares of Insull Insulation Company $50 par-value common stock received a cash dividend of $1.60 a share and a stock dividend of 5%. The stock was selling for $63 a share. What was the total value of the dividend which he received? By how much did the corporation reduce their retained earnings?

SECTION 4—DISTRIBUTION OF PARTNERSHIP PROFITS

A *partnership* is a business enterprise owned by two or more individuals. In a *general partnership*, each individual has unlimited liability: in case of business failure, creditors may look to the personal property of the general partners as well as to the business assets for satisfaction of their claims against the business. In addition to general partners, there may be *limited partners*, who are liable to creditors for only the amount of their investment in the business. They can take no part in managing the operation.

Every partnership should have a written agreement setting forth the nature of the contribution of each partner to the business and the basis for sharing profits or losses. In the absence of a written contract, the law states that they shall share equally in profits or losses irrespective of their contribution to the business in terms of money, time, skills, or knowledge.

There are many ways in which partners may agree to share profits and losses. The most common are:

1. equal distribution
2. agreed ratio
3. return on investment, with balance in an agreed ratio
4. salary for services, with balance in an agreed ratio
5. return on investment, salary for services, and balance in an agreed ratio

equal distribution

To illustrate this method, assume that John Baker, James Clark, and Ralph   *Example*
Dodge are general partners. Baker invested $40,000 in the business, Clark $30,000, and Dodge, $10,000. The net profit for the first year was $12,000.

The partners felt that differences in their individual investments were off-set by other, less tangible contributions to the business. Consequently, they decided upon equal distribution of profits or losses:

(*a*) First-year profit of $12,000:

$$1 + 1 + 1 = 3 \text{ parts}$$

Baker: $\frac{1}{3}$ × $12,000 = $ 4,000

Clark: $\frac{1}{3}$ × $12,000 =   4,000

Dodge: $\frac{1}{3}$ × $12,000 = $\underline{\quad 4,000}$
$12,000 Profit

(*b*) Second-year loss of $2,100:

Baker: $\frac{1}{3}$ × $2,100 = $ 700

Clark: $\frac{1}{3}$ × $2,100 =   700

Dodge: $\frac{1}{3}$ × $2,100 = $\underline{\quad 700}$
$2,100 Loss

agreed ratio

Example   Using the same partners and investments as in the preceding example, assume instead that a ratio was agreed upon after considering not only the amount of investment, but also the amount of time, ideas, and services contributed by each. The ratio was 5:3:2. The distribution was as follows:

$$5 + 3 + 2 = 10 \text{ parts}$$

Baker: $\frac{5}{10}$ X $12,000 = $ 6,000

Clark: $\frac{3}{10}$ X $12,000 =   3,600

Dodge: $\frac{2}{10}$ X $12,000 = $\underline{2,400}$
$\overline{\$12,000}$ Profit

return on investment, with balance in agreed ratio

Example   Again using the same initial facts as in the first example, assume instead that the partners decided to handle the investment factor on a return of 6% a year. The balance was to be distributed in the ratio 4:6:2 based on services rendered.

(*a*) Constant investment:

	Baker	Clark	Dodge	Totals
Return @6%				
$40,000 X $\frac{6}{100}$ X 1 =	$2,400			
$30,000 X $\frac{6}{100}$ X 1 =		$1,800		
$10,000 X $\frac{6}{100}$ X 1 =			$ 600	
Total returns				$ 4,800
Balance for distribution: $7,200				
Ratio for services:				
4:6:2 = 12 parts				
$\frac{4}{12}$ X $7,200 =	2,400			
$\frac{6}{12}$ X $7,200 =		3,600		
$\frac{2}{12}$ X $7,200 =			1,200	
				7,200
Total distribution	$4,800	$5,400	$1,800	$12,000

(*b*) The amount of investment in part (*a*), above, was considered to be constant throughout the year. If additions or withdrawals of investment are made, however, the 6% would be applied to each investment amount for the period of time it was available to the business. Assuming such a variance in investment periods, the distribution would be altered as follows:

	Baker	Clark	Dodge	Totals
January 1	$30,000	$20,000	$5,000	$55,000
April 1	10,000			65,000
July 13		15,000		80,000
October 1		−5,000	5,000	80,000

Return @6%:

$30,000 \times \frac{6}{100} \times 1 = \$1,800$

$10,000 \times \frac{6}{100} \times \frac{9}{12} = \underline{\quad 450}$ $2,250

$20,000 \times \frac{6}{100} \times 1 = \$1,200$

$15,000 \times \frac{6}{100} \times \frac{80}{360} = 200$

$10,000 \times \frac{6}{100} \times \frac{3}{12} = \underline{\quad 150}$ $1,550

$5,000 \times \frac{6}{100} \times 1 = \$300$

$5,000 \times \frac{6}{100} \times \frac{3}{12} = \underline{\quad 75}$ $ 375

Total returns $ 4,175

Balance for distribution: $7,825

Ratio for services:

4:6:2 = 12 parts

$\frac{4}{12} \times \$7,825 =$ $2,608

$\frac{6}{12} \times \$7,825 =$ $3,913

$\frac{2}{12} \times \$7,825 =$ $1,304

Total services $ 7,825

Total distribution $\overline{\$4,858}$ $\overline{\$5,463}$ $\overline{\$1,679}$ $\overline{\$12,000}$

salary for services, with balance in an agreed ratio

Example

Assuming the same initial information as in the preceding three examples, suppose that the three partners decided that the emphasis on distribution of profits should be on a salary basis for services rendered to the business. The balance would be distributed in accordance with the ratio of their individual investment to total investment or 4:3:1.

	Baker	Clark	Dodge	Totals
Salary allocations	$2,000	$3,000	$1,000	$ 6,000
Balance for distribution: $6,000				
Ratio for investments:				
4:3:1 = 8 parts				
$\frac{4}{8} \times \$6,000 =$	3,000			
$\frac{3}{8} \times \$6,000 =$		2,250		
$\frac{1}{8} \times \$6,000 =$			750	
Total investment-ratio returns				6,000
Total distribution	$5,000	$5,520	$1,750	$12,000

return on investment, salary for services, and balance in an agreed ratio

Example   Assume that the partners in the four preceding examples instead decided to combine the return on investment and salary concepts of distribution and to share the balance in an agreed ratio—in this case, equally.
(*a*) First-year profit of $12,000:

	Baker	Clark	Dodge	Totals
Return @6%:				
$\$40,000 \times \frac{6}{100} \times 1 =$	$2,400			
$\$30,000 \times \frac{6}{100} \times 1 =$		$1,800		
$\$10,000 \times \frac{6}{100} \times 1 =$			$ 600	
Total returns				$ 4,800
Salaries	2,000	3,000	1,000	6,000
Balance for distribution $1,200				
Shared equally	400	400	400	1,200
	$4,800	$5,200	$2,000	$12,000

(*b*) The same method as above was used the following year, but the business had a profit of $2,100. In absence of any other agreement, when earnings are insufficient to cover the allocation for return and salaries, the deficiency would be borne equally just as the excess was borne equally.

	Baker	Clark	Dodge	Totals
Return @6%	$2,400	$1.800	$ 600	$ 4,800
Salaries	2,000	3,000	1,000	6,000
Total allocations	$4,400	$4,800	$1,600	$10,800
Allocations $10,800				
Less: profit 2,100				
Deficiency $ 8,700				
Equal sharing of $8,700	2,900	2,900	2,900	8,700
Adjustment in partner's allocation	$ 1,500	$ 1,900	$ 1,300	$ 2,100

In view of the above, it would behoove Dodge to insist upon a different formula for distribution of losses. This could be by investment ratio after allocations, salary ratio after allocations, or even equally without allocations. The possible methods for distribution are numberless.

EXERCISE 7-8 DISTRIBUTION OF PARTNERSHIP PROFITS

	Partner	Investment	Distribution Method	Profit	Distribution
1.	A	$10,000	agreed ratio 3:2	$ 1,600	_____
	B	5,000			_____
2.	A	8,000	6% return on investments	5,450	_____
	B	6,000	balance equally		_____
3.	A	14,000	salary: A—$1,000	9,680	_____
	B	2,000	B—$4,000		_____
			balance 7:1		
4.	A	17,500	$6\frac{1}{2}$% return on investment	12,500	_____
	B	4,375	salary: A—$5,000		_____
			B—$3,500		
			balance equally		
5.	A	6,500	$5\frac{1}{2}$% return on investment	6,000	_____
	B	4,500	salary: A—$4,000		_____
			B—$3,000		
			balance equally		

EXERCISE 7-9 PROBLEMS ON DISTRIBUTION OF PARTNERSHIP PROFITS

Adams, Bailey, and Carter formed a partnership with each of them as general partners. Adams invested $20,000, Bailey $10,000, and Carter $5,000. The net profit for the first year was $10,000. How would the profit be distributed under each of the following methods?

1. Equal distribution
2. An agreed ratio of 3:2:1
3. A return on investment of 7% with the balance in the ratio 4:5:1
4. Salaries: Adams, $2,200; Bailey, $4,200; Carter, $600; balance in ratio 4:2:1
5. A return on investment of 5% plus salary—Adams, $1,800; Bailey, $4,200 Carter, $1,000; balance shared equally

EXERCISE 7-10 PROBLEMS ON DISTRIBUTION OF PARTNERSHIP PROFITS

1. Ray Walker and LeRoy Youngren invested $15,000 apiece in a small store. They were each to receive a 7% return on their investment. Walker was to receive a salary of $2,000 and Youngren $6,000. Any balance of profits was to be shared equally. If profits for the year were $11,200, how much did each receive?

2. Cox, Dublin, and Eaton distributed their partnership profits on the basis of an 8% return on their investments with the balance shared equally between them. How would a profit of $14,000 be distributed if their investments were: Cox, $100,000; Dublin, $80,000; and Eaton, $60,000?

3. Wilcox, Xavier, Yberra, and Zeman distributed their profits on a $6\frac{1}{2}$% return on their investments with the balance shared equally. Determine the distribution of $15,000 of profit using the following investment schedule.

Wilcox:	$10,000	Jan. 1	Yberra:	$4,000	Jan. 1
	$5,000	July 1		$4,000	Apr. 1
Xavier:	$10,000	Jan. 1	Zeman:	$3,000	Jan. 1
	-$2,000	July 1		$2,000	Oct. 1

4. Madison invested $7,500 in a business and his partner, Osborne, invested $5,000. They were to receive a 6% return on their investment, after which Madison was to receive a salary of $10,000. How much would each partner receive if profits were $9,750?

5. Barrett and Schmidt were to receive an 8% return on their investment in their partnership. Further distribution was to be by a $7,500 salary to Barrett and a $6,000 salary to Schmidt. Any remainder was to be divided by a ratio of 7:5. With the following investment schedule, how would a profit of $22,000 be shared?

Barrett:	$70,000	Jan. 1	Schmidt:	$50,000	Jan. 1
	10,000	July 1		5,000	Apr. 1
	- 5,000	Oct. 1		10,000	July 1
	7,500	Dec. 11		-5,000	Dec. 6

appendix I

arithmetic review

This appendix is a complete review of the fundamental arithmetic processes involving whole numbers and fractions. Every problem in the text can be solved by using one or more of the arithmetic processes explained in this appendix.

SECTION 1—THE DECIMAL SYSTEM

The number system we use is called the *decimal system*. It is well named, since the word *decimal* comes from the Latin *decem*, which means "ten," and the system makes use of 10 digits or symbols (0 to 9). In other words, the decimal system is a *base-10 system*. This is true because it takes 10 digits in any one column in table I-1 to equal 1 in the next place to the right or left of the decimal point: 10 units = 1 in the tens place; ten 10s = 1 in the hundreds place, etc.

Some of the positions occupied by numbers in our decimal system are named and shown in table I-1.

TABLE I-1 positions in the decimal system

billions	hundred millions	ten millions	millions	hundred thousands	ten thousands	thousands	hundreds	tens	units	•decimal point	tenths	hundredths	thousandths	ten thousandths	hundred thousandths	millionths	ten millionths	hundred millionths	billionths

| whole numbers | decimal fractions |

239

Whole numbers occupy positions to the left of the decimal point, while decimal numbers (fractions) are located on the right side of the decimal point. Once the position of the digit to the far left and/or right is named, the number can be read and understood. This is one reason why it is so important to know for sure the precise location of the decimal point.

Example

$$\begin{array}{ccc} \text{hundreds} & \text{tens} & \text{units} \\ \hline 3 & 4 & 7 \end{array}$$

In the above example, we understand that someone is talking about the quantity "three hundred forty-seven," or three groups of 100, four groups of 10, and seven units. The notation *347* has no practical meaning of course, until we are told what sort of persons, places, or things it represents. In practice, no decimal point is written unless there is a part of a unit (a fraction) in the total. Still, the decimal point is understood to be located at the end of any whole number.

If the above example were written 34.7, the reading is changed to "thirty-four and seven tenths." Notice here that the word "and" is used to represent the decimal point. Ideally, the word "and" should never be pronounced unless there is a digit or digits to the right of the decimal point.

Example   The number 62,758 should be read, "sixty-two thousand, seven hundred fifty-eight." If we add .34 to it, it would be read "sixty-two thousand, seven hundred fifty-eight *and* thirty-four hundredths."

When writing numbers that occupy positions to the right of the decimal point, we can choose how we want these numbers to appear on paper. Numbers to the right of the decimal point can be called *decimals* or *fractions*. The term *fraction* seems preferable because it denotes a number which is less than one whole unit. We shall refer to fractions as being expressed in *common* or *decimal* form. Depending upon the calculation required, one of these forms will be more convenient to use.

Example

.3   Decimal form

$\frac{3}{10}$ Common form

Both of the above expressions represent a certain fractional part of one unit. Both are read as "three tenths." Given either form, it is clear that we are talking about a number occupying the first position to the right of the decimal point. It is easy to prove that both of these expressions represent the same quantity:

$$\frac{3}{10} = 10 \,\overline{\smash{)}3.0}^{\,.3} = .3$$

We must be careful in writing fractions.

48.7 may be written $48\frac{7}{10}$ but when written $48.\frac{7}{10}$ the value has been | *Example* changed because 48 and $\frac{7}{10}$ of $\frac{1}{10}$ = 48 and $\frac{7}{100}$ or 48.07.

A number which occupies positions to the left and the right of the decimal point is called a mixed number. This represents a whole number plus a decimal fraction, like 48.7 in the example above.

Rounding off numbers

The decision as to how far to round off a number is usually left up to the individual who works out the problem or reports the data. Business, banks, insurance companies, taxing authorities, and other institutions have their own rules for rounding off numbers. In essence, we tend to round off numbers to the nearest significant digit for a given context. The basic rule is: When the number immediately to the right of the significant digit is 5 or more, the significant digit is raised by 1; otherwise it is left unchanged. When talking in terms of billions of dollars for example, we frequently round off to the nearest billion, dropping the "insignificant millions." Psychology sometimes plays a role here. A woman showing her husband the new hat she bought might say, "It was only $11.98," and he may reply, "You spent $12 for that?" She wouldn't think of rounding off that number to $12.

Following are some examples of rounding off numbers to the nearest significant digit:

To Nearest 1,000	To Nearest 100
9,270 to 9,000	810 to 800
3,865 to 4,000	473 to 500
7,250 to 7,000	236.7 to 200

To Nearest Unit	To Nearest 100th
82.7 to 83	64.938 to 64.94
12.2 to 12	3,286.67 to 3,286.67
3.832 to 4	.02956 to .03

EXERCISE I-1   ROUNDING OFF

1. Round off these numbers to the nearest 100.

638 _____   877 _____

97 _____	685 _____
$352\frac{1}{2}$ _____	32,841 _____
4,226 _____	659,319 _____

2. Round off these numbers to the nearest 10th.

33.862 _____	.06325 _____
4.75 _____	57.388 _____
.6271 _____	$.07\frac{1}{8}$ _____
958.8 _____	$.7\frac{2}{3}$ _____

3. Round off these numbers to the nearest 100th.

.4537 _____	166.248 _____
1.777 _____	.0565 _____
38.006 _____	$.007\frac{2}{3}$ _____
975.97 _____	7.41138 _____

SECTION 2—ADDITION

Adding whole numbers and decimal fractions

Addition is the process of combining numbers (quantities) and expressing the result as a single quantity or *sum*. The old adage about adding oranges to oranges and apples to apples will remind us to keep the columns arranged in precise vertical or horizontal order so that we add tenths to tenths, hundreds to hundreds and so forth.

Example

```
48,596.257
 3,941.800
   726.320
     5.843
    75.000
53,345.220
```

Improved skill in adding numbers involves increasing speed without decreasing accuracy. Any technique that can help accomplish this is worth adopting. Combining numbers that total 10 is one helpful technique.

combinations of ten

There are only five pairs of numbers that total 10:

$$\begin{array}{ccccc} 1 & 2 & 3 & 4 & 5 \\ 9 & 8 & 7 & 6 & 5 \end{array}$$

Everytime one of these combinations shows up in a column of digits, we can immediately add 10. This technique, of course, works for adding whole numbers, decimal fractions, and *mixed numbers* (quantities containing a whole number and fraction).

Grouping by 10's *Example*

```
798
462
684
529
531
200
875
4,079
```

Units Column:
10 (8 + 2) + 10 (9 + 1) = 20 + 9 = 29

Tenths Column:
Carry the 2 + 9 = 11 + 10 (8 + 2) = 21 + 10
    (7 + 3) = 31 + 6 = 37

Hundreds Column:
Carry the 3 + 7 = 10 + 10 (4 + 6) = 20 + 10
    (5 + 5) = 30 + 10 (8 + 2) = 40

As you gain increased speed by employing this technique, other combinations will become equally familiar. Before long, the process should involve adding number combinations rather than each number to the next one.

```
7.7
4.3
5.8
6.4
5.6
2.5
32.3
```

Grouping by 10's *Example*

Tenths Column
10 (7 + 3) + 10 (4 + 6) = 20 + 8 = 28 + 5 = 33

Units Column
Carry the 3 + 7 = 10 + 10 (4 + 6)
    = 20 + 10 (5 + 5) = 30 + 2 = 32

Horizontal addition

When quantities are written in a horizontal direction, there is no need to recopy the numbers vertically before adding. However, the technique of using combinations of 10 or other combinations may not work as smoothly when numbers are arranged horizontally.

Example

$45.22 + $32.95 + $48.50 + $29.64 + $81.17 + $62.33 = $297.81

Mentally left to right	2	7	11	18	21		=		1
Carry 2	4	13	18	24	25	28	=		8
Carry 2	7	9	17	24	25	27	=		7
Carry 2	6	9	13	15	23	29	=	29	

$297.81

Checking for accuracy in addition

The most practical way to check the accuracy of a sum is to add the columns again, but in the reverse direction. If you keep getting a different answer from your original one, rearrange the numbers in some new order and add them again.

Adding common fractions

Common fractions are expressed with one number (the *numerator*) written over a dividing line, below which is written the *denominator* (also called the *divisor*).

Examples are $\frac{1}{2}, \frac{2}{3}, \frac{5}{8}, \frac{11}{32}$, etc. Fractions like these which have values less than the whole number 1 are called *proper fractions*, while those having a value greater than 1 are called *improper fractions*—e.g., $\frac{15}{8}, \frac{5}{2}, \frac{19}{5}$. Fractions which do not contain any whole number are called *simple fractions* $\left(\text{e.g.,} \frac{3}{5}, \frac{21}{38}, \frac{19}{4}\right)$, while fractions which include a whole number either in the numerator or denominator or both are called *complex fractions*—for example,

$$\frac{2\frac{3}{4}}{9\frac{1}{2}}, \quad \frac{16}{2\frac{1}{4}}, \quad \frac{19\frac{4}{5}}{10}$$

The process of adding common fractions requires finding the *lowest common denominator* (LCD). This is the smallest number into which all of the denominators of the fractions to be added can be divided evenly.

Example

$$3\frac{1}{5} + 8\frac{1}{2} + 6\frac{1}{4}$$

Solution

We cannot add fifths, halves, and fourths. We need a denominator which is common to all three of them. The easiest way to arrive at the lowest common denominator is to start with the largest denominator given (fifths) and count by 5s until we get a number into which all three denominators can be divided evenly. The process is similar to adding pigs, cows, and goats and expressing the answer in terms of livestock: $5 + 5 = 10$, $10 + 5 = 15$, $15 + 5 = 20$, which is the lowest denominator common to all three. Now we express $\frac{1}{5}, \frac{1}{2}$, and $\frac{1}{4}$ in 20ths, and then add the numerators to get $\frac{19}{20}$:

$$
\begin{array}{cc}
3\frac{1}{5} & \frac{4}{20} \\
8\frac{1}{2} & \frac{10}{20} \\
6\frac{1}{4} & \frac{5}{20} \\
\hline
17 + & \frac{19}{20} = 17\frac{19}{20}
\end{array}
$$

other techniques for finding the lowest common denominator

1. When the denominators are all *prime* to one another (have no divisor common to each other except the number 1), their product will be the lowest common denominator.

Example

$$\frac{7}{9} + \frac{5}{7} + \frac{1}{2} \qquad 9 \times 7 \times 2 = 126 \text{ LCD}$$

2. When the denominators are not all prime to each other, their lowest common denominator can be found as follows:

Step 1. Write down the denominators in a horizontal row.
Step 2. Omit any denominator which can be divided evenly into one of the others.

Step 3. Divide the smallest number possible (other than 1) into 2 or more of the denominators and bring the answers down directly below, along with any denominators that cannot be evenly divided by this number.

Step 4. Continue dividing into 2 or more denominators using the smallest number possible (other than 1) until no other divisor can be used.

Step 5. Multiply all the divisors and the final answers together. The product of these numbers will be the lowest common denominator.

$$\frac{4}{9} + \frac{5}{7} + \frac{7}{10} + \frac{3}{18} + \frac{11}{15} + \frac{17}{27}$$ *Example*

Step 1. 9 7 10 18 15 27
Step 2. Omit the denominator 9.
Steps 3 and 4.

3	7	10	18	15	27
3	7	10	6	5	9
2	7	10	2	5	3
5	7	5	1	5	3
	7	1	1	1	3

Step 5. $3 \times 3 \times 2 \times 5 \times 7 \times 1 \times 1 \times 1 \times 3 = 1890$ (LCD)

Changing fractions to more convenient terms

In working with fractions, it is frequently advantageous to change them into more convenient terms.

Reducing to lower terms. Here the process is one of finding the largest divisor common to numerator and denominator. This divisor is known as the *greatest common factor*.

$$\frac{16}{24} = \frac{2}{3}$$ *Example*

The numbers 2, 4, and 8 will all divide evenly into both numerator and denominator. Dividing each by 8 will reduce this fraction to its lowest terms $\left(\frac{2}{3}\right)$. Therefore, 8 is the greatest common factor for 16 and 24.

Changing improper fractions to whole or mixed numbers. The procedure here is to divide the denominator into the numerator and write the remainder (if any) as a fraction.

$$\frac{15}{5} = 3 \qquad \frac{9}{2} = 4\frac{1}{2} \qquad \frac{33}{8} = 4\frac{1}{8}$$ *Examples*

Changing mixed numbers to improper fractions. The procedure is to multiply the whole number by the denominator of the fraction then add the numerator of the fraction and express the sum in terms of the fraction's denominator.

Examples
$$7\frac{4}{5} = \frac{39}{5} \qquad 12\frac{2}{3} = \frac{38}{3}$$

Changing fractions to higher terms. We have already seen how this was done in the process of adding fractions. Obviously, when the numerator and denominator are both multiplied by the same number, the value of the fraction is not changed. The fraction is merely stated in higher terms.

Example
$$\frac{3}{5} = \frac{18\,(3 \times 6)}{30\,(5 \times 6)}$$
$$\frac{5}{8} = \frac{?}{24}$$
$$24 = 8 \times 3$$

So,
$$5 \times 3 = 15 \qquad \frac{5}{8} = \frac{15}{24}$$

EXERCISE I-2 ADDITION BY COMBINATIONS OF TEN

Add, using combinations of 10. Prove your answer by reverse-order addition.

1. 6	2. 1	3. 3	4. 77	5. 72	6. 83
8	2	6	83	11	34
3	3	4	34	28	56
1	8	6	56	39	77
2	9	7			
6	6	3			
4	4	1			
		8			
		4			
		7			

7. 19	8. 42	9. 126	10. 204	11. 798
71	38	348	816	2,009
82	13	984	603	5,632
56	31	732	497	981
34	96	188	297	
23	73			
95	85			
	27			
	92			
	18			

12.	5,421	13.	43.87	14.	1,487	15.	28,364
	5,460		67.19		3,822		12,447
	569		102.21		7,203		80,793
	823		66.66		2,690		94,601
			81.76		8,678		72,688
							26,319

16.	$ 769.56	17.	59,302	18.	602.75	19.	396,475
	3,645.98		32,176		91.03		87,213
	5,038.47		87,653		427.311		621,438
	76.84		74,548		8.9		932,209
			90,132		62.073		36,721
			33,919		3,875.5		305,006
			46,784		962.		283,417
			81,009		.482		

20. 37.22
     98.56
     47.17
     32.25
     86.75
     42.18
     38.88
      9.98
    212.90

EXERCISE I-3 ADDITION PRACTICE

A. Add these figures mentally.
1. 3 + 8 + 2 + 5 + 9 + 4 + 3 + 1 =   _____
2. 20 + 8 + 5 + 13 + 62 + 45 + 3 + 9 =   _____
3. 38 + 19 + 42 + 64 + 88 + 72 + 26 =   _____
4. 638 + 472 + 395 + 716 =   _____
5. 774 + 127 + 918 + 758 =   _____
6. $1.14 + $1.83 =   _____
7. $20.67 + $1.81 =   _____
8. $1.92 + $.75 + $6.88 + $3.17 + $.62 =   _____
9. $32.50 + $86.25 + $19.77 + $8.45 + $16.70 =   _____
10. $364.58 + $827.33 + $724.15 + $528.62 =   _____

B. Complete this daily sales report. (All sales are cash.)

Department	Mon.	Tues.	Wed.	Thurs.	Fri.	Sat.	Total
22	$ 836.22	$ 938.14	$ 584.19	$ 627.34	$ 758.85	$1,033.21	_____
43	237.15	209.95	368.45	412.92	575.20	608.33	_____
71	1,588.77	1,242.21	1,187.53	1,209.91	1,356.75	1,400.19	_____
35	164.18	182.94	207.71	315.51	300.95	342.12	_____
Total	_____	_____	_____	_____	_____	_____	_____

C. Complete this payroll report.

Employee	Mon.	Tues.	Wed.	Thurs.	Fri.	Sat.	Total
Caro, R.	$16.82	$14.75	$21.60	$19.65	$24.20	$15.50	_____
Nash, A.	16.12	14.50	18.45	20.25	21.60	17.10	_____
Oliva, M.	13.87	16.95	22.50	19.85	24.20	13.85	_____
Tatarion, L.	16.00	16.50	19.95	18.10	17.50	12.95	_____
Wycoff, A.	20.00	21.00	17.40	16.80	15.55	15.25	_____
Total	_____	_____	_____	_____	_____	_____	_____

EXERCISE I-4   ADDING FRACTIONS AND MIXED NUMBERS

A. Add these proper fractions.

1. $\frac{2}{5} + \frac{1}{5}$

2. $\frac{2}{10} + \frac{7}{10}$

3. $\frac{5}{7} + \frac{2}{3}$

4. $\frac{3}{8} + \frac{1}{3}$

5. $\frac{7}{8} + \frac{3}{5}$

6. $\frac{2}{7} + \frac{1}{3}$

7. $\frac{1}{10} + \frac{1}{12}$

8. $\frac{11}{16} + \frac{3}{32}$

9. $\frac{2}{3} + \frac{5}{9} + \frac{4}{27}$

10. $\frac{7}{8} + \frac{5}{8} + \frac{5}{12}$

11. $\frac{7}{16} + \frac{5}{32} + \frac{3}{8} + \frac{1}{4}$

12. $\frac{7}{16} + \frac{3}{4} + \frac{1}{8} + \frac{1}{2}$

B. Add these mixed numbers.

1. $5\frac{1}{4} + 4\frac{3}{4}$

2. $12\frac{1}{2} + 27\frac{2}{3}$

3. $6\frac{1}{9} + 5\frac{8}{33} + 7\frac{3}{11}$

4. $12\frac{2}{3} + 3\frac{4}{5}$

5. $6\frac{3}{4} + 7\frac{5}{8} + 2\frac{1}{2}$

6. $24\frac{7}{8} + 42\frac{3}{4} + 26\frac{5}{16}$

7. $24\frac{1}{2} + 9\frac{3}{4} + 11\frac{1}{16} + 21\frac{1}{3}$

8. $56\frac{2}{3} + 24\frac{1}{2} + 94\frac{1}{4} + 76\frac{11}{12}$

9. $36\frac{2}{3} + 72\frac{5}{6} + 93\frac{9}{10} + 85\frac{2}{5}$

10. $7\frac{3}{15} + 18\frac{37}{30} + 8\frac{4}{10}$

EXERCISE I-5   REDUCING AND CONVERTING FRACTIONS

A. Change these mixed numbers to improper fractions.

1. $5\frac{1}{2}$ 6. $8\frac{11}{42}$

2. $2\frac{1}{3}$ 7. $62\frac{5}{9}$

3. $6\frac{1}{8}$ 8. $91\frac{3}{10}$

4. $22\frac{3}{5}$ 9. $15\frac{21}{35}$

5. $4\frac{13}{20}$ 10. $265\frac{2}{3}$

B. Reduce these fractions to their lowest terms.

1. $\frac{7}{14}$ 7. $\frac{12}{30}$

2. $\frac{12}{32}$ 8. $\frac{40}{72}$

3. $\frac{7}{56}$ 9. $\frac{42}{189}$

4. $\frac{14}{49}$ 10. $\frac{35}{84}$

5. $\frac{16}{56}$ 11. $\frac{56}{70}$

6. $\frac{60}{75}$ 12. $\frac{16}{40}$

C. Reduce these fractions to the denominator given.

1. $\frac{4}{5} = \frac{}{65}$ 7. $\frac{3}{8} = \frac{}{1,000}$

2. $\frac{1}{6} = \frac{}{78}$ 8. $\frac{72}{350} = \frac{}{700}$

3. $\frac{9}{16} = \frac{}{96}$ 9. $7\frac{1}{2} = \frac{}{30}$

4. $\frac{8}{9} = \frac{}{27}$ 10. $2\frac{1}{2} = \frac{}{100}$

5. $\frac{7}{8} = \frac{}{72}$ 11. $\frac{75}{50} = \frac{}{400}$

6. $\frac{2}{9} = \frac{}{45}$ 12. $\frac{17}{24} = \frac{}{144}$

SECTION 3—SUBTRACTION

Subtracting whole numbers and decimal fractions

Subtraction is essentially the opposite of addition. It is the arithmetic process of finding the difference between two quantities. Some new nomenclature is involved in subtraction:

$$\begin{array}{r} 85{,}426 \ \ \text{Minuend} \\ -\ 37{,}591 \ \ \text{Subtrahend} \\ \hline 47{,}835 \ \ \text{Difference} \end{array}$$

In the example above, before 9 (tens) can be subtracted from 2 (tens) 1 (hundred) must be borrowed from the 4 (hundreds). This results in merely exchanging 1 (hundred) for 10 (tens), allowing us to subtract 9 (tens) from 12 (tens):

100s	10s	Units
3	12	6
−5	9	1
	3	5

This same borrowing procedure must be performed two more times before the subtracting process can be completed in this example.

Subtracting decimal fractions or mixed numbers entails the same arithmetic procedure demonstrated above for whole numbers.

Checking accuracy in subtraction

Checking the accuracy of subtraction is a simple matter of adding the difference to the subtrahend. The sum obtained should equal the minuend.

Example

$$\begin{array}{r} 85{,}426.73 \ \ \text{Minuend} \\ -\ 37{,}591.42 \ \ \text{Subtrahend} \\ \hline 47{,}835.31 \ \ \text{Difference} \\ 85{,}426.73 \end{array}$$

Subtracting common fractions

The process of subtracting common fractions involves precisely the same steps already described for adding fractions in the preceding section, except that the numerators are subtracted rather than added.

Example

$$27\tfrac{3}{8} \ = \ 27\tfrac{27}{72} \ = \ 26\tfrac{27}{72} + \tfrac{72}{72} \ = \ 26\tfrac{99}{72}$$
$$-\ 13\tfrac{7}{9} \ = \ 13\tfrac{56}{72} \qquad\qquad = \ -13\tfrac{56}{72}$$
$$\hline$$
$$13\tfrac{43}{72}$$

Here it was necessary to borrow 1 whole unit from the whole number 27, convert that one unit to 72nds and add it to $\frac{27}{72}$ to get $26\frac{99}{72}$. After this, the subtraction process could be completed.

EXERCISE I-6 SUBTRACTION

A. Subtract the following. Check your accuracy by adding the difference to the subtrahend to get the minuend.

1. 87	2. 69	3. 95	4. 98	5. 586	6. 763	7. 126
46	28	64	87	368	674	49

8. 512	9. 695	10. $87.17	11. $71.65	12. $91.76
328	307	34.96	65.43	9.81

13. $6,487.50	14. $80,706.04	15. 3.873	16. 27.345
2,225.15	23,456.18	.521	1.722

17. 362.58	18. 4,389	19. 8,095	20. 648,372
.07	1,895	3,381	5,031

B. Subtract horizontally.

	Minuend	Subtrahend	Difference
1.	78	52	_____
2.	36	19	_____
3.	425	27	_____
4.	923	871	_____
5.	569	187	_____
6.	$32.45	$19.16	_____
7.	$75.28	$16.45	_____
8.	$256.19	$37.52	_____
9.	7,456	5,123	_____
10.	6,034	1,978	_____
11.	3.475	.241	_____
12.	72.956	.043	_____

C. Complete this check record. Beginning balance is $647.50.

Date	Amount of Check	Balance
2/3	$ 72.50	_____
2/6	41.78	_____
2/9	13.85	_____
2/9	7.95	_____
2/9	21.16	_____
2/12	88.75	_____
2/13	5.44	_____
2/15	3.83	_____
2/21	102.22	_____
2/28	33.81	_____

D. Find the difference and reduce answers to lowest terms.

1. $\frac{5}{8} - \frac{3}{8}$

2. $\frac{7}{8} - \frac{1}{4}$

3. $\frac{9}{16} - \frac{5}{16}$

4. $\frac{3}{4} - \frac{2}{3}$

5. $\frac{5}{6} - \frac{3}{4}$

6. $\frac{4}{5} - \frac{1}{3}$

7. $25 - 18\frac{2}{3}$

8. $29 - \frac{7}{8}$

9. $46\frac{2}{3} - 23\frac{5}{6}$

10. $35\frac{17}{30} - 19\frac{3}{5}$

11. $84\frac{99}{100} - 37\frac{2}{7}$

12. $26\frac{9}{8} - 13\frac{11}{6}$

13. $12\frac{5}{36} - \frac{6}{5}$

14. $14\frac{3}{4} - 10\frac{1}{6}$

15. $488\frac{3}{8} - 291\frac{5}{12}$

SECTION IV—MULTIPLICATION

Multiplying whole numbers and decimal fractions

The arithmetic process called multiplication is essentially a speeded-up version of addition. When doing multiplication, we may not be conscious of the fact that we are really adding numbers. For example, if we should forget that $3 \times 6 = 18$, we could write down the number 3 six times, add, and get the sum of 18, which is the quantity 3 taken 6 times. One important law of multiplication states that the *product* (result of multiplication) of two or more numbers multiplied by each other will be the same regardless of the order in which they are multiplied.

$$5 \times 7 = 35$$
$$7 \times 5 = 35$$
$$122 \times 4 \times 2 = 976$$
$$2 \times 4 \times 122 = 976$$
$$4 \times 122 \times 2 = 976$$
$$122 \times 2 \times 4 = 976$$

Examples

In the first example, 5 is technically called the *multiplicand*, while 7 is called the *multiplier*. On the third line, 122 is the multiplicand; both 4 and 2 are multipliers.

multiplying with a zero in the multiplier

Whenever a zero appears in the multiplier, the process of multiplying by zero can be eliminated, since the product will always be zero.

Example 1

(a)	(b)
283	283
×106	×106
1698	1698
283	000
29,998	283
	29,998

Notice that, in part (a), although we did not multiply by zero, we left a place for it so that when we began multiplying by 1 we put the product of 1 × 3 under the 6 in 1698.

Example 2

(a)	(b)
283	283
×160	×160
16980	000
283	1698
45,280	283
	45,280

In part (a), we start by leaving a place for the product of 0 × 283, which of course is 0. Then we continue to multiply by the other digits in the multiplier. Obviously, part (a) can be performed faster than part (b), and this method avoids the confusion sometimes brought about by the presence of zeros in the multiplier. Had the problem been given as 160 × 283, we would be wise to reverse it before multiplying, as in part (a), above.

placing the decimal point

In multiplying decimal fractions or mixed numbers, care must be exercised when placing the decimal point in the product. The rule is that there must be as many places to the right of the decimal point in the product as there are *total* places to the right of the decimal point in the multiplicand and multiplier.

Example

$$
\begin{array}{r r l}
38.52 & \text{(2 places)} \\
\times\ 1.74 & \text{(2 places)} \\
\hline
15408 \\
26964 \\
3852 \\
\hline
67.0248 & \text{(4 places)}
\end{array}
$$

In the above example, the whole number 38 plus 52 hundredths is multiplied by the whole number 1 plus 74 hundredths. The fractional part of the product must go to the ten-thousandths place because

$$
\frac{1}{100} \times \frac{1}{100} = \frac{1}{10,000} \qquad (100 \times 100 = 10,000)
$$

Example

$$
\begin{array}{r r l}
.4762 & \text{(4 places)} \\
\times\ \ .25 & \text{(2 places)} \\
\hline
23810 \\
9524 \\
\hline
.119050 & \text{(6 places)}
\end{array}
$$

Although we might want to round off the product to .1191 or .119, the original result must carry to the sixth place to the right of the decimal point. Here, a quantity given in ten-thousandths was multiplied by a quantity of hundredths. When we have $1/10,000 \times 1/100$, the answer must be in millionths $(10,000 \times 100 = 1,000,000)$, and the sixth place to the right of the decimal point is the millionths place.

multiplying by powers of 10

Each *power* of 10 means that 10 is taken (multiplied by itself) the number of times indicated by the superscript.

Example

$10^1 =$ 10 is taken once $=$ 10
$10^2 =$ 10 is taken twice $=$ $10 \times 10 = 100$
$10^3 =$ 10 is taken 3 times $=$ $10 \times 10 \times 10 = 1,000$

To multiply by any power of 10, all that needs to be done is add to the multiplicand the number of zeros present in the multiplier.

Example

$47 \times 10 \qquad (10^1) = 470$
$47 \times 100 \quad\ \ (10^2) = 4,700$
$47 \times 1,000 \ (10^3) = 47,000$

The effect of this procedure is to move the decimal point 1 place to the right for each zero in the multiplier.

Example

$264 \times 10^2 = 264 \times 100 = 26,400$
$26.4 \times 10^2 = 26.4 \times 100 = 2,640$
(decimal point moved 2 places to right)

$$6.423 \times 10^3 = 6.423 \times 1,000 = 6,423$$
$$.0438 \times 10^3 = .0438 \times 1,000 = 43.8$$
(decimal point moved 3 places to right)

Checking the accuracy of multiplication

Short of adding the multiplicand to itself the number of times indicated by the multiplier, there are better and faster ways to check the accuracy of multiplication.

method 1

Reverse the multiplier and multiplicand, then multiply again.

method 2

Divide the product by the multiplier to obtain the multiplicand or vice versa.

Example

$$\begin{array}{r} 27 \\ \times 13 \\ \hline 81 \\ 27 \\ \hline 351 \end{array}$$

$$\frac{351}{13} = 27$$

Proof

or

$$\frac{351}{27} = 13$$

method 3

Convert the multiplier into two numbers which are more convenient for multiplication purposes, then add or subtract the products obtained after multiplying these two numbers by the multiplicand.

(a) 327 × 101: $\left(\begin{array}{r} 327 \times 100 \\ +327 \times 1 \end{array}\right)$ = $\begin{array}{r} 32,700 \\ +327 \\ \hline 33,027 \text{ (Product)} \end{array}$

Examples

(b) 327 × 99: $\left(\begin{array}{r} 327 \times 100 \\ -327 \times 1 \end{array}\right)$ = $\begin{array}{r} 32,700 \\ -327 \\ \hline 32,373 \text{ (Product)} \end{array}$

(c) 327 × 90: $\left(\begin{array}{r} 327 \times 100 \\ -327 \times 10 \end{array}\right)$ = $\begin{array}{r} 32,700 \\ -3,270 \\ \hline 29,430 \text{ (Product)} \end{array}$

(d) 327 × 110: $\left(\begin{array}{l}327 \times 100 \\ +327 \times 10\end{array}\right)$ = $\begin{array}{r}32,700 \\ +3,270 \\ \hline 35,970\end{array}$ (Product)

(e) 327 × 125: $\left(\begin{array}{l}327 \times 100 \\ +\;\frac{1}{4} \times 32,700\end{array}\right)$ = $\begin{array}{r}32,700 \\ +8,175 \\ \hline 40,875\end{array}$ (Product)

(f) 327 × $16\frac{2}{3}$: $\left(\begin{array}{l}327 \times 100 \\ \frac{1}{6} \times 32,700\end{array}\right)$ = $\begin{array}{r}32,700 \\ 5,450\end{array}$ (Product)

As you become more familiar with number relationships, you may want to perform multiplication in this fashion and use the conventional procedure to check your accuracy. This is more likely to happen when you have committed to memory the aliquot parts of 100 listed in Section 6, Aliquot Parts!

Multiplying common fractions

The procedure for multiplying common fractions is

1. find the product of the numerators;
2. find the product of the denominators; and
3. reduce the result to its lowest terms—or do this before step 1 by finding the *greatest common factor* (see page 235) for all the fractions involved, as in example (d), below.

Examples

(a) $\dfrac{3}{5} \times \dfrac{2}{9} = \dfrac{\overset{2}{\cancel{6}}}{\underset{15}{\cancel{45}}} = \dfrac{2}{15}$ (lowest terms)

(b) $2\frac{7}{8} \times 6\frac{1}{2} = \frac{23}{8} \times \frac{13}{2} = \frac{299}{16} = 18\frac{11}{16}$

(c) $\frac{1}{4} \times \frac{5}{8} \times \frac{13}{32} = \frac{65}{1024}$

(d) $\dfrac{\overset{1}{\cancel{3}}}{\underset{4}{\cancel{8}}} \times \dfrac{\overset{1}{\cancel{2}}}{\underset{1}{\cancel{3}}} = \dfrac{1}{4}$

EXERCISE I-7   MULTIPLICATION

A. Find the product of each of the following. Check your answer by reverse multiplication.

1. 11 × 13

2. 12 × 8

3. 13 × 14

4. 300 × 9

5. 28 × 12

6. 575 × 8

7. 416 × 28

8. 129 × 94

9. 806 $\times$ 63

10. 393 $\times$ 94

11. 5,346 $\times$ 9

12. 1,288 $\times$ 16

13. 8,329 $\times$ 584

14. 11,821 $\times$ 403

15. $12.16 $\times$ $.05

16. 6.845 $\times$ 21.03

17. .078 $\times$ 3.652

18. $3.85 $\times$ 76

19. .726 $\times$ .0047

20. .000673 $\times$ .01047

21. 3.727 $\times$ .1077

B. Multiply mentally by moving the decimal point.

1. 378 $\times$ 10

2. 6,640 $\times$ 100

3. 16 $\times$ .1

4. .943 $\times$ 100

5. 10 $\times$ $92.75

6. 1,000 $\times$ .7

7. 1,000 $\times$ 5.837

8. 100 $\times$ .03

9. 396 $\times$ .001

10. .0023 $\times$ 10

11. .0475 $\times$ 100

12. 6.2 $\times$ 10,000

C. Find the product, using 10 or a power of 10 as a shortcut.

1. 15 $\times$ 50

2. 84 $\times$ 500

3. 362.5 $\times$ 50

4. $12.16 $\times$ .05

5. 1.902 $\times$ .05

6. 41.325 $\times$ 200

7. 84 $\times$ .5

8. 1.115 $\times$ 4000

9. 2.656 $\times$ .0004

D. Find the product and reduce to lowest terms.

1. $\frac{1}{2} \times \frac{1}{4}$

2. $\frac{3}{4} \times \frac{5}{9}$

3. $\frac{1}{4} \times \frac{8}{9}$

4. $\frac{2}{3} \times \frac{7}{8}$

5. $2\frac{1}{2} \times 3\frac{1}{2}$

6. $10\frac{1}{2} \times 3\frac{1}{7}$

7. $\frac{2}{15} \times \frac{5}{11}$

8. $\frac{7}{12} \times 38$

9. $\frac{5}{9} \times \frac{2}{3} \times 54$

10. $\frac{2}{27} \times 45 \times \frac{3}{5}$

11. $7\frac{5}{8} \times 72$

12. $\frac{14}{36} \times \frac{27}{50} \times \frac{5}{7}$

13. $\frac{10}{3} \times \frac{19}{24} \times \frac{49}{5} \times \frac{12}{21}$

14. 360 $\times$ $133\frac{1}{3}$

15. $540 \times 1\frac{1}{5}$ ¢ 　　　　17. $9\frac{1}{2} \times 73\frac{1}{2}$

16. $612\frac{1}{4} \times 13\frac{1}{2}$ 　　　　18. $417\frac{4}{5} \times \frac{19}{20}$

SECTION 5—DIVISION

Dividing whole numbers and decimal fractions

Just as multiplication is a speeded-up version of addition, division is essentially a speeded-up version of subtraction. When we seek to divide one quantity by another, we are really finding out how many times one number can be subtracted from the other number. For example: $50 \div 10 = 5$ means the quantity 10 can be subtracted exactly 5 times from the quantity 50. In this example, 50 is called the *dividend*, 10 is the *divisor*, and the answer 5 is called the *quotient*. The procedure of dividing a whole number into another whole number can be illustrated by another example:

$$
\begin{array}{r}
27 \\
15\overline{\smash{)}405} \\
30 \\
\hline
105 \\
105 \\
\end{array}
$$

Steps	Solution
	(15 will not divide into 4)
1. Divide	15 into 40 = 2
2. Multiply	15 × 2 = 30
3. Subtract	40 − 30 = 10
4. Compare	10 is less than the divisor 15
5. Bring down	5 is brought down to make 105
6. Repeat steps 1–4, and 5 if necessary	

When dividing decimal fractions or mixed numbers, the procedure is the same as for whole numbers. However, before dividing, the divisor is made a whole number by moving the decimal point all the way to the right and the decimal point in the dividend is likewise moved the same number of places.

Example

$$
\begin{array}{r}
123.55 \\
6.22\overline{\smash{)}768.4860} \\
622 \\
\hline
1464 \\
1244 \\
\hline
2208 \\
1866 \\
\hline
3426 \\
3110 \\
\hline
3160 \\
3110 \\
\hline
50 \\
\end{array}
$$

Before dividing, 6.22 was made into the whole number 622 by moving the decimal point 2 places to the right. In order to preserve the value relationship between the divisor and dividend, the decimal point in the dividend must likewise be moved 2 places to the right. You will recognize that this is the same as multiplying both quantities by 100. Nautrally, their relationship to each other has not changed.

The quotient was carried out to the hundredths place for greater accuracy. As a rule of thumb, it makes sense to carry out the quotient at least as many places as there originally were in the divisor.

$$2.786 \div 3.4 = .8194$$ *Example*

$$.8194 \times 3.4 = 2.78596 = 2.786$$ *Proof*

Note: Here there is a remainder of $\frac{4}{34}$ or $\frac{2}{17}$, which cannot be conveniently added. The proof is so close, however, that the remainder can be ignored.

dividing by powers of 10

The procedure here is the reverse of that described for multiplication by powers of 10. For whole numbers and decimal fractions, move the decimal point to the left the same number of decimal places as there are zeros in the divisor.

$$275 \div 10 = 27.5$$ *Examples*
$$275 \div 100 = 2.75$$
$$275 \div 1,000 = .275$$

$$368.2 \div 10 = 36.82$$
$$368.2 \div 100 = 3.682$$
$$368.2 \div 1,000 = .3682$$

The process of division can often be speeded up by first dividing by 10 or some power of 10.

Checking accuracy in division

To check the accuracy of a quotient, multiply the quotient by the divisor and add the remainder (if any). The result should equal the dividend.

$$648 \div 5 = 129 \text{ and a remainder of } 3$$ *Example 1*

$$129 \times 5 = 645 + 3 = 648$$ *Proof*

(*a*) $7,436 \div 20 = ?$ *Example 2*
   Think: $7,436 \div 100$
   Write: 74.36×5 (100 is 5 times larger than 20) $= 371.8$
(*b*) $62,380 \div 250 = ?$
   Think: $62,380 \div 1,000$
   Write: 6.238×4 (1,000 is 4 times larger than 250) $= 24.952$

Dividing common fractions

The procedure for dividing common fractions is

1. invert the divisor;
2. find the product of the numerators;
3. find the product of the denominators; and
4. reduce the result to its lowest terms—or do this immediately after step 1 by finding the greatest common factor for all of the fractions involved, as in parts (c) and (d) of the example below.

Note: After inverting the divisor, the procedure is exactly the same as multiplying common fractions.

Examples (a) $\frac{3}{5} \div \frac{5}{8} = \frac{3}{5} \times \frac{8}{5} = \frac{24}{25}$

(b) $12 \div \frac{1}{6} = 12 \times \frac{6}{1} = 72$

(c) $\frac{3}{8} \div \frac{3}{4} = \overset{1}{\underset{2}{\cancel{3}}} \times \overset{1}{\underset{1}{\cancel{4}}} = \frac{1}{2}$

(d) $31\frac{1}{5} \div 8\frac{2}{3} = \frac{\overset{6}{\cancel{156}}}{5} \times \frac{3}{\underset{1}{\cancel{26}}} = \frac{18}{5} = 3\frac{3}{5}$

(e) $\frac{\frac{5}{12}}{9\frac{4}{5}} \div 4\frac{1}{3} = \frac{5}{12} \times \frac{5}{49} = \frac{25}{588}$ (Divide the dividend first)

Then:

$$\frac{25}{\underset{196}{\cancel{588}}} \times \frac{\overset{1}{\cancel{3}}}{13} = \frac{25}{2,548}$$

EXERCISE I-8 DIVISION

A. Divide the following. For whole numbers, reduce remainders to lowest terms; for decimal fractions carry out to the hundredths place.

1. 984 ÷ 3

2. 2,185 ÷ 5

3. 316 ÷ 16

4. 895 ÷ 45

5. 3,768 ÷ 6

6. 69,032 ÷ 8

7. 14,628 ÷ 46

8. 964,284 ÷ 321

9. 75,893 ÷ 96

10. 543,531 ÷ 6

11. 39,579 ÷ 63

12. 54,896 ÷ 817

13. 41,351 ÷ 725

14. 893,394 ÷ 1,349

15. 3.8 ÷ 2

16. 264.6 ÷ 6

17. 2.845 ÷ .07

18. $36.80 ÷ 20

19. 538.24 ÷ 1.691

20. .02953 ÷ .006

21. 300 ÷ 700

22. 48.6 ÷ 1.85.2

23. 8,364.75 ÷ 21

24. 9.86 ÷ 1,000

B. Divide the following by moving the decimal point the correct number of places to the left.

1. 28 ÷ 10

2. 6.7 ÷ 10

3. 248 ÷ 100

4. 75.5 ÷ 100

5. 32 ÷ 1,000

6. 9 ÷ 1,000

7. $8,625 ÷ 1,000

8. .057 ÷ 10

9. 6.822 ÷ 100

10. 462.357 ÷ 1,000

C. Divide the following by first dividing by 10 or a power of 10.

1. 566 ÷ 20

2. 48.8 ÷ 25

3. 15 ÷ 300

4. 2,438 ÷ 200

5. 346,825 ÷ 50

6. .669 ÷ 30

7. 24.78 ÷ 500

8. 96,000 ÷ 4,000

9. .384 ÷ 600

D. Divide the following. Reduce quotients to their lowest terms.

1. $\frac{4}{5} \div \frac{3}{10}$

2. $\frac{3}{8} \div \frac{5}{16}$

3. $\frac{7}{12} \div \frac{3}{4}$

4. $\frac{2}{3} \div \frac{1}{9}$

5. $\frac{9}{16} \div 5$

6. $\frac{15}{16} \div 3$

7. $\frac{3}{16} \div \frac{5}{8}$

8. $6\frac{2}{3} \div \frac{2}{3}$

9. $93 \div 7\frac{5}{12}$

10. $236\frac{3}{7} \div 5$

11. $482 \div 166\frac{2}{3}$

12. $\frac{1}{5} \div \frac{1}{5}$

13. $8\frac{2}{3} \div 6\frac{1}{2}$

14. $\frac{11}{24} \div 2\frac{9}{10}$

15. $96\frac{5}{8} \div 3\frac{2}{3}$

18. $\dfrac{6\frac{4}{5}}{10\frac{1}{8}} \div \dfrac{25}{3}$

16. $\dfrac{\frac{3}{5}}{7} \div 2$

19. $\dfrac{\frac{35}{7}}{8\frac{1}{4}} \div \dfrac{4\frac{1}{8}}{6}$

17. $\dfrac{\frac{2}{7}}{5\frac{1}{4}} \div \dfrac{5}{8}$

20. $\dfrac{75}{400} \div \dfrac{\frac{9}{11}}{2\frac{1}{3}}$

SECTION 6—ALIQUOT PARTS

An *aliquot part* is a quantity (number) that is contained in another quantity (number) an exact number of times. Another way of saying this is that an aliquot part is a number which can be *factored* into another number. For

TABLE I-2 common aliquot parts of 1, 10, 100, 1,000, and 10,000

Aliquot Fractions and Multiples	Base Number or Divisor				
	1	10	100	1,000	10,000
$\frac{1}{2}$	.5	5	50	500	5,000
$\frac{1}{3}$	$.33\frac{1}{3}$	$3.3\frac{1}{3}$	$33\frac{1}{3}$	$333\frac{1}{3}$	$3,333\frac{1}{3}$
$\frac{2}{3}$	$.66\frac{2}{3}$	$6.66\frac{2}{3}$	$66\frac{2}{3}$	$666\frac{2}{3}$	$6,666\frac{2}{3}$
$\frac{1}{4}$	.25	2.5	25	250	2,500
$\frac{3}{4}$	.75	7.5	75	750	7,500
$\frac{1}{5}$	.2	2	20	200	2,000
$\frac{1}{6}$	$.16\frac{2}{3}$	$1.66\frac{2}{3}$	$16\frac{2}{3}$	$166\frac{2}{3}$	$1,666\frac{2}{3}$
$\frac{5}{6}$	$.83\frac{1}{3}$	$8.33\frac{1}{3}$	$83\frac{1}{3}$	$833\frac{1}{3}$	$8,333\frac{1}{3}$
$\frac{1}{8}$	.125	1.25	$12\frac{1}{2}$	125	1,250
$\frac{3}{8}$	.375	3.75	$37\frac{1}{2}$	375	3,750
$\frac{5}{8}$	.625	6.25	$62\frac{1}{2}$	625	6,250
$\frac{7}{8}$	.875	8.75	$87\frac{1}{2}$	875	8,750
$\frac{1}{10}$	.1	1	10	100	1,000
$\frac{1}{7}$	$.14\frac{2}{7}$	$1\frac{3}{7}$	$14\frac{2}{7}$	$142\frac{6}{7}$	$1,428\frac{4}{7}$
$\frac{1}{12}$	$.08\frac{1}{3}$	$.8\frac{1}{3}$	$8\frac{1}{3}$	$83\frac{1}{3}$	$833\frac{1}{3}$
$\frac{1}{16}$	.0625	.625	6.25	62.5	625

Note: Technically, only those fractions that divide evenly into 1, 10, and the powers of 10 are aliquot fractions (they all have 1 for a numerator). The other fractions in the first column are multiples of aliquot fractions.

example, $\frac{1}{2}$ is contained exactly two times in 1, $3\frac{1}{2}$ is contained exactly two times in 7, 200 is contained exactly five times in 1,000, and $16\frac{2}{3}$ is contained exactly six times in 100; in other words, in each case the division of the smaller number into the larger leaves no remainder. The list of aliquot parts in table I-2 includes the most common aliquot parts of 1, 10, and the powers of 10 up to 10,000. These aliquot parts are confronted frequently in business computations. In many cases, their use makes multiplication and division much easier. Once you have memorized the aliquot parts of 100, it is a simple matter to determine all of the others shown in the table.

In Table I-2, notice that when any aliquot part (columns 2-6) is divided by the base number at the top of the same column, the quotient in column 1 is the corresponding aliquot fraction or multiple of that fraction. For example, when $8.33\frac{1}{3}$ (an aliquot part of 10) is divided by 10, the quotient is the multiple aliquot fraction, $\frac{5}{6}$ $\left(\frac{25}{3} \div 10 = \frac{25}{3} \times \frac{1}{10} = \frac{25}{30} = \frac{5}{6}\right)$.

Multiplication by aliquot parts

When any quantity (number) is to be multiplied by an aliquot part, the number becomes the multiplicand; the aliquot part, the multiplier, then:

1. Multiply the multiplicand by the base number of the aliquot part
2. Multiply the resulting product by the aliquot fraction or its multiple.

(a) $273.68 \times 12\frac{1}{2}$:   *Examples*

$$\left(12\frac{1}{2} \text{ is } \frac{1}{8} \text{ of } 100\right)$$

$273.68 \times 100 = 27.368$ (Product of multiplicand and base number)

$27.368 \times \frac{1}{8} = 3.421$ (Multiply product by aliquot fraction or its multiple)

(b) $372 \times 333\frac{1}{3}$:

$$\left(333\frac{1}{3} \text{ is } \frac{1}{3} \text{ of } 1,000\right)$$

$$372 \times 1,000 = 372,000$$

$$372,000 \times \frac{1}{3} = 124,000$$

(c) $97.5 \times 62\frac{1}{2}$:

$$\left(62\frac{1}{2} \text{ is } \frac{5}{8} \text{ of } 100\right)$$

$$97.5 \times 100 = 9,750$$

$$\frac{\overset{4,875}{\cancel{9,750}}}{1} \times \frac{5}{\cancel{8}} = \frac{24,375}{4} = 6,093\frac{3}{4}$$

Division by aliquot parts

The procedure is the opposite when dividing by an aliquot part or its multiple.

Examples   (*a*) 685.28 ÷ 25:

$$\left(25 \text{ is } \tfrac{1}{4} \text{ of } 100\right)$$

685.28 ÷ 100 = 6.8528   (Divide dividend by base number)

$6.8528 \div \tfrac{1}{4}$ = 6.8528 × $\tfrac{4}{1}$ (Divide quotient by the aliquot
     = 27.4112   fraction or its multiple)

(*b*) 8,600 ÷ $87\tfrac{1}{2}$:

$$\left(87\tfrac{1}{2} \text{ is } \tfrac{7}{8} \text{ of } 100\right)$$

8,600 ÷ 100 = 86

$86 \div \tfrac{7}{8}$ = 86 × $\tfrac{8}{7}$

$= \tfrac{688}{7} = 98\tfrac{2}{7}$

(*c*) 395 ÷ 625:

$$\left(625 \text{ is } \tfrac{5}{8} \text{ of } 1,000\right)$$

395 ÷ 1,000 = .395

$.395 \div \tfrac{5}{8}$ = .395 × $\tfrac{8}{5}$

$= \dfrac{3,160}{5} = .632$

EXERCISE I-9 MULTIPLICATION AND DIVISION BY ALIQUOT PARTS

A. Multiply the following by using the aliquot-parts method.

1. 69 × $33\tfrac{1}{3}$ 9. 362 @90¢

2. 72 × $12\tfrac{1}{2}$ 10. 372 doz. @$33\tfrac{1}{3}$¢

3. 64 × 25   11. 64 yd. @$62\tfrac{1}{2}$¢

4. 32 doz. @75¢   12. 184 gal. @75¢

5. 45 lb. @60¢   13. 28 × 375

6. 25 oz. @20¢   14. $7.84 × $87\tfrac{1}{2}$

7. 264 yd. @$8\tfrac{1}{3}$¢   15. 5,625 @$37.50

8. 200 @40¢

B. Divide the following by using the aliquot-parts method.

1. $400 \div 25$
2. $825 \div 50$
3. $270 \div 3.3\frac{1}{3}$
4. $295 \div 200$
5. $855 \div 62\frac{1}{2}$
6. $12,960 \div 250$

7. $18 \div 3.75$
8. $360 \div .125$
9. $9,675 \div 8.33\frac{1}{3}$
10. $248.71 \div 666\frac{2}{3}$
11. $86,420 \div 125$
12. $127,246 \div 500$

SECTION 7—RATIO AND PROPORTION

When quantities are compared to each other by the operation of division, their relationship is called a *ratio*. For example, the ratio of 3 to 9 is $\frac{1}{3}$, which can also be written $1/3$, $3:9$, $\frac{3}{9}$, or, in its lowest terms, $1:3$.

Proportion is the term given to two equal ratios or fractions. It involves four quantities so related that the ratio of one pair is equal to the ratio of the other. Hence, $\frac{3}{9} = \frac{6}{18}$ is a *proportion*. The same proportion may also be expressed in this way: $3:9::6:18$, which is said, "three is to nine as six is to eighteen." When a proportional expression has a missing value, it can be found by the following procedure:

1. Divide the larger of the known value by its counterpart in the other fraction; and
2. multiply the quotient just found by the other known value.

(a) $\dfrac{3}{5} = \dfrac{x}{20}$ or $3:5::x:20$ *Examples*

Step 1: Divide the larger known value by its counterpart in the other fraction:

$$20 \div 5 = 4$$

Step 2: Multiply the quotient by the other known value:

$$4 \times 3 = 12$$
$$\frac{3}{5} = \frac{12}{20}$$

(b) $\dfrac{3}{7} = \dfrac{9}{x}$

$$9 \div 3 = 3$$
$$3 \times 7 = 21$$
$$\frac{3}{7} = \frac{9}{21}$$

(c) $\dfrac{6}{8} = \dfrac{x}{12}$

$$12 \div 8 = 1\tfrac{1}{2}$$

$$1\tfrac{1}{2} \times 6 = 9$$

$$\frac{6}{8} = \frac{9}{12}$$

Problems in *proportion* may also be solved in the manner illustrated below. The rule is: the product of the means equals the product of the extremes. The *extremes* are the 1st and 4th terms of the proportion, the *means* are the 2nd and 3rd terms.

Example

6 is to 12 as x is to 24

$$\frac{6}{12} = \frac{x}{24}$$

$12x = 144$ (Product of means, 12 times x, equals product of extremes, 6 times 24)

Divide by 12 to solve for x only:

$$x = \frac{144}{12} = 12$$

Direct Proportion occurs when both quantities increase or decrease at the same rate.

Example   A swimming pool fills at the rate of 400 gallons every 60 minutes. How long will it take to fill it with 3,600 gallons?

$$\frac{60}{x} = \frac{400}{3,600}$$ (60 minutes is to x minutes as 400 gallons is to 3,600 gallons)

$$400x = \frac{216,000}{400}$$

$x = 540$ minutes   (9 hours)

Inverse Proportion occurs when one quantity increases and the other quantity decreases—or vice versa—at the same rate.

Example   If a man can run from his house to the drug store in 10 minutes at the rate of 12 miles per hour, how long will it take him to cover the same distance if he runs 8 miles per hour?

$$\frac{10}{x} = \frac{8}{12} \qquad \text{(10 minutes is to } x \text{ minutes as}$$
$$\qquad\qquad\qquad 8 \text{ miles per hour is to 12 miles per hour)}$$

$$8x = \frac{120}{8}$$

$$x = 15 \text{ minutes}$$

Notice in these proportion problems that the left and right sides of the proportion (each ratio) must possess like quantities (i.e., days with days or gallons with gallons, etc.). Also, notice that in *direct* proportion the relationship between the two variables is expressed horizontally, whereas when the proportion is *inverse*, this relationship is expressed diagonally.

(*a*) Direct: *Examples*

horizontal

$$\frac{60 \text{ minutes}}{x \text{ minutes}} = \frac{400 \text{ gallons}}{3,600 \text{ gallons}}$$

Here the 60 minutes goes with the 400 gallons.

(*b*) Inverse:

diagonal

$$\frac{10 \text{ minutes}}{x \text{ minutes}} = \frac{8 \text{ miles per hour}}{12 \text{ miles per hour}}$$

Here the 10 minutes goes with the 12 miles per hour.

Before attempting to solve any problems in proportion, first decide whether the relationship is direct or inverse. If it is direct, set up the two variables horizontal to each other; if inverse, set up the two variables diagonal to each other. In either case, make sure that like quantities are on the same side of the equals sign.

Using proportion to solve common-ownership problems

Problems which require the distribution of wealth among co-owners can be readily solved by the use of proportion.

A total of 484 acres of property are owned by Mr. A, Mr. B, and Mr. C in   *Example* shares of $\frac{1}{4}, \frac{5}{8}$, and $\frac{1}{8}$ respectively. How many acres does each man own?

Rule: Reduce the fractions to their lowest common denominator. The numerators of these fractions will be the required ratio.

$$\frac{1}{4} + \frac{5}{8} + \frac{1}{8} = \overset{A}{\frac{2}{8}} + \overset{B}{\frac{5}{8}} + \overset{C}{\frac{1}{8}},$$

then,

$$2 + 5 + 1 = 8$$

A's share: $\dfrac{2}{8} = \dfrac{x}{424}$

$$8x = \dfrac{848}{8}$$

$$x = 106 \text{ acres}$$

B's share: $\dfrac{5}{8} = \dfrac{x}{424}$

$$8x = \dfrac{2,120}{8}$$

$$x = 265 \text{ acres}$$

C's share: $\dfrac{1}{8} = \dfrac{x}{424}$

$$8x = \dfrac{424}{8}$$

$$x = 53 \text{ acres}$$

Check:
```
A =  106
B =  265
C =   53
Total 424
```

In calculating problems of this type, there is no requirement to make the ownership shares total the whole number 1, as was the case in the above example. In the example which follows, the ownership shares actually total $1\frac{4}{15}$. The same method is used.

Example   A plot of 912 acres of property is owned by Mr. A, Mr. B, and Mr. C in shares of $\frac{1}{6}, \frac{3}{5}$, and $\frac{1}{2}$ respectively. How many acres does each man own?

Rule: Reduce the fractions to their lowest common denominator. The *numerators* of these fractions will be the required ratio.

$$\frac{1}{6} + \frac{3}{5} + \frac{1}{2} = \overset{A}{\frac{5}{30}} + \overset{B}{\frac{18}{30}} + \overset{C}{\frac{15}{30}}$$

Then,

$$5 + 18 + 15 = 38$$

$$\text{A's share:} \quad \frac{5}{38} = \frac{x}{912}$$

$$38x = \frac{4,560}{38}$$

$$x = 120 \text{ acres}$$

$$\text{B's share:} \quad \frac{18}{38} = \frac{x}{912}$$

$$38x = \frac{16,416}{38}$$

$$x = 432 \text{ acres}$$

$$\text{C's share:} \quad \frac{15}{38} = \frac{x}{912}$$

$$38x = \frac{13,680}{38}$$

$$x = 360 \text{ acres}$$

Check:

```
A =  120
B =  432
C =  360
Total 912
```

EXERCISE I-10 RATIO AND PROPORTION

A. Express the following ratios as common fractions reduced to their lowest terms.

1. 315 to 45

2. 17 to 51

3. $22\frac{1}{2}$ to 9

4. $5\frac{1}{9}$ to $31\frac{17}{18}$

5. $\frac{1}{7}$ to $\frac{3}{16}$

6. $\frac{17}{10}$ to $\frac{13}{8}$

7. $\frac{5}{16}$ to 31.25

8. $6.9\frac{1}{3}$ to 10.4

9. 625 to $\dfrac{7\frac{1}{2}}{15}$

B. Find the missing quantities in the following proportions.

1. $\dfrac{12}{6} = \dfrac{x}{18}$

2. $\dfrac{5}{3} = \dfrac{35}{x}$

3. $\dfrac{20}{3} = \dfrac{12}{x}$

4. $\dfrac{2,400}{300} = \dfrac{2,000}{x}$

5. $\dfrac{624}{104} = \dfrac{x}{50}$

8. $\dfrac{\frac{9}{8}}{\frac{3}{4}} = \dfrac{x}{8\frac{1}{2}}$

6. $\dfrac{\frac{3}{4}}{\frac{1}{8}} = \dfrac{\frac{5}{6}}{x}$

9. $\dfrac{58}{\frac{1}{5}} = \dfrac{x}{1\frac{4}{5}}$

7. $\dfrac{x}{3\frac{3}{4}} = \dfrac{24}{36}$

EXERCISE I-11 PROBLEMS ON RATIO AND PROPORTION

A. Problems in direct proportion:
   1. If an investment of $3,090 returns a profit of $618, what would have been the profit on a $2,400 investment?
   2. If rain falls at the rate of 3 inches in 18 hours, how many inches of rain will fall in 3 full days?
   3. The Oakland A's baseball team used 21 baseballs for a 9-inning game. At the same rate, how many balls would they have used if the game had gone 15 innings?
   4. A lady can iron 38 shirts in a 4-hour period. How many hours would it take her to iron 57 shirts?
   5. A ballplayer got 24 hits in his first 72 trips to the plate. If he continues this same pace, how many times will he have to bat to reach 100 hits?
B. Problems in inverse proportion:
   1. A piece-work operation requires the labor of 21 men for 15 days. How many men could complete the job in 9 days?
   2. A bus travels from Pillar to Post in 160 minutes at the rate of 50 miles per hour. How long will it take to make the return trip if the bus averages 65 miles per hour?
   3. If a store can sell 72 chairs at $100 each, then, assuming that more chairs can be sold when the price per chair is reduced, how many chairs will be sold at $60 each?
   4. A store had expenses of $20,000 one month and profits of $5,000. Assuming this relationship continues, what would be the profit for a month when expenses were $15,000?
C. Problems in ratio and proportion:
   1. In a partnership, A invested $7,500, B invested $6,000, and C invested $4,500. If the partnership earned $10,500, what will be each partner's share of profits if profits are divided according to each partner's share of the total investment?
   2. The Model Linen Supply Co. insured its plant for $35,000 with the National Insurance Co., for $15,000 with the General Insurance Co. and for $10,000 with the Liberty Insurance Co. A fire caused $18,600 worth of

damage to the plant. Assume each insurance company will pay part of the loss. Assume also that each company will pay in proportion to its share of the total insurance on the property. How much of the loss will each company pay?

3. A farmer rented his farm for $\frac{1}{4}$ of the proceeds on the sale of the crop. If he received $1,320, how much more would he have received had he rented for $\frac{1}{3}$ of the proceeds?

4. A profit of $13,200 is divided among A, B, and C in the ratios of $\frac{5}{6}$, $\frac{3}{4}$, and $\frac{4}{5}$ respectively. How much will each man receive?

5. A piece of property is sold for $12,750 for the benefit of four brothers. The brothers will divide the proceeds in the ratios of $\frac{1}{2}$, $\frac{2}{3}$, $\frac{3}{5}$, and $\frac{1}{3}$. What will be the amount of each share?

SECTION 8—PERCENT

Percent is probably the most useful arithmetic concept in the field of business mathematics. A complete understanding of this concept is necessary for solving problems in markup, property tax, insurance, interest, stocks and bonds, financial statement analysis, and every other problem wherein something is compared to something else.

Percent comes from the Latin *per centum* meaning "per hundred." This is well worth remembering, because the relationship between two quantities is expressed as so many per 100. Percent, then is the relationship between two quantities, based on 100. Instead of expressing the relationship of 50 to 100 as the fraction $\frac{50}{100}$, or in decimal form as .50, it is often more convenient to express it as 50%. All three of these expressions are equivalent (.50 = $\frac{50}{100}$ = 50%). In English usage, the same relationship might be stated as "one out of

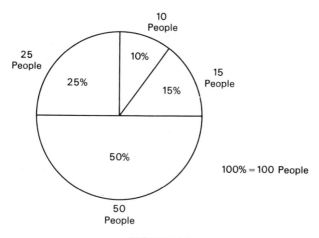

FIGURE I-1

two" or "every other." Thus, percent involves nothing more than comparing quantities to each other and expressing their relationship as so many parts out of 100. Since any quantity can be divided into 100 parts, the concept of percent may be shown as in figure I-1.

Converting percents to common and decimal fractions

We already know that a percent is really a fraction having the denominator of 100. In order to multiply or divide by a percent, it must first be converted to either a common or decimal fraction. The following rules apply:

Rule A To convert a common fraction to a decimal fraction, divide the numerator by the denominator.

Examples

$$\frac{1}{2} = 2\overline{\smash{\big)}1.0}^{\,.5} \qquad \frac{2}{5} = 5\overline{\smash{\big)}2.0}^{\,.4}$$

$$\frac{5}{8} = 8\overline{\smash{\big)}5.000}^{\,.625} \qquad \frac{3}{2} = 2\overline{\smash{\big)}3.0}^{\,1.5}$$

Rule B To convert a common or decimal fraction to a percent, multiply by 100 and add the percent sign (%).

Examples

$$.5 \times 100 = 50\% \qquad .4 \times 100 = 40\%$$
$$.625 \times 100 = 62.5\% \qquad 1.5 \times 100 = 150\%$$
$$\frac{3}{8} \times 100 = 37\frac{1}{2}\%$$

Rule C To convert a percent to a decimal fraction, remove the percent sign (%) and divide by 100.

Examples

$$\left. \begin{array}{l} 62.5\% = .625 \\ .273\frac{2}{3}\% = .00273\frac{2}{3} \\ 14.322\% = .14322 \end{array} \right\}$$ (With decimal fractions, move the decimal point 2 places to the left)

$$\left. \begin{array}{l} \frac{3}{4}\% = \frac{3}{4} \div 100 = \frac{3}{4} \times \frac{1}{100} = \frac{3}{400} \\[2mm] 7\frac{1}{5}\% = 7\frac{1}{5} \div 100 = \frac{36}{5} \times \frac{1}{100} = \frac{36}{500} = \frac{9}{125} \\[2mm] \qquad\qquad \text{or} \\[2mm] = 7.20\% = .0720 = \frac{720}{10,000} = \frac{9}{125} \\[2mm] \qquad\qquad \text{or} \\[2mm] = \frac{(5 \times 7) + 1}{5} = \frac{36}{500} \ \ (\text{Add 2 zeros}) = \frac{9}{125} \end{array} \right\}$$ (With fractional percents, it is quicker to add 2 zeros to the denominator)

Because any quantity may be compared to any other, the key question to ask before solving a percent problem is, "What is being compared to what?" The quantity which serves as the basis of comparison is defined as the *base*, and the base quantity is *always* equal to 100%. The quantity being compared is called the *percentage*, and the relationship between them is called the *percent*. Because of the confusion between the terms "percent" and "percentage," the percent is often called the *rate*.

The basic equation in all percent problems is percentage (P) = rate (R) × base (B). It is recommended that, at least at first, this "percentage statement" be written before solving each problem.

Solving for the percentage

(*a*) A man had $85 and spent 35% of it. How much did he spend?   *Example*

Step 1: What is being compared to what?
$x spent is being compared to $85. Therefore, the $85 is the base.

Step 2: Write the percentage statement:
What is 35% of $85?

Step 3:

$$P = R \times B$$

Step 4:

$$P = .35 \times \$85 = \$29.73$$

(*b*) Of 300 students attending a meeting, 28% were sophomores. How many sophomores were there?

Step 1: What is being compared to what?
The number of sophomores is being compared to the total of 300 students.

Step 2: Write the percentage statement:
What is 28% of 300?

Step 3:

$$P = R \times B$$

Step 4:

$$P = .28 \times 300 = 84 \text{ sophomores}$$

Solving for the rate

When both quantities in a percent problem are known, their relationship to each other may be expressed as a percent value (so many out of every 100). In this case we are solving for the rate. Since $P = R \times B$, then $R = P/B$. Remember that the base quantity is the one which serves as the basis of comparison, while the percentage quantity is the quantity being compared.

Examples   (*a*) An automobile dealer sold 5 of the 20 cars on his showroom floor this week. What percent of the total did he sell?

Step 1: What is being compared to what?
        5 cars sold compared to 20 cars on hand

Step 2: Write the percentage statement or equation:
        5 is ?% of 20.

Step 3:

$$R = \frac{P}{B}$$

Step 4:

$$R = \tfrac{5}{20} = \tfrac{1}{4} = .25 \times 100 = 25\%$$

The answer means he has sold cars at the rate of 25 out of every 100.

(*b*) In a group of 250 students, 30 were freshmen. What percent were not freshmen?

Step 1: What is being compared to what?
        220 nonfreshmen students compared to 250 students

Step 2: Write the percentage statement:
        220 is ?% of 250.

Step 3:

$$R = \frac{P}{B}$$

Step 4:

$$R = \tfrac{220}{250} = .88 \times 100 = 88\%$$

The answer means that 88 students out of every 100 are not freshmen.

(*c*) A store had sales of $2,000 in March of 1969. In March of 1970, sales were $3,000. What percent are March 1970 sales compared to those of March 1969?

Step 1: What is being compared to what?
        $3,000 March 1970 sales compared to $2,000 March 1969 sales

Step 2: Write the percentage statement:
        $3,000 is ?% of $2,000.

Step 3:

$$R = \frac{P}{B}$$

Step 4:

$$R = \frac{\$3,000}{\$2,000} = 1.50 \times 100 = 150\%$$

The answer means that sales this March are $1\frac{1}{2}$ times the amount of sales for the previous March, or that $150 of sales were made this March for every $100 of sales last March.

Notice that *the base number can be smaller or larger than the quantity being compared to it.*

Solving for the base

When the rate and the percentage are known, the base can be found by using the formula $B = P/R$. Again, the key question is, "What is being compared to what?" The percentage statement "a quantity is a certain % of another quantity" is of great value at this point. In this percentage statement the base is always the number following the phrase "% of."

(*a*) In a shipment of dresses, it was discovered that 16 dresses were in- *Examples* correctly labeled. If these represented 10% of the total, how many dresses were shipped?

Step 1: What is being compared to what?
16 dresses are being compared to the total. Therefore, the total number of dresses shipped is the base.

Step 2: Write the percentage statement:
16 is 10% of what?

Step 3:

$$B = \frac{P}{R}$$

Step 4:

$$B = \frac{16}{.10} = 160 \text{ dresses}$$

(*b*) The cheering squad of Disco Tech has 12 members, which is only $\frac{1}{5}$ of the members it had last year. How big was the cheering squad last year?

Step 1: What is being compared to what?
12 members are being compared to the number of members last year. Therefore, last year's membership is the base.

Step 2: Write the percentage statement:
12 is 20% of what?

Step 3:

$$B = \frac{P}{R}$$

Step 4:

$$B = \frac{12}{.20} = 60 \text{ members last year}$$

The formulas used for finding the rate and base in percentage problems are derived from the basic percentage equation: percentage = rate X base. Once the problem has been carefully read and the missing value defined as either the base, the rate, or the percentage, the graphic device shown below can serve as a reminder of how to proceed arithmetically.

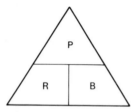

$$P = R \times B$$
$$R = \frac{P}{B}$$
$$B = \frac{P}{R}$$

Percent problems involving an increase or decrease

Percent problems involving increases or decreases in quantities are common in the business world. Although solving them requires no change in the basic procedure explained above, extra care must be taken in making sure these problems are understood correctly before a solution is attempted. This is the reason for giving them special attention here.

finding the rate (percent) of increase or decrease

Examples   (a) A salesman's commission earnings were $850 in April and $650 in March. What was the rate of increase in his earnings from March to April?

Step 1: What is being compared to what?
The increase in earnings is being compared to the March earnings. Therefore, March earnings serve as the base.

Step 2: Write the percentage statement:
$200 (the increase) is ?% of $650.

Step 3:

$$R = \frac{P}{B}$$

Step 4:

$$R = \frac{200}{650} = .3075 \times 100 = 30.8\% \quad \text{(Increase)}$$

(*b*) A town had a population of 8,000 people in 1960. In 1970 the population was 6,400. What was the rate of decrease?

Step 1: What is being compared to what?
The decrease in population is being compared to the population in 1960.

Step 2: Write the percentage statement:
1,600 (the decrease) is ?% of 8,000.

Step 3:

$$R = \frac{P}{B}$$

Step 4:

$$R = \frac{1,600}{8,000} = \frac{1}{5} = .20 = 20\%$$

finding the percentage (amount) of increase or decrease

The procedure to follow in problems of this kind is either

When the given quantity is *greater than* the missing quantity, *add* the percent of increase to the base. *Rule A*

or

When the given quantity is *less than* the missing quantity, *subtract* the percent of decrease from the base. *Rule B*

(*a*) The cheering squad of Disco Tech increased its membership by 20%. *Examples* If it now has 12 members, by how many members did the squad increase?

Step 1: What is being compared to what?
The 12-man squad is being compared to the original size of the squad. Therefore, the original size is the base.

Step 2: Write the percentage statement following rule A, above:
12 is 120% of what?

Step 3:

$$B = \frac{P}{R}$$

Step 4:

$$B = \frac{12}{1.20} = 10 \text{ students}$$

Step 5:

$$12 - 10 = 2 \text{ students} \quad \text{(Increase)}$$

Note: This problem could have been written, "12 is 20% greater than what number?"

(b) An appliance salesman earned $180 this week, which was 20% less than he earned last week. How much did he earn last week?

Step 1: What is being compared to what?
$180 is being compared to last week's earnings. Therefore, last week's earnings is the base.

Step 2: Write the percentage statement following rule B, above:
$180 is 80% of what?

Step 3:

$$B = \frac{P}{R}$$

Step 4:

$$B = \frac{\$180}{.80} = \$225$$

Note: This problem could have been written, "$180 is 20% less than what amount?"

(c) A store sells a certain style wallet at $6 apiece, which is 25% more than it pays for them. How much does the store pay for each wallet?

Step 1: What is being compared to what?
$6 selling price is being compared to the store's cost. Therefore, the store's cost is the base.

Step 2: Write the percentage statement following rule A, above:
$6 is 125% of what?

Step 3:

$$B = \frac{P}{R}$$

Step 4:

$$B = \frac{\$6}{1.25} = \$4.80$$

EXERCISE 1-12 PERCENT EQUIVALENTS

A. Find the percent that is equivalent to these quantities.

1. .67

2. 3.3

3. .095

4. 8.62

5. .006

6. $3\frac{1}{2}$

7. .01

8. .0475

9. 1.6267

10. .00404

11. $\frac{3}{4}$

12. $\frac{9}{8}$

13. $2\frac{2}{9}$

14. $16\frac{2}{3}$

15. $1.05\frac{1}{4}$

16. $\frac{3}{20}$

17. $3\frac{1}{8}$

18. $\frac{13}{57}$

B. Change these percents to their equivalent whole numbers, mixed numbers, or fractions, reducing them to their lowest terms.

1. 32%

2. $3\frac{1}{2}$%

3. .05%

4. 100%

5. 275%

6. $\frac{3}{5}$%

7. .91%

8. $12\frac{1}{8}$%

9. 40%

10. $\frac{3}{100}$%

11. 18.25%

12. $41\frac{2}{3}$%

13. $43\frac{3}{4}$%

14. $68\frac{3}{4}$%

15. 360%

16. $118\frac{3}{4}$%

17. 98%

18. $42\frac{6}{7}$%

EXERCISE 1-13 FINDING PERCENTAGE, RATE AND BASE

A. Find the indicated percentages below. Use the table of aliquot parts (table 1-2) when possible. Round off all money answers to the nearest cent.

1. 75% of 28

2. $12\frac{1}{2}$% of 72

3. $16\frac{2}{3}$% of 84

4. $62\frac{1}{2}$% of 64

5. 36% of $843

6. $3\frac{1}{4}$% of $4,350

7. 8.75% of 98.1

8. $3\frac{1}{3}$% of 330

9. $22\frac{2}{9}$% of $213

10. 115% of $37.60

11. 3.05% of $37,000

12. $62\frac{1}{2}$% of .24

13. $\frac{1}{5}$% of 90

14. $.375\frac{1}{3}$% of $887

15. .07% of 2.85

B. Find the rate to the nearest tenth of a percent.

1. 15 is what percent of 60?

2. 13 is what percent of 39?

3. 18 is what percent of 81?

4. $.36 is what percent of $4.20?

5. 750 is what percent of 250?

6. $.12 is what percent of $1.44?

7. $61 is what percent of $427?

8. $32 is what percent of $112?

9. $6\frac{2}{5}$ is what percent of $18\frac{5}{6}$?

10. $\frac{3}{5}$ is what percent of $\frac{2}{5}$?

11. 90 is what percent of 3?

12. $21\frac{1}{2}$ is what percent of $38\frac{1}{10}$?

13. What percent of 50 is 150?

14. What percent of 9.6 is 3.3?

15. $\frac{21}{8}$ is what percent of $\frac{7}{16}$?

C. Find the base. Round off all money answers to the nearest cent, all others to the nearest hundredth.

1. 50 is 5% of what quantity?

2. 64 is 16% of what quantity?

3. $.60 is 120% of what quantity?

4. $81 is $37\frac{1}{2}$% of what quantity?

5. $63 is $112\frac{1}{2}$% of what quantity?

6. $18 is 120% of what quantity?

7. $37.56 is $2\frac{1}{2}$% of what quantity?

8. 300% of what quantity is $46?

9. 144% of what quantity is $72?

10. $\frac{3}{4}$ is 9% of what quantity?

11. $2\frac{2}{7}$ is 36% of what quantity?

12. $88 is 110% of what quantity?

13. 3.42 is 216% of what quantity?

14. 16 compared to what quantity is 25%?

15. 300% is the relationship between 270 and what other quantity?

D. Find the percent of increase (to the nearest tenth) in each of the following.

1. 16 increased to 32

2. $2\frac{1}{2}$ increased to $7\frac{1}{2}$

3. 20 increased to 25

4. $13\frac{1}{3}$ increased to 80

5. 81 increased by 10

6. 200 increased by 25

7. $.35 increased by $.05

8. 330 increased to 550

9. $460 increased to $494.50

10. $2.85 increased to $160

E. Find the percent of decrease (to the nearest tenth) in the following.

1. 80 decreased to 72
2. 68 decreased to 57.8
3. $240 decreased to 80
4. 5 decreased by 2
5. $18\frac{2}{9}$ decreased by $\frac{2}{9}$

6. 7,000 decreased by 150
7. 625 decreased to 20
8. $88 reduced to $60
9. from 90 to 75
10. from $16.98 to $11.77

F. Find the amount of increase or decrease in the following. Carry out two places for money, one place for all other answers.

1. 3 increased 20%
2. 6% more than 150
3. 75 plus 80%
4. 25% off $35.00
5. $8 plus 40%

6. 19 less 2%
7. 30% more than 10
8. 250% more than 50
9. 40 is 20% less than what?
10. 16 is 60% more than what?

EXERCISE I-14 PROBLEMS ON PERCENT

1. Five dinner plates received in a store shipment of 144 came in damaged. What percent of the shipment was damaged?
2. Al Cummings withdrew 26% of the funds from his savings account. If his account had a balance of $460, what is the balance now?
3. If a company had cash on hand of $75,420 on March 1 and $48,200 on April 1 of the same year, what was the percent of decrease?
4. A car consumed 8 gallons of gasoline on a trip. If its tank was full with 20 gallons at the start of the trip, what percent of the gasoline is still in the tank?
5. At Thornton High, 35% of the students drove cars to school. If the enrollment is 2,600, how many drove cars to school?
6. Three men combined to make an investment of $10,000. If partners A and B put up equal amounts, and partner C put up $\frac{1}{4}$ of the total amount, what percent of the total did A and B contribute and what were the contributions of each partner?
7. An investment of $9,500 returned a profit of $725. What was the percent return on this investment?
8. If an investment produced a return of $800 and this was a 12% gain, what was the amount invested?
9. A service station reduced the price of a discontinued style of tires from $15.95 to $11.95. What percent off the old price could the buyer save?
10. Membership in a discount department store increased 15% in 1 year. If there are now 16,385 members, how many were there before this increase?
11. A store had cash receipts of $26,835.24 for the month of February. If state tax is 4% of sales and city tax is 1% of sales, what part of these

cash receipts must be forwarded to the state governm nt? What part to the city government?

12. An upholsterer finds that he must allow for a 15% excess in material before starting a job. If he calculates that it w il take $8\frac{1}{2}$ yards of material to upholster a sofa, how much material will be wasted?

13. If a merchant can sell wallets for $5 each and realize a profit of 40% of the selling price, how much does he pay for these wallets?

14. Jim Jones sold his automobile for $600, which was 65% less than he paid for it. The used-car price was how much less than the price Jim paid for the car?

15. A real estate investor sold a piece of property for 128% of what it cost him. What was his percent of gain?

16. The Arnold Co. had expenses this month equaling 32% of its sales of $86,247.53. How much were expenses?

17. A property owner sold 4% of his property. He now has 48 acres remaining. How many acres did he sell?

18. An employee's federal income tax takes 16% of his wages. What percent is his take-home pay based on his gross earnings?

19. An office products store sold 24 typewriters, bringing in a total revenue of $2,112. If $\frac{1}{3}$ of the typewriters sold at $112 each, $\frac{1}{5}$ for $82 each, and $\frac{1}{8}$ for $75 each, find (a) the sales volume produced by the remaining typewriters, and (b) the per-unit price of the remaining typewriters.

20. If a store gains $\frac{1}{4}$ more than it paid by selling eggs at 45¢ a dozen, what price would it have to charge to gain $\frac{1}{3}$ more than it pays per dozen?

21. Three ounces of 100% acid are added to 5 ounces of a 25%-acid solution, What percent (to the nearest tenth) of acid does the solution now have?

22. A silver bracelet is 12 parts silver and 2 parts nickel. What percent of the bracelet is pure silver?

23. A man contemplating the purchase of a luxurious 10-unit apartment building has determined the following: he can rent each unit for $210 per month; repairs and maintenance will be approximately $200 per unit per year; other expenses, including taxes and insurance, will run about 20% of the rental income. If he desires a 15% annual return on his investment, what would be the maximum price he should pay for the building?

24. A man increased his entertainment budget by 20%. This meant that each month he was spending 15% more on entertainment than on insurance. His insurance expense was $25 per month. (a) How much does he spend per month on entertainment? (b) How much was he spending on entertainment before he increased it?

25. The consumer price index rose from 122.6 to 128.7 from one year to another. What was the percent of increase? What is the cost, after the increase, of an item that cost 83 cents before the increase?

appendix II

graphical presentation
of business data

All business transactions are summarized in numbers. Business decisions must be based upon analysis and interpretation of the masses of numerical data generated by business. It is essential, therefore, that the best possible methods be employed to present data in a manner which will aid its comprehension and interpretation. In this text, percents and ratios are used to compare quantities. This is a step toward a special branch of mathematics called *statistics*, which deals with the interpretation of data. Of particular concern are certain statistical methods such as statistical averages, tables, and graphs.

Assembling of raw data

Numerical data are usually received in an unorganized manner, and it is thus necessary to arrange them systematically. The first step is to develop an *array* which puts the data in ascending or descending order. Let us say that the offer price per share of 100 mutual funds varies from $3.32 to $12.82. The difference between the two extremes ($9.50) is called the *range* of the data. Further useful classification or grouping of the data may be done on the basis of quantity or in accordance with time of occurrence. If classes or groups of data are established in a quantitative manner and a tabulation made of the number of cases falling into each class, the result is called a *frequency distribution*. If some characteristic is measured at specified intervals of time, the relationship between the measurements constitutes a *time series*.

Frequency distributions

The groups in a frequency distribution are called *class intervals*, with the lower number of each interval being the *lower class limit* and the higher number being the *upper class limit*. The number of cases falling within the range of the lower and upper limits (limits inclusive) is the *class frequency*.

The size of a single class interval is established by dividing the range of values by the number of intervals desired. Thus, the intervals in table II-1 were established by dividing a price range of $9.50 (i.e., from $3.32 to $12.82) by 10 and rounding off to $1.00. To insure no overlap of intervals, the lower limits were set at even dollars with the upper limits ending in 99¢. However, it is to be noted in table II-1 that there are 100¢ in each class interval since both the upper and lower limits are included. Once the classes were established, the number of prices falling into each class interval was done by tally.

TABLE II-1   offer prices per share of 100
             mutual funds on August 28,
             1970

Price per Share	Tally	Total Number of Prices
$ 3.00– 3.99	|||	3
4.00– 4.99	THL ||	7
5.00– 5.99	THL THL	10
6.00– 6.99	THL THL THL THL ||||	24
7.00– 7.99	THL THL THL ||	17
8.00– 8.99	THL THL THL	15
9.00– 9.99	THL THL		11
10.00–10.99	THL		6
11.00–11.99	THL	5
12.00–12.99	||	2
		100

graphical presentation of frequency distributions

An example of a graphical presentation of a frequency distribution is shown in figure II-1 which was constructed using the information in table II-1.

A graph has a horizontal line called the *X*-axis and a vertical line drawn perpendicular to it and called the *Y*-axis. Class intervals, which are termed *independent variables*, are marked on the *X*-axis. The *Y*-axis is scaled appropriately for the frequencies, which are the *dependent variables*. The number of cases within each class interval is indicated by a mark directly over that class interval at a height equal to the appropriate frequency indicated on the *Y*-axis. When these plotted points are connected, the result is a *frequency polygon*.

Rectangles may be drawn for each class interval, with the height being the

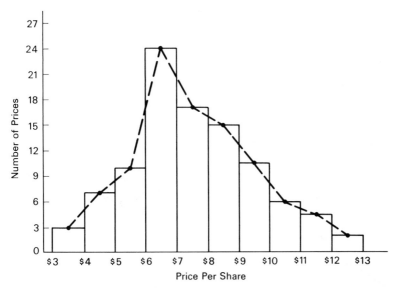

FIGURE II-1   distribution of offer prices per share for 100 mutual
funds on August 28, 1970

plotted frequency for that interval. A graph of such rectangles is called a *histo-gram* or a *rectangular frequency polygon*.

cumulative-frequency distributions

A graphical representation of a distribution in which the frequencies are cumulated from the lowest through the highest class is an *ogive*. A *"less-than"* *ogive* is one in which the frequencies of values less than the upper limit of a series of classes are presented (table II-2; figure II-2). A *"more-than"* *ogive* is one in which the frequencies of values greater than the lower limit of a series of classes are presented (table II-3; figure II-3).

TABLE II-2   cumulative-frequency table

Price per Share	Number of Prices
less than $ 4.00	3
less than 5.00	10
less than 6.00	20
less than 7.00	44
less than 8.00	61
less than 9.00	76
less than 10.00	87
less than 11.00	93
less than 12.00	98
less than 13.00	100

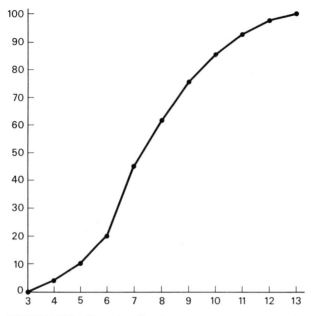

FIGURE II-2 "less-than" ogive

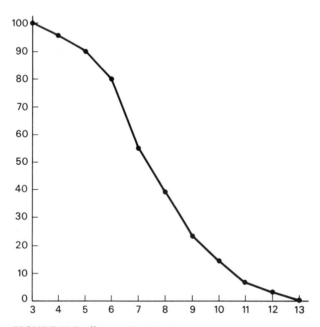

FIGURE II-3 "more-than" ogive

TABLE II-3 cumulative-frequency table

Price per Share	Number of Prices
more than $ 3.00	100
more than 4.00	97
more than 5.00	90
more than 6.00	80
more than 7.00	56
more than 8.00	39
more than 9.00	24
more than 10.00	13
more than 11.00	7
more than 12.00	2
more than 13.00	0

EXERCISE II-1 FREQUENCY DISTRIBUTION, FREQUENCY POLYGON, HISTOGRAM

The following are the earnings per share of 40 issues of common stock in the investment portfolio of a retired business man. Construct a frequency distribution, a frequency polygon, and a histogram for this data.

$1.70	$1.18	$1.24	$1.45	$1.49
1.25	1.38	1.29	1.45	1.46
1.40	1.45	1.48	1.77	1.40
1.65	1.47	1.43	1.37	1.38
1.35	1.53	1.36	1.46	1.34
1.30	1.50	1.40	1.52	1.40
1.55	1.76	1.51	1.57	1.42
1.60	1.63	1.44	1.62	1.56

types of frequency curves

Frequency curves may take a variety of shapes depending upon the distribution of the values being charted. Those in figure II-4 are some of the more common types.

The degree of peakedness of a curve is called *kurtosis*. The variation in the size of the frequencies or the degree to which they tend to spread about an average value is called *dispersion*. The tendency for data from measurements in nature or in the business world to group about a certain point permits the calculation of an average value which is typical of the total set of data. Knowing how to calculate such averages, called *measures of central tendency*, is essential for analysis of numerical data.

Measures of central tendency

the arithmetic mean

When most people use the term *average*, they are referring specifically to the *arithmetic mean* (or simply *mean*), which is the sum of a series of values

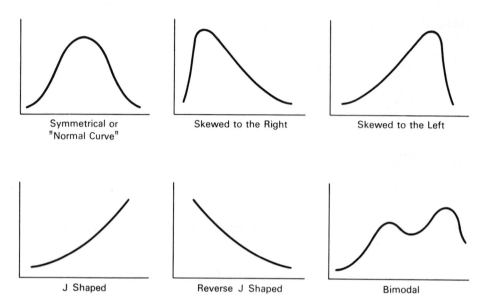

Symmetrical or "Normal Curve"	Skewed to the Right	Skewed to the Left
J Shaped	Reverse J Shaped	Bimodal

FIGURE II-4

divided by the number of values in the series. The formula for computing the arithmetic mean is

$$M = \frac{\Sigma X}{N}$$

where M = mean
        X = individual values
        Σ = "sum of"
        N = number of values in the series

If the number of values is large, it would be tedious to total them. An easier way is to arrange the data into a frequency distribution and then compute the mean for the distribution.

Finding the mean by the long method. The data in table II-1 are rearranged in table II-4 for computation of the mean by the long method. Each frequency is multiplied by the *midpoint* of its class interval. This means that all of the cases in a class interval are treated as though they were exactly halfway between the lower and upper limits of that interval. The product obtained is the total value for all cases in the class interval. The products are then totaled and divided by the total number of cases (N). Thus,

$$M = \frac{\Sigma Mf}{N} = \frac{\$758.00}{100} = \$7.58$$

Finding the mean by the short method. To further simplify the calculation of the mean—especially when many cases are involved—the short method or

TABLE II-4 computation of arithmetic mean by long method (offer price per share of 100 mutual funds on August 28, 1970)

Price per Share: Class Interval	Midpoint (M)	Number of Prices: Frequency (f)	Midpoint × Frequency (Mf)
$ 3.00-3.99	$ 3.50	3	$ 10.50
4.00-4.99	4.50	7	31.50
5.00-5.99	5.50	10	55.00
6.00-6.99	6.50	24	156.00
7.00-7.99	7.50	17	127.50
8.00-8.99	8.50	15	127.50
9.00-9.99	9.50	11	104.50
10.00-10.99	10.50	6	63.00
11.00-11.99	11.50	5	57.50
12.00-12.99	12.50	2	25.00
		100	$758.00

TABLE II-5 computation of arithmetic mean by short method (offer price per share of 100 mutual funds on August 28, 1970)

Price per Share: Class Interval	Midpoint (M)	Number of Prices: Frequency (f)	Deviation (d)	Frequency × Deviation (fd)	
$ 3.00-3.99	$ 3.50	3	−5	−15	
4.00-4.99	4.50	7	−4	−28	
5.00-5.99	5.50	10	−3	−30	
6.00-6.99	6.50	24	−2	−48	
7.00-7.99	7.50	17	−1	−17	
					Subtotal −138
8.00-8.99	8.50	15	0	0	
9.00-9.99	9.50	11	+1	+11	
10.00-10.99	10.50	6	+2	+12	
11.00-11.99	11.50	5	+3	+15	
12.00-12.99	12.50	2	+4	+8	
					Subtotal + 46
					Total − 92

group-deviation method may be used. In table II-5 a guess is made that the mean is the $8.50 midpoint of the class interval $8.00–$8.99. The guess need not be right. How far each class interval deviates, in terms of number of intervals, from the interval containing the assumed mean indicated is noted in the "Deviation" column. The deviations less than the midpoint $8.50 are indicated as negative because they would tend to lower the mean below the assumed point. The deviations greater than the midpoint $8.50 are indicated as positive because they would tend to raise the mean above the assumed point.

The deviations are then multiplied by the frequencies and the resultant products totaled. The result is the total deviation from the guessed mean of all values, which is then divided by the number of cases to obtain the average deviation from the guessed mean. The deviation may, of course, be either positive or negative. Thus, from table II-5,

$$\frac{\Sigma fd}{N} = \frac{-92}{100} = -.92$$

This value is then added to the assumed mean (A) to obtain the true mean:

$$M = A + \frac{\Sigma fd}{N} = \$8.50 + \frac{-92}{100}$$

$$= \$8.50 - .92 = \$7.58$$

Although the arithmetical mean is commonly used and relatively simple to compute, it may not always be appropriate. Its value may be greatly distorted by extreme values and may therefore not be typical of the data under consideration.

EXERCISE II-2 ARITHMETIC MEAN

From the information in exercise II-1, calculate the arithmetic mean (a) by the long method, and (b) by the short method.

the median

After data has been put into an array, the middle value is called the *median.* If there are an even number of cases, then the median is the arithmetic mean of the two middle values. The median designates the position of a value in an array, whereas the mean is a calculated average of the values.

As an example of determining the median from ungrouped data, consider the following 9 figures representing prices per share of 9 mutual funds: $5.47, $4.32, $8.90, $7.74, $3.19, $11.65, $9.32, $10.12, $6.38.

The first step is to arrange the prices in order of size—i.e., in an array:

$3.19, $4.32, $5.47, $6.38, $7.74, $8.90, $9.32, $10.12, $11.65

Since there are 9 prices, the 5th price is the middle one, with 4 prices above it and 4 below it. Therefore, the $7.74 price is the middle value or median. If one more price of $12.25 were added, then there would be 10 prices, an even number. The median would then lie between (or be the arithmetic mean of) the 2 middle values of $7.74 and $8.90.

$$\text{Median} = \frac{\$7.74 + \$8.90}{2} = \$8.32$$

TABLE II-6 computation of median offer price
(per share of 100 mutual funds on
August 28, 1970)

Price per Share: Class Interval	Number of Prices: Frequency (f)	Cumulated Frequency (Σf)
$ 3.00–3.99	3	3
4.00–4.99	7	10
5.00–5.99	10	20
6.00–6.99	24	44
7.00–7.99	17	61
8.00–8.99	15	76
9.00–9.99	11	87
10.00–10.99	6	93
11.00–11.99	5	98
12.00–12.99	2	100
	100	

The median of grouped data. The calculation of the median from grouped data may be illustrated by referring to table II-6:

1. Divide the total number of prices by 2, giving the numbered position of the median price:

$$\frac{N}{2} = \frac{100}{2}$$

$$= 50$$

2. Add the frequencies cumulatively until the lower limit of the class containing the median value is reached. Thus, as shown in the last column in table II-6, there are 44 prices below the lower class limit of $7.00 and 61 prices up to and including the upper class limit of $7.99, and the median value lies within the class interval.
3. Divide the number of prices needed to reach the 50th price by the number of prices in the class interval: 6/17. This indicates the fractional part of the class interval needed to arrive at the median position.
4. Multiply the class interval by the fraction arrived at in step 3:

$$\frac{6}{17} \times 1.00 = \frac{6.00}{17} = .353$$

5. Adding this value to the lower limit of the class gives the median value of $7.35.
   By formula,

$$\text{Median} = I_l + \left[\frac{i}{fm} \ C \right]$$

where L_1 = lower class limit of median class interval
         i = number of values needed in class to equal $N/2$
         fm = total number of cases in median class interval
         C = size of median class interval

Thus,

$$\text{Median} = \$7.00 + \left[\tfrac{6}{17} \times 1.00 \right] = \$7.353 \text{ rounded to } \$7.35$$

As a check, the process may be reversed by counting down from the interval with the highest value. When the upper class limit of $7.99 is reached, the cumulative total of prices is 39. Thus, $\tfrac{11}{17}$ of the interval must be subtracted from the upper limit to arrive at the median:

$$\tfrac{11}{17} \times 1.00 = \tfrac{11}{17} = .647$$
$$\$7.99 - .647 = 7.352 \text{ rounded to } \$7.35$$

Note: The upper limit had to be extended to three places (7.999) to accommodate the subtrahend. Because of this, the upper class interval limit is often carried one place further than any of the individual cases.

The median is easily calculated once the data has been placed in an array. It is not distorted by extreme values as is the case with the arithmetic mean, but it is not so well adapted to algebraic manipulation.

EXERCISE II-3 MEDIAN

From the information in exercise II-1, calculate the median (a) with the data put into an array but not grouped, and (b) with the data grouped by class interval.

the mode

A third measure of central tendency is the *mode*, which may sometimes only be approximated. It is the value which occurs most often in a group of values. In a frequency distribution, the modal class interval is that with the largest number of frequencies. If there are two intervals with a high number of frequencies, the data is termed *bimodal*.

In table II-6 the modal interval is $6.00–6.99, where 24 cases occur, the highest number in the group. The value of the mode may be approximated by the following formula:

$$\text{Mode} = L_1 + \left(\frac{fa}{fa + fb} \right) C$$

where L_1 = lower class limit of modal interval
         fa = frequency of class interval above modal interval
         fb = frequency of class interval below modal interval
         C = size of modal class interval

Therefore,

$$\text{Mode} = \$6.00 + \left(\frac{17}{17 + 10}\right)\$1.00$$
$$= \$6.00 + .63 = \$6.63$$

The mode has no significance unless there are a large number of values with a distinct central tendency.

relationship between mean, median and mode

In a perfectly symmetrical distribution, the mean, median, and mode will coincide. If the distribution is asymmetrical, the mean is pulled away from the mode in the direction of the extreme values or *skewness*, and the median will lie between these two measures. The values of the mean and the median may be determined exactly, and in cases of moderately asymmetrical distribution the mode may be approximated as follows:

$$\text{Mode} = \text{Mean} - 3(\text{Mean} - \text{Median})$$

Applying the values calculated in the examples for the offer price per share of 100 mutual funds (using tables II-4, II-5, and II-6),

$$\text{Mode} = \$7.58 - 3(\$7.58 - \$7.35)$$
$$= \$7.58 - .69 = \$6.89$$

The relationship may also be indicated as shown in figure II-5.

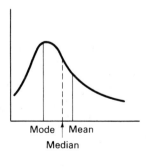 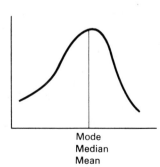 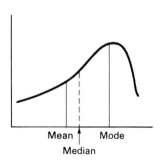

FIGURE II-5

EXERCISE II-4 MEAN, MEDIAN AND MODE FROM UNGROUPED DATA

Calculate the mean, the median, and the mode of each of the following groups of values.

(a)	(b)	(c)	(d)	(e)
48	9	23	11	7
16	36	18	32	14
27	48	15	8	9
32	16	45	10	23
19	11	37	32	6
12	41	15	27	8
32	26	29	43	11
43	41	10	11	29
38	39	15	34	33
22	43	12	37	42

EXERCISE II-5 MODE

Using the array and the frequency distribution developed in exercise II-4, calculate the mode (a) from the ungrouped data, and (b) from the grouped data.

Other types of graphical presentations

In discussing frequency distributions and measures of central tendency, it was necessary to include pictorial as well as verbal illustrations. Thus, we were introduced to graphing. A *graph* or *chart* is a method of presenting statistical data in picture form. It shows the relationship between two variables or two sets of values. The types of graphs most commonly used are line graphs, bar charts, and pie charts.

The following points should be considered in making graphs:

1. Select the type of graph which will present the most faithful picture of the data.
2. Title the graph clearly to aid interpretation. This usually includes information concerning the nature of the data, the geographical location of occurrences, and the time period covered.
3. Caption each scale designating the units of measurement.
   a. The caption on the X-axis (horizontal scale) should be centered below it. The independent variable or data which changes in determined increments, such as time, is usually scaled on the X-axis.
   b. The caption on the Y-axis (vertical scale) should be placed at the top of the scaled units. The dependent variable or data which is related to the increments of the independent variable is usually scaled on the Y-axis.
4. The zero point on the Y-axis should be shown at the bottom of the

scale and the highest value at the top of the scale. On the X-axis the lowest value should be on the left and the highest on the right.
5. Choose a scale adapted to the space used so that the results are in proportions which will not distort the data.

line graphs

In figure II-1, when the plotted frequencies for each class interval were connected, the result was a frequency polygon, referring to the area between the connecting line and the base line. This would also be a type of line graph. Since the points were connected with straight lines causing irregularities in the total line, this type of presentation is called a *broken-line graph*. When a smooth line is fitted to a series of points, as in figure II-4, the result is called a *curve graph*.

The most common use of line graphs is in presenting time series where the units of time are shown on the X-axis. The determination of the unit value for

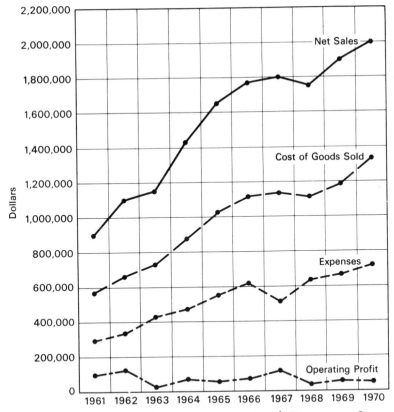

FIGURE II-6 elements of profit for Buffington's Department Store Inc., for the year 1961 through 1970

the Y-axis can be made by dividing the largest value by the number of spaces required for good proportion. If the highest value were $1,875 and 10 spaces were to be used, then the unit value of each space would be $187.50. This would be a bit awkward, so the unit value should be rounded off to $200. If it were rounded off to $180, then the highest value would extend above the top of the chart.

An example of a line graph is shown in figure II-6, which has been developed from the data in table II-7.

TABLE II-7   elements of profit for Buffington's Department Store Inc. for the years 1961 through 1970

	Net Sales	Cost of Goods Sold	Expenses	Operating Profit
1961	$ 950,000	$ 570,000	$304,000	$ 76,000
1962	1,100,000	665,500	363,000	71,500
1963	1,150,000	741,150	407,025	1,825
1964	1,435,000	882,525	487,900	64,575
1965	1,650,000	1,023,000	569,250	57,750
1966	1,775,000	1,109,375	603,500	62,125
1967	1,800,000	1,134,000	540,000	126,000
1968	1,750,000	1,111,250	612,500	26,250
1969	1,900,000	1,196,000	650,000	54,000
1970	2,000,000	1,280,000	670,000	50,000

EXERCISE II-6   BROKEN-LINE GRAPH

Prepare a broken-line graph for the following data:

Average Gross Sale for Year

	Furniture	Floor Covering	Household Appliances	Radios & TV
1961	$ 86.48	$44.90	$51.43	$107.49
1962	84.10	41.15	54.65	102.90
1963	79.17	37.80	59.75	95.15
1964	80.35	40.15	60.50	89.40
1965	85.42	48.75	58.14	100.50
1966	98.58	55.18	57.25	106.72
1967	114.73	60.27	52.60	114.90
1968	123.19	63.59	54.90	123.65
1969	136.95	69.73	55.30	132.56
1970	142.30	76.25	57.50	139.85

bar chart

In figure II-1, when rectangles were drawn for each class frequency to the height of the frequency, the result was a rectangular frequency polygon or histogram. A histogram is similar to a bar chart except that the former is intended to illustrate a frequency distribution, while bar charts contrast quantities which are represented by bars of varying lengths but of uniform width.

A *simple bar chart* is one in which solid bars are used for the factor being depicted. Thus, a comparison of expenses of different departments of a company might be shown by a simple bar chart. A *subdivided bar chart* is one in which the bars are subdivided in accordance with component parts of the basic factor. The expenses of different departments might be broken into components—such as selling, buying, occupancy, and administrative expenses—and each shown as a subdivision of the department expense bar.

An example of a subdivided bar chart is shown in figure II-7, which has been developed from the data in table II-8.

TABLE II-8   current assets as percents of total assets for the Crescent Department Stores as of January 31, 1971

	Cash	Receivables	Inventory	Other	Total
Buffington's	15.0%	25.4%	33.3%	1.3%	75.0%
Cohn's	18.8	27.0	31.5	2.2	79.5
Fox	21.4	16.2	28.0	1.0	66.6
King's	12.5	23.8	35.4	1.2	72.9
Spring	10.0	18.5	25.5	.5	54.5
United	14.6	22.5	30.5	1.0	68.6

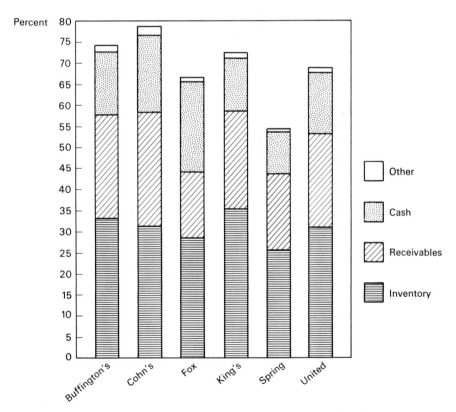

FIGURE II-7   Current assets as percents of total assets for the Crescent Department Stores as of January 31, 1971

EXERCISE II-7 BAR CHART

Prepare a subdivided vertical bar chart for the following data:

Branch Store Sales of the Silver Furniture Co. for the Year 1971

	Furniture	Floor Covering	Appliances	Radio & TV
Branch 1	$140,700	$ 70,000	$55,000	$ 75,000
Branch 2	75,000	30,000	40,000	55,000
Branch 3	175,500	55,000	83,000	70,500
Branch 4	115,000	50,000	54,000	60,000
Branch 5	165,000	80,000	75,500	82,600
Branch 6	222,500	130,000	95,000	100,000

pie charts

A *pie chart* is a circle divided into sections as pieces of a pie. The size of each section depicts its relationship to the whole. Pie charts are particularly useful in presenting distribution of finances, such as where each tax dollar goes or to show the relationship between the parts of a total quantity such as the chemical composition of a compound. They are also appropriate when quantities are compared on a percent basis, using the whole circle to represent 100%. In constructing a pie chart, since the circle contains $360°$, each percent occupies $3.6°$; consequently, instead of a ruler, a protractor is the essential instrument for constructing this type of chart.

The following points should be observed in making a pie chart:

1. Arrange the sectors clockwise from the top center of the circle in order of decreasing size.
2. Try to place all wording horizontally. If this is not possible, then have wording radiating toward the center so that the chart will always be turned clockwise for reading.
3. The comparison of sectors is enhanced if cross-hatching, coloring, or shading is used.

An example of a pie chart is shown in figure II-8, which has been developed from the data in table II-9.

TABLE II-9 Buffington's Department Store Inc. allocation of advertising budget for the year 1971

	Percent	Dollars	Degrees
Women's dresses	25%	$15,000	90.0
Men's wear	17	10,200	61.2
Housewares	15	9,000	54.0
Furniture	12	7,200	43.2
Women's suits & coats	10	6,000	36.0
Drugs & jewelry	8	4,800	28.8
Lingerie	5	3,000	18.0
Shoes	5	3,000	18.0
Notions	3	1,800	10.8
	100%	$60,000	360.0

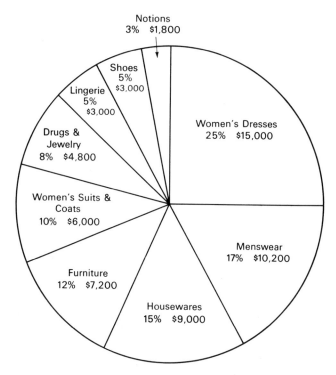

FIGURE II-8 Buffington's Department Store Inc. allocation of advertising budget for the year 1971

EXERCISE II-8 PIE CHART

Prepare a pie chart for the following data:

Expenses of Randolph Co. for the year 1971

Salaries	$17,000
Rent	3,000
Advertising	1,200
Utiliites	800
Supplies	400
Other	1,600

appendix III

number systems

Although the decimal (base-10) system (see appendix I) is common for much computation, it is by no means the only number system in use today. Some other commonly used number systems are the binary (base-2), octal (base-8), duodecimal (base-12), and hexidecimal (base-16) systems. Bases 2, 8, and 16 are used in computer mathematics, and base 12 applies to common measurements such as the dozen, the number of inches in a foot, and the 24 hours in the day.

In this appendix, we shall look briefly at some different number systems and the operations of addition, subtraction, multiplication, and division using them.

Concept of base

The *base* of a number system is the number of different digits which can occur in each position in the number system. For example, the decimal system, with its base of 10, has 10 different digits (0, 1, 2, ..., 9), any of which may be used in each position in a number. Stated another way, it takes b symbols to write a base-b number system, the last digit in the system always being one less than the base.

Number systems with bases above 10 must employ other symbols as digits. The letters of the alphabet are commonly used.

Counting in bases other than 10

Counting in bases other than 10 follows the same method as counting in base 10: simply group the objects to be counted. For example, to count in base 7, simply count in groups of 7:

This yields two groups of 7 and one 1, which is written 21_{seven} or 21_7 ("two-one base seven").

When working in bases other than 10, it is very important to indicate by means of the subscript which base is being used. (The subscript 10 need not be used when working in base 10.)

EXERCISE III-1 COUNTING IN DIFFERENT BASES

A. Count and write in base 6.

```
X X X X
X X X X
X X X X
X X X
```

B. Count and write in base 3.

```
X X X X X X
X X X X X X
X X X X X
```

C. Count and write in base 4.

```
X X
```

Positional notation

A number in any base is represented as follows:

$$... + a_4 b^4 + a_3 b^3 + a_2 b^2 + a_1 b^1 + a_0 b^0$$

where b represents the base, b^0 always equals 1 regardless of the numerical value of b, and a_4, a_3, etc. are the digits in the numeral.

For example, 243_{10} means

$$2 \times 10^2 + 4 \times 10 + 3 \times 1$$

or

$$2b^2 + 4b + 3$$

and 243_5 means

$$2 \times 5^2 + 4 \times 5 + 3 \times 1$$

and 243_7 means

$$2 \times 7^2 + 4 \times 7 + 3 \times 1$$

Conversion from one base to another

converting from a base other than 10 to base 10

To convert to base 10 from any other base,

1. write the number in positional notation, and
2. multiply and add the result.

It is often helpful to write the number to be converted in the following form, especially when it involves powers of b greater than 2:

...	b^4	b^3	b^2	b^1	b^0
	a_4	a_3	a_2	a_1	a_0

where b is the base and the a's are the digits in the numeral.

Convert 234_5 to base 10.

Example 1

b^2	b^1	b^0
25	5	1
2	3	4
a_2	a_1	a_0

$$\begin{aligned} 2 \times 25 &+ 3 \times 5 + 4 \times 1 \\ = 50 \quad &+ 15 \quad + 4 \\ = 69_{10} \end{aligned}$$

Convert 1101101_2 to base 10.

Example 2

b^6	b^5	b^4	b^3	b^2	b^1	b^0
64	32	16	8	4	2	1
1	1	0	1	1	0	1

$$\begin{aligned} &1(64) + 1(32) + 0(16) + 1(8) + 1(4) + 0(2) + 1(1) \\ = \ &64 \quad + 32 \quad + 0 \quad + 8 \quad + 4 \quad + 0 \quad + 1 \\ = \ &109_{10} \end{aligned}$$

Example 3

Convert 666_7 to base 10.

$$\begin{array}{c|c|c}49 & 7 & 1 \\ \hline 6 & 6 & 6\end{array}$$

$$\begin{aligned}6(49) &+ 6(7) + 6(1) \\ = 294 & + 42 + 6 \\ = 346_{10}\end{aligned}$$

EXERCISE III-2 CONVERTING TO BASE 10

Convert 311 in bases 4, 5, 6, 7, 8, and 9 to base 10.

converting from base 10 to any other base

To convert from base 10 to any other base,

1. divide the base-10 number by the highest power of base b possible;
2. divide the remainder from step 1 by the next highest power of b possible;
3. continue this procedure until the remainder is less than b.

Always be sure to use a zero to indicate place value.

Example 1

Convert 82 to base 5.

$$\begin{aligned}b^0 &= 1 \\ b^1 &= 5 \\ b^2 &= 25\end{aligned}$$

$$\begin{array}{r}3 \\ 25\overline{)82} \\ 75 \\ \hline 7\end{array} \quad \begin{array}{r}1 \\ 5\overline{)7} \\ 5 \\ \hline 2\end{array} \quad 2 < 5 \quad \therefore 82_{10} = 312_5$$

Example 2

Convert 18 to base 2.

$$\begin{aligned}b^0 &= 1 \\ b^1 &= 2 \\ b^2 &= 4 \\ b^3 &= 8 \\ b^4 &= 16\end{aligned}$$

$$\begin{array}{r}1 \\ 16\overline{)18} \\ 16 \\ \hline 2\end{array} \quad \begin{array}{r}1 \\ 2\overline{)2} \\ 2 \\ \hline 0\end{array} \quad \therefore 18_{10} = 10010_2$$

It was necessary to use zeros to indicate that there are no groups of 8 or 4, and no 1s in this number.

Example 3

Convert 64 to base 4.

$$\begin{aligned}b^0 &= 1 \\ b^1 &= 4 \\ b^2 &= 16 \\ b^3 &= 64\end{aligned}$$

$$\begin{array}{r}1 \\ 64\overline{)64} \\ 64 \\ \hline 0\end{array} \quad \therefore 64_{10} = 1000_4$$

Again, the zeros are necessary to indicate no groups of 16 or 4, and no 1s.

EXERCISE III-3 CONVERTING FROM BASE 10 TO OTHER BASES

A. Convert 265 to base 5.
B. Convert 4,846 to base 6.
C. Convert 1,583 to base 9.

Other conversions

It is possible to convert from base 2 directly to base 8 (since $2^3 = 8$), and to convert from base 3 directly to base 9 (since $3^2 = 9$).

Example 1

$$101_2 = 5_8$$

That is,

$$1(4) + 0(2) + 1 = 4 + 0 + 1 = 5_8$$

$$65_8 = 110101_2$$

Example 2

$$
\begin{aligned}
65_8 &= 6(8) + 5(1) \\
&= [(32) + (16) + (0)] + [(4) + (0) + (1)] \\
&= 2^5 + 2^4 + 0 + 2^2 + 0 + 1 \\
&= 110101_2
\end{aligned}
$$

$$88_9 = 2222_3$$

Example 3

$$
\begin{aligned}
88_9 &= 8(9) + 8(1) \\
&= [(54) + (18)] + [(6) + (1)] \\
&= [2(27) + 2(9)] + [2(3) + (2)] \\
&= 2(3^3) + 2(3^2) + 2(3) + 2 \\
&= 2222_3
\end{aligned}
$$

$$2112_3 = 75_9$$

Example 4

$$
\begin{aligned}
2(27) + 1(9) + 1(3) + 2 &= (54 + 9) + (3 + 2) \\
&= 63 + 5 \\
&= 7(9) + 5 = 75_9
\end{aligned}
$$

Operations in bases other than 10

The operations of addition, subtraction, multiplication, and division are carried out in bases other than 10 just as they are in base 10. The important thing to remember is in what base you are grouping.

(1) $11_5 + 23_5 = 34_5$

(2) $23_5 + 34_5 = 57_5$

In base 5, 7 means 1 group with a remainder of 2 ones. Write the 2 in the ones column and carry one group of five to the fives column.

Then $57_5 = 62_5$

But, in base 5, 6 means 1 group of five with a remainder of 1.

So, $62_5 = 112_5$

Hence, $23_5 + 34_5 = 112_5$

(3) $111_2 + 101_2 = 1100_2$

EXERCISE III-4 ADDING IN DIFFERENT BASES

Add the following.

1. 44_8	2. 432_5	3. 432_7	4. 432_9	5. 43_6	6. 43_8
36_8	341_5	341_7	341_9	25_6	25_8
	243_5	243_7	243_9	32_6	32_8
				41_6	41_8

Subtraction is simply the inverse of addition.

Examples

(1) $23_5 - 11_5 = 12_5$

(2) $43_5 - 24_5 = 14_5$

Borrow a group of 5 from the fives column to yield 8 ones and 3 fives i.e., $43_5 = 38_5$ and

$$38_5 - 24_5 = 14_5$$

(3) $100_2 - 11_2 = 1_2$

Think of this problem as $20_2 - 11_2$; then borrow and subtract

EXERCISE III-5 SUBTRACTING IN DIFFERENT BASES

Subtract the following.

1. 53_7	2. 1001_2	3. 13_6
-24_7	-101_2	-4_6

4. 432_8	5. 601_9	6. 30102_4
-154_8	-487_9	-12323_4

multiplication

The operation of multiplication is performed the same way in all bases. Again, remember what base you are working in.

Multiplication tables, such as tables III-1, III-2, and III-3, may be helpful when working in unfamiliar bases.

TABLE III-1
base 2
multiplication table

X	0	1
0	0	0
1	0	1

TABLE III-2
base 5
multiplication table

X	0	1	2	3	4
0	0	0	0	0	0
1	0	1	2	3	4
2	0	2	4	11	13
3	0	3	11	14	22
4	0	4	13	22	31

TABLE III-3
base 6
multiplication table

X	0	1	2	3	4	5
0	0	0	0	0	0	0
1	0	1	2	3	4	5
2	0	2	4	10	12	14
3	0	3	10	13	20	23
4	0	4	12	20	24	32
5	0	5	14	23	32	41

Examples

$$\begin{array}{r} 23_5 \\ \times 11_5 \\ \hline 23_5 \\ 23_5 \\ \hline 303_5 \end{array} \qquad \begin{array}{r} 11_2 \\ \times 11_2 \\ \hline 11_2 \\ 11_2 \\ \hline 1001_2 \end{array} \qquad \begin{array}{r} 42_6 \\ \times 3_6 \\ \hline 210_6 \end{array}$$

EXERCISE III-6 MULTIPLYING IN DIFFERENT BASES

A. Multiply the following.

1. 234_5 2. 1100_2 3. 234_5 4. 424_6 5. 245_7
   $\times 3_5$ $\times 1010_2$ $\times 23_5$ $\times 21_6$ $\times 36_7$

B. Make a multiplication table for base 8 and then solve

$$\begin{array}{r} 66_8 \\ \times 71_8 \end{array}$$

division

Division is the inverse of multiplication. Just as multiplication can be thought of as repeated addition, division can be thought of as repeated subtraction. This concept often helps when working in bases other than 10. Referring to the multiplication tables (tables III-1, III-2, and III-3) also helps.

Examples

Base 5	Base 6	Base 2

$$
\begin{array}{r}
2\ r1 \\
11\overline{)23} \\
22 \\
\hline
1
\end{array}
\qquad
\begin{array}{r}
13\ r2 \\
23\overline{)345} \\
23 \\
\hline
115 \\
113 \\
\hline
2
\end{array}
\qquad
\begin{array}{r}
101 \\
101\overline{)11001} \\
101 \\
\hline
101 \\
101 \\
\hline
\end{array}
$$

EXERCISE III-7 DIVIDING IN DIFFERENT BASES

Divide the following

1. $23_5\sqrt{4234_5}$ 2. $23_4\sqrt{3021_4}$ 3. $32_5\sqrt{3442_5}$

4. $23_4\sqrt{2211_4}$ 5. $42_7\sqrt{6456_7}$ 6. $74_8\sqrt{6747_8}$

Note: All calculations in bases other than 10 can be checked by converting the problem to a base–10 problem.

appendix IV

compound interest and annuity tables

By permission of:
Financial Publishing Co.
Boston, Mass.

RATE **½%**	P E R I O D S	AMOUNT OF 1 *How $1 left at compound interest will grow.*	AMOUNT OF 1 PER PERIOD *How $1 deposited periodically will grow.*	SINKING FUND *Periodic deposit that will grow to $1 at future date.*
	1	1.005 000 0000	1.000 000 0000	1.000 000 0000
	2	1.010 025 0000	2.005 000 0000	.498 753 1172
.005	3	1.015 075 1250	3.015 025 0000	.331 672 2084
	4	1.020 150 5006	4.030 100 1250	.248 132 7930
per period	5	1.025 251 2531	5.050 250 6256	.198 009 9750
	6	1.030 377 5094	6.075 501 8788	.164 595 4556
	7	1.035 529 3969	7.105 879 3881	.140 728 5355
	8	1.040 707 0439	8.141 408 7851	.122 828 8649
	9	1.045 910 5791	9.182 115 8290	.108 907 3606
	10	1.051 140 1320	10.228 026 4082	.097 770 5727
	11	1.056 395 8327	11.279 166 5402	.088 659 0331
	12	1.061 677 8119	12.335 562 3729	.081 066 4297
	13	1.066 986 2009	13.397 240 1848	.074 642 2387
	14	1.072 321 1319	14.464 226 3857	.069 136 0860
	15	1.077 682 7376	15.536 547 5176	.064 364 3640
	16	1.083 071 1513	16.614 230 2552	.060 189 3669
	17	1.088 486 5070	17.697 301 4065	.056 505 7902
	18	1.093 928 9396	18.785 787 9135	.053 231 7305
	19	1.099 398 5843	19.879 716 8531	.050 302 5273
ANNUALLY	20	1.104 895 5772	20.979 115 4373	.047 666 4520
If compounded *annually* nominal annual rate is	21	1.110 420 0551	22.084 011 0145	.045 281 6293
	22	1.115 972 1553	23.194 431 0696	.043 113 7973
	23	1.121 552 0161	24.310 403 2250	.041 134 6530
½%	24	1.127 159 7762	25.431 955 2411	.039 320 6103
	25	1.132 795 5751	26.559 115 0173	.037 651 8570
	26	1.138 459 5530	27.691 910 5924	.036 111 6289
	27	1.144 151 8507	28.830 370 1453	.034 685 6456
	28	1.149 872 6100	29.974 521 9961	.033 361 6663
	29	1.155 621 9730	31.124 394 6060	.032 129 1390
SEMIANNUALLY	30	1.161 400 0829	32.280 016 5791	.030 978 9184
If compounded *semiannually* nominal annual rate is	31	1.167 207 0833	33.441 416 6620	.029 903 0394
	32	1.173 043 1187	34.608 623 7453	.028 894 5324
	33	1.178 908 3343	35.781 666 8640	.027 947 2727
1%	34	1.184 802 8760	36.960 575 1983	.027 055 8560
	35	1.190 726 8904	38.145 378 0743	.026 215 4958
	36	1.196 680 5248	39.336 104 9647	.025 421 9375
	37	1.202 663 9274	40.532 785 4895	.024 671 3861
	38	1.208 677 2471	41.735 449 4170	.023 960 4464
	39	1.214 720 6333	42.944 126 6640	.023 286 0714
QUARTERLY	40	1.220 794 2365	44.158 847 2974	.022 645 5186
If compounded *quarterly* nominal annual rate is	41	1.226 898 2077	45.379 641 5338	.022 036 3133
	42	1.233 032 6987	46.606 539 7415	.021 456 2163
	43	1.239 197 8622	47.839 572 4402	.020 903 1969
2%	44	1.245 393 8515	49.078 770 3024	.020 375 4086
	45	1.251 620 8208	50.324 164 1539	.019 871 1696
	46	1.257 878 9249	51.575 784 9747	.019 388 9439
	47	1.264 168 3195	52.833 663 8996	.018 927 3264
	48	1.270 489 1611	54.097 832 2191	.018 485 0290
	49	1.276 841 6069	55.368 321 3802	.018 060 8690
	50	1.283 225 8149	56.645 162 9871	.017 653 7580
MONTHLY	51	1.289 641 9440	57.928 388 8020	.017 262 6931
If compounded *monthly* nominal annual rate is	52	1.296 090 1537	59.218 030 7460	.016 886 7486
	53	1.302 570 6045	60.514 120 8997	.016 525 0686
	54	1.309 083 4575	61.816 691 5042	.016 176 8606
6%	55	1.315 628 8748	63.125 774 9618	.015 841 3897
	56	1.322 207 0192	64.441 403 8366	.015 517 9735
$i = .005$	57	1.328 818 0543	65.763 610 8558	.015 205 9777
$j_{(2)} = .01$	58	1.335 462 1446	67.092 428 9100	.014 904 8114
$j_{(4)} = .02$	59	1.342 139 4553	68.427 891 0546	.014 613 9240
$j_{(12)} = .06$	60	1.348 850 1525	69.770 030 5099	.014 332 8015
	n	$s=(1+i)^n$	$s_{\overline{n}\|}=\dfrac{(1+i)^n-1}{i}$	$\dfrac{1}{s_{\overline{n}\|}}=\dfrac{i}{(1+i)^n-1}$

PRESENT WORTH OF 1 *What $1 due in the future is worth today.*	PRESENT WORTH OF 1 PER PERIOD *What $1 payable periodically is worth today.*	PARTIAL PAYMENT *Annuity worth $1 today.* *Periodic payment necessary to pay off a loan of $1.*	PERIODS	RATE $\frac{1}{2}\%$
.995 024 8756	.995 024 8756	1.005 000 0000	1	
.990 074 5031	1.985 099 3787	.503 753 1172	2	
.985 148 7593	2.970 248 1380	.336 672 2084	3	.005
.980 247 5217	3.950 495 6597	.253 132 7930	4	
.975 370 6684	4.925 866 3281	.203 009 9750	5	*per period*
.970 518 0780	5.896 384 4061	.169 595 4556	6	
.965 689 6298	6.862 074 0359	.145 728 5355	7	
.960 885 2038	7.822 959 2397	.127 828 8649	8	
.956 104 6804	8.779 063 9201	.113 907 3606	9	
.951 347 9407	9.730 411 8608	.102 770 5727	10	
.946 614 8664	10.677 026 7272	.093 659 0331	11	
.941 905 3397	11.618 932 0668	.086 066 4297	12	
.937 219 2434	12.556 151 3103	.079 642 2387	13	
.932 556 4611	13.488 707 7714	.074 136 0860	14	
.927 916 8768	14.416 624 6482	.069 364 3640	15	
.923 300 3749	15.339 925 0231	.065 189 3669	16	
.918 706 8407	16.258 631 8637	.061 505 7902	17	
.914 136 1599	17.172 768 0236	.058 231 7305	18	
.909 588 2188	18.082 356 2424	.055 302 5273	19	
.905 062 9043	18.987 419 1467	.052 666 4520	20	ANNUALLY If compounded *annually* nominal annual rate is
.900 560 1037	19.887 979 2504	.050 281 6293	21	
.896 079 7052	20.784 058 9556	.048 113 7973	22	
.891 621 5972	21.675 680 5529	.046 134 6530	23	
.887 185 6689	22.562 866 2218	.044 320 6103	24	
.882 771 8098	23.445 638 0316	.042 651 8570	25	$\frac{1}{2}\%$
.878 379 9103	24.324 017 9419	.041 111 6289	26	
.874 009 8610	25.198 027 8029	.039 685 6456	27	
.869 661 5532	26.067 689 3561	.038 361 6663	28	
.865 334 8788	26.933 024 2349	.037 129 1390	29	
.861 029 7302	27.794 053 9651	.035 978 9184	30	SEMIANNUALLY If compounded *semiannually* nominal annual rate is
.856 746 0002	28.650 799 9653	.034 903 0394	31	
.852 483 5823	29.503 283 5475	.033 894 5324	32	
.848 242 3704	30.351 525 9179	.032 947 2727	33	
.844 022 2591	31.195 548 1771	.032 055 8560	34	
.839 823 1434	32.035 371 3205	.031 215 4958	35	1%
.835 644 9188	32.871 016 2393	.030 421 9375	36	
.831 487 4814	33.702 503 7207	.029 671 3861	37	
.827 350 7278	34.529 854 4484	.028 960 4464	38	
.823 234 5550	35.353 089 0034	.028 286 0714	39	
.819 138 8607	36.172 227 8641	.027 645 5186	40	QUARTERLY If compounded *quarterly* nominal annual rate is
.815 063 5430	36.987 291 4070	.027 036 3133	41	
.811 008 5005	37.798 299 9075	.026 456 2163	42	
.806 973 6323	38.605 273 5398	.025 903 1969	43	
.802 958 8381	39.408 232 3779	.025 375 4086	44	
.798 964 0180	40.207 196 3959	.024 871 1696	45	2%
.794 989 0727	41.002 185 4686	.024 388 9439	46	
.791 033 9031	41.793 219 3717	.023 927 3264	47	
.787 098 4111	42.580 317 7828	.023 485 0290	48	
.783 182 4986	43.363 500 2814	.023 060 8690	49	
.779 286 0683	44.142 786 3497	.022 653 7580	50	MONTHLY If compounded *monthly* nominal annual rate is
.775 409 0231	44.918 195 3728	.022 262 6931	51	
.771 551 2668	45.689 746 6396	.021 886 7486	52	
.767 712 7033	46.457 459 3429	.021 525 0686	53	
.763 893 2371	47.221 352 5800	.021 176 8606	54	
.760 092 7732	47.981 445 3532	.020 841 3897	55	$.6\%$
.756 311 2171	48.737 756 5704	.020 517 9735	56	
.752 548 4748	49.490 305 0452	.020 205 9777	57	
.748 804 4525	50.239 109 4977	.019 904 8114	58	$i\ \ =.005$
.745 079 0572	50.984 188 5549	.019 613 9240	59	$j_{(2)}=.01$
.741 372 1962	51.725 560 7511	.019 332 8015	60	$j_{(4)}=.02$ $j_{(12)}=.06$
$v^n = \dfrac{1}{(1+i)^n}$	$a_{\overline{n}|} = \dfrac{1-v^n}{i}$	$\dfrac{1}{a_{\overline{n}|}} = \dfrac{i}{1-v^n}$	n	

RATE	P E R I O D S	AMOUNT OF 1 *How $1 left at compound interest will grow.*	AMOUNT OF 1 PER PERIOD *How $1 deposited periodically will grow.*	SINKING FUND *Periodic deposit that will grow to $1 at future date.*
1%	1	1.010 000 0000	1.000 000 0000	1.000 000 0000
	2	1.020 100 0000	2.010 000 0000	.497 512 4378
.01	3	1.030 301 0000	3.030 100 0000	.330 022 1115
	4	1.040 604 0100	4.060 401 0000	.246 281 0939
per period	5	1.051 010 0501	5.101 005 0100	.196 039 7996
	6	1.061 520 1506	6.152 015 0601	.162 548 3667
	7	1.072 135 3521	7.213 535 2107	.138 628 2829
	8	1.082 856 7056	8.285 670 5628	.120 690 2920
	9	1.093 685 2727	9.368 527 2684	.106 740 3628
	10	1.104 622 1254	10.462 212 5411	.095 582 0766
	11	1.115 668 3467	11.566 834 6665	.086 454 0757
	12	1.126 825 0301	12.682 503 0132	.078 848 7887
	13	1.138 093 2804	13.809 328 0433	.072 414 8197
	14	1.149 474 2132	14.947 421 3238	.066 901 1717
	15	1.160 968 9554	16.096 895 5370	.062 123 7802
	16	1.172 578 6449	17.257 864 4924	.057 944 5968
	17	1.184 304 4314	18.430 443 1373	.054 258 0551
	18	1.196 147 4757	19.614 747 5687	.050 982 0479
	19	1.208 108 9504	20.810 895 0444	.048 051 7536
	20	1.220 190 0399	22.019 003 9948	.045 415 3149
ANNUALLY If compounded *annually* nominal annual rate is **1%**	21	1.232 391 9403	23.239 194 0347	.043 030 7522
	22	1.244 715 8598	24.471 585 9751	.040 863 7185
	23	1.257 163 0183	25.716 301 8348	.038 885 8401
	24	1.269 734 6485	26.973 464 8532	.037 073 4722
	25	1.282 431 9950	28.243 199 5017	.035 406 7534
	26	1.295 256 3150	29.525 631 4967	.033 868 8776
	27	1.308 208 8781	30.820 887 8117	.032 445 5287
	28	1.321 290 9669	32.129 096 6898	.031 124 4356
	29	1.334 503 8766	33.450 387 6567	.029 895 0198
	30	1.347 848 9153	34.784 891 5333	.028 748 1132
SEMIANNUALLY If compounded *semiannually* nominal annual rate is **2%**	31	1.361 327 4045	36.132 740 4486	.027 675 7309
	32	1.374 940 6785	37.494 067 8531	.026 670 8857
	33	1.388 690 0853	38.869 008 5316	.025 727 4318
	34	1.402 576 9862	40.257 698 6170	.024 839 9694
	35	1.416 602 7560	41.660 275 6031	.024 003 6818
	36	1.430 768 7836	43.076 878 3592	.023 214 3098
	37	1.445 076 4714	44.507 647 1427	.022 468 0491
	38	1.459 527 2361	45.952 723 6142	.021 761 4958
	39	1.474 122 5085	47.412 250 8503	.021 091 5951
	40	1.488 863 7336	48.886 373 3588	.020 455 5980
QUARTERLY If compounded *quarterly* nominal annual rate is **4%**	41	1.503 752 3709	50.375 237 0924	.019 851 0232
	42	1.518 789 8946	51.878 989 4633	.019 275 6260
	43	1.533 977 7936	53.397 779 3580	.018 727 3705
	44	1.549 317 5715	54.931 757 1515	.018 204 4058
	45	1.564 810 7472	56.481 074 7231	.017 705 0455
	46	1.580 458 8547	58.045 885 4703	.017 227 7499
	47	1.596 263 4432	59.626 344 3250	.016 771 1103
	48	1.612 226 0777	61.222 607 7682	.016 333 8354
	49	1.628 348 3385	62.834 833 8459	.015 914 7393
	50	1.644 631 8218	64.463 182 1844	.015 512 7309
MONTHLY If compounded *monthly* nominal annual rate is **12%**	51	1.661 078 1401	66.107 814 0062	.015 126 8048
	52	1.677 688 9215	67.768 892 1463	.014 756 0329
	53	1.694 465 8107	69.446 581 0678	.014 399 5570
	54	1.711 410 4688	71.141 046 8784	.014 056 5826
	55	1.728 524 5735	72.852 457 3472	.013 726 3730
$i = .01$ $j_{(2)} = .02$ $j_{(4)} = .04$ $j_{(12)} = .12$	56	1.745 809 8192	74.580 981 9207	.013 408 2440
	57	1.763 267 9174	76.326 791 7399	.013 101 5595
	58	1.780 900 5966	78.090 059 6573	.012 805 7272
	59	1.798 709 6025	79.870 960 2539	.012 520 1950
	60	1.816 696 6986	81.669 669 8564	.012 244 4477
	n	$s=(1+i)^n$	$s_{\overline{n}|}=\dfrac{(1+i)^n-1}{i}$	$\dfrac{1}{s_{\overline{n}|}}=\dfrac{i}{(1+i)^n-1}$

PRESENT WORTH OF 1 — *What $1 due in the future is worth today.*	PRESENT WORTH OF 1 PER PERIOD — *What $1 payable periodically is worth today.*	PARTIAL PAYMENT — *Annuity worth $1 today. Periodic payment necessary to pay off a loan of $1.*	PERIODS	RATE
.990 099 0099	.990 099 0099	1.010 000 0000	1	**1%**
.980 296 0494	1.970 395 0593	.507 512 4378	2	
.970 590 1479	2.940 985 2072	.340 022 1115	3	.01
.960 980 3445	3.901 965 5517	.256 281 0939	4	*per period*
.951 465 6876	4.853 431 2393	.206 039 7996	5	
.942 045 2353	5.795 476 4746	.172 548 3667	6	
.932 718 0547	6.728 194 5293	.148 628 2829	7	
.923 483 2225	7.651 677 7518	.130 690 2920	8	
.914 339 8242	8.566 017 5760	.116 740 3628	9	
.905 286 9547	9.471 304 5307	.105 582 0766	10	
.896 323 7175	10.367 628 2482	.096 454 0757	11	
.887 449 2253	11.255 077 4735	.088 848 7887	12	
.878 662 5993	12.133 740 0728	.082 414 8197	13	
.869 962 9696	13.003 703 0423	.076 901 1717	14	
.861 349 4748	13.865 052 5172	.072 123 7802	15	
.852 821 2622	14.717 873 7794	.067 944 5968	16	
.844 377 4873	15.562 251 2667	.064 258 0551	17	
.836 017 3142	16.398 268 5809	.060 982 0479	18	
.827 739 9150	17.226 008 4959	.058 051 7536	19	
.819 544 4703	18.045 552 9663	.055 415 3149	20	ANNUALLY *If compounded annually nominal annual rate is*
.811 430 1687	18.856 983 1349	.053 030 7522	21	
.803 396 2066	19.660 379 3415	.050 863 7185	22	
.795 441 7887	20.455 821 1302	.048 885 8401	23	
.787 566 1274	21.243 387 2576	.047 073 4722	24	
.779 768 4430	22.023 155 7006	.045 406 7534	25	**1%**
.772 047 9634	22.795 203 6640	.043 868 8776	26	
.764 403 9241	23.559 607 5881	.042 445 5287	27	
.756 835 5684	24.316 443 1565	.041 124 4356	28	
.749 342 1470	25.065 785 3035	.039 895 0198	29	
.741 922 9178	25.807 708 2213	.038 748 1132	30	SEMIANNUALLY *If compounded semiannually nominal annual rate is*
.734 577 1463	26.542 285 3676	.037 675 7309	31	
.727 304 1053	27.269 589 4729	.036 670 8857	32	
.720 103 0745	27.989 692 5474	.035 727 4378	33	
.712 973 3411	28.702 665 8885	.034 839 9694	34	
.705 914 1991	29.408 580 0876	.034 003 6818	35	**2%**
.698 924 9496	30.107 505 0373	.033 214 3098	36	
.692 004 9006	30.799 509 9379	.032 468 0491	37	
.685 153 3670	31.484 663 3048	.031 761 4958	38	
.678 369 6702	32.163 032 9751	.031 091 5951	39	
.671 653 1389	32.834 686 1140	.030 455 5980	40	QUARTERLY *If compounded quarterly nominal annual rate is*
.665 003 1078	33.499 689 2217	.029 851 0232	41	
.658 418 9186	34.158 108 1403	.029 275 6260	42	
.651 899 9194	34.810 008 0597	.028 727 3705	43	
.645 445 4648	35.455 453 5245	.028 204 4058	44	
.639 054 9156	36.094 508 4401	.027 705 0455	45	**4%**
.632 727 6392	36.727 236 0793	.027 227 7499	46	
.626 463 0091	37.353 699 0884	.026 771 1103	47	
.620 260 4051	37.973 959 4935	.026 333 8354	48	
.614 119 2129	38.588 078 7064	.025 914 7393	49	
.608 038 8247	39.196 117 5311	.025 512 7309	50	MONTHLY *If compounded monthly nominal annual rate is*
.602 018 6383	39.798 136 1694	.025 126 8048	51	
.596 058 0577	40.394 194 2271	.024 756 0329	52	
.590 156 4928	40.984 350 7199	.024 399 5570	53	
.584 313 3592	41.568 664 0791	.024 056 5826	54	
.578 528 0784	42.147 192 1576	.023 726 3730	55	**12%**
.572 800 0776	42.719 992 2352	.023 408 2440	56	
.567 128 7898	43.287 121 0250	.023 101 5595	57	
.561 513 6532	43.848 634 6782	.022 805 7272	58	$i\ =.01$
.555 954 1121	44.404 588 7903	.022 520 1950	59	$j_{(2)}=.02$
.550 449 6159	44.955 038 4062	.022 244 4477	60	$j_{(4)}=.04$ $j_{(12)}=.12$
$v^n=\dfrac{1}{(1+i)^n}$	$a_{\overline{n}\rceil}=\dfrac{1-v^n}{i}$	$\dfrac{1}{a_{\overline{n}\rceil}}=\dfrac{i}{1-v^n}$	n	

RATE **1½%** .015 *per period* ANNUALLY If compounded *annually* nominal annual rate is **1½%** SEMIANNUALLY If compounded *semiannually* nominal annual rate is **3%** QUARTERLY If compounded *quarterly* nominal annual rate is **6%** MONTHLY If compounded *monthly* nominal annual rate is **18%** $j = .015$ $j_{(2)} = .03$ $j_{(4)} = .06$ $j_{(12)} = .18$	P E R I O D S	AMOUNT OF 1 *How $1 left at compound interest will grow.*	AMOUNT OF 1 PER PERIOD *How $1 deposited periodically will grow.*	SINKING FUND *Periodic deposit that will grow to $1 at future date.*
	1	1.015 000 0000	1.000 000 0000	1.000 000 0000
	2	1.030 225 0000	2.015 000 0000	.496 277 9156
	3	1.045 678 3750	3.045 225 0000	.328 382 9602
	4	1.061 363 5506	4.090 903 3750	.244 444 7860
	5	1.077 284 0039	5.152 266 9256	.194 089 3231
	6	1.093 443 2639	6.229 550 9295	.160 525 2146
	7	1.109 844 9129	7.322 994 1935	.136 556 1645
	8	1.126 492 5866	8.432 839 1064	.118 584 0246
	9	1.143 389 9754	9.559 331 6929	.104 609 8234
	10	1.160 540 8250	10.702 721 6683	.093 434 1779
	11	1.177 948 9374	11.863 262 4934	.084 293 8442
	12	1.195 618 1715	13.041 211 4308	.076 679 9929
	13	1.213 552 4440	14.236 829 6022	.070 240 3574
	14	1.231 755 7307	15.450 382 0463	.064 723 3186
	15	1.250 232 0667	16.682 137 7770	.059 944 3557
	16	1.268 985 5477	17.932 369 8436	.055 765 0778
	17	1.288 020 3309	19.201 355 3913	.052 079 6569
	18	1.307 340 6358	20.489 375 7221	.048 805 7818
	19	1.326 950 7454	21.796 716 3580	.045 878 4701
	20	1.346 855 0066	23.123 667 1033	.043 245 7359
	21	1.367 057 8316	24.470 522 1099	.040 865 4950
	22	1.387 563 6991	25.837 579 9415	.038 703 3152
	23	1.408 377 1546	27.225 143 6407	.036 730 7520
	24	1.429 502 8119	28.633 520 7953	.034 924 1020
	25	1.450 945 3541	30.063 023 6072	.033 263 4539
	26	1.472 709 5344	31.513 968 9613	.031 731 9599
	27	1.494 800 1774	32.986 678 4957	.030 315 2680
	28	1.517 222 1801	34.481 478 6732	.029 001 0765
	29	1.539 980 5128	35.998 700 8533	.027 778 7802
	30	1.563 080 2205	37.538 681 3661	.026 639 1883
	31	1.586 526 4238	39.101 761 5865	.025 574 2954
	32	1.610 324 3202	40.688 288 0103	.024 577 0970
	33	1.634 479 1850	42.298 612 3305	.023 641 4375
	34	1.658 996 3727	43.933 091 5155	.022 761 8855
	35	1.683 881 3183	45.592 087 8882	.021 933 6303
	36	1.709 139 5381	47.275 969 2065	.021 152 3955
	37	1.734 776 6312	48.985 108 7446	.020 414 3673
	38	1.760 798 2806	50.719 885 3758	.019 716 1329
	39	1.787 210 2548	52.480 683 6564	.019 054 6298
	40	1.814 018 4087	54.267 893 9113	.018 427 1017
	41	1.841 228 6848	56.081 912 3199	.017 831 0610
	42	1.868 847 1151	57.923 141 0047	.017 264 2571
	43	1.896 879 8218	59.791 988 1198	.016 724 6488
	44	1.925 333 0191	61.688 867 9416	.016 210 3801
	45	1.954 213 0144	63.614 200 9607	.015 719 7604
	46	1.983 526 2096	65.568 413 9751	.015 251 2458
	47	2.013 279 1028	67.551 940 1848	.014 803 4238
	48	2.043 478 2893	69.565 219 2875	.014 374 9996
	49	2.074 130 4637	71.608 697 5768	.013 964 7841
	50	2.105 242 4206	73.682 828 0405	.013 571 6832
	51	2.136 821 0569	75.788 070 4611	.013 194 6887
	52	2.168 873 3728	77.924 891 5180	.012 832 8700
	53	2.201 406 4734	80.093 764 8908	.012 485 3664
	54	2.234 427 5705	82.295 171 3642	.012 151 3812
	55	2.267 943 9840	84.529 598 9346	.011 830 1756
	56	2.301 963 1438	86.797 542 9186	.011 521 0635
	57	2.336 492 5909	89.099 506 0624	.011 223 4068
	58	2.371 539 9798	91.435 998 6534	.010 936 6116
	59	2.407 113 0795	93.807 538 6332	.010 660 1241
	60	2.443 219 7757	96.214 651 7126	.010 393 4274
	n	$s = (1+i)^n$	$s_{\overline{n}\rvert} = \dfrac{(1+i)^n - 1}{i}$	$\dfrac{1}{s_{\overline{n}\rvert}} = \dfrac{i}{(1+i)^n - 1}$

PRESENT WORTH OF 1 _What $1 due in the future is worth today._	PRESENT WORTH OF 1 PER PERIOD _What $1 payable periodically is worth today._	PARTIAL PAYMENT _Annuity worth $1 today._ _Periodic payment necessary to pay off a loan of $1._	P E R I O D S	RATE $1\frac{1}{2}\%$
.985 221 6749	.985 221 6749	1.015 000 0000	1	
.970 661 7486	1.955 883 4235	.511 277 9156	2	
.956 316 9937	2.912 200 4173	.343 382 9602	3	.015
.942 184 2303	3.854 384 6476	.259 444 7860	4	_per period_
.928 260 3254	4.782 644 9730	.209 089 3231	5	
.914 542 1925	5.697 187 1655	.175 525 2146	6	
.901 026 7907	6.598 213 9561	.151 556 1645	7	
.887 711 1238	7.485 925 0799	.133 584 0246	8	
.874 592 2402	8.360 517 3201	.119 609 8234	9	
.861 667 2317	9.222 184 5519	.108 434 1779	10	
.848 933 2332	10.071 117 7851	.099 293 8442	11	
.836 387 4219	10.907 505 2070	.091 679 9929	12	
.824 027 0166	11.731 532 2236	.085 240 3574	13	
.811 849 2775	12.543 381 5011	.079 723 3186	14	
.799 851 5049	13.343 233 0060	.074 944 3557	15	
.788 031 0393	14.131 264 0453	.070 765 0778	16	
.776 385 2604	14.907 649 3057	.067 079 6569	17	
.764 911 5866	15.672 560 8924	.063 805 7818	18	
.753 607 4745	16.426 168 3669	.060 878 4701	19	
.742 470 4182	17.168 638 7851	.058 245 7359	20	
.731 497 9490	17.900 136 7341	.055 865 4950	21	ANNUALLY _If compounded annually nominal annual rate is_
.720 687 6345	18.620 824 3685	.053 703 3152	22	
.710 037 0783	19.330 861 4468	.051 730 7520	23	
.699 543 9195	20.030 405 3663	.049 924 1020	24	
.689 205 8320	20.719 611 1984	.048 263 4539	25	$1\frac{1}{2}\%$
.679 020 5242	21.398 631 7225	.046 731 9599	26	
.668 985 7381	22.067 617 4606	.045 315 2680	27	
.659 099 2494	22.726 716 7100	.044 001 0765	28	
.649 358 8664	23.376 075 5763	.042 778 7802	29	
.639 762 4299	24.015 838 0062	.041 639 1883	30	
.630 307 8127	24.646 145 8189	.040 574 2954	31	SEMIANNUALLY _If compounded semiannually nominal annual rate is_
.620 992 9189	25.267 138 7379	.039 577 0970	32	
.611 815 6837	25.878 954 4216	.038 641 4375	33	
.602 774 0726	26.481 728 4941	.037 761 8855	34	
.593 866 0814	27.075 594 5755	.036 933 6303	35	3%
.585 089 7353	27.660 684 3109	.036 152 3955	36	
.576 443 0890	28.237 127 3999	.035 414 3673	37	
.567 924 2256	28.805 051 6255	.034 716 1329	38	
.559 531 2568	29.364 582 8822	.034 054 6298	39	
.551 262 3219	29.915 845 2042	.033 427 1017	40	
.543 115 5881	30.458 960 7923	.032 831 0610	41	QUARTERLY _If compounded quarterly nominal annual rate is_
.535 089 2494	30.994 050 0417	.032 264 2571	42	
.527 181 5265	31.521 231 5681	.031 724 6488	43	
.519 390 6665	32.040 622 2346	.031 210 3804	44	
.511 714 9423	32.552 337 1770	.030 719 7604	45	6%
.504 152 6526	33.056 489 8295	.030 251 2458	46	
.496 702 1207	33.553 191 9503	.029 803 4238	47	
.489 361 6953	34.042 553 6456	.029 374 9996	48	
.482 129 7491	34.524 683 3947	.028 964 7841	49	
.475 004 6789	34.999 688 0736	.028 571 6832	50	
.467 984 9053	35.467 672 9789	.028 194 6887	51	MONTHLY _If compounded monthly nominal annual rate is_
.461 068 8722	35.928 741 8511	.027 832 8700	52	
.454 255 0465	36.382 996 8977	.027 485 3664	53	
.447 541 9178	36.830 538 8154	.027 151 3812	54	
.440 927 9978	37.271 466 8132	.026 830 1756	55	18%
.434 411 8205	37.705 878 6337	.026 521 0635	56	
.427 991 9414	38.133 870 5751	.026 223 4068	57	
.421 666 9373	38.555 537 5124	.025 936 6116	58	$i = .015$
.415 435 4062	38.970 972 9186	.025 660 1241	59	$j_{(2)} = .03$ $j_{(4)} = .06$
.409 295 9667	39.380 268 8853	.025 393 4274	60	$j_{(12)} = .18$
$v^n = \dfrac{1}{(1+i)^n}$	$a_{\overline{n}|} = \dfrac{1-v^n}{i}$	$\dfrac{1}{a_{\overline{n}|}} = \dfrac{i}{1-v^n}$	n	

RATE **2%** .02 *per period*	P E R I O D S	AMOUNT OF 1 *How $1 left at compound interest will grow.*	AMOUNT OF 1 PER PERIOD *How $1 deposited periodically will grow.*	SINKING FUND *Periodic deposit that will grow to $1 at future date.*
	1	1.020 000 0000	1.000 000 0000	1.000 000 0000
	2	1.040 400 0000	2.020 000 0000	.495 049 5050
	3	1.061 208 0000	3.060 400 0000	.326 754 6726
	4	1.082 432 1600	4.121 608 0000	.242 623 7527
	5	1.104 080 8032	5.204 040 1600	.192 158 3941
	6	1.126 162 4193	6.308 120 9632	.158 525 8123
	7	1.148 685 6676	7.434 283 3825	.134 511 9561
	8	1.171 659 3810	8.582 969 0501	.116 509 7991
	9	1.195 092 5686	9.754 628 4311	.102 515 4374
	10	1.218 994 4200	10.949 720 9997	.091 326 5279
	11	1.243 374 3084	12.168 715 4197	.082 177 9428
	12	1.268 241 7946	13.412 089 7281	.074 559 5966
	13	1.293 606 6305	14.680 331 5227	.068 118 3527
	14	1.319 478 7631	15.973 938 1531	.062 601 9702
	15	1.345 868 3383	17.293 416 9162	.057 825 4723
	16	1.372 785 7051	18.639 285 2545	.053 650 1259
	17	1.400 241 4192	20.012 070 9596	.049 969 8408
	18	1.428 246 2476	21.412 312 3788	.046 702 1022
	19	1.456 811 1725	22.840 558 6264	.043 781 7663
	20	1.485 947 3960	24.297 369 7989	.041 156 7181
ANNUALLY If compounded *annually* nominal annual rate is **2%**	21	1.515 666 3439	25.783 317 1949	.038 784 7689
	22	1.545 979 6708	27.298 983 5388	.036 631 4005
	23	1.576 899 2642	28.844 963 2096	.034 668 0976
	24	1.608 437 2495	30.421 862 4738	.032 871 0973
	25	1.640 605 9945	32.030 299 7232	.031 220 4384
	26	1.673 418 1144	33.670 905 7177	.029 699 2308
	27	1.706 886 4766	35.344 323 8321	.028 293 0862
	28	1.741 024 2062	37.051 210 3087	.026 989 6716
	29	1.775 844 6903	38.792 234 5149	.025 778 3552
	30	1.811 361 5841	40.568 079 2052	.024 649 9223
SEMIANNUALLY If compounded *semiannually* nominal annual rate is **4%**	31	1.847 588 8158	42.379 440 7893	.023 596 3472
	32	1.884 540 5921	44.227 029 6051	.022 610 6073
	33	1.922 231 4039	46.111 570 1972	.021 686 5311
	34	1.960 676 0320	48.033 801 6011	.020 818 6728
	35	1.999 889 5527	49.994 477 6331	.020 002 2092
	36	2.039 887 3437	51.994 367 1858	.019 232 8526
	37	2.080 685 0906	54.034 254 5295	.018 506 7789
	38	2.122 298 7924	56.114 939 6201	.017 820 5663
	39	2.164 744 7682	58.237 238 4125	.017 171 1439
	40	2.208 039 6636	60.401 983 1807	.016 555 7478
QUARTERLY If compounded *quarterly* nominal annual rate is **8%**	41	2.252 200 4569	62.610 022 8444	.015 971 8836
	42	2.297 244 4660	64.862 223 3012	.015 417 2945
	43	2.343 189 3553	67.159 467 7673	.014 889 9334
	44	2.390 053 1425	69.502 657 1226	.014 387 9391
	45	2.437 854 2053	71.892 710 2651	.013 909 6161
	46	2.486 611 2894	74.330 564 4704	.013 453 4159
	47	2.536 343 5152	76.817 175 7598	.013 017 9220
	48	2.587 070 3855	79.353 519 2750	.012 601 8355
	49	2.638 811 7932	81.940 589 6605	.012 203 9639
	50	2.691 588 0291	84.579 401 4537	.011 823 2097
MONTHLY If compounded *monthly* nominal annual rate is **24%**	51	2.745 419 7897	87.270 989 4828	.011 458 5615
	52	2.800 328 1854	90.016 409 2724	.011 109 0856
	53	2.856 334 7492	92.816 737 4579	.010 773 9189
	54	2.913 461 4441	95.673 072 2070	.010 452 2618
	55	2.971 730 6730	98.586 533 6512	.010 143 3732
$i = .02$ $j_{(2)} = .04$ $j_{(4)} = .08$ $j_{(12)} = .24$	56	3.031 165 2865	101.558 264 3242	.009 846 5645
	57	3.091 788 5922	104.589 429 6107	.009 561 1957
	58	3.153 624 3641	107.681 218 2029	.009 286 6706
	59	3.216 696 8513	110.834 842 5669	.009 022 4335
	60	3.281 030 7884	114.051 539 4183	.008 767 9658
	n	$s=(1+i)^n$	$s_{\overline{n}\rvert}=\dfrac{(1+i)^n-1}{i}$	$\dfrac{1}{s_{\overline{n}\rvert}}=\dfrac{i}{(1+i)^n-1}$

PRESENT WORTH OF 1	PRESENT WORTH OF 1 PER PERIOD	PARTIAL PAYMENT	P E R I O D S	RATE
What $1 due in the future is worth today.	*What $1 payable periodically is worth today.*	*Annuity worth $1 today.* *Periodic payment necessary to pay off a loan of $1.*		**2%**
.980 392 1569	.980 392 1569	1.020 000 0000	1	
.961 168 7812	1.941 560 9381	.515 049 5050	2	
.942 322 3345	2.883 883 2726	.346 754 6726	3	.02
.923 845 4260	3.807 728 6987	.262 623 7527	4	*per period*
.905 730 8098	4.713 459 5085	.212 158 3941	5	
.887 971 3822	5.601 430 8907	.178 525 8123	6	
.870 560 1786	6.471 991 0693	.154 511 9561	7	
.853 490 3712	7.325 481 4405	.136 509 7991	8	
.836 755 2659	8.162 236 7064	.122 515 4374	9	
.820 348 2999	8.982 585 0062	.111 326 5279	10	
.804 263 0391	9.786 848 0453	.102 177 9428	11	
.788 493 1756	10.575 341 2209	.094 559 5966	12	
.773 032 5251	11.348 373 7460	.088 118 3527	13	
.757 875 0246	12.106 248 7706	.082 601 9702	14	
.743 014 7300	12.849 263 5006	.077 825 4723	15	
.728 445 8137	13.577 709 3143	.073 650 1259	16	
.714 162 5625	14.291 871 8768	.069 969 8408	17	
.700 159 3750	14.992 031 2517	.066 702 1022	18	
.686 430 7598	15.678 462 0115	.063 781 7663	19	
.672 971 3331	16.351 433 3446	.061 156 7181	20	ANNUALLY
.659 775 8168	17.011 209 1614	.058 784 7689	21	If compounded
.646 839 0361	17.658 048 1974	.056 631 4005	22	*annually*
.634 155 9177	18.292 204 1151	.054 668 0976	23	nominal annual rate is
.621 721 4879	18.913 925 6031	.052 871 0973	24	
.609 530 8705	19.523 456 4736	.051 220 4384	25	**2%**
.597 579 2848	20.121 035 7584	.049 699 2308	26	
.585 862 0440	20.706 897 8024	.048 293 0862	27	
.574 374 5529	21.281 272 3553	.046 989 6716	28	
.563 112 3068	21.844 384 6620	.045 778 3552	29	
.552 070 8890	22.396 455 5510	.044 649 9223	30	SEMIANNUALLY
.541 245 9696	22.937 701 5206	.043 596 3472	31	If compounded
.530 633 3035	23.468 334 8241	.042 610 6073	32	*semiannually*
.520 228 7289	23.988 563 5530	.041 686 5311	33	nominal annual rate is
.510 028 1656	24.498 591 7187	.040 818 6728	34	
.500 027 6134	24.998 619 3320	.040 002 2092	35	**4%**
.490 223 1504	25.488 842 4824	.039 232 8526	36	
.480 610 9317	25.969 453 4141	.038 506 7789	37	
.471 187 1880	26.440 640 6021	.037 820 5663	38	
.461 948 2235	26.902 588 8256	.037 171 1439	39	
.452 890 4152	27.355 479 2407	.036 555 7478	40	QUARTERLY
.444 010 2110	27.799 489 4517	.035 971 8836	41	If compounded
.435 304 1284	28.234 793 5801	.035 417 2945	42	*quarterly*
.426 768 7533	28.661 562 3334	.034 889 9334	43	nominal annual rate is
.418 400 7386	29.079 963 0720	.034 387 9391	44	
.410 196 8025	29.490 159 8745	.033 909 6161	45	**8%**
.402 153 7280	29.892 313 6025	.033 453 4159	46	
.394 268 3607	30.286 581 9632	.033 017 9220	47	
.386 537 6086	30.673 119 5718	.032 601 8355	48	
.378 958 4398	31.052 078 0115	.032 203 9639	49	
.371 527 8821	31.423 605 8937	.031 823 2097	50	MONTHLY
.364 243 0217	31.787 848 9153	.031 458 5615	51	If compounded
.357 101 0017	32.144 949 9170	.031 109 0856	52	*monthly*
.350 099 0212	32.495 048 9382	.030 773 9189	53	nominal annual rate is
.343 234 3345	32.838 283 2728	.030 452 2618	54	
.336 504 2496	33.174 787 5223	.030 143 3732	55	**24%**
.329 906 1270	33.504 693 6494	.029 846 5645	56	
.323 437 3794	33.828 131 0288	.029 561 1957	57	
.317 095 4700	34.145 226 4988	.029 286 6706	58	$i = .02$
.310 877 9118	34.456 104 4106	.029 022 4335	59	$j_{(2)} = .04$
.304 782 2665	34.760 886 6770	.028 767 9658	60	$j_{(4)} = .08$ $j_{(12)} = .24$
$v^n = \dfrac{1}{(1+i)^n}$	$a_{\overline{n}|} = \dfrac{1-v^n}{i}$	$\dfrac{1}{a_{\overline{n}|}} = \dfrac{i}{1-v^n}$	n	

RATE **2½%** .025 *per period* ANNUALLY If compounded *annually* nominal annual rate is **2½%** SEMIANNUALLY If compounded *semiannually* nominal annual rate is **5%** QUARTERLY If compounded *quarterly* nominal annual rate is **10%** MONTHLY If compounded *monthly* nominal annual rate is **30%** $i = .025$ $j_{(2)} = .05$ $j_{(4)} = .1$ $j_{(12)} = .3$	P E R I O D S	AMOUNT OF 1 *How $1 left at compound interest will grow.*	AMOUNT OF 1 PER PERIOD *How $1 deposited periodically will grow.*	SINKING FUND *Periodic deposit that will grow to $1 at future date.*
	1	1.025 000 0000	1.000 000 0000	1.000 000 0000
	2	1.050 625 0000	2.025 000 0000	.493 827 1605
	3	1.076 890 6250	3.075 625 0000	.325 137 1672
	4	1.103 812 8906	4.152 515 6250	.240 817 8777
	5	1.131 408 2129	5.256 328 5156	.190 246 8609
	6	1.159 693 4182	6.387 736 7285	.156 549 9711
	7	1.188 685 7537	7.547 430 1467	.132 495 4296
	8	1.218 402 8975	8.736 115 9004	.114 467 3458
	9	1.248 862 9699	9.954 518 7979	.100 456 8900
	10	1.280 084 5442	11.203 381 7679	.089 258 7632
	11	1.312 086 6578	12.483 466 3121	.080 105 9558
	12	1.344 888 8242	13.795 552 9699	.072 487 1270
	13	1.378 511 0449	15.140 441 7941	.066 048 2708
	14	1.412 973 8210	16.518 952 8390	.060 536 5249
	15	1.448 298 1665	17.931 926 6599	.055 766 4561
	16	1.484 505 6207	19.380 224 8264	.051 598 9886
	17	1.521 618 2612	20.864 730 4471	.047 927 7699
	18	1.559 658 7177	22.386 348 7083	.044 670 0805
	19	1.598 650 1856	23.946 007 4260	.041 760 6151
	20	1.638 616 4403	25.544 657 6116	.039 147 1287
	21	1.679 581 8513	27.183 274 0519	.036 787 3273
	22	1.721 571 3976	28.862 855 9032	.034 646 6061
	23	1.764 610 6825	30.584 427 3008	.032 696 3781
	24	1.808 725 9496	32.349 037 9833	.030 912 8204
	25	1.853 944 0983	34.157 763 9329	.029 275 9210
	26	1.900 292 7008	36.011 708 0312	.027 768 7467
	27	1.947 800 0183	37.912 000 7320	.026 376 8722
	28	1.996 495 0188	39.859 800 7503	.025 087 9327
	29	2.046 407 3942	41.856 295 7690	.023 891 2685
	30	2.097 567 5791	43.902 703 1633	.022 777 6407
	31	2.150 006 7686	46.000 270 7424	.021 739 0025
	32	2.203 756 9378	48.150 277 5109	.020 768 3123
	33	2.258 850 8612	50.354 034 4487	.019 859 3819
	34	2.315 322 1327	52.612 885 3099	.019 006 7508
	35	2.373 205 1861	54.928 207 4426	.018 205 5823
	36	2.432 535 3157	57.301 412 6287	.017 451 5767
	37	2.493 348 6986	59.733 947 9444	.016 740 8992
	38	2.555 682 4161	62.227 296 6430	.016 070 1180
	39	2.619 574 4765	64.782 979 0591	.015 436 1534
	40	2.685 063 8384	67.402 553 5356	.014 836 2332
	41	2.752 190 4343	70.087 617 3740	.014 267 8555
	42	2.820 995 1952	72.839 807 8083	.013 728 7567
	43	2.891 520 0751	75.660 803 0035	.013 216 8833
	44	2.963 808 0770	78.552 323 0786	.012 730 3683
	45	3.037 903 2789	81.516 131 1556	.012 267 5106
	46	3.113 850 8609	84.554 034 4345	.011 826 7568
	47	3.191 697 1324	87.667 885 2954	.011 406 6855
	48	3.271 489 5607	90.859 582 4277	.011 005 9938
	49	3.353 276 7997	94.131 071 9884	.010 623 4847
	50	3.437 108 7197	97.484 348 7881	.010 258 0569
	51	3.523 036 4377	100.921 457 5078	.009 908 6956
	52	3.611 112 3486	104.444 493 9455	.009 574 4635
	53	3.701 390 1574	108.055 606 2942	.009 254 4944
	54	3.793 924 9113	111.756 996 4515	.008 947 9856
	55	3.888 773 0341	115.550 921 3628	.008 654 1932
	56	3.985 992 3599	119.439 694 3969	.008 372 4260
	57	4.085 642 1689	123.425 686 7568	.008 102 0412
	58	4.187 783 2231	127.511 328 9257	.007 842 4404
	59	4.292 477 8037	131.699 112 1489	.007 593 0656
	60	4.399 789 7488	135.991 589 9526	.007 353 3959
	n	$s=(1+i)^n$	$s_{\overline{n}|}=\dfrac{(1+i)^n-1}{i}$	$\dfrac{1}{s_{\overline{n}|}}=\dfrac{i}{(1+i)^n-1}$

PRESENT WORTH OF 1 *What $1 due in the future is worth today.*	PRESENT WORTH OF 1 PER PERIOD *What $1 payable periodically is worth today.*	PARTIAL PAYMENT *Annuity worth $1 today.* *Periodic payment necessary to pay off a loan of $1.*	P E R I O D S	RATE $2\frac{1}{2}\%$
.975 609 7561	.975 609 7561	1.025 000 0000	1	
.951 814 3962	1.927 424 1523	.518 827 1605	2	
.928 599 4109	2.856 023 5632	.350 137 1672	3	.025
.905 950 6448	3.761 974 2080	.265 817 8777	4	*per period*
.883 854 2876	4.645 828 4956	.215 246 8609	5	
.862 296 8660	5.508 125 3616	.181 549 9711	6	
.841 265 2351	6.349 390 5967	.157 495 4296	7	
.820 746 5708	7.170 137 1675	.139 467 3458	8	
.800 728 3618	7.970 865 5292	.125 456 8900	9	
.781 198 4017	8.752 063 9310	..114 258 7632	10	
.762 144 7822	9.514 208 7131	.105 105 9558	11	
.743 555 8850	10.257 764 5982	.097 487 1270	12	
.725 420 3757	10.983 184 9738	.091 048 2708	13	
.707 727 1958	11.690 912 1696	.085 536 5249	14	
.690 465 5568	12.381 377 7264	.080 766 4561	15	
.673 624 9335	13.055 002 6599	.076 598 9886	16	
.657 195 0571	13.712 197 7170	.072 927 7699	17	
.641 165 9093	14.353 363 6264	.069 670 0805	18	
.625 527 7164	14.978 891 3428	.066 760 6151	19	
.610 270 9429	15.589 162 2856	.064 147 1287	20	ANNUALLY *If compounded annually* nominal annual rate is
.595 386 2857	16.184 548 5714	.061 787 3273	21	
.580 864 6690	16.765 413 2404	.059 646 6061	22	
.566 697 2380	17.332 110 4784	.057 696 3781	23	
.552 875 3542	17.884 985 8326	.055 912 8204	24	
.539 390 5894	18.424 376 4220	.054 275 9210	25	$2\frac{1}{2}\%$
.526 234 7214	18.950 611 1434	.052 768 7467	26	
.513 399 7282	19.464 010 8717	.051 376 8722	27	
.500 877 7836	19.964 888 6553	.050 087 9327	28	
.488 661 2523	20.453 549 9076	.048 891 2685	29	
.476 742 6852	20.930 292 5928	.047 777 6407	30	
.465 114 8148	21.395 407 4076	.046 739 0025	31	SEMIANNUALLY *If compounded semiannually* nominal annual rate is
.453 770 5510	21.849 177 9586	.045 768 3123	32	
.442 702 9766	22.291 880 9352	.044 859 3819	33	
.431 905 3430	22.723 786 2783	.044 006 7508	34	
.421 371 0664	23.145 157 3447	.043 205 5823	35	5%
.411 093 7233	23.556 251 0680	.042 451 5767	36	
.401 067 0471	23.957 318 1151	.041 740 8992	37	
.391 284 9240	24.348 603 0391	.041 070 1180	38	
.381 741 3893	24.730 344 4284	.040 436 1534	39	
.372 430 6237	25.102 775 0521	.039 836 2332	40	QUARTERLY *If compounded quarterly* nominal annual rate is
.363 346 9499	25.466 122 0020	.039 267 8555	41	
.354 484 8292	25.820 606 8313	.038 728 7567	42	
.345 838 8578	26.166 445 6890	.038 216 8833	43	
.337 403 7637	26.503 849 4527	.037 730 3683	44	
.329 174 4036	26.833 023 8563	.037 267 5106	45	10%
.321 145 7596	27.154 169 6159	.036 826 7568	46	
.313 312 9362	27.467 482 5521	.036 406 6855	47	
.305 671 1573	27.773 153 7094	.036 005 9938	48	
.298 215 7632	28.071 369 4726	.035 623 4847	49	
.290 942 2080	28.362 311 6805	.035 258 0569	50	MONTHLY *If compounded monthly* nominal annual rate is
.283 846 0566	28.646 157 7371	.034 908 6956	51	
.276 922 9820	28.923 080 7191	.034 574 4635	52	
.270 168 7629	29.193 249 4821	.034 254 4944	53	
.263 579 2809	29.456 828 7630	.033 947 9856	54	
.257 150 5180	29.713 979 2810	.033 654 1932	55	30%
.250 878 5541	29.964 857 8351	.033 372 4260	56	
.244 759 5650	30.209 617 4001	.033 102 0412	57	
.238 789 8195	30.448 407 2196	.032 842 4404	58	$i = .025$
.232 965 6776	30.681 372 8972	.032 593 0656	59	$j_{(2)} = .05$
.227 283 5879	30.908 656 4851	.032 353 3959	60	$j_{(4)} = .1$ $j_{(12)} = .3$
$v^n=\dfrac{1}{(1+i)^n}$	$a_{\overline{n}|}=\dfrac{1-v^n}{i}$	$\dfrac{1}{a_{\overline{n}|}}=\dfrac{i}{1-v^n}$	n	

RATE **3%**	P E R I O D S	AMOUNT OF 1 *How $1 left at compound interest will grow.*	AMOUNT OF 1 PER PERIOD *How $1 deposited periodically will grow.*	SINKING FUND *Periodic deposit that will grow to $1 at future date.*
.03 *per period*	1	1.030 000 0000	1.000 000 0000	1.000 000 0000
	2	1.060 900 0000	2.030 000 0000	.492 610 8374
	3	1.092 727 0000	3.090 900 0000	.323 530 3633
	4	1.125 508 8100	4.183 627 0000	.239 027 0452
	5	1.159 274 0743	5.309 135 8100	.188 354 5714
	6	1.194 052 2965	6.468 409 8843	.154 597 5005
	7	1.229 873 8654	7.662 462 1808	.130 506 3538
	8	1.266 770 0814	8.892 336 0463	.112 456 3888
	9	1.304 773 1838	10.159 106 1276	.098 433 8570
	10	1.343 916 3793	11.463 879 3115	.087 230 5066
	11	1.384 233 8707	12.807 795 6908	.078 077 4478
	12	1.425 760 8868	14.192 029 5615	.070 462 0855
	13	1.468 533 7135	15.617 790 4484	.064 029 5440
	14	1.512 589 7249	17.086 324 1618	.058 526 3390
	15	1.557 967 4166	18.598 913 8867	.053 766 5805
	16	1.604 706 4391	20.156 881 3033	.049 610 8493
	17	1.652 847 6323	21.761 587 7424	.045 952 5294
	18	1.702 433 0612	23.414 435 3747	.042 708 6959
	19	1.753 506 0531	25.116 868 4359	.039 813 8806
	20	1.806 111 2347	26.870 374 4890	.037 215 7076
ANNUALLY If compounded *annually* nominal annual rate is **3%**	21	1.860 294 5717	28.676 485 7236	.034 871 7765
	22	1.916 103 4089	30.536 780 2954	.032 747 3948
	23	1.973 586 5111	32.452 883 7042	.030 813 9027
	24	2.032 794 1065	34.426 470 2153	.029 047 4159
	25	2.093 777 9297	36.459 264 3218	.027 427 8710
	26	2.156 591 2675	38.553 042 2515	.025 938 2903
	27	2.221 289 0056	40.709 633 5190	.024 564 2103
	28	2.287 927 6757	42.930 922 5246	.023 293 2334
	29	2.356 565 5060	45.218 850 2003	.022 114 6711
	30	2.427 262 4712	47.575 415 7063	.021 019 2593
SEMIANNUALLY If compounded *semiannually* nominal annual rate is **6%**	31	2.500 080 3453	50.002 678 1775	.019 998 9288
	32	2.575 082 7557	52.502 758 5228	.019 046 6183
	33	2.652 335 2384	55.077 841 2785	.018 156 1219
	34	2.731 905 2955	57.730 176 5169	.017 321 9633
	35	2.813 862 4544	60.462 081 8124	.016 539 2916
	36	2.898 278 3280	63.275 944 2668	.015 803 7942
	37	2.985 226 6778	66.174 222 5948	.015 111 6244
	38	3.074 783 4782	69.159 449 2726	.014 459 3401
	39	3.167 026 9825	72.234 232 7508	.013 843 8516
	40	3.262 037 7920	75.401 259 7333	.013 262 3779
QUARTERLY If compounded *quarterly* nominal annual rate is **12%**	41	3.359 898 9258	78.663 297 5253	.012 712 4089
	42	3.460 695 8935	82.023 196 4511	.012 191 6731
	43	3.564 516 7703	85.483 892 3446	.011 698 1103
	44	3.671 452 2734	89.048 409 1149	.011 229 8469
	45	3.781 595 8417	92.719 861 3884	.010 785 1757
	46	3.895 043 7169	96.501 457 2300	.010 362 5378
	47	4.011 895 0284	100.396 500 9469	.009 960 5065
	48	4.132 251 8793	104.408 395 9753	.009 577 7738
	49	4.256 219 4356	108.540 647 8546	.009 213 1383
	50	4.383 906 0187	112.796 867 2902	.008 865 4944
MONTHLY If compounded *monthly* nominal annual rate is **36%**	51	4.515 423 1993	117.180 773 3089	.008 533 8232
	52	4.650 885 8952	121.696 196 5082	.008 217 1837
	53	4.790 412 4721	126.347 082 4035	.007 914 7059
	54	4.934 124 8463	131.137 494 8756	.007 625 5841
	55	5.082 148 5917	136.071 619 7218	.007 349 0710
$i = .03$ $j_{(2)} = .06$ $j_{(4)} = .12$ $j_{(12)} = .36$	56	5.234 613 0494	141.153 768 3135	.007 084 4726
	57	5.391 651 4409	146.388 381 3629	.006 831 1432
	58	5.553 400 9841	151.780 032 8038	.006 588 4819
	59	5.720 003 0136	157.333 433 7879	.006 355 9281
	60	5.891 603 1040	163.053 436 8015	.006 132 9587
	n	$s=(1+i)^n$	$s_{\overline{n}\rceil}=\dfrac{(1+i)^n-1}{i}$	$\dfrac{1}{s_{\overline{n}\rceil}}=\dfrac{i}{(1+i)^n-1}$

PRESENT WORTH OF 1 *What $1 due in the future is worth today.*	PRESENT WORTH OF 1 PER PERIOD *What $1 payable periodically is worth today.*	PARTIAL PAYMENT *Annuity worth $1 today.* *Periodic payment necessary to pay off a loan of $1.*	P E R I O D S	RATE **3%**
.970 873 7864	.970 873 7864	1.030 000 0000	1	
.942 595 9091	1.913 469 6955	.522 610 8374	2	
.915 141 6594	2.828 611 3549	.353 530 3633	3	.03
.888 487 0479	3.717 098 4028	.269 027 0452	4	*per period*
.862 608 7844	4.579 707 1872	.218 354 5714	5	
.837 484 2567	5.417 191 4439	.184 597 5005	6	
.813 091 5113	6.230 282 9552	.160 506 3538	7	
.789 409 2343	7.019 692 1895	.142 456 3888	8	
.766 416 7323	7.786 108 9219	.128 433 8570	9	
.744 093 9149	8.530 202 8368	.117 230 5066	10	
.722 421 2766	9.252 624 1134	.108 077 4478	11	
.701 379 8802	9.954 003 9936	.100 462 0855	12	
.680 951 3400	10.634 955 3336	.094 029 5440	13	
.661 117 8058	11.296 073 1394	.088 526 3390	14	
.641 861 9474	11.937 935 0868	.083 766 5805	15	
.623 166 9392	12.561 102 0260	.079 610 8493	16	
.605 016 4458	13.166 118 4718	.075 952 5294	17	
.587 394 6076	13.753 513 0795	.072 708 6959	18	
.570 286 0268	14.323 799 1063	.069 813 8806	19	
.553 675 7542	14.877 474 8605	.067 215 7076	20	ANNUALLY If compounded *annually* nominal annual rate is
.537 549 2759	15.415 024 1364	.064 871 7765	21	
.521 892 5009	15.936 916 6372	.062 747 3948	22	
.506 691 7484	16.443 608 3857	.060 813 9027	23	
.491 933 7363	16.935 542 1220	.059 047 4159	24	
.477 605 5693	17.413 147 6913	.057 427 8710	25	**3%**
.463 694 7274	17.876 842 4587	.055 938 2903	26	
.450 189 0558	18.327 031 4745	.054 564 2103	27	
.437 076 7532	18.764 108 2277	.053 293 2334	28	
.424 346 3623	19.188 454 5900	.052 114 6711	29	
.411 986 7595	19.600 441 3495	.051 019 2593	30	SEMIANNUALLY If compounded *semiannually* nominal annual rate is.
.399 987 1452	20.000 428 4946	.049 998 9288	31	
.388 337 0341	20.388 765 5288	.049 046 6182	32	
.377 026 2467	20.765 791 7755	.048 156 1219	33	
.366 044 8997	21.131 836 6752	.047 321 9633	34	
.355 383 3978	21.487 220 0731	.046 539 2916	35	**6%**
.345 032 4251	21.832 252 4981	.045 803 7942	36	
.334 982 9369	22.167 235 4351	.045 111 6244	37	
.325 226 1524	22.492 461 5874	.044 459 5874	38	
.315 753 5460	22.808 215 1334	.043 843 8516	39	
.306 556 8408	23.114 771 9742	.043 262 3779	40	QUARTERLY If compounded *quarterly* nominal annual rate is
.297 628 0008	23.412 399 9750	.042 712 4089	41	
.288 959 2240	23.701 359 1990	.042 191 6731	42	
.280 542 9360	23.981 902 1349	.041 698 1103	43	
.272 371 7825	24.254 273 9174	.041 229 8469	44	
.264 438 6238	24.518 712 5412	.040 785 1757	45	**12%**
.256 736 5279	24.775 449 0691	.040 362 5378	46	
.249 258 7650	25.024 707 8341	.039 960 5065	47	
.241 998 8009	25.266 706 6350	.039 577 7738	48	
.234 950 2922	25.501 656 9272	.039 213 1383	49	
.228 107 0798	25.729 764 0070	.038 865 4944	50	MONTHLY If compounded *monthly* nominal annual rate is
.221 463 1843	25.951 227 1913	.038 533 8232	51	
.215 012 8003	26.166 239 9915	.038 217 1837	52	
.208 750 2915	26.374 990 2830	.037 914 7059	53	
.202 670 1859	26.577 660 4690	.037 625 5841	54	
.196 767 1708	26.774 427 6398	.037 349 0710	55	**36%**
.191 036 0882	26.965 463 7279	.037 084 4726	56	
.185 471 9303	27.150 935 6582	.036 831 1432	57	
.180 069 8352	27.331 005 4934	.036 588 4819	58	$i = .03$
.174 825 0827	27.505 830 5761	.036 355 9281	59	$j_{(2)} = .06$
.169 733 0900	27.675 563 6661	.036 132 9587	60	$j_{(4)} = .12$ $j_{(12)} = .36$
$v^n = \dfrac{1}{(1+i)^n}$	$a_{\overline{n}\rvert} = \dfrac{1-v^n}{i}$	$\dfrac{1}{a_{\overline{n}\rvert}} = \dfrac{i}{1-v^n}$	n	

RATE $3\frac{1}{2}\%$ .035 *per period*	P E R I O D S	AMOUNT OF 1 *How $1 left at compound interest will grow.*	AMOUNT OF 1 PER PERIOD *How $1 deposited periodically will grow.*	SINKING FUND *Periodic deposit that will grow to $1 at future date.*
	1	1.035 000 0000	1.000 000 0000	1.000 000 0000
	2	1.071 225 0000	2.035 000 0000	.491 400 4914
	3	1.108 717 8750	3.106 225 0000	.321 934 1806
	4	1.147 523 0006	4.214 942 8750	.237 251 1395
	5	1.187 686 3056	5.362 465 8756	.186 481 3732
	6	1.229 255 3263	6.550 152 1813	.152 668 2087
	7	1.272 279 2628	7.779 407 5076	.128 544 4938
	8	1.316 809 0370	9.051 686 7704	.110 476 6465
	9	1.362 897 3533	10.368 495 8073	.096 446 0051
	10	1.410 598 7606	11.731 393 1606	.085 241 3679
	11	1.459 969 7172	13.141 991 9212	.076 091 9658
	12	1.511 068 6573	14.601 961 6385	.068 483 9493
	13	1.563 956 0604	16.113 030 2958	.062 061 5726
	14	1.618 694 5225	17.676 986 3562	.056 570 7287
	15	1.675 348 8308	19.295 680 8786	.051 825 0694
	16	1.733 986 0398	20.971 029 7094	.047 684 8306
	17	1.794 675 5512	22.705 015 7492	.044 043 1317
	18	1.857 489 1955	24.499 691 3004	.040 816 8408
	19	1.922 501 3174	26.357 180 4960	.037 940 3252
ANNUALLY If compounded *annually* nominal annual rate is	20	1.989 788 8635	28.279 681 8133	.035 361 0768
	21	2.059 431 4737	30.269 470 6768	.033 036 5870
	22	2.131 511 5753	32.328 902 1505	.030 932 0742
	23	2.206 114 4804	34.460 413 7257	.029 018 8042
$3\frac{1}{2}\%$	24	2.283 328 4872	36.666 528 2061	.027 272 8303
	25	2.363 244 9843	38.949 856 6933	.025 674 0354
	26	2.445 958 5587	41.313 101 6776	.024 205 3963
	27	2.531 567 1083	43.759 060 2363	.022 852 4103
	28	2.620 171 9571	46.290 627 3446	.021 602 6452
	29	2.711 877 9756	48.910 799 3017	.020 445 3825
SEMIANNUALLY If compounded *semiannually* nominal annual rate is	30	2.806 793 7047	51.622 677 2772	.019 371 3316
	31	2.905 031 4844	54.429 470 9819	.018 372 3998
	32	3.006 707 5863	57.334 502 4663	.017 441 5048
	33	3.111 942 3518	60.341 210 0526	.016 572 4221
7%	34	3.220 860 3342	63.453 152 4044	.015 759 6583
	35	3.333 590 4459	66.674 012 7386	.014 998 3473
	36	3.450 266 1115	70.007 603 1845	.014 284 1628
	37	3.571 025 4254	73.457 869 2959	.013 613 2454
	38	3.696 011 3152	77.028 894 7213	.012 982 1414
	39	3.825 371 7113	80.724 906 0365	.012 387 7506
QUARTERLY If compounded *quarterly* nominal annual rate is	40	3.959 259 7212	84.550 277 7478	.011 827 2823
	41	4.097 833 8114	88.509 537 4690	.011 298 2174
	42	4.241 257 9948	92.607 371 2804	.010 798 2765
	43	4.389 702 0246	96.848 629 2752	.010 325 3914
14%	44	4.543 341 5955	101.238 331 2998	.009 877 6816
	45	4.702 358 5513	105.781 672 8953	.009 453 4334
	46	4.866 941 1006	110.484 031 4467	.009 051 0817
	47	5.037 284 0392	115.350 972 5473	.008 669 1944
	48	5.213 588 9805	120.388 256 5864	.008 306 4580
	49	5.396 064 5948	125.601 845 5670	.007 961 6665
MONTHLY If compounded *monthly* nominal annual rate is	50	5.584 926 8557	130.997 910 1618	.007 633 7096
	51	5.780 399 2956	136.582 837 0175	.007 321 5641
	52	5.982 713 2710	142.363 236 3131	.007 024 2854
	53	6.192 108 2354	148.345 949 5840	.006 740 9997
42%	54	6.408 832 0237	154.538 057 8195	.006 470 8979
	55	6.633 141 1445	160.946 889 8432	.006 213 2297
	56	6.865 301 0846	167.580 030 9877	.005 967 2981
	57	7.105 586 6225	174.445 332 0722	.005 732 4549
$i\ =.035$ $j_{(2)}=.07$ $j_{(4)}=.14$ $j_{(12)}=.42$	58	7.354 282 1543	181.550 918 6948	.005 508 0966
	59	7.611 682 0297	188.905 200 8491	.005 293 6605
	60	7.878 090 9008	196.516 882 8788	.005 088 6213
	n	$s=(1+i)^n$	$s_{\overline{n}\|}=\dfrac{(1+i)^n-1}{i}$	$\dfrac{1}{s_{\overline{n}\|}}=\dfrac{i}{(1+i)^n-1}$

PRESENT WORTH OF 1 *What $1 due in the future is worth today.*	PRESENT WORTH OF 1 PER PERIOD *What $1 payable periodically is worth today.*	PARTIAL PAYMENT *Annuity worth $1 today.* *Periodic payment necessary to pay off a loan of $1.*	P E R I O D S	RATE $3\frac{1}{2}\%$
.966 183 5749	.966 183 5749	1.035 000 0000	1	
.933 510 7004	1.899 694 2752	.526 400 4914	2	
.901 942 7057	2.801 636 9809	.356 934 1806	3	.035
.871 442 2277	3.673 079 2086	.272 251 1395	4	*per period*
.841 973 1669	4.515 052 3755	.221 481 3732	5	
.813 500 6443	5.328 553 0198	.187 668 2087	6	
.785 990 9607	6.114 543 9805	.163 544 4938	7	
.759 411 5562	6.873 955 5367	.145 476 6465	8	
.733 730 9722	7.607 686 5089	.131 446 0051	9	
.708 918 8137	8.316 605 3226	.120 241 3679	10	
.684 945 7137	9.001 551 0363	.111 091 9658	11	
.661 783 2983	9.663 334 3346	.103 483 9493	12	
.639 404 1529	10.302 738 4875	.097 061 5726	13	
.617 781 7903	10.920 520 2778	.091 570 7287	14	
.596 890 6186	11.517 410 8964	.086 825 0694	15	
.576 705 9117	12.094 116 8081	.082 684 8306	16	
.557 203 7794	12.651 320 5876	.079 043 1317	17	
.538 361 1396	13.189 681 7271	.075 816 8408	18	
.520 155 6904	13.709 837 4175	.072 940 3252	19	
.502 565 8844	14.212 403 3020	.070 361 0768	20	
.485 570 9028	14.697 974 2048	.068 036 5870	21	ANNUALLY
.469 150 6308	15.167 124 8355	.065 932 0742	22	If compounded *annually*
.453 285 6336	15.620 410 4691	.064 018 8042	23	nominal annual rate is
.437 957 1339	16.058 367 6030	.062 272 8303	24	
.423 146 9893	16.481 514 5923	.060 674 0354	25	$3\frac{1}{2}\%$
.408 837 6708	16.890 352 2631	.059 205 3963	26	
.395 012 2423	17.285 364 5054	.057 852 4103	27	
.381 654 3404	17.667 018 8458	.056 602 6452	28	
.368 748 1550	18.035 767 0008	.055 445 3825	29	
.356 278 4106	18.392 045 4114	.054 371 3316	30	SEMIANNUALLY
.344 230 3484	18.736 275 7598	.053 372 3998	31	If compounded *semiannually*
.332 589 7086	19.068 865 4684	.052 441 5048	32	nominal annual rate is
.321 342 7136	19.390 208 1820	.051 572 4221	33	
.310 476 0518	19.700 684 2338	.050 759 6583	34	
.299 976 8617	20.000 661 0955	.049 998 3473	35	7%
.289 832 7166	20.290 493 8121	.049 284 1628	36	
.280 031 6102	20.570 525 4223	.048 613 2454	37	
.270 561 9422	20.841 087 3645	.047 982 1414	38	
.261 412 5046	21.102 499 8691	.047 387 7506	39	
.252 572 4682	21.355 072 3373	.046 827 2823	40	QUARTERLY
.244 031 3702	21.599 103 7075	.046 298 2174	41	If compounded *quarterly*
.235 779 1017	21.834 882 8092	.045 798 2765	42	nominal annual rate is
.227 805 8953	22.062 688 7046	.045 325 3914	43	
.220 102 3143	22.282 791 0189	.044 877 6816	44	
.212 659 2409	22.495 450 2598	.044 453 4334	45	14%
.205 467 8656	22.700 918 1254	.044 051 0817	46	
.198 519 6769	22.899 437 8023	.043 669 1944	47	
.191 806 4511	23.091 244 2535	.043 306 4580	48	
.185 320 2426	23.276 564 4961	.042 961 6665	49	
.179 053 3745	23.455 617 8706	.042 633 7096	50	MONTHLY
.172 998 4295	23.628 616 3001	.042 321 5641	51	If compounded *monthly*
.167 148 2411	23.795 764 5412	.042 024 2854	52	nominal annual rate is
.161 495 8851	23.957 260 4263	.041 740 9997	53	
.156 034 6716	24.113 295 0978	.041 470 8979	54	
.150 758 1368	24.264 053 2346	.041 213 2297	55	42%
.145 660 0355	24.409 713 2702	.040 967 2981	56	
.140 734 3339	24.550 447 6040	.040 732 4549	57	$i\ \ =.035$
.135 975 2018	24.686 422 8058	.040 508 0966	58	$j_{(2)}\ =.07$
.131 377 0066	24.817 799 8124	.040 293 6605	59	$j_{(4)}\ =.14$
.126 934 3059	24.944 734 1182	.040 088 6213	60	$j_{(12)}=.42$
$v^n=\dfrac{1}{(1+i)^n}$	$a_{\overline{n}\|}=\dfrac{1-v^n}{i}$	$\dfrac{1}{a_{\overline{n}\|}}=\dfrac{i}{1-v^n}$	n	

	P E R I O D S	AMOUNT OF 1 *How $1 left at compound interest will grow.*	AMOUNT OF 1 PER PERIOD *How $1 deposited periodically will grow.*	SINKING FUND *Periodic deposit that will grow to $1 at future date.*
RATE **4%** .04 *per period*	1 2 3 4 5	1.040 000 0000 1.081 600 0000 1.124 864 0000 1.169 858 5600 1.216 652 9024	1.000 000 0000 2.040 000 0000 3.121 600 0000 4.246 464 0000 5.416 322 5600	1.000 000 0000 .490 196 0784 .320 348 5392 .235 490 0454 .184 627 1135
	6 7 8 9 10	1.265 319 0185 1.315 931 7792 1.368 569 0504 1.423 311 8124 1.480 244 2849	6.632 975 4624 7.898 294 4809 9.214 226 2601 10.582 795 3105 12.006 107 1230	.150 761 9025 .126 609 6120 .108 527 8320 .094 492 9927 .083 290 9443
	11 12 13 14 15	1.539 454 0563 1.601 032 2186 1.665 073 5073 1.731 676 4476 1.800 943 5055	13.486 351 4079 15.025 805 4642 16.626 837 6828 18.291 911 1901 20.023 587 6377	.074 149 0393 .066 552 1727 .060 143 7278 .054 668 9731 .049 941 1004
	16 17 18 19 20	1.872 981 2457 1.947 900 4956 2.025 816 5154 2.106 849 1760 2.191 123 1430	21.824 531 1432 23.697 512 3889 25.645 412 8845 27.671 229 3998 29.778 078 5758	.045 819 9992 .042 198 5221 .038 993 3281 .036 138 6184 .033 581 7503
ANNUALLY If compounded *annually* nominal annual rate is **4%**	21 22 23 24 25	2.278 768 0688 2.369 918 7915 2.464 715 5432 2.563 304 1649 2.665 836 3315	31.969 201 7189 34.247 969 7876 36.617 888 5791 39.082 604 1223 41.645 908 2872	.031 280 1054 .029 198 8111 .027 309 0568 .025 586 8313 .024 011 9628
	26 27 28 29 30	2.772 469 7847 2.883 368 5761 2.998 703 3192 3.118 651 4519 3.243 397 5100	44.311 744 6187 47.084 214 4034 49.967 582 9796 52.966 286 2987 56.084 937 7507	.022 567 3805 .021 238 5406 .020 012 9752 .018 879 9342 .017 830 0991
SEMIANNUALLY If compounded *semiannually* nominal annual rate is **8%**	31 32 33 34 35	3.373 133 4104 3.508 058 7468 3.648 381 0967 3.794 316 3406 3.946 088 9942	59.328 335 2607 62.701 468 6711 66.209 527 4180 69.857 908 5147 73.652 224 8553	.016 855 3524 .015 948 5897 .015 103 5665 .014 314 7715 .013 577 3224
	36 37 38 39 40	4.103 932 5540 4.268 089 8561 4.438 813 4504 4.616 365 9884 4.801 020 6279	77.598 313 8495 81.702 246 4035 85.970 336 2596 90.409 149 7100 95.025 515 6984	.012 886 8780 .012 239 5655 .011 631 9191 .011 060 8274 .010 523 4893
QUARTERLY If compounded *quarterly* nominal annual rate is **16%**	41 42 43 44 45	4.993 061 4531 5.192 783 9112 5.400 495 2676 5.616 515 0783 5.841 175 6815	99.826 536 3264 104.819 597 7794 110.012 381 6906 115.412 876 9582 121.029 392 0365	.010 017 3765 .009 540 2007 .009 089 8859 .008 664 5444 .008 262 4558
	46 47 48 49 50	6.074 822 7087 6.317 815 6171 6.570 528 2418 6.833 349 3714 7.106 683 3463	126.870 567 7180 132.945 390 4267 139.263 206 0438 145.833 734 2855 152.667 083 6570	.007 882 0488 .007 521 8855 .007 180 6476 .006 857 1240 .006 550 2004
MONTHLY If compounded *monthly* nominal annual rate is **48%**	51 52 53 54 55	7.390 950 6801 7.686 588 7073 7.994 052 2556 8.313 814 3459 8.646 366 9197	159.773 767 0032 167.164 717 6834 174.851 306 3907 182.845 358 6463 191.159 172 9922	.006 258 8497 .005 982 1236 .005 719 1451 .005 469 1025 .005 231 2426
i = .04 $j_{(2)}$ = .08 $j_{(4)}$ = .16 $j_{(12)}$ = .48	56 57 58 59 60	8.992 221 5965 9.351 910 4603 9.725 986 8787 10.115 026 3539 10.519 627 4081	199.805 539 9119 208.797 761 5083 218.149 671 9687 227.875 658 8474 237.990 685 2013	.005 004 8662 .004 789 3234 .004 584 0087 .004 388 3581 .004 201 8451
	n	$s=(1+i)^n$	$s_{\overline{n}|}=\dfrac{(1+i)^n-1}{i}$	$\dfrac{1}{s_{\overline{n}|}}=\dfrac{i}{(1+i)^n-1}$

PRESENT WORTH OF 1 *What $1 due in the future is worth today.*	PRESENT WORTH OF 1 PER PERIOD *What $1 payable periodically is worth today.*	PARTIAL PAYMENT *Annuity worth $1 today.* *Periodic payment necessary to pay off a loan of $1.*	P E R I O D S	RATE **4%**
.961 538 4615	.961 538 4615	1.040 000 0000	1	
.924 556 2130	1.886 094 6746	.530 196 0784	2	
.888 996 3587	2.775 091 0332	.360 348 5392	3	.04
.854 804 1910	3.629 895 2243	.275 490 0454	4	
.821 927 1068	4.451 822 3310	.224 627 1135	5	*per period*
.790 314 5257	5.242 136 8567	.190 761 9025	6	
.759 917 8132	6.002 054 6699	.166 609 6120	7	
.730 690 2050	6.732 744 8750	.148 527 8320	8	
.702 586 7356	7.435 331 6105	.134 492 9927	9	
.675 564 1688	8.110 895 7794	.123 290 9443	10	
.649 580 9316	8.760 476 7109	.114 149 0393	11	
.624 597 0496	9.385 073 7605	.106 552 1727	12	
.600 574 0861	9.985 647 8466	.100 143 7278	13	
.577 475 0828	10.563 122 9295	.094 668 9731	14	
.555 264 5027	11.118 387 4322	.089 941 1004	15	
.533 908 1757	11.652 295 6079	.085 819 9992	16	
.513 373 2459	12.165 668 8537	.082 198 5221	17	
.493 628 1210	12.659 296 9747	.078 993 3281	18	
.474 642 4240	13.133 939 3988	.076 138 6184	19	
.456 386 9462	13.590 326 3450	.073 581 7503	20	
.438 833 6021	14.029 159 9471	.071 280 1054	21	ANNUALLY
.421 955 3867	14.451 115 3337	.069 198 8111	22	If compounded *annually*
.405 726 3333	14.856 841 6671	.067 309 0568	23	nominal annual rate is
.390 121 4743	15.246 963 1414	.065 586 8313	24	
.375 116 8023	15.622 079 9437	.064 011 9628	25	**4%**
.360 689 2329	15.982 769 1766	.062 567 3805	26	
.346 816 5701	16.329 585 7467	.061 238 5406	27	
.333 477 4713	16.663 063 2180	.060 012 9752	28	
.320 651 4147	16.983 714 6327	.058 879 9342	29	
.308 318 6680	17.292 033 3007	.057 830 0991	30	SEMIANNUALLY
.296 460 2577	17.588 493 5583	.056 855 3524	31	If compounded *semiannually*
.285 057 9401	17.873 551 4984	.055 948 5897	32	nominal annual rate is
.274 094 1731	18.147 645 6715	.055 103 5665	33	
.263 552 0896	18.411 197 7611	.054 314 7715	34	
.253 415 4707	18.664 613 2318	.053 577 3224	35	**8%**
.243 668 7219	18.908 281 9537	.052 886 8780	36	
.234 296 8479	19.142 578 8016	.052 239 5655	37	
.225 285 4307	19.367 864 2323	.051 631 9191	38	
.216 620 6064	19.584 484 8388	.051 060 8274	39	
.208 289 0447	19.792 773 8834	.050 523 4893	40	QUARTERLY
.200 277 9276	19.993 051 8110	.050 017 3765	41	If compounded *quarterly*
.192 574 9303	20.185 626 7413	.049 540 2007	42	nominal annual rate is
.185 168 2023	20.370 794 9436	.049 089 8859	43	
.178 046 3483	20.548 841 2919	.048 664 5444	44	
.171 198 4118	20.720 039 7038	.048 262 4558	45	**16%**
.164 613 8575	20.884 653 5613	.047 882 0488	46	
.158 282 5553	21.042 936 1166	.047 521 8855	47	
.152 194 7647	21.195 130 8814	.047 180 6476	48	
.146 341 1199	21.341 472 0013	.046 857 1240	49	
.140 712 6153	21.482 184 6167	.046 550 2004	50	MONTHLY
.135 300 5917	21.617 485 2083	.046 258 8497	51	If compounded *monthly*
.130 096 7228	21.747 581 9311	.045 982 1236	52	nominal annual rate is
.125 093 0027	21.872 674 9337	.045 719 1451	53	
.120 281 7333	21.992 956 6671	.045 469 1025	54	
.115 655 5128	22.108 612 1799	.045 231 2426	55	**48%**
.111 207 2239	22.219 819 4037	.045 004 8662	56	
.106 930 0229	22.326 749 4267	.044 789 3234	57	$i = .04$
.102 817 3297	22.429 566 7564	.044 584 0087	58	$j_{(2)} = .08$
.098 862 8171	22.528 429 5735	.044 388 3581	59	$j_{(4)} = .16$
.095 060 4010	22.623 489 9745	.044 201 8451	60	$j_{(12)} = .48$
$v^n = \dfrac{1}{(1+i)^n}$	$a_{\overline{n}|} = \dfrac{1-v^n}{i}$	$\dfrac{1}{a_{\overline{n}|}} = \dfrac{i}{1-v^n}$	n	

RATE **4½%**	P E R I O D S	AMOUNT OF 1 How $1 left at compound interest will grow.	AMOUNT OF 1 PER PERIOD How $1 deposited periodically will grow.	SINKING FUND Periodic deposit that will grow to $1 at future date.
.045 *per period*	1	1.045 000 0000	1.000 000 0000	1.000 000 0000
	2	1.092 025 0000	2.045 000 0000	.488 997 5550
	3	1.141 166 1250	3.137 025 0000	.318 773 3601
	4	1.192 518 6006	4.278 191 1250	.233 743 6479
	5	1.246 181 9377	5.470 709 7256	.182 791 6395
	6	1.302 260 1248	6.716 891 6633	.148 878 3875
	7	1.360 861 8305	8.019 151 7881	.124 701 4680
	8	1.422 100 6128	9.380 013 6186	.106 609 6533
	9	1.486 095 1404	10.802 114 2314	.092 574 4700
	10	1.552 969 4217	12.288 209 3718	.081 378 8217
	11	1.622 853 0457	13.841 178 7936	.072 248 1817
	12	1.695 881 4328	15.464 031 8393	.064 666 1886
	13	1.772 196 0972	17.159 913 2721	.058 275 3528
	14	1.851 944 9216	18.932 109 3693	.052 820 3160
	15	1.935 282 4431	20.784 054 2909	.048 113 8081
	16	2.022 370 1530	22.719 336 7340	.044 015 3694
	17	2.113 376 8099	24.741 706 8870	.040 417 5833
	18	2.208 478 7664	26.855 083 6970	.037 236 8975
	19	2.307 860 3108	29.063 562 4633	.034 407 3443
	20	2.411 714 0248	31.371 422 7742	.031 876 1443
ANNUALLY If compounded *annually* nominal annual rate is **4½%**	21	2.520 241 1560	33.783 136 7990	.029 600 5669
	22	2.633 652 0080	36.303 377 9550	.027 545 6461
	23	2.752 166 3483	38.937 029 9629	.025 682 4930
	24	2.876 013 8340	41.689 196 3113	.023 987 0299
	25	3.005 434 4565	44.565 210 1453	.022 439 0280
	26	3.140 679 0071	47.570 644 6018	.021 021 3674
	27	3.282 009 5624	50.711 323 6089	.019 719 4616
	28	3.429 699 9927	53.993 333 1713	.018 520 8051
	29	3.584 036 4924	57.423 033 1640	.017 414 6147
	30	3.745 318 1345	61.007 069 6564	.016 391 5429
SEMIANNUALLY If compounded *semiannually* nominal annual rate is **9%**	31	3.913 857 4506	64.752 387 7909	.015 443 4459
	32	4.089 981 0359	68.666 245 2415	.014 563 1962
	33	4.274 030 1825	72.756 226 2774	.013 744 5281
	34	4.466 361 5407	77.030 256 4599	.012 981 9119
	35	4.667 347 8100	81.496 618 0005	.012 270 4478
	36	4.877 378 4615	86.163 965 8106	.011 605 7796
	37	5.096 860 4922	91.041 344 2720	.010 984 0206
	38	5.326 219 2144	96.138 204 7643	.010 401 6920
	39	5.565 899 0790	101.464 423 9787	.009 855 6712
	40	5.816 364 5376	107.030 323 0577	.009 343 1466
QUARTERLY If compounded *quarterly* nominal annual rate is **18%**	41	6.078 100 9418	112.846 687 5953	.008 861 5804
	42	6.351 615 4842	118.924 788 5371	.008 408 6759
	43	6.637 438 1810	125.276 404 0213	.007 982 3492
	44	6.936 122 8991	131.913 842 2022	.007 580 7056
	45	7.248 248 4296	138.849 965 1013	.007 202 0184
	46	7.574 419 6089	146.098 213 5309	.006 844 7107
	47	7.915 268 4913	153.672 633 1398	.006 507 3395
	48	8.271 455 5734	161.587 901 6311	.006 188 5821
	49	8.643 671 0742	169.859 357 2045	.005 887 2235
	50	9.032 636 2725	178.503 028 2787	.005 602 1459
MONTHLY If compounded *monthly* nominal annual rate is **54%**	51	9.439 104 9048	187.535 664 5512	.005 332 3191
	52	9.863 864 6255	196.974 769 4560	.005 076 7923
	53	10.307 738 5337	206.838 634 0815	.004 834 6867
	54	10.771 586 7677	217.146 372 6152	.004 605 1886
	55	11.256 308 1722	227.917 959 3829	.004 387 5437
i = .045 $j_{(2)}$ = .09 $j_{(4)}$ = .18 $j_{(12)}$ = .54	56	11.762 842 0400	239.174 267 5551	.004 181 0518
	57	12.292 169 9318	250.937 109 5951	.003 985 0622
	58	12.845 317 5787	263.229 279 5269	.003 798 9695
	59	13.423 356 8698	276.074 597 1056	.003 622 2094
	60	14.027 407 9289	289.497 953 9753	.003 454 2558
	n	$s=(1+i)^n$	$s_{\overline{n}\rceil}=\dfrac{(1+i)^n-1}{i}$	$\dfrac{1}{s_{\overline{n}\rceil}}=\dfrac{i}{(1+i)^n-1}$

PRESENT WORTH OF 1 *What $1 due in the future is worth today.*	PRESENT WORTH OF 1 PER PERIOD *What $1 payable periodically is worth today.*	PARTIAL PAYMENT *Annuity worth $1 today.* *Periodic payment necessary to pay off a loan of $1.*	P E R I O D S	RATE $4\frac{1}{2}\%$
.956 937 7990	.956 937 7990	1.045 000 0000	1	
.915 729 9512	1.872 667 7503	.533 997 5550	2	
.876 296 6041	2.748 964 3543	.363 773 3601	3	.045
.838 561 3436	3.587 525 6979	.278 743 6479	4	*per period*
.802 451 0465	4.389 976 7444	.227 791 6395	5	
.767 895 7383	5.157 872 4827	.193 878 3875	6	
.734 828 4577	5.892 700 9404	.169 701 4680	7	
.703 185 1270	6.595 886 0674	.151 609 6533	8	
.672 904 4277	7.268 790 4951	.137 574 4700	9	
.643 927 6820	7.912 718 1771	.126 378 8217	10	
.616 198 7388	8.528 916 9159	.117 248 1817	11	
.589 663 8649	9.118 580 7808	.109 666 1886	12	
.564 271 6410	9.682 852 4218	.103 275 3528	13	
.539 972 8622	10.222 825 2840	.097 820 3160	14	
.516 720 4423	10.739 545 7263	.093 113 8081	15	
.494 469 3228	11.234 015 0491	.089 015 3694	16	
.473 176 3854	11.707 191 4346	.085 417 5833	17	
.452 800 3688	12.159 991 8034	.082 236 8975	18	
.433 301 7884	12.593 293 5918	.079 407 3443	19	
.414 642 8597	13.007 936 4515	.076 876 1443	20	ANNUALLY If compounded *annually* nominal annual rate is
.396 787 4255	13.404 723 8770	.074 600 5669	21	
.379 700 8857	13.784 424 7627	.072 545 6461	22	
.363 350 1298	14.147 774 8925	.070 682 4930	23	
.347 703 4735	14.495 478 3660	.068 987 0299	24	
.332 730 5967	14.828 208 9627	.067 439 0280	25	$4\frac{1}{2}\%$
.318 402 4849	15.146 611 4476	.066 021 3674	26	
.304 691 3731	15.451 302 8206	.064 719 4616	27	
.291 570 6919	15.742 873 5126	.063 520 8051	28	
.279 015 0162	16.021 888 5288	.062 414 6147	29	
.267 000 0155	16.288 888 5443	.061 391 5429	30	
.255 502 4072	16.544 390 9515	.060 443 4459	31	SEMIANNUALLY If compounded *semiannually* nominal annual rate is
.244 499 9112	16.788 890 8627	.059 563 1962	32	
.233 971 2069	17.022 862 0695	.058 744 5281	33	
.223 895 8917	17.246 757 9613	.057 981 9119	34	
.214 254 4419	17.461 012 4031	.057 270 4478	35	9%
.205 028 1740	17.666 040 5772	.056 605 7796	36	
.196 199 2096	17.862 239 7868	.055 984 0206	37	
.187 750 4398	18.049 990 2266	.055 401 6920	38	
.179 665 4926	18.229 655 7192	.054 855 6712	39	
.171 928 7011	18.401 584 4203	.054 343 1466	40	QUARTERLY If compounded *quarterly* nominal annual rate is
.164 525 0728	18.566 109 4931	.053 861 5804	41	
.157 440 2611	18.723 549 7542	.053 408 6759	42	
.150 660 5369	18.874 210 2911	.052 982 3492	43	
.144 172 7626	19.018 383 0536	.052 580 7056	44	
.137 964 3661	19.156 347 4198	.052 202 0184	45	18%
.132 023 3169	19.288 370 7366	.051 844 7107	46	
.126 338 1023	19.414 708 8389	.051 507 3395	47	
.120 897 7055	19.535 606 5444	.051 188 5821	48	
.115 691 5842	19.651 298 1286	.050 887 2235	49	
.110 709 6500	19.762 007 7785	.050 602 1459	50	MONTHLY If compounded *monthly* nominal annual rate is
.105 942 2488	19.867 950 0273	.050 332 3191	51	
.101 380 1424	19.969 330 1697	.050 076 7923	52	
.097 014 4903	20.066 344 6600	.049 834 6867	53	
.092 836 8328	20.159 181 4928	.049 605 1886	54	
.088 839 0745	20.248 020 5673	.049 387 5437	55	54%
.085 013 4684	20.333 034 0357	.049 181 0518	56	
.081 352 6013	20.414 386 6370	.048 985 0622	57	
.077 849 3793	20.492 236 0163	.048 798 9695	58	$i = .045$
.074 497 0137	20.566 733 0299	.048 622 2094	59	$j_{(2)} = .09$
.071 289 0083	20.638 022 0382	.048 454 2558	60	$j_{(4)} = .18$
$v^n = \dfrac{1}{(1+i)^n}$	$a_{\overline{n}|} = \dfrac{1-v^n}{i}$	$\dfrac{1}{a_{\overline{n}|}} = \dfrac{i}{1-v^n}$	n	$j_{(12)} = .54$

RATE 5%	P E R I O D S	AMOUNT OF 1 *How $1 left at compound interest will grow.*	AMOUNT OF 1 PER PERIOD *How $1 deposited periodically will grow.*	SINKING FUND *Periodic deposit that will grow to $1 at future date.*
.05 *per period*	1	1.050 000 0000	1.000 000 0000	1.000 000 0000
	2	1.102 500 0000	2.050 000 0000	.487 804 8780
	3	1.157 625 0000	3.152 500 0000	.317 208 5646
	4	1.215 506 2500	4.310 125 0000	.232 011 8326
	5	1.276 281 5625	5.525 631 2500	.180 974 7981
	6	1.340 095 6406	6.801 912 8125	.147 017 4681
	7	1.407 100 4227	8.142 008 4531	.122 819 8184
	8	1.477 455 4438	9.549 108 8758	.104 721 8136
	9	1.551 328 2160	11.026 564 3196	.090 690 0800
	10	1.628 894 6268	12.577 892 5355	.079 504 5750
	11	1.710 339 3581	14.206 787 1623	.070 388 8915
	12	1.795 856 3260	15.917 126 5204	.062 825 4100
	13	1.885 649 1423	17.712 982 8465	.056 455 7652
	14	1.979 931 5994	19.598 631 9888	.051 023 9695
	15	2.078 928 1794	21.578 563 5882	.046 342 2876
	16	2.182 874 5884	23.657 491 7676	.042 269 9080
	17	2.292 018 3178	25.840 366 3560	.038 699 1417
	18	2.406 619 2337	28.132 384 6738	.035 546 2223
	19	2.526 950 1954	30.539 003 9075	.032 745 0104
ANNUALLY *If compounded annually nominal annual rate is*	20	2.653 297 7051	33.065 954 1029	.030 242 5872
	21	2.785 962 5904	35.719 251 8080	.027 996 1071
	22	2.925 260 7199	38.505 214 3984	.025 970 5086
	23	3.071 523 7559	41.430 475 1184	.024 136 8219
5%	24	3.225 099 9437	44.501 998 8743	.022 470 9008
	25	3.386 354 9409	47.727 098 8180	.020 952 4573
	26	3.555 672 6879	51.113 453 7589	.019 564 3207
	27	3.733 456 3223	54.669 126 4468	.018 291 8599
	28	3.920 129 1385	58.402 582 7692	.017 122 5304
	29	4.116 135 5954	62.322 711 9076	.016 045 5149
	30	4.321 942 3752	66.438 847 5030	.015 051 4351
SEMIANNUALLY *If compounded semiannually nominal annual rate is*	31	4.538 039 4939	70.760 789 8782	.014 132 1204
	32	4.764 941 4686	75.298 829 3721	.013 280 4189
	33	5.003 188 5420	80.063 770 8407	.012 490 0437
10%	34	5.253 347 9691	85.066 959 3827	.011 755 4454
	35	5.516 015 3676	90.320 307 3518	.011 071 7072
	36	5.791 816 1360	95.836 322 7194	.010 434 4571
	37	6.081 406 9428	101.628 138 8554	.009 839 7945
	38	6.385 477 2899	107.709 545 7982	.009 284 2282
	39	6.704 751 1544	114.095 023 0881	.008 764 6242
QUARTERLY *If compounded quarterly nominal annual rate is*	40	7.039 988 7121	120.799 774 2425	.008 278 1612
	41	7.391 988 1477	127.839 762 9546	.007 822 2924
	42	7.761 587 5551	135.231 751 1023	.007 394 7131
	43	8.149 666 9329	142.993 338 6575	.006 993 3328
20%	44	8.557 150 2795	151.143 005 5903	.006 616 2506
	45	8.985 007 7935	159.700 155 8699	.006 261 7347
	46	9.434 258 1832	168.685 163 6633	.005 928 2036
	47	9.905 971 0923	178.119 421 8465	.005 614 2109
	48	10.401 269 6469	188.025 392 9388	.005 318 4306
	49	10.921 333 1293	198.426 662 5858	.005 039 6453
MONTHLY *If compounded monthly nominal annual rate is*	50	11.467 399 7858	209.347 995 7151	.004 776 7355
	51	12.040 769 7750	220.815 395 5008	.004 528 6697
	52	12.642 808 2638	232.856 165 2759	.004 294 4966
	53	13.274 948 6770	245.498 973 5397	.004 073 3368
60%	54	13.938 696 1108	258.773 922 2166	.003 864 3770
	55	14.635 630 9164	272.712 618 3275	.003 666 8637
$i\ =.05$ $j_{(2)}=.1$ $j_{(4)}=.2$ $j_{(12)}=.6$	56	15.367 412 4622	287.348 249 2439	.003 480 0978
	57	16.135 783 0853	302.715 661 7060	.003 303 4300
	58	16.942 572 2396	318.851 444 7913	.003 136 2568
	59	17.789 700 8515	335.794 017 0309	.002 978 0161
	60	18.679 185 8941	353.583 717 8825	.002 828 1845
	n	$s=(1+i)^n$	$s_{\overline{n}|}=\dfrac{(1+i)^n-1}{i}$	$\dfrac{1}{s_{\overline{n}|}}=\dfrac{i}{(1+i)^n-1}$

PRESENT WORTH OF 1 *What $1 due in the future is worth today.*	PRESENT WORTH OF 1 PER PERIOD *What $1 payable periodically is worth today.*	PARTIAL PAYMENT *Annuity worth $1 today.* *Periodic payment necessary to pay off a loan of $1.*	PERIODS	RATE **5%**
.952 380 9524	.952 380 9524	1.050 000 0000	1	
.907 029 4785	1.859 410 4308	.537 804 8780	2	
.863 837 5985	2.723 248 0294	.367 208 5646	3	.05
.822 702 4748	3.545 950 5042	.282 011 8326	4	
.783 526 1665	4.329 476 6706	.230 974 7981	5	*per period*
.746 215 3966	5.075 692 0673	.197 017 4681	6	
.710 681 3301	5.786 373 3974	.172 819 8184	7	
.676 839 3620	6.463 212 7594	.154 721 8136	8	
.644 608 9162	7.107 821 6756	.140 690 0800	9	
.613 913 2535	7.721 734 9292	.129 504 5750	10	
.584 679 2891	8.306 414 2183	.120 388 8915	11	
.556 837 4182	8.863 251 6364	.112 825 4100	12	
.530 321 3506	9.393 572 9871	.106 455 7652	13	
.505 067 9530	9.898 640 9401	.101 023 9695	14	
.481 017 0981	10.379 658 0382	.096 342 2876	15	
.458 111 5220	10.837 769 5602	.092 269 9080	16	
.436 296 6876	11.274 066 2478	.088 699 1417	17	
.415 520 6549	11.689 586 9027	.085 546 2223	18	
.395 733 9570	12.085 320 8597	.082 745 0104	19	
.376 889 4829	12.462 210 3425	.080 242 5872	20	ANNUALLY If compounded *annually* nominal annual rate is
.358 942 3646	12.821 152 7072	.077 996 1071	21	
.341 849 8711	13.163 002 5783	.075 970 5086	22	
.325 571 3058	13.488 573 8841	.074 136 8219	23	
.310 067 9103	13.798 641 7943	.072 470 9008	24	
.295 302 7717	14.093 944 5660	.070 952 4573	25	**5%**
.281 240 7350	14.375 185 3010	.069 564 3207	26	
.267 848 3190	14.643 033 6200	.068 291 8599	27	
.255 093 6371	14.898 127 2571	.067 122 5304	28	
.242 946 3211	15.141 073 5782	.066 045 5149	29	
.231 377 4487	15.372 451 0269	.065 051 4351	30	SEMIANNUALLY If compounded *semiannually* nominal annual rate is
.220 359 4749	15.592 810 5018	.064 132 1204	31	
.209 866 1666	15.802 676 6684	.063 280 4189	32	
.199 872 5396	16.002 549 2080	.062 490 0437	33	
.190 354 7996	16.192 904 0076	.061 755 4454	34	
.181 290 2854	16.374 194 2929	.061 071 7072	35	**10%**
.172 657 4146	16.546 851 7076	.060 434 4571	36	
.164 435 6330	16.711 287 3405	.059 839 7945	37	
.156 605 3647	16.867 892 7053	.059 284 2282	38	
.149 147 9664	17.017 040 6717	.058 764 6242	39	
.142 045 6823	17.159 086 3540	.058 278 1612	40	QUARTERLY If compounded *quarterly* nominal annual rate is
.135 281 6022	17.294 367 9562	.057 822 2924	41	
.128 839 6211	17.423 207 5773	.057 394 7131	42	
.122 704 4011	17.545 911 9784	.056 993 3328	43	
.116 861 3344	17.662 773 3128	.056 616 2506	44	
.111 296 5089	17.774 069 8217	.056 261 7347	45	**20%**
.105 996 6752	17.880 066 4968	.055 928 2036	46	
.100 949 2144	17.981 015 7113	.055 614 2109	47	
.096 142 1090	18.077 157 8203	.055 318 4306	48	
.091 563 9133	18.168 721 7336	.055 039 6453	49	
.087 203 7270	18.255 925 4606	.054 776 7355	50	MONTHLY If compounded *monthly* nominal annual rate is
.083 051 1685	18.338 976 6291	.054 528 6697	51	
.079 096 3510	18.418 072 9801	.054 294 4966	52	
.075 329 8581	18.493 402 8382	.054 073 3368	53	
.071 742 7220	18.565 145 5602	.053 864 3770	54	
.068 326 4019	18.633 471 9621	.053 666 8637	55	**60%**
.065 072 7637	18.698 544 7258	.053 480 0978	56	
.061 974 0607	18.760 518 7865	.053 303 4300	57	
.059 022 9149	18.819 541 7014	.053 136 2568	58	$i = .05$
.056 212 2999	18.875 754 0013	.052 978 0161	59	$j_{(2)} = .1$ $j_{(4)} = .2$
.053 535 5237	18.929 289 5251	.052 828 1845	60	$j_{(12)} = .6$
$v^n = \dfrac{1}{(1+i)^n}$	$a_{\overline{n}\rceil} = \dfrac{1-v^n}{i}$	$\dfrac{1}{a_{\overline{n}\rceil}} = \dfrac{i}{1-v^n}$	n	

RATE 6% .06 per period	P E R I O D S	AMOUNT OF 1 How $1 left at compound interest will grow.	AMOUNT OF 1 PER PERIOD How $1 deposited periodically will grow.	SINKING FUND Periodic deposit that will grow to $1 at future date.
	1	1.060 000 0000	1.000 000 0000	1.000 000 0000
	2	1.123 600 0000	2.060 000 0000	.485 436 8932
	3	1.191 016 0000	3.183 600 0000	.314 109 8128
	4	1.262 476 9600	4.374 616 0000	.228 591 4924
	5	1.338 225 5776	5.637 092 9600	.177 396 4004
	6	1.418 519 1123	6.975 318 5376	.143 362 6285
	7	1.503 630 2590	8.393 837 6499	.119 135 0181
	8	1.593 848 0745	9.897 467 9088	.101 035 9426
	9	1.689 478 9590	11.491 315 9834	.087 022 2350
	10	1.790 847 6965	13.180 794 9424	.075 867 9582
	11	1.898 298 5583	14.971 642 6389	.066 792 9381
	12	2.012 196 4718	16.869 941 1973	.059 277 0294
	13	2.132 928 2601	18.882 137 6691	.052 960 1053
	14	2.260 903 9558	21.015 065 9292	.047 584 9090
	15	2.396 558 1931	23.275 969 8850	.042 962 7640
	16	2.540 351 6847	25.672 528 0781	.038 952 1436
	17	2.692 772 7858	28.212 879 7628	.035 444 8042
	18	2.854 339 1529	30.905 652 5485	.032 356 5406
	19	3.025 599 5021	33.759 991 7015	.029 620 8604
ANNUALLY If compounded annually nominal annual rate is 6%	20	3.207 135 4722	36.785 591 2035	.027 184 5570
	21	3.399 563 6005	39.992 726 6758	.025 004 5467
	22	3.603 537 4166	43.392 290 2763	.023 045 5685
	23	3.819 749 6616	46.995 827 6929	.021 278 4847
	24	4.048 934 6413	50.815 577 3545	.019 679 0050
	25	4.291 870 7197	54.864 511 9957	.018 226 7182
	26	4.549 382 9629	59.156 382 7155	.016 904 3467
	27	4.822 345 9407	63.705 765 6784	.015 697 1663
	28	5.111 686 6971	68.528 111 6191	.014 592 5515
	29	5.418 387 8990	73.639 798 3162	.013 579 6135
SEMIANNUALLY If compounded semiannually nominal annual rate is 12%	30	5.743 491 1729	79.058 186 2152	.012 648 9115
	31	6.088 100 6433	84.801 677 3881	.011 792 2196
	32	6.453 386 6819	90.889 778 0314	.011 002 3374
	33	6.840 589 8828	97.343 164 7133	.010 272 9350
	34	7.251 025 2758	104.183 754 5961	.009 598 4254
	35	7.686 086 7923	111.434 779 8719	.008 973 8590
	36	8.147 251 9999	119.120 866 6642	.008 394 8348
	37	8.636 087 1198	127.268 118 6640	.007 857 4274
	38	9.154 252 3470	135.904 205 7839	.007 358 1240
	39	9.703 507 4879	145.058 458 1309	.006 893 7724
QUARTERLY If compounded quarterly nominal annual rate is 24%	40	10.285 717 9371	154.761 965 6188	.006 461 5359
	41	10.902 861 0134	165.047 683 5559	.006 058 8551
	42	11.557 032 6742	175.950 544 5692	.005 683 4152
	43	12.250 454 6346	187.507 577 2434	.005 333 1178
	44	12.985 481 9127	199.758 031 8780	.005 006 0565
	45	13.764 610 8274	212.743 513 7907	.004 700 4958
	46	14.590 487 4771	226.508 124 6181	.004 414 8527
	47	15.465 916 7257	241.098 612 0952	.004 147 6805
	48	16.393 871 7293	256.564 528 8209	.003 897 6549
	49	17.377 504 0330	272.958 400 5502	.003 663 5619
MONTHLY If compounded monthly nominal annual rate is 72%	50	18.420 154 2750	290.335 904 5832	.003 444 2864
	51	19.525 363 5315	308.756 058 8582	.003 238 8028
	52	20.696 885 3434	328.281 422 3897	.003 046 1669
	53	21.938 698 4640	348.978 307 7331	.002 865 5076
	54	23.255 020 3718	370.917 006 1970	.002 696 0209
	55	24.650 321 5941	394.172 026 5689	.002 536 9634
$i = .06$ $j_{(2)} = .12$ $j_{(4)} = .24$ $j_{(12)} = .72$	56	26.129 340 8898	418.822 348 1630	.002 387 6472
	57	27.697 101 3432	444.951 689 0528	.002 247 4350
	58	29.358 927 4238	472.648 790 3959	.002 115 7359
	59	31.120 463 0692	502.007 717 8197	.001 992 0012
	60	32.987 690 8533	533.128 180 8889	.001 875 7215
	n	$s=(1+i)^n$	$s_{\overline{n}|}=\dfrac{(1+i)^n-1}{i}$	$\dfrac{1}{s_{\overline{n}|}}=\dfrac{i}{(1+i)^n-1}$

PRESENT WORTH OF 1 *What $1 due in the future is worth today.*	PRESENT WORTH OF 1 PER PERIOD *What $1 payable periodically is worth today.*	PARTIAL PAYMENT *Annuity worth $1 today.* *Periodic payment necessary to pay off a loan of $1.*	P E R I O D S	RATE **6%**
.943 396 2264	.943 396 2264	1.060 000 0000	1	
.889 996 4400	1.833 392 6664	.545 436 8932	2	
.839 619 2830	2.673 011 9495	.374 109 8128	3	.06
.792 093 6632	3.465 105 6127	.288 591 4924	4	*per period*
.747 258 1729	4.212 363 7856	.237 396 4004	5	
.704 960 5404	4.917 324 3260	.203 362 6285	6	
.665 057 1136	5.582 381 4396	.179 135 0181	7	
.627 412 3713	6.209 793 8110	.161 035 9426	8	
.591 898 4635	6.801 692 2745	.147 022 2350	9	
.558 394 7769	7.360 087 0514	.135 867 9582	10	
.526 787 5254	7.886 874 5768	.126 792 9381	11	
.496 969 3636	8.383 843 9404	.119 277 0294	12	
.468 839 0222	8.852 682 9626	.112 960 1053	13	
.442 300 9644	9.294 983 9270	.107 584 9090	14	
.417 265 0607	9.712 248 9877	.102 962 7640	15	
.393 646 2837	10.105 895 2715	.098 952 1436	16	
.371 364 4186	10.477 259 6901	.095 444 8042	17	
.350 343 7911	10.827 603 4812	.092 356 5406	18	
.330 513 0105	11.158 116 4917	.089 620 8604	19	
.311 804 7269	11.469 921 2186	.087 184 5570	20	
.294 155 4027	11.764 076 6213	.085 004 5467	21	ANNUALLY If compounded *annually* nominal annual rate is
.277 505 0969	12.041 581 7182	.083 045 5685	22	
.261 797 2612	12.303 378 9794	.081 278 4847	23	
.246 978 5483	12.550 357 5278	.079 679 0050	24	
.232 998 6305	12.783 356 1583	.078 226 7182	25	**6%**
.219 810 0288	13.003 166 1870	.076 904 3467	26	
.207 367 9517	13.210 534 1387	.075 697 1663	27	
.195 630 1431	13.406 164 2818	.074 592 5515	28	
.184 556 7388	13.590 721 0206	.073 579 6135	29	
.174 110 1309	13.764 831 1515	.072 648 9115	30	
.164 254 8405	13.929 085 9920	.071 792 2196	31	SEMIANNUALLY If compounded *semiannually* nominal annual rate is
.154 957 3967	14.084 043 3887	.071 002 3374	32	
.146 186 2233	14.230 229 6119	.070 272 9350	33	
.137 911 5314	14.368 141 1433	.069 598 4254	34	
.130 105 2183	14.498 246 3616	.068 973 8590	35	**12%**
.122 740 7720	14.620 987 1336	.068 394 8348	36	
.115 793 1811	14.736 780 3147	.067 857 4274	37	
.109 238 8501	14.846 019 1648	.067 358 1240	38	
.103 055 5190	14.949 074 6838	.066 893 7724	39	
.097 222 1877	15.046 296 8715	.066 461 5359	40	
.091 719 0450	15.138 015 9165	.066 058 8551	41	QUARTERLY If compounded *quarterly* nominal annual rate is
.086 527 4010	15.224 543 3175	.065 683 4152	42	
.081 629 6235	15.306 172 9410	.065 333 1178	43	
.077 009 0788	15.383 182 0198	.065 006 0565	44	
.072 650 0743	15.455 832 0942	.064 700 4958	45	**24%**
.068 537 8060	15.524 369 9002	.064 414 8527	46	
.064 658 3075	15.589 028 2077	.064 147 6805	47	
.060 998 4033	15.650 026 6110	.063 897 6549	48	
.057 545 6635	15.707 572 2746	.063 663 5619	49	
.054 288 3618	15.761 860 6364	.063 444 2864	50	
.051 215 4357	15.813 076 0721	.063 238 8028	51	MONTHLY If compounded *monthly* nominal annual rate is
.048 316 4488	15.861 392 5208	.063 046 1669	52	
.045 581 5554	15.906 974 0762	.062 865 5076	53	
.043 001 4674	15.949 975 5436	.062 696 0209	54	
.040 567 4221	15.990 542 9657	.062 536 9634	55	**72%**
.038 271 1529	16.028 814 1186	.062 387 6472	56	
.036 104 8612	16.064 918 9798	.062 247 4350	57	
.034 061 1898	16.098 980 1696	.062 115 7359	58	$i \quad = .06$
.032 133 1979	16.131 113 3676	.061 992 0012	59	$j_{(2)} \ = .12$
.030 314 3377	16.161 427 7052	.061 875 7215	60	$j_{(4)} \ = .24$ $j_{(12)} = .72$
$v^n = \dfrac{1}{(1+i)^n}$	$a_{\overline{n}|} = \dfrac{1-v^n}{i}$	$\dfrac{1}{a_{\overline{n}|}} = \dfrac{i}{1-v^n}$	n	

RATE 7%	P E R I O D S	AMOUNT OF 1 How $1 left at compound interest will grow.	AMOUNT OF 1 PER PERIOD How $1 deposited periodically will grow.	SINKING FUND Periodic deposit that will grow to $1 at future date.
.07 per period	1 2 3 4 5	1.070 000 0000 1.144 900 0000 1.225 043 0000 1.310 796 0100 1.402 551 7307	1.000 000 0000 2.070 000 0000 3.214 900 0000 4.439 943 0000 5.750 739 0100	1.000 000 0000 .483 091 7874 .311 051 6657 .225 228 1167 .173 890 6944
	6 7 8 9 10	1.500 730 3518 1.605 781 4765 1.718 186 1798 1.838 459 2124 1.967 151 3573	7.153 290 7407 8.654 021 0925 10.259 802 5690 11.977 988 7489 13.816 447 9613	.139 795 7998 .115 553 2196 .097 467 7625 .083 486 4701 .072 377 5027
	11 12 13 14 15	2.104 851 9523 2.252 191 5890 2.409 845 0002 2.578 534 1502 2.759 031 5407	15.783 599 3186 17.888 451 2709 20.140 642 8598 22.550 487 8600 25.129 022 0102	.063 356 9048 .055 901 9887 .049 650 8481 .044 344 9386 .039 794 6247
	16 17 18 19 20	2.952 163 7486 3.158 815 2110 3.379 932 2757 3.616 527 5350 3.869 684 4625	27.888 053 5509 30.840 217 2995 33.999 032 5105 37.378 964 7862 40.995 492 3212	.035 857 6477 .032 425 1931 .029 412 6017 .026 753 0148 .024 392 9257
ANNUALLY If compounded annually nominal annual rate is 7%	21 22 23 24 25	4.140 562 3749 4.430 401 7411 4.740 529 8630 5.072 366 9534 5.427 432 6401	44.865 176 7837 49.005 739 1586 53.436 140 8997 58.176 670 7627 63.249 037 7160	.022 289 0017 .020 405 7732 .018 713 9263 .017 189 0207 .015 810 5172
	26 27 28 29 30	5.807 352 9249 6.213 867 6297 6.648 838 3638 7.114 257 0492 7.612 255 0427	68.676 470 3562 74.483 823 2811 80.697 690 9108 87.346 529 2745 94.460 786 3237	.014 561 0279 .013 425 7340 .012 391 9283 .011 448 6518 .010 586 4035
SEMIANNUALLY If compounded semiannually nominal annual rate is 14%	31 32 33 34 35	8.145 112 8956 8.715 270 7983 9.325 339 7542 9.978 113 5370 10.676 581 4846	102.073 041 3664 110.218 154 2621 118.933 425 0604 128.258 764 8146 138.236 878 3516	.009 796 9061 .009 072 9155 .008 408 0653 .007 796 7381 .007 233 9596
	36 37 38 39 40	11.423 942 1885 12.223 618 1417 13.079 271 4117 13.994 820 4105 14.974 457 8392	148.913 459 8363 160.337 402 0248 172.561 020 1665 185.640 291 5782 199.635 111 9887	.006 715 3097 .006 236 8480 .005 795 0515 .005 386 7616 .005 009 1389
QUARTERLY If compounded quarterly nominal annual rate is 28%	41 42 43 44 45	16.022 669 8880 17.144 256 7801 18.344 354 7547 19.628 459 5875 21.002 451 7587	214.609 569 8279 230.632 239 7158 247.776 496 4959 266.120 851 2507 285.749 310 8382	.004 659 6245 .004 335 9072 .004 035 8953 .003 757 6913 .003 499 5710
	46 47 48 49 50	22.472 623 3818 24.045 707 0185 25.728 906 5098 27.529 929 9655 29.457 025 0631	306.751 762 5969 329.224 385 9787 353.270 092 9972 378.998 999 5070 406.528 929 4724	.003 259 9650 .003 037 4421 .002 830 6953 .002 638 5294 .002 459 8495
MONTHLY If compounded monthly nominal annual rate is 84%	51 52 53 54 55	31.519 016 8175 33.725 347 9947 36.086 122 3543 38.612 150 9191 41.315 001 4835	435.985 954 5355 467.504 971 3530 501.230 319 3477 537.316 441 7021 575.928 592 6212	.002 293 6519 .002 139 0147 .001 995 0908 .001 861 1007 .001 736 3264
	56 57 58 59 60	44.207 051 5873 47.301 545 1984 50.612 653 3623 54.155 539 0977 57.946 426 8345	617.243 594 1047 661.450 645 6920 708.752 190 8905 759.364 844 2528 813.520 383 3505	.001 620 1059 .001 511 8286 .001 410 9304 .001 316 8900 .001 229 2255

$i = .07$
$j_{(2)} = .14$
$j_{(4)} = .28$
$j_{(12)} = .84$

n	$s=(1+i)^n$	$s_{\overline{n}|}=\dfrac{(1+i)^n-1}{i}$	$\dfrac{1}{s_{\overline{n}|}}=\dfrac{i}{(1+i)^n-1}$

PRESENT WORTH OF 1	PRESENT WORTH OF 1 PER PERIOD	PARTIAL PAYMENT	P E R I O D S	RATE
What $1 due in the future is worth today.	*What $1 payable periodically is worth today.*	*Annuity worth $1 today.* *Periodic payment necessary to pay off a loan of $1.*		**7%**
.934 579 4393	.934 579 4393	1.070 000 0000	1	
.873 438 7283	1.808 018 1675	.553 091 7874	2	
.816 297 8769	2.624 316 0444	.381 051 6657	3	.07
.762 895 2120	3.387 211 2565	.295 228 1167	4	
.712 986 1795	4.100 197 4359	.243 890 6944	5	*per period*
.666 342 2238	4.766 539 6598	.209 795 7998	6	
.622 749 7419	5.389 289 4016	.185 553 2196	7	
.582 009 1046	5.971 298 5062	.167 467 7625	8	
.543 933 7426	6.515 232 2488	.153 486 4701	9	
.508 349 2921	7.023 581 5409	.142 377 5027	10	
.475 092 7964	7.498 674 3373	.133 356 9048	11	
.444 011 9592	7.942 686 2966	.125 901 9887	12	
.414 964 4479	8.357 650 7444	.119 650 8481	13	
.387 817 2410	8.745 467 9855	.114 344 9386	14	
.362 446 0196	9.107 914 0051	.109 794 6247	15	
.338 734 5978	9.446 648 6029	.105 857 6477	16	
.316 574 3905	9.763 222 9934	.102 425 1931	17	
.295 863 9163	10.059 086 9097	.099 412 6017	18	
.276 508 3330	10.335 595 2427	.096 753 0148	19	
.258 419 0028	10.594 014 2455	.094 392 9257	20	
.241 513 0867	10.835 527 3323	.092 289 0017	21	ANNUALLY
.225 713 1652	11.061 240 4974	.090 405 7732	22	If compounded
.210 946 8833	11.272 187 3808	.088 713 9263	23	*annually*
.197 146 6199	11.469 334 0007	.087 189 0207	24	nominal annual rate is
.184 249 1775	11.653 583 1783	.085 810 5172	25	**7%**
.172 195 4930	11.825 778 6713	.084 561 0279	26	
.160 930 3673	11.986 709 0386	.083 425 7340	27	
.150 402 2124	12.137 111 2510	.082 391 9283	28	
.140 562 8154	12.277 674 0664	.081 448 6518	29	
.131 367 1172	12.409 041 1835	.080 586 4035	30	SEMIANNUALLY
.122 773 0067	12.531 814 1902	.079 796 9061	31	If compounded
.114 741 1277	12.646 555 3179	.079 072 9155	32	*semiannually*
.107 234 6988	12.753 790 0168	.078 408 0653	33	nominal annual rate is
.100 219 3447	12.854 009 3615	.077 796 7381	34	
.093 662 9390	12.947 672 3004	.077 233 9596	35	**14%**
.087 535 4570	13.035 207 7574	.076 715 3097	36	
.081 808 8383	13.117 016 5957	.076 236 8480	37	
.076 456 8582	13.193 473 4539	.075 795 0515	38	
.071 455 0077	13.264 928 4616	.075 386 7616	39	
.066 780 3810	13.331 708 8426	.075 009 1389	40	QUARTERLY
.062 411 5710	13.394 120 4137	.074 659 6245	41	If compounded
.058 328 5711	13.452 448 9847	.074 335 9072	42	*quarterly*
.054 512 6832	13.506 961 6680	.074 035 8953	43	nominal annual rate is
.050 946 4329	13.557 908 1009	.073 757 6913	44	
.047 613 4887	13.605 521 5896	.073 499 5710	45	**28%**
.044 498 5876	13.650 020 1772	.073 259 9650	46	
.041 587 4650	13.691 607 6423	.073 037 4421	47	
.038 866 7898	13.730 474 4320	.072 830 6953	48	
.036 324 1026	13.766 798 5346	.072 638 5294	49	
.033 947 7594	13.800 746 2940	.072 459 8495	50	MONTHLY
.031 726 8780	13.832 473 1720	.072 293 6519	51	If compounded
.029 651 2878	13.862 124 4598	.072 139 0147	52	*monthly*
.027 711 4839	13.889 835 9437	.071 995 0908	53	nominal annual rate is
.025 898 5831	13.915 734 5269	.071 861 1007	54	
.024 204 2833	13.939 938 8102	.071 736 3264	55	**84%**
.022 620 8255	13.962 559 6357	.071 620 1059	56	
.021 140 9584	13.983 700 5941	.071 511 8286	57	
.019 757 9051	14.003 458 4991	.071 410 9304	58	$i\ \ =.07$
.018 465 3318	14.021 923 8310	.071 316 8900	59	$j_{(2)}=.14$
.017 257 3195	14.039 181 1504	.071 229 2255	60	$j_{(4)}=.28$
$v^n=\dfrac{1}{(1+i)^n}$	$a_{\overline{n}}=\dfrac{1-v^n}{i}$	$\dfrac{1}{a_{\overline{n}}}=\dfrac{i}{1-v^n}$	n	$j_{(12)}=.84$

RATE 8%	PERIODS	AMOUNT OF 1 — How $1 left at compound interest will grow.	AMOUNT OF 1 PER PERIOD — How $1 deposited periodically will grow.	SINKING FUND — Periodic deposit that will grow to $1 at future date.
.08 per period	1	1.080 000 0000	1.000 000 0000	1.000 000 0000
	2	1.166 400 0000	2.080 000 0000	.480 769 2308
	3	1.259 712 0000	3.246 400 0000	.308 033 5140
	4	1.360 488 9600	4.506 112 0000	.221 920 8045
	5	1.469 328 0768	5.866 600 9600	.170 456 4546
	6	1.586 874 3229	7.335 929 0368	.136 315 3862
	7	1.713 824 2688	8.922 803 3597	.112 072 4014
	8	1.850 930 2103	10.636 627 6285	.094 014 7606
	9	1.999 004 6271	12.487 557 8388	.080 079 7092
	10	2.158 924 9973	14.486 562 4659	.069 029 4887
	11	2.331 638 9971	16.645 487 4632	.060 076 3421
	12	2.518 170 1168	18.977 126 4602	.052 695 0169
	13	2.719 623 7262	21.495 296 5771	.046 521 8052
	14	2.937 193 6243	24.214 920 3032	.041 296 8528
	15	3.172 169 1142	27.152 113 9275	.036 829 5449
	16	3.425 942 6433	30.324 283 0417	.032 976 8720
	17	3.700 018 0548	33.750 225 6850	.029 629 4315
	18	3.996 019 4992	37.450 243 7398	.026 702 0959
	19	4.315 701 0591	41.446 263 2390	.024 127 6275
ANNUALLY — If compounded annually nominal annual rate is 8%	20	4.660 957 1438	45.761 964 2981	.021 852 2088
	21	5.033 833 7154	50.422 921 4420	.019 832 2503
	22	5.436 540 4126	55.456 755 1573	.018 032 0684
	23	5.871 463 6456	60.893 295 5699	.016 422 1692
	24	6.341 180 7372	66.764 759 2155	.014 977 9616
	25	6.848 475 1962	73.105 939 9527	.013 678 7791
	26	7.396 353 2119	79.954 415 1490	.012 507 1267
	27	7.988 061 4689	87.350 768 3609	.011 448 0962
	28	8.627 106 3864	95.338 829 8297	.010 488 9057
	29	9.317 274 8973	103.965 936 2161	.009 618 5350
SEMIANNUALLY — If compounded semiannually nominal annual rate is 16%	30	10.062 656 8891	113.283 211 1134	.008 827 4334
	31	10.867 669 4402	123.345 868 0025	.008 107 2841
	32	11.737 082 9954	134.213 537 4427	.007 450 8132
	33	12.676 049 6350	145.950 620 4381	.006 851 6324
	34	13.690 133 6059	158.626 670 0732	.006 304 1101
	35	14.785 344 2943	172.316 803 6790	.005 803 2646
	36	15.968 171 8379	187.102 147 9733	.005 344 6741
	37	17.245 625 5849	203.070 319 8112	.004 924 4025
	38	18.625 275 6317	220.315 945 3961	.004 538 9361
	39	20.115 297 6822	238.941 221 0278	.004 185 1297
QUARTERLY — If compounded quarterly nominal annual rate is 32%	40	21.724 521 4968	259.056 518 7100	.003 860 1615
	41	23.462 483 2165	280.781 040 2068	.003 561 4940
	42	25.339 481 8739	304.243 523 4233	.003 286 8407
	43	27.366 640 4238	329.583 005 2972	.003 034 1370
	44	29.555 971 6577	356.949 645 7210	.002 801 5156
	45	31.920 449 3903	386.505 617 3787	.002 587 2845
	46	34.474 085 3415	418.426 066 7690	.002 389 9085
	47	37.232 012 1688	452.900 152 1105	.002 207 9922
	48	40.210 573 1423	490.132 164 2793	.002 040 2660
	49	43.427 418 9937	530.342 737 4217	.001 885 5731
MONTHLY — If compounded monthly nominal annual rate is 96%	50	46.901 612 5132	573.770 156 4154	.001 742 8582
	51	50.653 741 5143	620.671 768 9286	.001 611 1575
	52	54.706 040 8354	671.325 510 4429	.001 489 5903
	53	59.082 524 1023	726.031 551 2783	.001 377 3506
	54	63.809 126 0304	785.114 075 3806	.001 273 7003
	55	68.913 856 1129	848.923 201 4111	.001 177 9629
	56	74.426 964 6019	917.837 057 5239	.001 089 5180
$i = .08$	57	80.381 121 7701	992.264 022 1259	.001 007 7963
$j_{(2)} = .16$	58	86.811 611 5117	1072.645 143 8959	.000 932 2748
$j_{(4)} = .32$	59	93.756 540 4326	1159.456 755 4076	.000 862 4729
$j_{(12)} = .96$	60	101.257 063 6672	1253.213 295 8402	.000 797 9488
	n	$s = (1+i)^n$	$s_{\overline{n}\|} = \dfrac{(1+i)^n - 1}{i}$	$\dfrac{1}{s_{\overline{n}\|}} = \dfrac{i}{(1+i)^n - 1}$

PRESENT WORTH OF 1 *What $1 due in the future is worth today.*	PRESENT WORTH OF 1 PER PERIOD *What $1 payable periodically is worth today.*	PARTIAL PAYMENT *Annuity worth $1 today.* *Periodic payment necessary to pay off a loan of $1.*	P E R I O D S	RATE **8%**
.925 925 9259	.925 925 9259	1.080 000 0000	1	
.857 338 8203	1.783 264 7462	.560 769 2308	2	
.793 832 2410	2.577 096 9872	.388 033 5140	3	.08
.735 029 8528	3.312 126 8400	.301 920 8045	4	*per period*
.680 583 1970	3.992 710 0371	.250 456 4546	5	
.630 169 6269	4.622 879 6640	.216 315 3862	6	
.583 490 3953	5.206 370 0592	.192 072 4014	7	
.540 268 8845	5.746 638 9437	.174 014 7606	8	
.500 248 9671	6.246 887 9109	.160 079 7092	9	
.463 193 4881	6.710 081 3989	.149 029 4887	10	
.428 882 8593	7.138 964 2583	.140 076 3421	11	
.397 113 7586	7.536 078 0169	.132 695 0169	12	
.367 697 9247	7.903 775 9416	.126 521 8052	13	
.340 461 0414	8.244 236 9830	.121 296 8528	14	
.315 241 7050	8.559 478 6879	.116 829 5449	15	
.291 890 4676	8.851 369 1555	.112 976 8720	16	
.270 268 9514	9.121 638 1069	.109 629 4315	17	
.250 249 0291	9.371 887 1360	.106 702 0959	18	
.231 712 0640	9.603 599 2000	.104 127 6275	19	
.214 548 2074	9.818 147 4074	.101 852 2088	20	ANNUALLY If compounded *annually* nominal annual rate is
.198 655 7476	10.016 803 1550	.099 832 2503	21	
.183 940 5070	10.200 743 6621	.098 032 0684	22	
.170 315 2843	10.371 058 9464	.096 422 1692	23	
.157 699 3373	10.528 758 2837	.094 977 9616	24	
.146 017 9049	10.674 776 1886	.093 678 7791	25	**8%**
.135 201 7638	10.809 977 9524	.092 507 1267	26	
.125 186 8183	10.935 164 7707	.091 448 0962	27	
.115 913 7207	11.051 078 4914	.090 488 9057	28	
.107 327 5192	11.158 406 0106	.089 618 5350	29	
.099 377 3325	11.257 783 3431	.088 827 4334	30	SEMIANNUALLY If compounded *semiannually* nominal annual rate is
.092 016 0487	11.349 799 3918	.088 107 2841	31	
.085 200 0451	11.434 999 4368	.087 450 8132	32	
.078 888 9306	11.513 888 3674	.086 851 6324	33	
.073 045 3061	11.586 933 6736	.086 304 1101	34	
.067 634 5427	11.654 568 2163	.085 803 2646	35	**16%**
.062 624 5766	11.717 192 7928	.085 344 6741	36	
.057 985 7190	11.775 178 5119	.084 924 4025	37	
.053 690 4806	11.828 868 9925	.084 538 9361	38	
.049 713 4080	11.878 582 4004	.084 185 1297	39	
.046 030 9333	11.924 613 3337	.083 860 1615	40	QUARTERLY If compounded *quarterly* nominal annual rate is
.042 621 2345	11.967 234 5683	.083 561 4940	41	
.039 464 1061	12.006 698 6743	.083 286 8407	42	
.036 540 8389	12.043 239 5133	.083 034 1370	43	
.033 834 1101	12.077 073 6234	.082 801 5156	44	
.031 327 8797	12.108 401 5032	.082 587 2845	45	**32%**
.029 007 2961	12.137 408 7992	.082 389 9085	46	
.026 858 6075	12.164 267 4067	.082 207 9922	47	
.024 869 0810	12.189 136 4877	.082 040 2660	48	
.023 026 9268	12.212 163 4145	.081 885 5731	49	
.021 321 2286	12.233 484 6431	.081 742 8582	50	MONTHLY If compounded *monthly* nominal annual rate is
.019 741 8783	12.253 226 5214	.081 611 1575	51	
.018 279 5169	12.271 506 0383	.081 489 5903	52	
.016 925 4786	12.288 431 5169	.081 377 3506	53	
.015 671 7395	12.304 103 2564	.081 273 7003	54	
.014 510 8699	12.318 614 1263	.081 177 9629	55	**96%**
.013 435 9906	12.332 050 1170	.081 089 5180	56	
.012 440 7321	12.344 490 8490	.081 007 7963	57	$i = .08$
.011 519 1964	12.356 010 0454	.080 932 2748	58	$j_{(2)} = .16$
.010 665 9226	12.366 675 9680	.080 862 4729	59	$j_{(4)} = .32$
.009 875 8542	12.376 551 8222	.080 797 9488	60	$j_{(12)} = .96$
$v^n = \dfrac{1}{(1+i)^n}$	$a_{\overline{n}|} = \dfrac{1-v^n}{i}$	$\dfrac{1}{a_{\overline{n}|}} = \dfrac{i}{1-v^n}$	n	

RATE 9%	P E R I O D S	AMOUNT OF 1 *How $1 left at compound interest will grow.*	AMOUNT OF 1 PER PERIOD *How $1 deposited periodically will grow.*	SINKING FUND *Periodic deposit that will grow to $1 at future date.*
.09 *per period*	1	1.090 000 0000	1.000 000 0000	1.000 000 0000
	2	1.188 100 0000	2.090 000 0000	.478 468 8995
	3	1.295 029 0000	3.278 100 0000	.305 054 7573
	4	1.411 581 6100	4.573 129 0000	.218 668 6621
	5	1.538 623 9549	5.984 710 6100	.167 092 4570
	6	1.677 100 1108	7.523 334 5649	.132 919 7833
	7	1.828 039 1208	9.200 434 6757	.108 690 5168
	8	1.992 562 6417	11.028 473 7966	.090 674 3778
	9	2.171 893 2794	13.021 036 4382	.076 798 8021
	10	2.367 363 6746	15.192 929 7177	.065 820 0899
	11	2.580 426 4053	17.560 293 3923	.056 946 6567
	12	2.812 664 7818	20.140 719 7976	.049 650 6585
	13	3.065 804 6121	22.953 384 5794	.043 566 5597
	14	3.341 727 0272	26.019 189 1915	.038 433 1730
	15	3.642 482 4597	29.360 916 2188	.034 058 8627
	16	3.970 305 8811	33.003 398 6784	.030 299 9097
	17	4.327 633 4104	36.973 704 5595	.027 046 2485
	18	4.717 120 4173	41.301 337 9699	.024 212 2907
	19	5.141 661 2548	46.018 458 3871	.021 730 4107
	20	5.604 410 7678	51.160 119 6420	.019 546 4750
ANNUALLY If compounded *annually* nominal annual rate is 9%	21	6.108 807 7369	56.764 530 4098	.017 616 6348
	22	6.658 600 4332	62.873 338 1466	.015 904 9930
	23	7.257 874 4722	69.531 938 5798	.014 381 8800
	24	7.911 083 1747	76.789 813 0520	.013 022 5607
	25	8.623 080 6604	84.700 896 2267	.011 806 2505
	26	9.399 157 9198	93.323 976 8871	.010 715 3599
	27	10.245 082 1326	102.723 134 8069	.009 734 9054
	28	11.167 139 5246	112.968 216 9396	.008 852 0473
	29	12.172 182 0818	124.135 356 4641	.008 055 7226
	30	13.267 678 4691	136.307 538 5459	.007 336 3514
SEMIANNUALLY If compounded *semiannually* nominal annual rate is 18%	31	14.461 769 5314	149.575 217 0150	.006 685 5995
	32	15.763 328 7892	164.036 986 5464	.006 096 1861
	33	17.182 028 3802	179.800 315 3356	.005 561 7255
	34	18.728 410 9344	196.982 343 7158	.005 076 5971
	35	20.413 967 9185	215.710 754 6502	.004 635 8375
	36	22.251 225 0312	236.124 722 5687	.004 235 0500
	37	24.253 835 2840	258.375 947 5999	.003 870 3293
	38	26.436 680 4595	282.629 782 8839	.003 538 1975
	39	28.815 981 7009	309.066 463 3434	.003 235 5500
	40	31.409 420 0540	337.882 445 0443	.002 959 6092
QUARTERLY If compounded *quarterly* nominal annual rate is 36%	41	34.236 267 8588	369.291 865 0983	.002 707 8853
	42	37.317 531 9661	403.528 132 9572	.002 478 1420
	43	40.676 109 8431	440.845 664 9233	.002 268 3675
	44	44.336 959 7290	481.521 774 7664	.002 076 7493
	45	48.327 286 1046	525.858 734 4954	.001 901 6514
	46	52.676 741 8540	574.186 020 6000	.001 741 5959
	47	57.417 648 6209	626.862 762 4540	.001 595 2455
	48	62.585 236 9967	684.280 411 0748	.001 461 3892
	49	68.217 908 3264	746.865 648 0716	.001 338 9289
	50	74.357 520 0758	815.083 556 3980	.001 226 8681
MONTHLY If compounded *monthly* nominal annual rate is 108%	51	81.049 696 8826	889.441 076 4738	.001 124 3016
	52	88.344 169 6021	970.490 773 3565	.001 030 4065
	53	96.295 144 8663	1058.834 942 9585	.000 944 4343
	54	104.961 707 9042	1155.130 087 8248	.000 865 7034
	55	114.408 261 6156	1260.091 795 7290	.000 793 5930
i = .09 $j_{(2)}$ = .18 $j_{(4)}$ = .36 $j_{(12)}$ =1.08	56	124.705 005 1610	1374.500 057 3447	.000 727 5373
	57	135.928 455 6255	1499.205 062 5057	.000 667 0202
	58	148.162 016 6318	1635.133 518 1312	.000 611 5709
	59	161.496 598 1287	1783.295 534 7630	.000 560 7595
	60	176.031 291 9602	1944.792 132 8917	.000 514 1938
	n	$s=(1+i)^n$	$s_{\overline{n}\|}=\dfrac{(1+i)^n-1}{i}$	$\dfrac{1}{s_{\overline{n}\|}}=\dfrac{i}{(1+i)^n-1}$

PRESENT WORTH OF 1 *What $1 due in the future is worth today.*	PRESENT WORTH OF 1 PER PERIOD *What $1 payable periodically is worth today.*	PARTIAL PAYMENT *Annuity worth $1 today.* *Periodic payment necessary to pay off a loan of $1.*	PERIODS	RATE
				9%
.917 431 1927	.917 431 1927	1.090 000 0000	1	
.841 679 9933	1.759 111 1859	.568 468 8995	2	
.772 183 4801	2.531 294 6660	.395 054 7573	3	.09
.708 425 2111	3.239 719 8771	.308 668 6621	4	*per period*
.649 931 3863	3.889 651 2634	.257 092 4570	5	
.596 267 3269	4.485 918 5902	.222 919 7833	6	
.547 034 2448	5.032 952 8351	.198 690 5168	7	
.501 866 2797	5.534 819 1147	.180 674 3778	8	
.460 427 7795	5.995 246 8943	.166 798 8021	9	
.422 410 8069	6.417 657 7012	.155 820 0899	10	
.387 532 8504	6.805 190 5515	.146 946 6567	11	
.355 534 7251	7.160 725 2766	.139 650 6585	12	
.326 178 6469	7.486 903 9235	.133 566 5597	13	
.299 246 4650	7.786 150 3885	.128 433 1730	14	
.274 538 0413	8.060 688 4299	.124 058 8827	15	
.251 869 7627	8.312 558 1925	.120 299 9097	16	
.231 073 1768	8.543 631 3693	.117 046 2485	17	
.211 993 7402	8.755 625 1094	.114 212 2907	18	
.194 489 6699	8.950 114 7793	.111 730 4107	19	
.178 430 8898	9.128 545 6691	.109 546 4750	20	
.163 698 0640	9.292 243 7331	.107 616 6348	21	ANNUALLY If compounded *annually* nominal annual rate is
.150 181 7101	9.442 425 4432	.105 904 9930	22	
.137 781 3854	9.580 206 8286	.104 381 8800	23	
.126 404 9408	9.706 611 7694	.103 022 5607	24	
.115 967 8356	9.822 579 6049	.101 806 2505	25	**9%**
.106 392 5097	9.928 972 1146	.100 715 3599	26	
.097 607 8070	10.026 579 9217	.099 734 9054	27	
.089 548 4468	10.116 128 3685	.098 852 0473	28	
.082 154 5384	10.198 282 9069	.098 055 7226	29	
.075 371 1361	10.273 654 0430	.097 336 3514	30	SEMIANNUALLY If compounded *semiannually* nominal annual rate is
.069 147 8313	10.342 801 8743	.096 685 5995	31	
.063 438 3773	10.406 240 2517	.096 096 1861	32	
.058 200 3462	10.464 440 5979	.095 561 7255	33	
.053 394 8130	10.517 835 4109	.095 076 5971	34	
.048 986 0670	10.566 821 4779	.094 635 8375	35	**18%**
.044 941 3459	10.611 762 8237	.094 235 0500	36	
.041 230 5925	10.652 993 4163	.093 870 3293	37	
.037 826 2317	10.690 819 6480	.093 538 1975	38	
.034 702 9648	10.725 522 6128	.093 235 5500	39	
.031 837 5824	10.757 360 1952	.092 959 6092	40	QUARTERLY If compounded *quarterly* nominal annual rate is
.029 208 7912	10.786 568 9865	.092 707 8853	41	
.026 797 0562	10.813 366 0426	.092 478 1420	42	
.024 584 4552	10.837 950 4978	.092 268 3675	43	
.022 554 5461	10.860 505 0439	.092 076 7493	44	
.020 692 2441	10.881 197 2880	.091 901 6514	45	**36%**
.018 983 7102	10.900 180 9981	.091 741 5959	46	
.017 416 2479	10.917 597 2460	.091 595 2455	47	
.015 978 2090	10.933 575 4550	.091 461 3892	48	
.014 658 9074	10.948 234 3624	.091 338 9289	49	
.013 448 5389	10.961 682 9013	.091 226 8681	50	MONTHLY If compounded *monthly* nominal annual rate is
.012 338 1091	10.974 021 0104	.091 124 3016	51	
.011 319 3661	10.985 340 3765	.091 030 4065	52	
.010 384 7396	10.995 725 1160	.090 944 4343	53	
.009 527 2840	11.005 252 4000	.090 865 7034	54	
.008 740 6275	11.013 993 0276	.090 793 5930	55	**108%**
.008 018 9243	11.022 011 9519	.090 727 5373	56	
.007 356 8113	11.029 368 7632	.090 667 0202	57	
.006 749 3682	11.036 118 1314	.090 611 5079	58	$i\ =\ .09$
.006 192 0809	11.042 310 2123	.090 560 7595	59	$j_{(2)}\ =\ .18$
.005 680 8082	11.047 991 0204	.090 514 1938	60	$j_{(4)}\ =\ .36$ $j_{(12)}\ =1.08$
$v^n = \dfrac{1}{(1+i)^n}$	$a_{\overline{n}\rceil} = \dfrac{1-v^n}{i}$	$\dfrac{1}{a_{\overline{n}\rceil}} = \dfrac{i}{1-v^n}$	n	

RATE **10%**	P E R I O D S	AMOUNT OF 1 *How $1 left at compound interest will grow.*	AMOUNT OF 1 PER PERIOD *How $1 deposited periodically will grow.*	SINKING FUND *Periodic deposit that will grow to $1 at future date.*
.1 *per period*	1	1.100 000 0000	1.000 000 0000	1.000 000 0000
	2	1.210 000 0000	2.100 000 0000	.476 190 4762
	3	1.331 000 0000	3.310 000 0000	.302 114 8036
	4	1.464 100 0000	4.641 000 0000	.215 470 8037
	5	1.610 510 0000	6.105 100 0000	.163 797 4808
	6	1.771 561 0000	7.715 610 0000	.129 607 3804
	7	1.948 717 1000	9.487 171 0000	.105 405 4997
	8	2.143 588 8100	11.435 888 1000	.087 444 0176
	9	2.357 947 6910	13.579 476 9100	.073 640 5391
	10	2.593 742 4601	15.937 424 6010	.062 745 3949
	11	2.853 116 7061	18.531 167 0611	.053 963 1420
	12	3.138 428 3767	21.384 283 7672	.046 763 3151
	13	3.452 271 2144	24.522 712 1439	.040 778 5238
	14	3.797 498 3358	27.974 983 3583	.035 746 2232
	15	4.177 248 1694	31.772 481 6942	.031 473 7769
	16	4.594 972 9864	35.949 729 8636	.027 816 6207
	17	5.054 470 2850	40.544 702 8499	.024 664 1344
	18	5.559 917 3135	45.599 173 1349	.021 930 2222
	19	6.115 909 0448	51.159 090 4484	.019 546 8682
	20	6.727 499 9493	57.274 999 4933	.017 459 6248
ANNUALLY If compounded *annually* nominal annual rate is **10%**	21	7.400 249 9443	64.002 499 4426	.015 624 3898
	22	8.140 274 9387	71.402 749 3868	.014 005 0630
	23	8.954 302 4326	79.543 024 3255	.012 571 8127
	24	9.849 732 6758	88.497 326 7581	.011 299 7764
	25	10.834 705 9434	98.347 059 4339	.010 168 0722
	26	11.918 176 5377	109.181 765 3773	.009 159 0386
	27	13.109 994 1915	121.099 941 9150	.008 257 6423
	28	14.420 993 6106	134.209 936 1065	.007 451 0132
	29	15.863 092 9717	148.630 929 7171	.006 728 0747
	30	17.449 402 2689	164.494 022 6889	.006 079 2483
SEMIANNUALLY If compounded *semiannually* nominal annual rate is **20%**	31	19.194 342 4958	181.943 424 9578	.005 496 2140
	32	21.113 776 7454	201.137 767 4535	.004 971 7167
	33	23.225 154 4199	222.251 544 1989	.004 499 4063
	34	25.547 669 8619	245.476 698 6188	.004 073 7064
	35	28.102 436 8481	271.024 368 4806	.003 689 7051
	36	30.912 680 5329	299.126 805 3287	.003 343 0638
	37	34.003 948 5862	330.039 485 8616	.003 029 9405
	38	37.404 343 4448	364.043 434 4477	.002 746 9250
	39	41.144 777 7893	401.447 777 8925	.002 490 9840
	40	45.259 255 5682	442.592 555 6818	.002 259 4144
QUARTERLY If compounded *quarterly* nominal annual rate is **40%**	41	49.785 181 1250	487.851 811 2499	.002 049 8028
	42	54.763 699 2375	537.636 992 3749	.001 859 9911
	43	60.240 069 1612	592.400 691 6124	.001 688 0466
	44	66.264 076 0774	652.640 760 7737	.001 532 2365
	45	72.890 483 6851	718.904 836 8510	.001 391 0047
	46	80.179 532 0536	791.795 320 5361	.001 262 9527
	47	88.197 485 2590	871.974 852 5897	.001 146 8221
	48	97.017 233 7849	960.172 337 8487	.001 041 4797
	49	106.718 957 1634	1057.189 571 6336	.000 945 9041
	50	117.390 852 8797	1163.908 528 7970	.000 859 1740
MONTHLY If compounded *monthly* nominal annual rate is **120%**	51	129.129 938 1677	1281.299 381 6766	.000 780 4577
	52	142.042 931 9844	1410.429 319 8443	.000 709 0040
	53	156.247 225 1829	1552.472 251 8287	.000 644 1339
	54	171.871 947 7012	1708.719 477 0116	.000 585 2336
	55	189.059 142 4713	1880.591 424 7128	.000 531 7476
$i\ =.1$ $j_{(2)}=.2$ $j_{(4)}=.4$ $j_{(12)}=1.2$	56	207.965 056 7184	2069.650 567 1841	.000 483 1734
	57	228.761 562 3902	2277.615 623 9025	.000 439 0556
	58	251.637 718 6293	2506.377 186 2927	.000 398 9822
	59	276.801 490 4922	2758.014 904 9220	.000 362 5796
	60	304.481 639 5414	3034.816 395 4142	.000 329 5092
	n	$s=(1+i)^n$	$s_{\overline{n}|}=\dfrac{(1+i)^n-1}{i}$	$\dfrac{1}{s_{\overline{n}|}}=\dfrac{i}{(1+i)^n-1}$

PRESENT WORTH OF 1	PRESENT WORTH OF 1 PER PERIOD	PARTIAL PAYMENT *Annuity worth $1 today.*	P E R I O D S	RATE
What $1 due in the future is worth today.	*What $1 payable periodically is worth today.*	*Periodic payment necessary to pay off a loan of $1.*		**10%**
.909 090 9091	.909 090 9091	1.100 000 0000	1	
.826 446 2810	1.735 537 1901	.576 190 4762	2	
.751 314 8009	2.486 851 9910	.402 114 8036	3	.1
.683 013 4554	3.169 865 4463	.315 470 8037	4	
.620 921 3231	3.790 786 7694	.263 797 4808	5	*per period*
.564 473 9301	4.355 260 6995	.229 607 3804	6	
.513 158 1182	4.868 418 8177	.205 405 4997	7	
.466 507 3802	5.334 926 1979	.187 444 0176	8	
.424 097 6184	5.759 023 8163	.173 640 5391	9	
.385 543 2894	6.144 567 1057	.162 745 3949	10	
.350 493 8995	6.495 061 0052	.153 963 1420	11	
.318 630 8177	6.813 691 8229	.146 763 3151	12	
.289 664 3797	7.103 356 2026	.140 778 5238	13	
.263 331 2543	7.366 687 4569	.135 746 2232	14	
.239 392 0494	7.606 079 5063	.131 473 7769	15	
.217 629 1358	7.823 708 6421	.127 816 6207	16	
.197 844 6689	8.021 553 3110	.124 664 1344	17	
.179 858 7899	8.201 412 1009	.121 930 2222	18	
.163 507 9908	8.364 920 0917	.119 546 8682	19	
.148 643 6280	8.513 563 7198	.117 459 6248	20	ANNUALLY
.135 130 5709	8.648 694 2907	.115 624 3898	21	If compounded *annually*
.122 845 9736	8.771 540 2643	.114 005 0630	22	nominal annual rate is
.111 678 1578	8.883 218 4221	.112 571 8127	23	
.101 525 5980	8.984 744 0201	.111 299 7764	24	
.092 295 9982	9.077 040 0182	.110 168 0722	25	**10%**
.083 905 4529	9.160 945 4711	.109 159 0386	26	
.076 277 6844	9.237 223 1556	.108 257 6423	27	
.069 343 3495	9.306 566 5051	.107 451 0132	28	
.063 039 4086	9.369 605 9137	.106 728 0747	29	
.057 308 5533	9.426 914 4670	.106 079 2483	30	SEMIANNUALLY
.052 098 6848	9.479 013 1518	.105 496 2140	31	If compounded *semiannually*
.047 362 4407	9.526 375 5926	.104 971 7167	32	nominal annual rate is
.043 056 7643	9.569 432 3569	.104 499 4063	33	
.039 142 5130	9.608 574 8699	.104 073 7064	34	
.035 584 1027	9.644 158 9726	.103 689 7051	35	**20%**
.032 349 1843	9.676 508 1569	.103 343 0638	36	
.029 408 3494	9.705 916 5063	.103 029 9405	37	
.026 734 8631	9.732 651 3694	.102 746 9250	38	
.024 304 4210	9.756 955 7903	.102 490 9840	39	
.022 094 9282	9.779 050 7185	.102 259 4144	40	QUARTERLY
.020 086 2983	9.799 137 0168	.102 049 8028	41	If compounded *quarterly*
.018 260 2712	9.817 397 2880	.101 859 9911	42	nominal annual rate is
.016 600 2465	9.833 997 5345	.101 688 0466	43	
.015 091 1332	9.849 088 6678	.101 532 2365	44	
.013 719 2120	9.862 807 ,8798	.101 391 0047	45	**40%**
.012 472 0109	9.875 279 8907	.101 262 9527	46	
.011 338 1918	9.886 618 0825	.101 146 8221	47	
.010 307 4470	9.896 925 5295	.101 041 4797	48	
.009 370 4064	9.906 295 9359	.100 945 9041	49	
.008 518 5513	9.914 814 4872	.100 859 1740	50	MONTHLY
.007 744 1375	9.922 558 6247	.100 780 4577	51	If compounded *monthly*
.007 040 1250	9.929 598 7498	.100 709 0040	52	nominal annual rate is
.006 400 1137	9.935 998 8634	.100 644 1339	53	
.005 818 2851	9.941 817 1486	.100 585 2336	54	
.005 289 3501	9.947 106 4987	.100 531 7476	55	**120%**
.004 808 5001	9.951 914 9988	.100 483 1734	56	
.004 371 3637	9.956 286 3626	.100 439 0556	57	
.003 973 9670	9.960 260 3296	.100 398 9822	58	$i = .1$
.003 612 6973	9.963 873 0269	.100 362 5796	59	$j_{(2)} = .2$
.003 284 2703	9.967 157 2972	.100 329 5092	60	$j_{(4)} = .4$
$v^n=\dfrac{1}{(1+i)^n}$	$a_{\overline{n}\rvert}=\dfrac{1-v^n}{i}$	$\dfrac{1}{a_{\overline{n}\rvert}}=\dfrac{i}{1-v^n}$	n	$j_{(12)} = 1.2$

index